The Fixers

The Fixers

Eddie Mannix, Howard Strickling and the MGM Publicity Machine

E.J. FLEMING

McFarland & Company, Inc., Publishers
Jefferson, North Carolina, and London

LIBRARY OF CONGRESS CATALOGUING-IN-PUBLICATION DATA

Fleming, E.J., 1954–
    The Fixers : Eddie Mannix, Howard Strickling and the MGM
publicity machine / E.J. Fleming.
        p.   cm.
    Includes bibliographical references and index.

    ISBN-13: 978-0-7864-2027-8
    softcover : 50# alkaline paper ∞

    1. Mannix, Eddie.   2. Strickling, Howard.   3. Theatrical
agents—United States—Biography.   4. Metro-Goldwyn-Mayer.
5. Motion picture industry—Public relations—California—Los
Angeles.   I. Title.
PN1998.2.F557   2005
791.43'092'273—dc22   2004025792

British Library cataloguing data are available

Front cover: Eddie Mannix and Howard Strickling *(Bison Archives,
Raleigh Studios, Hollywood, CA);* background ©2005 PhotoSpin

Manufactured in the United States of America

*McFarland & Company, Inc., Publishers
    Box 611, Jefferson, North Carolina 28640
    www.mcfarlandpub.com*

This is for my family and for our friends
who have heard all the stories.
Now you can interrupt me when
I repeat one and say, "I have the book."

Acknowledgments

My interest in the movies and Hollywood history goes back over twenty years, and for those twenty years my family and friends have offered ears for (probably) seemingly unending stories and have given ongoing encouragement. For that I want to thank them individually and as a group. Thank you to Barb and the kids, Mom and Dad, my brother Tony for his unending assistance with all things computer, my friends Dick and Lemoyne Rhoades, Mitch Gibney (who still lends me his apartment ten years later), and people like Barb and Gerry Tax, George and Judy Tujowski, Don and Nancy Burke and Scott Davis, who listen patiently as I ramble on.

I also want to thank the staff at the Herrick Library at the Academy of Motion Picture Arts and Sciences, who treat every researcher — important and not — as if they were famous. Also, the people at the UCLA Library and the Beverly Hills and Los Angeles Public libraries are universally helpful and encouraging.

A number of people shared recollections and confirmed many of the stories in this book that had previously been just rumor, particularly the late Maurice Rapf. His remembrances of the earliest days of MGM and Hollywood were invaluable and insightful. Maurice was in a unique position to confirm many of the unconfirmed rumors about Eddie Mannix and Howard Strickling, having known them personally growing up in early Hollywood before being blacklisted during the McCarthy era. Kevin Apodaca in Los Angeles and Maurice's daughter Joanna in New Hampshire were both instrumental in arranging for me to speak with her father.

Also a special thank you to Jack Larson for sharing his stories of growing up in Hollywood among the European expatriate community and his lifelong friendship with Eddie and Toni Mannix. His personal involvement in the life and tragic death of George Reeves, and knowledge of Reeves' relationship with Toni Mannix, made him an invaluable source of information and confirmation. Reeves researchers and writers Jim Hambrick and Jim Nolt also offered their opinions and thoughts about that section of the book. Thanks also to the wonderful writer David Stenn for his gracious offer of reviewing the manuscript and for his direction and thoughts. His books about Jean Harlow and Clara Bow are two of the best Hollywood biographies available.

The late Col. Barney Oldfield offered numerous insights into the personalities of Howard and Gail Strickling and many of the people in the book and patiently and thoughtfully responded to my every query. Both he and Cecil Jones were instrumental in helping track down photographs, and for that I thank them both. Lita Grey Chaplin offered some interesting stories of the silent era, for which I am grateful.

Chicago
November 2004

Contents

Acknowledgments   vii

Preface   1

Prologue — Call Mr. Strickling   3

One — The Movies Find Hollywood   5

Two — Building the Emerald City   19

Three — Omens, and the Twenties End Roaring   53

Four — The 1930s: The Golden Age of Trouble   87

Five — The 1940s: War Inside and Out   189

Six — The 1950s: Relics and the Last Big Secret   232

Postscript — Fade Out   275

Notes   281

Selected Bibliography   293

Index   299

Gossip columnist Louella Parsons, to fellow writer Hedda Hopper, hearing that Hopper was writing an autobiography:

"What are you going to write about?"

Hopper to Parsons: "I'm going to tell the truth."

Parsons to Hopper: "Oh, dear, that's what I was afraid of."

"We told stars what they could say, and they did what we said because they knew we knew best..."

— *Howard Strickling*

"Strickling and Mannix were just pimps for Louis B. Mayer..."

— *Maurice Rapf*

"In other businesses it's different, like if an editor gets drunk you hire another one. Well, if you got John Barrymore in a picture you can't say throw the bum out. You got Gable and Taylor and Garbo, but there's only one of each so you work things out."

— *Howard Strickling*

Preface

The names Eddie Mannix and Howard Strickling are virtually unknown outside of Hollywood, and today perhaps little-remembered even there except by old-timers. But like Cecil B. DeMille, Louis B. Mayer, and David O. Selznick, during the golden age of Hollywood and the movies, theirs were household names. They helped lord over some of the most famous names in the movies: Garbo. Gable. Lombard. Beery. Garland. Gilbert. And hundreds of other names and faces recognized by the hundreds of millions of moviegoers over four decades.

The names Mannix and Strickling first came to my attention while researching and writing other books dealing with aspects of the history of Hollywood and the movies. They are both often mentioned in literally hundreds of biographies of MGM stars and production employees such as directors, producers, and cameramen. But they are not mentioned in their capacities as general manager (Mannix) or director of publicity (Strickling). What initially struck me was that their names always arose *when someone got into trouble.*

From the 1920s through the early 1950s, the studios actually owned their stars, signing them to contracts that allowed the studio to control almost every aspect of their lives. Unlike today, when a star can work with anyone willing to pay their price or decline an offer from anyone they dislike, during the early years of the industry the studio system allowed MGM to force any employee to do almost anything it demanded. And those demands were often far and above typical employer requirements. Abortions. Studio-prescribed drugs. Even marriages.

Stars such as Clark Gable and Greta Garbo were worth untold millions to MGM, and the loss of such an asset could easily doom the studio. If fans knew that Gable fathered an illegitimate child or ran over and killed a pedestrian with his car, if Wallace Beery was known as a murderer, if Garbo was known to be an active bisexual, the results would have been

1

disastrous. So MGM had to keep the secrets. Make the arrangements. "Fix" things. Mannix and Strickling were "the fixers."

Anybody in a position to help was paid. Lawyers. Doctors and medical people. Policemen. Judges. District attorneys. Photographers and writers. In a time when information flow could be more easily controlled than it could be today, people like Eddie and Howard controlled what happened, and what people heard. And everyone believed them.

This is the story of Eddie and Howard and their work. It is impossible to document everything they were involved in. Secrecy was imperative, and until they died both men steadfastly refused to tell their stories. But while writers and researchers have been able to chronicle the results of their work, their personal stories have never been told until now. I wanted to try to tell the story within the context of the growth of MGM and the movies, amidst the maelstrom that so often characterized movie stars' lives. They both were unflinchingly loyal to Louis B. Mayer and MGM, while at the same time saddled with often-amoral stars who had unlimited opportunities for problems. The results were probably to be expected.

There are hundreds of stories not detailed within this work. Many of them are undoubtedly true, but unless some firm background could be found and confirmed they were not included. The stories told here are all supported by a combination of written records, personal accounts, interviews, and other source materials as noted. Research was conducted at a number of movie industry archive sites and interviews conducted with former studio employees, many involved in the individual events. Whenever possible, specific attribution is noted. In a small number of cases wherein I take issue with the conventional wisdom or historically-accepted conclusion, my own opinion is offered and noted as such.

Eddie Mannix was a New Jersey bricklayer whose closest friends were mobsters. Howard Strickling was the son of a small-town grocer. Eddie Mannix and Howard Strickling were involved in some of the most spectacular cover-ups in the history of MGM, Hollywood, and the movies. This is their story.

Prologue

Call Mr. Strickling

John Carmichael and his wife Winifred got off the bus on Benedict Canyon Drive and silently trudged arm in arm up steep and winding Easton Street. Even on such a brilliantly clear summer morning the canopy of trees hanging over the narrow street left more cool shade than warm sunlight on the gravel road. So narrow that if a car happened by they had to step onto someone's front steps to allow it to pass, Easton was also so steep that John's wife of twenty years had to hold tightly onto his arm as they made their way to work.

Approaching the gate to 9820, the Carmichaels shared friendly greetings with gardener Clifton Davis as he came out of his apartment inside the garage on the street. The couple continued inside and took the narrow path even further up the hill toward the main house. Early every morning, the Carmichaels got the house ready for Mr. Paul. Mr. Paul was an executive at the biggest movie studio in Hollywood, and his car would be at the drive to take him to work in an hour. The early morning Los Angeles heat hadn't yet overtaken the secluded hillside estate, and the smell of bougainvillea and the dew-covered woods filled the air as the couple made their way past the pool.

Tiny red flowers floated calmly in the water, distorting the reflection of the beautiful house with its slate roof, brass gutters, and hand-carved rainspouts featuring likenesses of Douglas Fairbanks, Charlie Chaplin and Mary Pickford. They walked past an empty champagne bottle and a single broken glass lying on the flagstone by the pool, silent witnesses to the loud poolside argument that Clifton had heard late the night before.

Noises traveled through these canyons like the birds— it was nearly impossible to tell exactly where in the hills sounds came from — but while Clifton had listened to the loud disagreement between Mr. Paul and his lady friend through open windows that offered him little relief from the late night heat, he had hoped aloud that the neighbors couldn't hear it too.

3

As the grand Tudor house rose directly above them between the trees over the pool, John noticed a lady's bathing suit, still wet, lying across a chair. Yes, Clifton had heard the swimming the night before, and then that terrible fight. A little while later, the studio limousine had taken the lady away, lumbering down the narrow, rutted street and disappearing down Benedict Canyon.

The quiet house reminded John and Winifred that Mr. Paul's new wife had spent the previous night with her mother down in the Beverly Hills flats below Sunset. Most days in the two months since she and Mr. Paul married, she was awake when the Carmichaels arrived, her friendly smile and sweetness belying the fact that she was such a big movie star. She was making a movie with Clark Gable — Clark Gable! — but she told them, "Call me Jean." Just "Jean." Not "Miss Harlow" — "Jean." They knew her friends called her "Baby." She was so sweet to everyone. Winifred liked the name "Baby."

While Winifred made coffee and breakfast for everyone, John got the house opened up and headed upstairs to make sure Mr. Paul's clothes were laid out for him. As he climbed the stairs to the second-floor master bedroom, John thought it strange that Mr. Paul wasn't yet up. He was usually in the shower by now. Even stranger, his bed hadn't been slept in.

Then he saw him — on the floor in the dressing room beyond the bed, lying on his side up against his big mirror. Naked. Eyes open. A bent arm tucked under his side. And blood everywhere: pooled on the floor, streaking his face. And those bloody tracks on the mirror and the wall. It was horrible, so horrible that John fainted dead away, falling in a heap on the floor next to Mr. Paul.

Looking for the men, Winifred came upstairs a few minutes later. The noise of her walking through the house calling his name stirred John awake, and he stumbled into his shocked wife's arms. After she saw Mr. Paul's body, they both knew exactly what they had to do. John ran downstairs and out of the house, past the broken glass by the pool and down the hill to find Clifton, and Winifred called Jean's mother. Mother Jean also knew what to do. She called Mr. Strickling.

One

The Movies Find Hollywood

How seemingly unremarkable men like Howard Strickling and Eddie Mannix, and the studio publicity departments they oversaw, became so powerful is a story that has as its origin a mixture of pure coincidence and accidental timing. Before finding the movie business— or more precisely, before the movie business found them — their individual careers were distinctly unimpressive.

Strickling and Mannix, and the movie-makers they worked for — Cecil B. DeMille, Marcus Loew, Samuel Goldwyn, Jesse Lasky, Louis B. Mayer, D.W. Griffith, Thomas Ince, Mack Sennett, Harry Cohn — were to a man only marginally successful in their pre-movie careers. They did, however, share a single common thread: they each had the singular realization that they were present at the birth of a business opportunity that had unlimited potential to generate huge amounts of money. That was more than enough to attract the attention of even the least motivated of the group.

All of these men realized at about the same time that there was a fortune to be made and no barriers to enter the business. There was nothing to stop anyone from getting into the movies. Nobody had any experience. Nobody's father or uncle or grandfather was in the business. Nepotism wasn't just absent; it did not even exist. There was no experience required. Indeed, there was not any experience to have been had!

In their early 20s, Mannix and Strickling were two anonymous men among the millions of faces walking the sidewalks of New York. Strickling, the son of a grocery store owner, was a newspaper reporter. Mannix was a carnival bouncer at Palisades Park, a distinctly blue collar amusement park.[1] Luckily, though, like the rest of the men who rode the movie industry to wealth and power in the early 1900s, they were at the right place at the right time when this brand new industry was born out of an incredible invention.

Indeed, the movies did not just appear; they fairly erupted. At the time of its birth, absolutely everything about motion pictures was not just new; it was totally unique — unheard-of. Nobody had ever seen actual *moving* pictures. To put it into an understandable context is difficult, but at the time, a significant portion of the world's population had probably only seen a few *photographs* during their lifetimes, and they had certainly never seen a camera. Pictures that actually *moved* was a stunning concept; literally unbelievable.

It was clear that people everywhere were terribly excited about this brand new "movie" thing, and that all that needed to be done was to put something—anything— on film. The men seemed to understand implicitly that, no matter what they put on film, people would pay to see it. It must have seemed almost too easy. Cameras could be rented fairly cheaply, there were not yet any big salaries, and almost all of the locations—from city streets to empty beaches to woodlands— were free. There was little risk. The men saw that, although it doesn't appear that any of them were gifted with unusual vision. None seemed to have any real cultural bent, nor did any of them originally approach the movie product as an artistic endeavor. Indeed, most of them were distinctly, almost comically, uncultured.

Russian-born Louis B. Mayer was a Boston scrap metal and junk dealer. D.W. Griffith, a Kentucky gentleman and son of a Civil War hero. Samuel Goldwyn, a New York glove maker. Adolph Zukor, a Pittsburgh fur seller. The Warner brothers— Jack, Harry, Sam and Al — sons of a bicycle maker in Youngstown, Ohio. Harry Cohn, a man so crude and uncultured that he was almost universally despised. William Fox, a New York suit lining cutter. Carl Laemmle, an Oshkosh, Wisconsin, clothing store owner. Mack Sennett, a boiler repairman and former stevedore who became world-renowned as "The King of Comedy." No business visionaries; no artists; no monumental success stories at all. But when it was over they were leading the industry, and were millionaires. They were ruthless, demanding, unforgiving taskmasters as their influence grew along with the fledgling industry.

The movies were born in 1881 when William K.L. Dickson walked into Thomas Edison's Menlo Park laboratory looking for a job. Young Dickson had more than a resume; he had an idea that in 1888 Edison said would do "for the eye what the phonograph does for the ear."[2] In 1894 he and Dickson offered the first workable version of their "kinetascope." The large machine allowed a single viewer to watch a 50-foot-long film, a 10-second moving picture.[3] The viewer looked into an eyepiece to see the image playing inside the machine on a single loop of film. Edison could not synchronize any sound, so the images played silently.

On April 23, 1894, Edison shipped 25 new machines to parlors in Atlantic City and Chicago, and 12 to a parlor that he himself opened in New York. He rented the former Koster and Bial's Music Parlor at Broadway and 34th and set up the cumbersome machines against the walls. Crowds began gathering as the machines were carted inside, and by the time the parlor opened the next morning there were hundreds of people waiting to come in.

The offerings, changed every few days, soon were a minute long. The first was Edison's film of Fred Ott sneezing. Another was a tooth extraction. Still another was *How the Porto Rico Girls Entertain Uncle Sam's Soldiers.*[4] The early slang terms, "movies" or "flickers"—referring to the flickering movement of the early films—are still used 100 years later. They were also called "chasers," since some early theater owners preferred vaudeville acts and used movies to get patrons out the door.

Improvements came quickly. Thomas Armat unveiled the "Vitascope," a machine that projected a series of backlit still pictures onto a wall fast enough to simulate movement. In 1895 Dickson left Edison's operation to start his own American Mutoscope and Biograph Company and developed a portable player that could be moved and operated easily. Movies were now portable, and instead of one person watching through the eyepiece of the kinetascope, an entire room could watch the Vitascope image on the wall.

One of Dickson's first "big-screen" offerings was the Empire State Express train silently rounding a curve toward the camera, smoke belching. The first time it was shown, the crowd screamed in fear as the locomotive rumbled toward them on screen. Armat's invention, with Dickson's improvements, had a huge impact upon moviemaking.[5] No longer were movies limited to 45- or 60-second shorts, the amount of time a person could comfortably lean and look through the eyepiece. With a seated audience, a number of separate short scenes could be connected as one long offering. Longer offerings meant longer lines and more money.

Edwin S. Porter, Edison's principal cameraman, was a prolific moviemaker during the first years, filming hundreds of titles. Among his work were the first films offering beginning-to-end plots and scenes strung together in a longer format.[6] His later classic *The Great Train Robbery* would become the first major success in the industry. Soon other moviemakers followed suit with similar longer, more involved offerings.

By 1898, 5,000 Vitascope parlors were attracting millions of eager viewers across North America. In a single year, 200 theaters opened in Boston, 100 in Pittsburgh, and 200 in Chicago. Considering how much smaller populations were then than today, these numbers are amazing. All of these small local outlets purchased films as quickly as they could be sourced, and once paid for, the owners owned them. Once the local audience became bored with a title, like today a new one had to be found. In 1905, to help theater owners get better access, Carl Laemmle — who began buying nickelodeon theaters in 1904 — opened a film exchange company, which allowed for better product distribution and lower costs to the theater owners. It immediately dawned on producers that there was more money to be made by renting the movies than by selling them.

The demand was insatiable. Dozens of small production companies— with exotic-sounding names like Essanay, Selig, Kalem and Pathé— began making movies. Actor G.M. Anderson, who had starred in Porter's *Great Train Robbery* just a few months earlier, opened Essanay Studio in New York. Porter's old boss Edison himself built a studio in Brooklyn, Biograph and Vitagraph opened in New York, and others opened in Chicago and Boston.

During 1907 and 1908, 25 million Americans— half the population — saw a nickelodeon feature at least once a week. By 1910, however, the nickelodeon network was quickly being replaced by what would soon become 10,000 full-fledged movie theaters. By 1915, that number stood at a remarkable 17,500.

Almost all of the early efforts were filmed around New York and Long Island. The "wilds" of the Orange Mountains in Cuddebackville, New York, or the beaches of Atlantic Highlands, New Jersey, were used for outdoor shots.[7] Within a few years, however, the larger production companies began moving their entire crews— actors, directors, and cameramen — west to Arizona or California to film during the winter months.

Each fall from the late 1890s into the early 1900s many of the New York– or Chicago-based movie studios packed up their entire staff and all of their equipment and loaded the lot onto trains. They arrived in Los Angeles hot and dusty after a four-day trip on the Twentieth Century Limited from Chicago. New Yorkers rode the Black Diamond Express on the Lehigh Valley Railroad to Chicago. When they arrived in L.A. they had still to endure a bumpy, one- to two-hour carriage ride to the outpost known as Hollywood. Until 1908 or 1909 all of the studios and their employees returned by train back to New York or Chicago when spring arrived.

The earliest movie companies in the L.A. area set up their camps in the eastern part of Hollywood, now known as the Silverlake area, just north of Elysian Park. At the time the area was known as Edendale, and what is now called Silver Lake was at the time called Echo Park Lake. Any sound was said to echo off the lake for miles through the empty hillsides. There were few residents and open, inexpensive land as far as the eye could see. The connection to L.A. was a seven-mile-long electric railroad line; Edendale was the end of the line from downtown L.A. Between 1900 and 1910 most movie production took place in the hills around Edendale and on the dusty main street dotted with a half dozen shops and the Clifford Street School.[8]

In 1906 Hollywood was still just a large ranch. The area had been divided by the Spanish government; to the west was Rancho La Brea and the east Rancho Los Feliz. The Ranchos were subdivided and sold in the 1880s. Most of Rancho La Brea was purchased by Daeida and Horace Henderson Wilcox in 1886. He was a millionaire real estate developer from Ohio, a religious fanatic, and a Prohibitionist. He devised a grid plan for his large tract and in 1887 began selling his version of a Christian community with a Methodist, Prohibitionist church on every block. Mrs. Wilcox named the area after a friend's Ohio estate: "Hollywood."

Wilcox offered free land to anyone who would put up a church on the property they were given. Because of this, almost every other Hollywood resident was directly involved in a church of some type. The typical Hollywood resident was markedly different than the movie people who overran the quiet village every winter during the early 1900s. Locals couldn't wait for the spring and the annual migration out of town. The everyday rules of the quiet village were strict. Alcohol was prohibited. Gambling was not allowed, even in people's homes. Bikes were not to be ridden on walking paths. Sunday was the Sabbath; a day of prayer. Any outside work on Sunday was frowned upon. The village didn't offer much in the way of amenities. There was a single small hotel with perhaps a dozen rooms, a general store, and a barbershop.

The Santa Monica Mountains, a seemingly endless wall of uninhabitable scrub-laden canyons full of bears, snakes and mountain lions, ringed Hollywood to the north. Highwaymen and Indians roamed the miles of mountain trails. There was no Beverly Hills. What is now the most expensive land in the U.S. was then a stark wasteland of bean fields and orange groves dotted with a few houses. The few locals called it Morocco Junction.

The first development came about by accident. By 1907 Boston-bred oilman Burton Green had spent several years drilling hundreds of dry oil wells around dusty Morocco Junction. His Rodeo Water and Land Company was nearly broke, so it was suggested the company sell land holdings to the growing numbers of people coming from the East Coast. The area was desolate; even in 1923 Charlie Chaplin said it looked like "an abandoned real estate development" with sidewalks disappearing into bean fields.[9] But, desperate, Green borrowed the name of his Beverly Farms, Massachusetts, home and began building a hotel surrounded by a housing project to recoup his mounting oil losses. He envisioned a luxury resort attracting wealthy travelers from around the world. Around the hotel, filling the farm tracts, would be dozens of homes. Green broke ground in late 1907. His first model home still stands, unchanged, at 515 Canon Drive. It took three years, but in early 1911 Green opened the crown jewel of his eleventh-hour gamble, the Beverly Hills Hotel. The building sat in pink splendor amid an endless expanse of bean fields, its green roof-tiles visible for miles. It was nestled under the Santa Monica Mountains, which locals had begun calling the Beverly Hills. Other than a half dozen of Green's small cottages, there were few houses for miles in any direction.

Gloria Swanson described the new hotel as "a quiet, secluded hotel a long way from town," but it was a popular spot, featuring the only bar in Morocco Junction. It helped fuel rapid growth in the newly renamed Beverly Hills, but it still boasted a population of only 550 souls in 1913. The movies would quickly change that. The first to take advantage of California as a year-round filming location was Chicagoan William Selig's Selig Film Company. His first Edendale studio was the rented back yard of a Chinese laundry. His directors borrowed clotheslines crisscrossing the yard to hang set walls and shading cloth when they weren't full of drying clothes.[10] Within a few months of his 1908 arrival Selig purchased a block of downtown Edendale and built the first California movie studio.

In 1910 D.W. Griffith's Biograph Studio arrived, renting a large vacant lot at the corner of Grand Avenue and Washington Street next to a lumberyard and a baseball field. He also rented a loft to store equipment. According to Mary Pickford the furniture consisted of "a table and three chairs."[11] Later arrivals included the Bison Studios, New York Moving Pictures Company, Norberg Pictures, and Mack Sennett's Keystone Studio, all in and around Edendale between 1910 and 1913. By 1913, little happened during the day in Edendale that wasn't movie-related. The once ghostly-quiet town had become busy with "movies."

More and more local families joined the movie business. Studios offered a variety of new opportunities with new lines of work in dozens of fields. The early East Coast movie crews visiting L.A. for winter filming were small groups, kept low in number to keep costs down. As more and more movies were made, the need for local labor became increasingly important. Carpenters and painters were needed to build sets, and in some cases the studios themselves. Tailors and dressmakers were needed for costumes and set decoration. Property ("prop") men were needed to supply the props. Cameramen, film technicians, cutters, editors and directors were needed to provide the finished motion pictures. Writers were needed.

In 1913 the Centaur Film Company became the first studio to relocate everything from the East Coast to downtown Hollywood. The company paid $40 a month to rent the dilapidated Blondeau Tavern Barbershop at the corner of Sunset and Gower. Filming began immediately, with nearby fields, corrals and storefronts becoming instant, and very realistic, movie sets.

Within months of Centaur's arrival, a Goldwyn-Lasky group arrived to film a Western, *The Squaw Man.* Coming west to use actual western locales— they couldn't afford to rent indoor facilities at home in New York anyway— the group initially intended to film in Flagstaff, Arizona. In December 1913 a small group left New York; production manager DeMille, director Oscar Apfel, cameraman Alfred Gandolfi, and the group's male star Dustin Farnum. Farnum was so unsure of the prospects that he made the company pay him in advance, in cash, his entire contract of $250 for five weeks' work.[12] Also along was Farnum's butler and dresser Fred Kley.

DeMille's brother turned down an offer to invest in the trip, saying he would need the money to pay Cecil's return fare when "the company folded up."[13] DeMille himself viewed the trip as little more than a free vacation west. Owner Lasky also decided against going, saying he had "no great personal faith in the project and I couldn't see myself wasting time in Arizona." As soon as DeMille stepped off the train in Arizona after the four-day trip he decided it was unsuitable. It was too flat and too much of a desert, not right for the scenes he envisioned. It was also unbearably hot, with oppressive heat baking the ground to 120°, and a rainy season that added floods to the awful humidity. There was also a range war going on between cattle ranchers and sheepmen. DeMille decided to proceed to California, so they headed through the southwestern wilderness to a place called Los Angeles. It may have been a dusty outpost at the end of the world, but when DeMille stepped off the train at the old Santa Fe depot in L.A. he knew he was right. The climate was more comfortable than Arizona and within a day's ride, cameramen could film mountains, deserts, and the ocean.

The group settled into the Alexandria Hotel, the finest downtown hotel at the time. Sitting in the hotel bar, DeMille met L.L. Burns and Harry Reiver, transplanted New Yorkers who had a film development laboratory in a place they said was "just ten miles away ... called Hollywood." They mentioned that the building next door to theirs might be usable as a studio, and drove DeMille up dusty Prospect Avenue to Hollywood. The building was a large, L-shaped, green barn, a failed farm that stood at the corner of Selma and Vine in "downtown" Hollywood.[14] Above the barn loomed Mount Lee. DeMille cabled boss Lasky in New York. In an ironic exchange of telegrams, DeMille noted, "Flagstaff no good. STOP. Want to rent barn in place called Hollywood. STOP. $75.00 a month. STOP. Cecil." Lasky, furious that DeMille had skipped Flagstaff without checking with him first, offered a terse reply: "OK on month to month only. STOP. Don't make any long commitments. STOP. Jesse."[15]

On December 29, 1913, just one day after his arrival, DeMille gathered his crew for a group photograph in front of the barn and set about filming *The Squaw Man*. DeMille and director Apfel had written the script during the train trip to Arizona. As soon as he opened his office he found extras standing by their horses at the corner every morning. One of his first hires was a cowboy named Hal Roach. Farnum worked with a cast of dozens of *real* cowboys and Indians. Shooting took just two weeks and the film made its New York debut on February 14. A crowd of film distributors and theater owners—among them Adolph Zukor and Louis B. Mayer—watched in amazement—the film's six reels. The film broke six times during viewing but the people were agog. DeMille's first California movie had cost $47,000—a gamble of more than twice the assets of the entire company—but within three months grossed more than $250,000. Within the next ten months, 325 movies were filmed in and around Hollywood. Every major studio was permanently located in L.A. within two years.

Although fascinated with the movies, the conservative locals didn't quickly warm to the outsiders. The Wilcoxes and their religious neighbors never intended the quiet hamlet to become a haven for eastern actors and their sinful ways. Even in 1913 the original residents were vocal in their distaste for anything related to the intruders with the cameras. Aside from having difficulty renting land on which to film, DeMille faced other challenges. While he filmed *The Squaw Man* he was shot at twice by angry locals for venturing too close to their farms. Duly warned, DeMille began carrying a handgun in a holster at all times. Most of the early filmmakers followed suit; it was unusual to find an unarmed director in Hollywood at that time. Just after the filming was finished an intruder broke into his shabby studio office during the night and sabotaged the first negative print of the film, removing it from film canisters and tearing and stomping on it until it was ruined.[16] Only a chance decision to have his cameraman make two copies every day saved DeMille's company from closing before it opened.[17]

The few local hotels—nothing more than ragged boarding houses, really—boasted signs that warned, "No dogs! No Jews! No Actors!" and "No Dogs or Movie People Allowed!"[18] Those sentiments were evident as late as 1923, when writer Francis Marion and her actor-husband Fred Thomson tried to buy Beverly Hills land from L.A. oilman Alphonso Bell, a former college classmate of Thomson's. Bell told him, "I'm terribly sorry you became an actor Fred, but I've made it a law; I won't sell an acre of my land to actors or Jews."[19] Even the word "movies" was a derogatory slur. DeMille had to lie so he could rent a home. He brought his wife along with him to look at houses, and told landlords and his potential neighbors that "those 'movies' are crazy." They rented to him thinking he was a salesman.

Carl Laemmle was the most improbable of the movie men, elf-like at barely five foot two, with a gap-toothed smile and big bald head.[20] Although he was the first to produce movies, he was the last to come to California. By the time his Universal Studios arrived in 1912 there was no land remaining near Hollywood. After first renting a small property in town, in 1913 he moved over the Santa Monica Mountains and into the San Fernando Valley. As he stood at the top of the Cahuenga Pass on his first three-hour trip over the mountains, Laemmle surveyed a 50-mile-wide valley bordered on the north by majestic snow-covered mountains. He bought a 300-acre chicken ranch in Lankersham (now North Hollywood) just above the valley floor. Two years later, the once scrub-littered hillside was covered with street facades, from New York ghettos to Chinatown to Western. His little city had its own fire and police departments, hospitals, stores, and home sites. It also housed the biggest zoo in California. On March 15, 1915, Universal City was dedicated as a municipality.[21]

To generate some money, for 25¢ the Universal Studio Tour offered a walk through the lot, the chance to see movies being made, and a bag lunch. Every day, over 500 fans traipsed through the crowded facility.[22] But Universal's movies were becoming less successful, so Laemmle asked his 19-year-old secretary, Irving Thalberg, to clean up the mess.

By 1915, the standard-bearers for the 17,500 movie theaters were massive exhibition halls. There were 30 of the giants across the country. Among the first was the Exeter Theater in Boston, which held 900 seats but was dwarfed by the Palace Theater in L.A. with 1,950, and the massive Strand Theater in New York, with over 2,985 seats. The money was unheard of; the original Vitagraph Studios, capitalized with $1,000 in 1897, was by 1910 netting $6 million a year. At a time when a family income of $750 yearly was considered comfortable, some of the moviemen were earning $20,000 a week.

Almost all of the creators of the American movie industry were immigrants. Most came from eastern Europe and almost all were Jewish. All were part of the massive immigration of the late 1800s as millions fled the oppression, bigotry and economic uncertainty of turn-of-the-century Europe. Their paths began aboard crowded boats crossing the Atlantic, in the lines passing through Ellis Island, and in the sweltering ghettos of Montreal and New York.

Carl Laemmle was born in Laupheim, Germany, in 1867, and left his Oshkosh, Wisconsin, clothing store to open nickelodeons and produce films in New York. His Independent Movie Production (IMP) company filmed two-reelers in a Brooklyn beer garden[23] and in 1912 was known as Universal Picture Company. As a favor to his wife, he hired her best friend's son. Irving Thalberg was born in 1899, just after his family arrived from Germany. Born with congenital heart problems, doctors predicted the sickly child would not live to his teens. The Laemmle and Thalberg families had adjoining cottages on Long Island, and on weekend evenings Laemmle hung a large sheet over his front porch and showed his latest movies for neighbors.[24] He wrote down their opinions and made production decisions based upon them. Even then, teenaged neighbor Thalberg had a keen intuition about his movies. Laemmle also liked Thalberg because, like him, he was barely above five feet tall.

Cecil B. DeMille was the son of a minister-turned-actor who became a Broadway producer who worked with impresario David Belasco. His older brother, an actor, married the daughter of philosopher Henry George.[25] When his father died suddenly his mother opened a private girls' school and small theater company in the family home. She eventually became a successful play broker in New York. The younger DeMille worked as a stagehand, did a little acting, and in 1900 had a role in an off-Broadway play. It was there that he met Jesse Lasky. Lasky and DeMille played coronets in vaudeville pit orchestras. Lasky made and lost several fortunes promoting Broadway shows with his Jesse L. Lasky Feature Play Company, and hired young workaholic DeMille as his general manager.

Samuel Goldwyn — born Samuel Goldfish — was a third generation Russian glove-maker. Losing his job one day in 1913, he was walking back to his rooming house when he wandered into the Herald Square Theater on 34th Street to watch one of the new movies.[26] In seconds he had decided on his new career and went from the movie theater to his brother-in-law's apartment in search of a partner. His brother-in-law was Jesse Lasky. The two founded a movie company and hired DeMille as a director. Lasky and Goldwyn were just 33, DeMille 32. Goldwyn thought films were too short. Rather than one- or two-reel shorts, he felt — correctly, it turned out — that audiences would pay more for longer, more involved stories. DeMille visited an Edison film set for less than ten minutes before telling his bosses, "If that's all it takes to make movies, we'll all be knighted in a month."

Hungarian-born Adolph Zukor was selling furs in Chicago when a friend convinced him to invest in a theater in New York in 1903. Within six months he owned 500-seat emporiums in Newark, Boston and Philadelphia. Zukor believed that "the only chance motion pictures had of being successful was if stories or plays could be produced which were like those on the stage or in magazines." He also thought European films would be more popular than American.

Between 1903 and 1910 Zukor and his partner Marcus Loew dominated the trade by importing movies from Europe and controlling all distribution to any other U.S. chains. In 1912 Zukor founded the Famous Players Company to produce European-style films in the U.S. and in 1916 merged his Famous Players Studio with Lasky's Feature Play Company to increase production.[27] Zukor believed the easiest way to grow was to buy smaller firms and drive others out of business. After buying his biggest distributor — Paramount Pictures Corporation — he controlled everything from production to sales to distribution.[28] His mergers and purchases resulted in Paramount Pictures. Loew left Zukor to start his own theater business.

The Zukor-Lasky merger had left Goldfish the odd man out. It didn't help that at the time he was embroiled in an ill-timed divorce from partner Lasky's younger sister. Forced out of the partnership that he had begged Lasky to invest in, he located another partner in New York film distributor Edgar Selwyn. Before finding films, Selwyn may have been the most pathetic of any of these men. Orphaned at 15, he hopped trains from New York to Chicago, but finding no work, the teenager tried to commit suicide by jumping into the Chicago River. He landed on an ice flow, breaking a leg. Struggling to shore, he was accosted by a thief who put a gun to his head and demanded, "Your money or your life!" Exhausted, Selwyn replied, "My life." The gunman felt so sorry he gave Selwyn money for food before walking off into the night.[29] Selwyn made his way back to New York and eventually become a successful playwright. On November 19, 1916, Sam Goldfish and Selwyn formed Goldwyn Pictures to make movies. Later in 1918 Goldfish took the new company's name as his own, legally becoming "Samuel Goldwyn."

Nicholas Schenck was a plump Russian immigrant, one of seven children, born in 1881. His family lived in a Lower East Side tenement. Nick and older brother Joe were opposites. Joe carried a perpetual frown, but was kind and generous, gave excellent advice[30] and was universally beloved. His eventual wife, Norma Talmadge, called him "Daddy." Joe was stylish;

Nick was drab. Joe was older and spoke without any accent; Nick managed to keep his. Joe would marry a glamorous movie star; Nick's first
wife was a Brooklyn cop, his second a vaudeville dancer named Pansy.[31]
They always worked together, first running errands and selling newspapers so they could attend pharmacy school at night. They worked in a
Bowery drugstore; by 1910 they had saved enough to buy it, and within
two years they added a second near Chinatown. The brothers were not
above selling opium and morphine on the side to increase revenues.[32]

They stumbled upon another venture after taking a trolley ride to
Fort George, an amusement park above Manhattan on the Hudson River,
one of 500 U.S. parks drawing millions of city-dwellers every weekend.
There were several thousand people milling about with nothing to do but
wait for a return trolley, so that day the Schenck brothers rented a beer
concession that cleared $2,000 in the first three weeks. They spent $800
for a stage the next summer, cleared $16,000, and bought the park. They
added to their renamed Paradise Park a Ferris wheel, a scenic railway, and
concessions. One was a boxcar-sized movie theater screening the one-reel
"scenic tours" popular at the time. Viewers sat in the railcar seats as images
rolled past the windows. By 1920 the park took in $100,000 during a sunny
weekend.[33] One of their original investors was Marcus Loew, who by 1912
was running a chain of nickelodeons and arcades; he was so impressed
with the brothers' business acumen that he bought a $10,000 piece of the
park (the equivalent of about $300,000 today).[34] They went to work for
Loew's theater chains in 1913, but they kept their parks.

As part of their deal with Loew, the Schencks acquired two suburban
movie houses from Loew's huge Consolidated Enterprises. Loew and the
Schencks shared profits and began a pattern of reinvesting in real estate
for nickelodeons, vaudeville theaters, and later, motion picture production. By 1919 Loews, Inc. owned 60 movie and vaudeville theaters. Joe was
running Loew's talent-booking offices while Nick ran the theater operations. His assistant was a barrel-chested tough guy named Edgar J. Mannix.

Loew purchased a small California movie-maker — Metro Studios —
in 1919. Prior to that, Metro's main products were short inexpensive films
shown between features, called fillers. Metro was run by Louis B. Mayer.
As an infant Mayer came from Russia to St. Johns, in New Brunswick,
Canada, with his family. By 12 he was scouring the streets of New Brunswick alone, negotiating to buy metal for his father's junkyard. He developed fierce negotiating skills that became famous. His father was a stern,
harsh disciplinarian. Louis grew attached to his mother, developing an
obsession for motherhood that he kept his entire life. When she died he

said her last words were, "I'll wait for you."[35] He believed all mothers were infallible, almost perfect. He never wavered from that ideal, and woe to anyone who disagreed. Some of the biggest stars in the movies paid a price for being disrespectful of mothers.

Around age 16 Mayer was in Boston, in his words, "without the price of a sandwich." For the next five years he tethered himself to a boat and collected junk from the bottom of the harbor. He developed huge muscles dragging large pieces of metal onto the boat, along with a deeply ingrained work ethic, which he demanded of almost everyone he met.[36] In 1904 he married Margaret Shenberg, the daughter of a cantor at the synagogue Mayer attended. The couple had two daughters. In 1907 he borrowed $650 from his sisters to pay the six-month lease on the Gem, a ratty 600-seat burlesque house in a mill town near Boston called Haverhill. Locals had nicknamed the eyesore "The Germ."[37] It was located in the worst part of Haverhill, an area called the Bowery.

He did the rehab work himself, and his Orpheum Theater opened Thanksgiving Day, November 28, 1907. It was the only movie theater for 20 miles, and did well from the start. He soon began searching for investors for new locations, but his conservative New England neighbors ignored his entreaties, and called him Crazy Louie because of his never-ending requests.[38] But the youthful Mayer — only 24 — knew he had stumbled on something special, so he kept asking until he got the money he needed. It took Mayer two years, but by 1910 he opened a second theater across the river in Bradford, New Hampshire. The immense Colonial Theater held 1,600 people. His two theaters were consistently sold out. In 1912 he became a naturalized American citizen. So proud was Mayer that when the judge asked his birthday he yelled, "The fourth of July, your honor!"[39]

In 1914 Mayer moved to Boston and founded the American Feature Film Corporation to make his own movies and in February 1915 teamed with Pittsburgh promoter Richard Rowland to form Metro Pictures Corporation. Metro would distribute the films of five small production companies: Columbia Pictures Corporation, Dyreda Art Film Company, Popular Plays and Players, Quality Pictures, and Rolfe's Picture Company.[40] The company would produce one film a week and signed some of the most popular stars of the day, including Francis X. Bushman, Mary Miles Minter, and Ethel and Lionel Barrymore.

By 1915, Mayer's company and his theaters were major distributors for several bigger producers. Even so, it was not until his screening of D.W. Griffith's monumental Civil War work *The Birth of a Nation* (1915) that Mayer realized the earnings potential from making movies versus showing them. Mayer had a unique ability to decide if a film would be popular or not, and he secured an exclusive contract to exhibit *Birth* through all of New England. It was not the first time he gambled on a film; in 1914 he paid $4,000 — a huge sum — for the rights to *Squaw Man*[41] and earned 20 times that. His gamble on *Birth* made him rich. Over 1 million people stood in theaters' lines every day across the country. In New York it ran for over 40 sold-out weeks and still commanded the unheard-of ticket price of $2 ($50 today).[42] It played for five to seven years—continuously— in some Southern theaters. It was the first-ever movie blockbuster. Conservative estimates place the *Birth* gross between $50 million and $70 million (nearly a *billion* dollars today).

Mayer's clever gambit earned him more in one month than he had made in all his previous months together, somewhere near $2 million. The profits bankrolled his decision to make movies himself, so Mayer founded his own production company, Louis B. Mayer Pictures and in 1918 moved to Hollywood to make movies for his own theater chain. He rented a small studio in Edendale that had belonged to movie pioneer "Colonel" William N. Selig. It included a small building, a barn and a corral. He shared the lot with William Fox's production people.

By the time of his arrival there were almost 75 film companies working full time in the area. Slowly, almost inexorably, the fates had brought these men to the movie business, most as early as 1913. More precisely, the movie business found them, and dragged each one in. To a man, however, they each somehow found it: some by accident, some after much convincing; a few were even begged. Eventually, though, they were all members of the very new, very exclusive club: They were all making movies.

Two

Building the Emerald City

Louis B. Mayer Pictures was a profitable little company during the first years, making movies and distributing them either through First National Pictures or through Loew's Metro Company on contract. Between 1918 and 1920 while the industry and the other studios were steadily growing in size, Mayer's company still remained relatively small. Even so, Mayer was surrounded with high-quality managers. His team was led by Irving Thalberg and production manager Harry Rapf.

In 1922 Mayer met 22-year-old Thalberg, already known as the Boy Wonder. The hiring of Thalberg was, like almost everything else, dumb luck. Thalberg was five foot six and weighed 115 pounds. He had a handsome face and though he had a well-built chest, his legs and arms were almost tiny.[1] His size and effeminate mannerisms belied his ruthlessness. Edward G. Robinson once fled a contract negotiation to throw up in the hall outside Thalberg's office.[2] Mannix said, "Thalberg was a sweet guy but he could piss ice water."[3]

Thalberg came to L.A. on a 1919 trip to Universal with Carl Laemmle. Within a month he proved his toughness during a battle with director Erich von Stroheim. Von Stroheim's father was an Austrian hat-maker and he never served in the military, but he wore a Prussian cavalry officer's uniform with sword and monocle. He was making *Foolish Wives,* the last of three erotic films set in post–World War I Europe. *Blind Husbands* and *The Devil's Pass Key* barely made money because he spent uncontrollably, often on unseen props. Socks worn under the costumes of 100 soldiers were hand-monogrammed silk. He built a life-size replica of Monaco's royal palace. He delayed filming a banquet scene with 250 extras because wine goblets had ½-inch solid gold rims instead of the ¾-inch rims he had ordered. His final version was six hours long, 25 reels versus the normal six.

Thalberg ordered him to finish the picture without added expense, but von Stroheim walked out of his office. Thalberg closed filming, hired someone to slash the film in half, and released it without von Stroheim's approval. When von Stroheim started *Merry-Go-Round* by building a replica of a 10-acre Vienna amusement park, Thalberg fired him. The industry was stunned when the 21-year-old newcomer fired the legendary director, but by standing up to von Stroheim, Thalberg forever altered the moviemaking landscape. The victory meant the studios were in charge, not the directors.

Mayer knew of the Thalberg-von Stroheim feud, but Thalberg also had his editor George Randolph Chester write a series for *The Saturday Evening Post* about the Boy Wonder; young immigrant "Izzy Izkovitch" working up to running a major studio.[4] Thalberg wasn't identified by name but the nickname "Boy Wonder" stuck. A family conflict with Laemmle led Thalberg to Mayer in 1922. For several years Laemmle had tried to arrange a relationship with Thalberg and his daughter Rosabelle. He approached Thalberg's mother but Henrietta didn't want Irving to marry, afraid the rigors of a sexual relationship would weaken his feeble heart. She once found him playing tennis and walked onto the court and took his racquet from his hands. When Irving rejected Rosabelle, her father denied a promised contract and raise. Thalberg's business credo was "Never remain in a job after you have everything from it that you can."[5] Coincidently, at that moment Mayer was looking for a studio manager and arranged a meeting at the home of their mutual lawyer, Edwin Loeb, just before Christmas 1922. When Thalberg mentioned how much he owed his mother, Mayer decided to hire him on the spot. He joined Louis B. Mayer Pictures on February 15, 1923, as vice president in charge of production, and went from $200 a week at Universal to $600. But Mayer's daughters were forbidden to date Thalberg; Mayer didn't "want any young widows."[6]

The birth of MGM had its beginnings in a series of mergers designed by Adolph Zukor and Marcus Loew. Zukor had built a production and distribution system from the Famous Players–Lasky-Paramount mergers, but in 1919 he needed better theaters to show his movies. Loew had parlayed his vaudeville chain into a national movie chain and was a major exhibitor, but desperately needed product. To obtain it he combined three smaller companies, first taking over Metro from Richard Rowland in 1919 and inheriting his small group of green-shuttered buildings at the corner of Cahuenga and Romaine. Loew didn't even know Mayer at the time; Loew inherited Mayer when he bought Metro because Mayer was making films for Metro. From 1919 to 1923, Loew's Metro churned out four or five movies a week, but Loew tired of management, films, and dealing with egomaniacal actors and directors. He just wanted to run his theaters and had passed on the day-to-day stuff to his two aides, Nicholas and Joe Schenck.

Loew didn't solicit the next merger, and in fact his mounting boredom was leading him toward selling the production side entirely. During a Florida vacation he mentioned his plan to a friend, Broadway impresario Lee Shubert. Unknown to Loew, Shubert owned a piece of Goldwyn Studios, and he suggested to Loew that rather than selling, he should buy Goldwyn and merge the two. Loew still wasn't thinking about Mayer's little company.[7] Goldwyn president F.J. Godsol wasn't a "movie person"; he was a deal-maker hired in 1919 to turn the studio around. He had no loyalty. Within a year founder Goldwyn was gone. In 1923, Godsol saw a merger as a way to save the company. The only assets were a large Culver City lot, their lion trademark, and a few good directors, but Shubert convinced Loew the studio was a bargain. Godsol came to Loew's Florida mansion and made the merger deal,[8] but Godsol's lawyer J. Robert Rubin sensed that nobody in the mix was capable of running the new entity. He mentioned Mayer; he had done several deals with him, and was impressed with Mayer's business and organizational acumen and his knack for picking good movies.

Rubin called Mayer on his own and suggested that Mayer hurry to New York and join the negotiations between Loew and Goldwyn. Mayer left L.A. by train that day, going straight to the Waldorf-Astoria to announce his interest in joining the merger. In two days, Rubin arranged a deal between Loew's Metro, Goldwyn Studios, and Mayer. Loew's absorbed both Goldwyn Pictures and Louis B. Mayer Studios, resulting in an entity named Metro-Goldwyn-Mayer. Thalberg biographer Roland Flamini described it as "the triple merger of a long-established but inefficient studio, a financially ailing one, and Mayer's smaller but thriving outfit."[9] Loew purchased all Goldwyn company stock and paid Mayer $87,000 (about $1 million today) for his studio and 24 unfinished films. The new MGM would be a division of Loew's. The West Coast operation would locate at the Goldwyn lot in Culver City. Mayer would run the company as West Coast head of operations and produce 15 movies in two years. The 35-year-old junk dealer from Russia was running a studio.

MGM would be produce and distribute films and Loew's would act as the primary exhibitor through their 125 theaters and 150,000 seats. It wasn't the largest U.S. chain but it dominated the heavily populated northeast.[10] MGM would also rent films to 25,000 non-Loew theaters. Mayer was installed as studio chief, Thalberg remained second-in-command and supervisor of production, and lawyer Rubin was corporate secretary. Rapf would continue as a production manager. Mayer reported to Loew and

Schenck. He was making $1,500 a week and Thalberg $650. A side agreement with Loew paid Mayer, Thalberg, and Rubin 20 percent of the new
MGM's profits; Mayer 10 percent, the other men 5 percent apiece.[11] It
would make all three men rich. The paperwork was signed on April 10,
1924.

The formal start date was to be May 17, 1924, but Mayer couldn't wait
and opened on April 26, a hot Saturday morning. Mayer's best director
Fred Niblo was the emcee. The Culver City site was draped with banners
and flags, a large key bearing the word "SUCCESS," and an eight-foot tall
picture of Loew. A squadron of Navy planes flew overhead in formation
and dropped thousands of roses. A 250-man military band played marches
as guests assembled, Will Rogers trotted in on a white horse, and Mayer
offered a typical homily using the Yiddish accent he reserved for important events. "MGM will reach a point of perfection never approached by
any other company. If there is one thing I insist upon, it is quality.... I
hope that it is given me to live up to this great trust. This is a great moment
for me. I accept this solemn trust and pledge the best that I have to give."[12]
In front of 500 people, he was crying.

The new studio had the most talent in Hollywood. MGM's directors
were the most impressive in the industry, and included Fred Niblo, Victor Fleming, Robert Z. Armstrong, Clarence Brown, Sidney Franklin, Sam
Wood, George Hill, Robert Leonard, and King Vidor. Woodbridge Strong
Van Dyke was called "One-Take" Van Dyke for the speed with which he
completed films. He made William Powell's *The Thin Man* in just 18 days.[13]

MGM boasted the largest group of "name" stars in the business. The
top were "stars" like Lon Chaney or John Gilbert. Below stars were "fea-
tured players" like Marion Davies or Blanche Sweet. Next were "leads" like
Florence Rice or Edmund Gwenn. Mayer's company brought in Chaney,
Norma Shearer, Renée Adorée, and Hedda Hopper, as well as directors like
Niblo and Hobart Henley. Metro brought Ramon Novarro, Alice Terry,
Viola Dana, Jackie Coogan, Buster Keaton, Mae Busch, and directors Rex
Ingram and Vidor. From Goldwyn came Gilbert, Sweet, Mae Murray, Conrad Nagel, Aileen Pringle, William Haines and Eleanor Boardman, and
directors Victor Seastrom and Thalberg nemesis Von Stroheim. Produc-
tion relationships with William Randolph Hearst's Cosmopolitan Pictures
brought Hearst mistress Marion Davies and director Marshall Neilan.

Mayer brought along a core group of writers and directors like Francis Marion and Carey Wilson, art director Cedric Gibbons (who came
from Edison and then Goldwyn) and costumer Gilbert Adrian. Lana
Turner described his department as "200 old women with gnarled fingers
at hundreds of tables."

Mayer's boss in New York was Nick Schenck. Schenck assigned Mayer an assistant, barrel-chested Edgar J. Mannix. In 1911, when the Schencks were building Paradise Park, Nick met the young New Jersey Irishman who would remain a trusted aid for 40 years. Eddie Mannix attended elementary school in Fort Lee but after a year in a Hackensack middle school, went to work. At Paradise Park, the 20-year-old Mannix was one of hundreds of tradesman working at the park. He was a carpenter, bricklayer and mason, and sold tickets. He was a rough and tumble Irishman, a short, tough fighter with thick arms and big fists. He earned the nickname "Bulldog" as a teenager. At MGM he would be "the Irishman" (for his heritage) or "the Chinaman" (for his somewhat slanted eyes),[14] but friends called him E.J.[15] He was a foul-mouthed "deez, dem and doze" guy with no social polish, a fondness for drinking and a weakness for women.[16]

It is lost to history how Nick and Eddie met, or what so impressed Schenck that he took Mannix off the construction crew and made him a bookkeeper. A youth spent running numbers in Hackensack had made him a master of "working books," which he did for the Schencks until the IRS questioned their accounting practices.[17] Mannix was appointed Paradise Park's chief bouncer instead. The unofficial bodyguard and "muscle" for the Schenck brothers, Eddie could take out five rowdies at a time. He had to rid the park of the unruly, make sure money was safe, deal with unscrupulous vendors, and protect the brothers from the anti-Semitic locals. Given the makeup of the crowd — thousands of blue-collar immigrants enjoying breaks from 12-hour workdays and crowded New York tenements—toughness was a requirement. He soon became Schenck's number-two man, the general manager responsible for day-to-day operations. When the brothers purchased the largest amusement park on the East Coast, Palisades Park, in 1911, Mannix ran that too. Their friend Marcus Loew financed the purchase.

In less than five years the Schencks parlayed a small drugstore into ownership of the most popular amusement parks in New York. Joe had begun making movies in 1913 after a chance meeting with Evelyn Nesbitt Thaw on a cruise. She was "The Girl on the Red Velvet Swing" that hung above her lover — architect Stanford White's— piano. Unfortunately, her cuckolded millionaire husband William Thaw murdered White. Schenck hired Thaw as his first lead actress and cast her in *Redemption* (1913). The film made Schenck $250,000. His small Comique Studios— managed by Eddie —churned out films from the third floor of a decrepit warehouse in a grimy neighborhood at 320 East Forty-Eighth Street and First Avenue. The train rumbled past every five minutes.

Mannix's fortunes increased with the Schencks'. When he went to

work for them Eddie was living in a three-room-flat in a Fort Lee tenement a block from his childhood home. By the time he met Bernice
Froomis, a cute blond Irish girl from Fort Lee, two years younger, he was
living in an upscale brownstone.[18] Eddie fell in love quickly and after a
short courtship they married in a small Catholic church during the summer of 1916. Even in the marriage's early years Eddie's wandering eye
caused problems but Bernice, ever the good Catholic girl, turned a blind
eye.[19] Divorce was out of the question.

When Loew founded MGM, Mannix was thrust into the middle of
the management team. From the beginning Loew refereed fights between
the New York and L.A. offices. Mayer thought Loew favored the New Yorkers and Schenck didn't trust the L.A. people. The arguments continued for
years, but the L.A. operation became very large, very fast. The MGM
empire would soon employ 10,000 people, and even though Nick Schenck
was the boss, Mayer's L.A. office steered the ship. Schenck openly disliked
Mayer, but since he was inexperienced with film production and had no
interest in moving to California, he had to plant spies to watch the L.A.
operation. He was worried about money because of the percentage deal
Mayer and his team had, so Schenck sent Mannix to L.A.[20] Who better to
spy on Mayer than Schenck's bodyguard and bouncer?

Nobody in the movies knew Mannix. No MGM employee had ever
heard of him. Even a dozen years later in 1936 he was described in the *International Motion Picture Almanac* as "connected with theatrical profession
for five years as manager of eastern shows and for fourteen consecutive
seasons as manager of Palisades Park. Entered pictures in 1916, affiliated
with Allen Dwan." It was noted by way of introduction that he had "connections and associations with Jos. and Nicholas Schenck."[21] But in 1924
Mannix was installed as financial comptroller and assistant to Irving Thalberg. Everyone in New York knew his first responsibility was to keep an
eye on Mayer. Mannix, gambler, womanizer, drinker and mob-connected
tough guy, was the eyes and ears for the Schencks. He had more power than
even Mayer, because he was watching everybody.

People at the L.A. studio knew Mannix was "a Schenck man" but
Mayer liked the pugnacious New Yorker anyway. They became friends right
away and in just a few months Mannix became "a Mayer man."[22] Eddie
and Bernice arrived in Hollywood at the end of November 1924. During
a meeting just after, between Mayer and Erich Von Strohiem, the director casually said, "all women are whores." When an enraged Mayer
knocked him out with one punch, he earned Eddie's undying respect.[23]
Eddie's assistantship to Thalberg meant he would be privy to virtually
everything since Thalberg was minutely involved in every production

detail. It also meant unlimited access to women. Eddie could never be faithful to Bernice.[24] His job at the amusement parks gave him the opportunity to bed park employees and visitors, and the California assignment meant Eddie was surrounded by beautiful women every day. Almost all would trade sex for even a remote chance at stardom. Mannix's affairs would continue for the rest of his life.

When MGM began Mayer was 33 but looked older; Thalberg was 23 but looked younger. The barrel-chested Mayer and the painfully skinny Thalberg were an unlikely pair. They had different styles but complemented each other. Mayer's management style and attitude toward employees was a view of his true personality. He was insecure and given to exaggeration verging on hyperbole, so it was sometimes difficult to divine the true from the visible Mayer. But he could be manipulative, cruel, and unforgiving, and he held a grudge forever.

Seemingly at odds with his insecure personality, Mayer insisted on hiring the best people he could. He often said, "Good people make me look good," and he believed it.[25] His managers were invariably smarter than he was, and were the best at their individual jobs. His management team was an eclectic mix. Harry Rapf was a former vaudevillian whose huge nose made him the butt of incessant jokes. He was emotional, and wept easily, and his butchery of the English language was famous; he once said to Thalberg about a story, "Take out the essentials and what do you have?"[26] But he was a consummate showman and knew how to find talent and exploit it.

Culver City needed a publicity director and from New York, Mayer inherited Howard Dietz, a fascinating Renaissance man. He quit school after the seventh grade but earned a journalism degree from Columbia. He served in the navy and was a newspaper reporter before joining Goldwyn in 1919, hired as a publicity writer. By 1924 he was the head of all publicity. Dietz was also responsible for several well-known MGM trademarks. It was his suggestion that the new MGM use Goldwyn's "Leo the Lion," that he had designed (Mayer wanted to use his eagle).[27] He also crafted the studio's "Ars Gratia Artis" motto, attributing the incorrect Latin translation "Art for Art's Sake."[28] He would later write the studio's "More Stars Than There Are in Heaven" slogan. But Dietz wanted to work from New York, and hated even visiting California, so Mayer and Thalberg hired Pete Smith, a Brooklyn native who owned a successful L.A. press agency. Smith was one of the first publicity agents in the movies, working for Famous Players–Lasky on the immensely popular Hobart Bosworth films.[29] He was a natural comic with a quick wit and a caustic delivery. His firm represented several studios and independent directors and writers.[30] His assistant was young West Virginia native Howard Strickling.

The Stricklings came from the German village of Haltern in the early fourteenth century, first appearing in the U.S. around 1760 when John Strickling settled northeast of Baltimore in Harford County, Maryland.[31] Their eldest son Joseph moved to the remote Shenandoah Valley in Virginia the early 1800s, marrying and fathering 11 children.[32] Ten would farm the area around Winchester for the rest of their lives. His oldest son John B. moved to Newport, in southeastern Ohio, an equally remote outpost alongside the Ohio River, where he fathered 11 children of his own after his 1836 marriage to 16-year-old Deborah Shuler.

For the rest of the nineteenth century, the Ohio Stricklings prospered in the small farming towns on either side of the river, running farms and businesses in hamlets like Newport and Beaverton, Ohio, or St. Mary's and Mineral Wells, Virginia (West Virginia became a state in 1863). During the Civil War the Shenandoah Valley was the site of dozens of battles, and the Virginia Stricklings played host to a number of actions around Winchester and Front Royal. Both the Ohio and Virginia Stricklings were able to weather the brutal war and keep their farms. John and Deborah Strickling's eldest son Joseph married Sophia Crandall in 1864.[33] The second of their five children, John Wesley, was born in 1869 and at age 20 moved across the river to tiny St. Mary's, West Virginia. He opened a small general store serving farm families along the river in towns such as Raven Rock, Ben's Run, and Friendly. In 1893 he married Margaret Cochran.[34] Four children were born there: Joseph Wesley in 1894, John Howard in 1897, Roy Eugene in 1899, and Margaret Edythe in 1902. John Howard was called Howard.

In early 1905, the family moved to California and settled in Gardena, a remote farming community of 450 souls about 50 dusty miles south of L.A. They lived in a small house at 112 Vermont Street at the corner of El Segundo Boulevard, the town's main street,[35] and the elder Strickling opened a grocery store. The post office incorrectly listed the family as "Strickland." Margaret and the children worked at the store during the day and Howard enrolled in Gardena Agricultural High School, intent on running his own farm. But his articles for the school's weekly newspaper *The Lark* showed a talent for writing.[36] In 1919 the family moved to even more remote San Bernardino County, further east to Ontario. They settled into a home at 215 West F Street in Ontario off Euclid Avenue.[37] Euclid was dotted with businesses and ranch houses and ran from deep in the valley until it disappeared into the snow-capped San Gabriel Mountains to the north. In October 1919, as his father opened another small grocery store, Howard headed for Hollywood.

Much of Strickling's early life can be confirmed through census records, birth and death records, and county archives. However, once Strickling began working in Hollywood the stories become muddled in a cloud of fictitious biographies written by Strickling himself. Like all studio bios, Strickling's was partial fiction. He usually described his father as a minister and claimed his first job as a newspaper errand boy and typesetter. Strickling supposedly worked as a sports writer for an Ontario newspaper, but no records confirm that. Within a few months of arriving in L.A. was working at the studios in "publicity."

When 25-year-old Strickling moved from Ontario to Hollywood in 1919, he rented a room from Alice Sweeney, a 45-year-old friend of his father. The elder Strickling knew the owner of the Hollywood grocery store where Sweeney and her brother worked. She owned a large house at 1801 Cherokee Avenue in the center of town, living with her brother and his three teenaged children and renting out rooms in the large house to boarders. Hotel rooms were scarce in early 1920s Hollywood, and it was common for people to take on boarders if they had the room.[38] Howard shared two large upstairs rooms with Harry Beassley, who managed a music store.

The block wasn't glamorous but was clean and quiet and a short stroll from busy Hollywood Boulevard and the studios. The residents were working people; store owners, cab drivers, carpenters and farm laborers.[39] Within a few days Strickling was hired as an office boy at Metro Studios and after a year or so moved to Goldwyn as a publicist, a simple title that Strickling used to describe his occupation on forms for the next 40 years. He shared a cramped office with a dozen writers who produced publicity for films and actors.

He was a favorite of manager Pete Smith. He was at heart a country boy, son of a grocer, with roots deep in the tiny West Virginia hamlets and farm towns in San Bernardino County. He was tall and ruggedly handsome, but steadfastly quiet. Like his father his hobbies were gardening and raising chickens and turkeys. Like Mayer, he adored his parents.[40]

Strickling and Mannix were opposites in almost everything. Mannix was gruff while Strickling was gentlemanly to a fault. Mannix had innumerable affairs while Strickling was married to the same woman for almost 50 years. Mannix had disdain for most of his charges—a sign on his desk warned "THE ONLY STAR AT MGM IS LEO THE LION!"[41]—but Strickling was genuinely concerned for their welfare. But before long Strickling and Mannix were responsible for shaping the destinies of the entire MGM family, and did so for four decades. Perhaps more than anyone else at the studio the two would determine the studio's fate and the fate of the biggest stars in the movies. In 1924 they were outsiders, but within a year they were running the inner circle. They would be "The Fixers." Everyone in Hollywood would know it.

Mayer and Thalberg were also opposites. During his tenure from 1924 to 1951, Mayer discovered many of the screen's finest actors and actresses and the most creative producers, writers, and directors. He told every hire, "Find your way around. A man must run before he walks, and walk before he runs."[42] Mayer had a simple grasp of what people liked. He described his decision-making by saying, "If a story makes me cry, it's good." His grandson Danny Selznick said, "He cried at *Lassie,* cried at *The Human Comedy.* He cried at *The Great Caruso.*"[43] According to Mayer only three emotions were important. He showed people what they were by tapping his forehead, his heart, and his genitals.[44] His original theaters were successful because he showed quality movies. An instinctive showman with a gut feeling for business and what would be popular, his experience with *The Birth of a Nation* led to a belief that bigger was better, that blockbusters were the way to go.

Mayer thought himself the "Father of the Studio" and treated employees like children who didn't know what was good for them. He said, "I don't operate a fly by night studio. People who do their jobs have a job for life." He told female hires to think of him as "your friend, your counselor, and your guide." As actress Ann Rutherford described the studio, "From the time you're signed at MGM you just felt you were in God's hands. Like somebody was looking after you."[45] Mayer ruled his company as if it were a family with a harsh father like his own, but made decisions like his mother. Writer Sam Marx said Mayer's job "permitted him to act as godhead to men and a father figure to women."

He was the father, MGM was home, and he took care of his children. Marx spent years as a story editor before leaving MGM for Columbia after a fight with Mayer. Years later he ran into Mayer at Saratoga Race Track, and though Mayer was with Marx's boss, Harry Cohn, he asked him, "When are you coming home, Sam?" In 1940, when Lionel Barrymore was crippled by arthritis and confined to a wheelchair (the reason his Mr. Potter sat in a wheelchair during *It's a Wonderful Life*), Mayer arranged for him to get cocaine to deaden the chronic pain.[46]

Mayer's attitude with employees developed from his dealings with the first director he hired in Hollywood, free-spirited Irishman Marshall Neilan. "Mickey" was originally D.W. Griffith's chauffeur and Griffith used him in over 100 films by 1916, before he began directing comedies. His biggest success was Mary Pickford, whom he directed in a dozen films and developed into a brilliant comedic actress. Every studio wanted Neilan but Mayer convinced him to join MGM in 1924. Neilan arrived at their first meeting four hours late, and drunk. Mayer disliked everything about Neilan's personality and Neilan taunted Mayer by making fun of his Puritanical views. He told Mayer he was going to sleep with every one of Mack Sennett's "Bathing Beauties," and offered Mayer regular updates with the names of his most recent conquests.[47] Neilan was eventually fired in 1926 but Mayer never forgot his introduction to what he considered "Hollywood types." Marx noted, "The backlash [from Neilan] would be felt by many great stars, writers, directors and executives in the decades ahead."

Mayer was disgusted when Neilan bragged about his affairs but wasn't opposed to them, particularly after Neilan's wife suffered permanent hormonal and mental imbalances following a 1930s hysterectomy.[48] He frequently availed himself of the contract actresses, who would do anything for him. They were afraid of him but unaware that he would never have cancelled an actress's contract because she wouldn't sleep with him. He usually fell in love with the big stars he slept with, including Jean Harlow, Grace Moore, Jeanette MacDonald, Ginny Simms, and Eleanor Powell.[49] He courted them as if he were the most eligible bachelor in Hollywood instead of a husband and father of two. He gave his lovers flowers and expensive gifts, trips for their families, and quiet romantic dinners.

Mayer's most interesting affair was his fling with Norma Shearer. She was beautiful and talented, but is remembered as Mrs. Irving Thalberg. Stories of her affairs with her bosses were common on the lot but the Mayer affair was a closely guarded secret, particularly after her ascension to "Queen of the Lot" by marrying Thalberg. Joan Crawford once said, "How can I get a role. She's sleeping with the boss."[50] At the time she was referring to Thalberg, but Shearer was *Mayer's* protégée long before she set her sights on Thalberg.

Mayer was a contradiction. With all of his personal foibles he had an acute sense of what made a movie good. His had no formal education but could quickly decipher and understand complicated issues. He possessed a rapid-fire wit that surprised contemporaries. And he understood in a very basic way what people liked. The 1940s *Andy Hardy* movies featured Lewis Stone as Judge Hardy, a wizened and beloved character Mayer modeled after himself. But Mayer never fooled himself into believing that movies were more than they were, saying, "Don't try to make pictures better. Just keep them the way they are." He told director Gottfried Reinhardt, who wanted to make an artsy picture, "You want to be an artist, but you want other people to starve for your art." He could also be comically simple in his decision-making. For example, he hated people who used cigarette holders; he thought it made users look "unwholesome, decadent, and potentially troublesome."[51] "Goddamn intellectuals," he once screamed, "with their cigarette holders!"

During the 1930s and 1940s he was a frequent visitor to MGM Sunday baseball games. Clad in a shirt and tie, Mayer always wanted to pitch. The league's organizer, Buster Keaton, hired Ernie Orsatti, an outfielder for the St. Louis Cardinals, as an assistant prop man. Orsatti spent the baseball off-season at MGM playing with Keaton every day at four.[52] If Mayer wanted to make an emotional point he fell back on two old ploys. First he cried. If that didn't work he "fainted." When he was young he over-dieted and during a disagreement with a director fainted dead away from hunger. The director thought Mayer died and after reviving him gave in. From that day forward, if his arguments didn't move an intractable opponent Mayer would fall to the floor in a phony faint.

Mayer's feelings for women and mothers directed his decisions. He rewarded obedience but punished even minor transgressions as personal betrayal. He was strict and authoritarian with actors, controlling every aspect of their lives. If they angered Mayer they were punished with equal severity, often with career-ending consequences. Producer Herman Mankiewicz said, "Mayer had the memory and hide of an elephant. The only difference was elephants are vegetarians and Mayer eats his fellow man."[53] John Gilbert was Mayer's most famous victim. Gilbert was an irreverent alcoholic and womanizer. At a party Gilbert described a childhood incident with his mother, stage actress Ada Adair. While he was walking behind her holding her dress, she slipped, and, Gilbert said, "she wasn't wearing any drawers. That was the last time I saw my mother's ass."[54] Mayer would have fired Gilbert, even though he made millions for MGM, but Gilbert and Thalberg were pals and Thalberg told Mayer, "We can't ignore talent because we don't like their personality."[55] Mayer spent years looking for a way to get rid of Gilbert.

Mary Pickford, at the time of her pre-marriage affair with Douglas Fairbanks. In her late 20s she was still playing teenagers.

Mayer's office was on the ground floor of the main building near the Washington Boulevard entrance. Secretary Ida Koverman and her two assistants sat outside. It was a huge all-white office copied from Harry Cohn, who himself copied Italian dictator Benito Mussolini's office. The phones, dictographs, and grand piano were all white. The office was "so long I could barely see the other end of it," according to Frank Capra.[56] Sam Goldwyn said, "You need an automobile to reach the desk."[57] Like Cohn and Mussolini, Mayer put his huge circular desk on a raised platform so visitors sat below. Also as in Cohn's office, the doorway was controlled by a button at his desk. Nobody entered or left unless he allowed it. But Mayer didn't need a button; he had Koverman.

Mayer met Ida Koverman when she was in California to rally the women's vote for Herbert Hoover; she had been Hoover's secretary when he was a San Francisco engineer. Mayer hired her when the studio first opened. On her desk was a photograph of the president inscribed "To my dear Ida, Herbert Hoover." Mayer thought she was Jewish and didn't know for years she was a Catholic. His grandson said she reminded Mayer of his mother.[58] She was actually a feisty Scottish widow who rarely smiled and hardly ever laughed. Mayer paid her $250 a week, the same salary paid to MGM stars. For the next 30 years "Kay" never asked for a raise, believing Mayer should offer her one. He never did, and to the day she died in 1953 she was paid $250 a week.

Kay was as powerful as her boss. She controlled who got to see him. She decided what problems were passed on and what problems went to Strickling or Mannix. A casual mention that Mayer should "take a look at" someone could make a career, and she was responsible for some of MGM's biggest finds. She overruled Mayer's first reaction to an unknown with big ears and bad teeth and convinced him to sign Clark Gable. She suggested Mayer hire Mario Lanza,[59] and it was her idea to hire Spangler Arlington Brugh and rename him Robert Taylor. She heard a teenaged mama's-boy singing in an L.A. choir and convinced Mayer to hire Nelson Eddy after he said, "He's too pretty and he can't act."[60] She was the in-house arbiter of good taste. Hedda Hopper said she was "the only living soul in Hollywood Mayer would listen to when she told him what to do."

Koverman also suggested the studio start a school for young actors; her "Little Red Schoolhouse" alumni included Jackie Cooper, Mickey Rooney, Judy Garland, Elizabeth Taylor, and Donna Reed. It was run for years by Miss McDonald, who could have come from central casting. She was a gray-haired, middle-aged spinster who terrified children. Actors attended school daily until their eighteenth birthday. But her power extended far beyond the studio. During a 1927 Pete Smith publicity stunt flying a lion to New York, the plane crashed somewhere in Arizona. Koverman arranged for 40 navy search planes to be dispatched to find the lost lion. When the Navy balked, Koverman asked President Hoover to make the call, and he did.

When MGM began, the New York office knew Mayer had to polish his personal skills and avoid his accented and profanity-laced everyday speech. Pete Smith wrote his letters and speeches and coached him not to ad lib in public.[61] Actor Conrad Nagel was hired to work on grammar and when that didn't work, New York quietly offered Koverman a bonus to help. Her value didn't go unnoticed. Howard Hughes offered her over $1,000 a week to work for RKO. She never mentioned the offer to Mayer. To gain entrance to Mayer's inner sanctum, visitors were required to wear a tie and jacket and women formal dress, makeup and hair. It didn't matter if the visitor were an international star, a writer, or a business associate.

Thalberg was the antithesis of Mayer in every respect; as a manager, decision-maker, businessman, and a person. As William Haines described them, "He [Thalberg] was a great, great man. I was blind when it came to him. It was just the opposite with Mayer. I remember everything good about the one, everything bad about the other." Close to both men, Sam Marx said, "Thalberg was naïve, Mayer was sharp. Thalberg was frail, Mayer was robust. Thalberg was retiring, Mayer was pugnacious. Thalberg was searching for new meanings in life, Mayer satisfied with the old. Thalberg was loyal but rarely emotional, Mayer was emotional but rarely loyal."[62]

Thalberg believed that a studio must control every aspect of the filmmaking process — everything. This unwavering core belief would direct Thalberg's entire career. He said, "In a business where no one had the courage of his own convictions, I knew I was right and I should make them do it my way." Thalberg had a photographic memory for details. When Harry Rapf accused Thalberg of not reading a scenario, Thalberg listed from memory 50 individual scenes in order. He then told an incredulous Rapf, "I can give you page numbers if you want them."[63]

As a person he was uniquely aloof. Everyone — even his closest managers — thought him unapproachable. Dietz said of him, "He was thoughtful when he thought of you, he just never thought of you unless you were useful."[64] He arrived every day at ten, went to his private bungalow for coffee and then to his office. He rarely left before one in the morning, staying until two most days. He preferred to work in anonymity, and his name never once graced an MGM film credit. Mayer, on the other hand, had an agreement with Loew that every picture would be released under the heading, "Louis B. Mayer Presents," followed by "A Louis B. Mayer Production." His name appeared on every piece of studio stationary and every press release. Thalberg negotiated his name *out* of everything, saying, "Credit you give yourself isn't worth having."[65] He allowed himself credit once, for the scenario of *The Dangerous Little Demon* (1920) for Marie Prevost. The writer was "I.R. Irving." His personal style mirrored his aloofness. He worked almost restlessly, pacing the room, twirling his watch chain and endlessly flipping a $20 gold piece he always carried.[66] He was a bubbling fountain of insightful and usually correct ideas.

Thalberg never surrounded himself with yes-men. While other managers were trailed by sycophantic hangers-on, Thalberg was fiercely independent, relying instead on his own opinions. Mayer always had six or eight managers following at his heels.[67] Thalberg had three rules: Never take any man's opinion as final. Never take your opinion as final. Never expect anyone to help you but yourself.[68] He had a half-dozen aides from whom he solicited advice and counsel. Unlike Mayer's yes-men, Thalberg's were hard working and intelligent, each bringing a specific expertise to their boss. Interestingly, the men in Thalberg's inner circle were older and well-educated, and short like him. They were an eclectic group.

He was closest to production assistant Bernie Hyman, an old friend from Universal, and to Paul Bern. Hyman was a gregarious, funny man with the face of a child, who always wore plaid sport coats. Paul Bern, a fellow German immigrant, was the creative source. Al Lewin was Thalberg's source of intellectual advice. He had a master's from Harvard, had left unfinished a doctoral dissertation at Columbia,[69] and moved to Hollywood after a stint as a movie critic for the *Jewish Chronicle*. Thalberg's interest in movies based on books prompted his hiring Lewin, who had an encyclopedic knowledge of the written word. He became Thalberg's personal assistant.[70] Kate Corbaloy was his chief writing assistant. Her husband abandoned her after the birth of their fourth daughter, and she worked as a librarian at Stanford University before moving to Hollywood to teach screenwriting at the Palmer Institute of Authorship. Thalberg found her there. Hunt Stromberg was a handsome Kentuckian with wiry hair and a nervous tic who had been the sports editor at the *St. Louis Times*. He was the sloppiest dresser at MGM; Thalberg could tell what he had for lunch by simply looking at his tie. Harry Rapf filled out the inner circle. He was an ex-vaudevillian who tolerated a lifetime of jokes about the size of his nose; he was "The Ant-eater," "Thalberg's sundial," and he could "keep a lit cigar dry in the shower."[71] He was also known for his Rapf-isms like "This is the best apple pie I ever ate with my whole mouth."[72] About a movie based on the Virgin Mary, "Can it be done in modern dress?" He once told Thalberg, "I woke up last night with a terrific idea for a movie, but I didn't like it."[73]

Even with their various eccentricities Thalberg valued their opinions and actively sought their counsel. But they were no different than any other employee when it came to getting an appointment. His office was in a corner of the second floor. He chose the spot because he didn't want to be too close to Mayer. His reception area was larger than the office itself. Secretaries Dorothy Howell, who came with him from Universal, and Vivian Newcomb sat outside, sharing desk space with secretaries for Mannix and Rapf. Thalberg's area was always crowded with people waiting to see him. Even Mayer rarely got in on his first attempt. Director Victor Seastrom once sat outside for three days just before Christmas waiting to see his boss. Then he went on vacation to Sweden for two weeks. When he returned he ran into Vivian Newcomb, who told him, "Oh, Mr. Seastrom, I think Mr. Thalberg can see you know."[74] Writer George Oppenheimer once sat in Thalberg's anteroom for four days.

Thalberg's inner office was large and wood-paneled, dominated by his oversized mahogany desk and large leather chair that sat on a raised platform. Visitor's chairs and sofas were small. According to Maurice Rapf, when you sat there it was like being a child in the principal's office. Adjacent to the desk was a massive fireplace.

Management styles and personal foibles aside, in the beginning the biggest challenge facing Mayer and his managers was operating in a creative environment. Most of the their employees were not business-minded. They were creative, easygoing verging on lazy, and indifferent to the commercial demands of the business. In short, what made the directors, writers and actors so special also made them difficult. Mayer had dealt with everything from old-line Boston financiers to New York bankers, but nothing had prepared him for his dealings with the film world.

The property that MGM inherited in 1924 was originally part of La Ballona Rancho, an eighteenth century Spanish land grant. In 1915 Harry H. Culver owned it and dreamt of a city covering the rolling hills. Between 1915 and 1920 he lured people to his Culver City by giving away free land to anyone to would build a movie studio on their gifted parcel. Culver's first taker was Thomas Ince, who received 12 free acres for Triangle Studios, which he owned with D.W. Griffith and Mack Sennett. It was on Washington Boulevard, a dirt road running through the hills from the ocean into town. The nearest building was St. Augustine's Catholic Church, across the street, and Slim's, a tiny coffee stand a block away. Just a few months later the Triangle partners were feuding; Sam Goldwyn leased their property and bought 25 extra acres for $2,000. He had a small three-story office building fronting six small glass-enclosed stages. Littered about the property were small buildings to store wardrobe, props, and equipment, and several locker-style dressing rooms for the stars. Goldwyn planted grass so it would look like a home and let Will Rogers borrow a small building to keep his horses stabled.

When he expanded in 1919, 20 acres that a few years earlier had been free cost $50,000. He enclosed the lot with a 15-foot-tall cement wall, a half mile of which ran down Washington Boulevard. The main area on Washington between Madison and Jackson was known as Lot 1. That area held the executive offices, projection rooms, laboratories for film developing, huge sound stages, quarters for writers, hundreds of dressing rooms, and all of the related technical departments. There were individual buildings for wardrobe, make-up, props, and others.

The new main gate was flanked by several dozen four-story-tall Corinthian columns built for Thomas Ince's 1915 *Intolerance* set. Within a few years, Goldwyn's back lot held 50 buildings and sets for every conceivable locale. Street sets of every kind were constructed; Western, oriental, European, and dozens of American versions. The main building was three low-slung stories tall. It would eventually be renamed for Irving Thalberg and nicknamed "The Iron Lung" for Thalberg's air conditioning.[75] The first floor was dominated by Mayer's office. The second floor offices were filled with Thalberg's people. His was on a corner, and when he moved there to get away from Mayer, Mannix was asked to move next to Thalberg to keep an eye on him. Mannix reported daily to Mayer the comings and goings at Thalberg's sanctuary. Harry Rapf was next door and Paul Bern just down the hall.

Next door was Ben Thau's casting office with his famous "private interview room" and separate entrance onto Washington. The casting offices were just west of the main entrance with a separate entrance so casting directors and staff could walk outside and check the lines that formed every morning before sunrise (it also offered a quick exit for unfortunates who endured the private interview rooms in the casting department). Most of the people in the casting lines carried costumes or were in costume if they knew of a particular type of film was being made, and casting people walked the lines choosing from among the hundreds of hopefuls. The money was good. Extras earned $5 for crowd scenes, $10 for small group shots, or $25 if they were seen in a closeup. Even higher rates prevailed for the lucky few who had spoken lines.

Outside the building near the front gate was a shoeshine stand operated by Harold "Slickem" Garrison, a black man with a fourth-grade education who nonetheless counseled his executive customers on everything from script decisions to casting questions. He was also Thalberg's driver.[76] Across the street stood four massive five-story-tall billboards. The studio's latest movie posters shone from each. Mayer and Thalberg used the promise of putting their names on the boards to bribe actors, directors, and producers.

Inside the gates, the area close to the main building resembled a military camp, dominated by half a dozen long, two-story buildings with porches running the length of the fronts. On one side stood one such building that housed the film editing offices. The building was connected to the main building by a large bridge that allowed executives easy access to the projection rooms to see the "dailies"; that day's film output. Above the projection rooms were editing rooms. The building also had a plain metal balcony running the entire length, and was used often as a movie set if army barracks were needed. If a prison were needed, the doors were removed and replaced by bars.

On the other side of the main entrance were a pair of two-story buildings that stretched 200 yards west down Washington. They held the dressing rooms. Each also had a balcony running the entire length of the building, and for privacy the side facing the street had no windows.[77] Most of the rooms were the same size, like hotel rooms with private baths, but bigger stars were given larger quarters closer to makeup or hairdressing. Stars didn't have separate dressing rooms until Marion Davies arrived in 1925.

Davies was a wonderful comedic actress and lifelong mistress of publisher William Randolph Hearst. Hearst purchased Cosmopolitan Films so that he could direct her career, hand-picking directors and always including a scene with Marion wearing slacks (dressing her as a man was one of his little-known fetishes). At Universal, Hearst built a 15-room stucco "bungalow" with an orange tile roof for her dressing room. It was luxurious, with brocade curtains and carpets, sunken bathtubs and two kitchens. On March 10, 1925, he had the 3,000-square-foot house disassembled and shipped via a caravan of trucks to MGM. Hearst would move the house twice more: when she left MGM in 1934 it went to Warner Brothers, and when she left Warners, onto an acre of land at 910 Benedict Canyon, where it still stands today.

Thalberg built a similar bungalow that had a dining room and kitchen for his private chef, where he hosted formal dinners for guests and daily lunches for his pals. Within a few years, every major star at MGM was given his or her own bungalow, and as with the original dressing rooms, the size was based upon his or her popularity.

The writers were housed in a large building near the entrance. A superb manager, Thalberg was stymied by writers. "Damn it," he told Anita Loos, "I can keep tabs on everyone else at the studio and can see if they are doing their jobs. But I can never tell what's going on with you writers." At one time in the 1930s, the lobby directory listed such literary greats as F. Scott Fitzgerald, Vicki Baum, Loos, Stephen Vincent Benet, Moss Hart, Aldous Huxley, George S. Kaufman, Dorothy Parker, and Robert Benchley.[78]

In addition to writers the building also housed story and research departments. The story department had 100 readers who combed through literary sources that might make a movie. The material was synopsized so the producers could decide from a one-page summary if they wanted to consider making a film. If there was interest, the story department dealt with the original writers and then the studio's writers. Supporting the departments were over 200 stenographers who spent their days huddled over typewriters transcribing meeting notes, scripts, script revisions, and anything else. Low-level writers toiled on scripts that would probably never be read, while high-profile writers under contract developed "real" scripts.

The research department provided writers with the historical information necessary for a script about a certain time period or event. Like a huge private library, the research department was staffed by dozens of elderly women silently patrolling aisle upon aisle of floor-to-ceiling bookcases and newspapers. Anita Loos shared quarters with actor Lionel Barrymore, who was given a first floor dressing room because arthritis prevented him from walking up stairs to a normal dressing room. Next door was a small building—once a Culver City grocery store—that was Koverman's schoolhouse. The noise was a constant irritant to the irascible Barrymore, who would stand by a window and yell at the children running by.

Next door was another two-story row building housing the directors and producers, nicknamed Director's Row. There were little wooden frames on the screen doors naming the resident. Every name, from successful directors like Tod Browning and King Vidor to unknowns, was handwritten in pen. It was a constant reminder of how easily they could be replaced.

Another building housed all of the cameramen, 25 on the payroll at all times. Some were retained so they wouldn't film for rival studios and some as pet cameramen demanded by certain stars. Norma Shearer let only Bill Daniels put her on film because he hid the droopy eye that had plagued her since childhood. Garbo demanded Oliver Marsh, and Jean Harlow would marry her favorite cameraman, Hal Rosson. Portrait photographers George Hurrell and Clarence Bull, among the portrait photographers assigned to the publicity department, became world famous. Publicity — by 1928 there were 100 employees — had a private three-story building near the main entrance.

There were dozens of other buildings housing everything from sculpture to animal-training, truck repair, and transportation. The thousands of employees needed to be fed, so a large commissary building was erected near the entrance. The main restaurant was known as the Plantation Café, managed for 30 years by hostess Frances Edwards. It was the social center and a gathering place for coworkers to chat about work, actors to meet with agents, and visitors to rub elbows with movie stars. The specialty was 35¢ chicken soup, a rich soup with huge pieces of chicken and vegetables, made fresh every morning. Mayer promised his mother that when he was rich she would always have chicken soup with real chicken. It was available whenever the commissary was open.[79]

The commissary was primarily for actors and studio managers. The backlot workers ate lunch at their sets or at their desks, rarely visiting the commissary. Several hundred people could visit at once. To keep things manageable, companies shooting were given staggered lunch times. In addition, a pecking order was in place for seating. The main room was dominated by two tables, one each for writers and directors. The directors' table was in the dead center of the large dining room, with all other tables arrayed in a circular pattern around that table. There were dozens of counter stools surrounding the room. There was a small screened-in porch that housed a single table and 12 chairs. It was the most sought-after lunch seat. Bill, a midget actor, served the table, lorded over by writer Joseph Farnham. Bill brought in a huge tray on his three-foot-tall shoulders loaded with 20 pounds of Russian rye bread, ham, chicken, and salads. Farnham then built a giant sandwich called "The Farnham"; it was the most expensive item on the menu. At the end of lunch, Bill brought a small silver birdcage that held three dice. The loser paid for lunch, the equivalent of $500.[80]

Thalberg and other executives ate in a small bungalow next to the commissary that was built as a private lunchroom. The executive bungalow held one long table and 12 chairs. The chair at the head of the table was always kept empty for Mayer. He seldom ate there; he had a private dining room near his office.

MGM had its own police department, run by Whitey Hendry. Strickling said that Mayer suggested hiring him, saying, "We needed a top cop who knew all the other top cops in the area and all over the United States, so he offered Whitey a lot of money."[81] Hendry was the middleman between the studio and police and worked closely with the publicity department, reporting directly to Thalberg. At the same time he was also chief of police for Culver City. Hendry usually just appeared at the site of an MGM problem. In the 1930s, director Busby Berkeley, who had several high-profile legal run-ins, simply listed him as "Whitey" in his address book, alongside Hendry's Santa Monica address and phone numbers.[82]

The studio fire department employed over 50 men protecting a five-square mile tinderbox. With the exception of the fireproof film negative building, the entire property was of very flammable wooden construction. A wide boulevard ran through the middle of the property, dubbed "The Alley." On a typical day it was bustling with activity, a parade of stars heading from dressing rooms to sets and sets moving from stage to stage.

Lot 2, one of the six back lots where 99 percent of MGM movies were filmed, was west of Lot 1, bordered by Washington and Elenda and containing dozens of permanent outdoor sets. There were city streets, Western scenes, suburban neighborhoods, and all manner of buildings. It was originally a huge gravel pit owned by Joe Schenck, and was filled in with dirt from Los Angeles's excavation of the La Brea tar pits.[83] Even larger outdoor sets were contained south of Washington in a vast lot that ran for a mile along Jefferson. These featured several lakes, a fully contained harbor, and a 15-acre jungle. Looming over the lakefront sets was an ingenious contraption of hundreds of movable barrels that could be turned upside down as quickly as they could be filled. The resulting waterfalls created huge waves when needed. Also hidden in Lot 2 were Stone Age sets, an operational French railway station with several dozen authentic European trains, and a dozen European villages. Amid the sets was a two-acre park of manicured lawns and eucalyptus trees named Cohn Park (after Joe Cohn, head of production).

Lot 3 was covered by natural forest surrounding a large lake (built by Cedric Gibbons) fed by an artificial river. The original MGM parcel covered 150 acres, but within ten years Mayer grew MGM to 25 huge sound stages and almost 225 acres. One of the more famous back lots was a triangular piece of land southeast of the main lot, 30 acres near the intersection of Jefferson Boulevard and Higuera Street. It was part of the original Ince holdings, nicknamed "The Forty Acres." Ince leased it to Cecil B. DeMille in 1925 to film *King of Kings*, and it was where DeMille built his full-size replica of the biblical city of Jerusalem. *King Kong* (1933) was filmed there, as were most outdoor scenes in *Gone with the Wind* (1939). David O. Selznick built his replica of Atlanta there and the "Tara" mansion. During the 1950s the *Superman* television series was filmed there, and in some episodes the façade of "Tara" is visible.

Mayer's day began the same way every day. Within minutes of his arrival Mannix walked in with a report of the studio's financial position. Meetings followed in order with Cohn on production, Rapf and Hyman on movie preparation, and individual appointments with contract players. But among the dozens of daily meetings, Mannix was always first — every day, for 30 years.

When they arrived in L.A. in the fall of 1924, Eddie and Bernice Mannix took an apartment near downtown with their niece Ruth. Six months later they stumbled upon the house they would share for the next decade. The house was built by Buster Keaton to surprise his wife Natalie Talmadge. The Keaton marriage was unhappy due to interference from Natalie's sisters Constance and Norma and their awful mother Peg.[84] Thalberg pursued Constance for years and Norma married Joe Schenck, but the Talmadge women and Keaton hated each other. His marriage became sexless after Natalie was convinced by her sisters to stop having sex after childbirth.[85] Norma herself was avoiding Schenck's requests for rough sex,[86] and sleeping with almost every actor she worked with. Worse, the Talmadges were living with the Keatons.

In a desperate bid to rid himself of the Talmadge women Buster secretly built a charming three-bedroom ranch house at 516 Linden Drive in the Beverly Hills flats, a dozen tree-lined streets running below Sunset. It was a quiet neighborhood with wide boulevards and good-sized lots but decidedly unglamorous. Keaton's neighbors were Joseph Pruig, a doctor for the Mexican embassy, William Fowler, who owned a bookstore, and an elderly couple, Oscar and Eva Blattner, who owned an orange grove. The only movie person in the area was James Hanley, who conducted a studio orchestra.[87] There were no stars. Buster and Natalie were friendly with Bernice and Eddie through Schenck, Eddie's boss and Buster's brother-in-law. Buster filled the house with furniture and the pool with water and invited Natalie and the Mannixes out for a drive to surprise Natalie. She hated the house, asking, "Where will the governess sleep?" and refused to move in. Bernice loved the house, and a disappointed Keaton said, "If you really like it Bernice, it's yours."[88] Eddie paid $37,500 and moved in. Natalie designed a 25-room mansion a few blocks away, spending the equivalent of $4 million.

Keaton's employment at MGM ended some years later when he was living in his studio trailer during a separation from Natalie. It was the site of nightly parties, and stories of wild drinking and sex reached Mayer. Mayer walked in on a party and a drunken Keaton threw him out. Mayer fired Keaton. Thalberg said, "I can't make stars as fast as L.B. can fire them."[89]

Eddie hired Jimmy and Priscilla Scott, newly arrived from Alabama.

They moved into quarters at the rear of 516, and Priscilla cooked and cleaned and Jimmy served as chauffeur and valet. Eddie, Bernice, niece Ruth and the Scotts lived there for the next decade.[90]

The studios discovered the power of publicity early. The first publicity stunt was arranged when the movies were young, when newspapers heralded releases but no actors' names were publicized. Distributors just bought titles. Actors did two or three short films a week, and as their exposure increased viewer preferences translated to ticket sales, but even as studios began offering contracts the names were still nowhere to be seen. There were reasons not driven by studios. In the beginning the actors didn't want their names publicized, because many were stage performers and movies were considered beneath them. They enjoyed the money but didn't want to jeopardize their stage careers.

As certain faces drew crowds they were put under contract. Zukor owned William Farnum, Mary Pickford, Mabel Normand, and Lillian and Dorothy Gish. Vitagraph owned Wallace Reid and Clara Kimball Young. Essanay owned Francis X. Bushman, and Pathé offered Pearl White's *Perils of Pauline* serial. D.W. Griffith and Biograph had Florence Lawrence. The studios knew the faces equaled money, but wouldn't publicize their stars— until Carl Laemmle.

Mary Pickford was recognized the world over, so she left Zukor's Famous Players when Laemmle promised to promote her by name at his Independent Moving Picture (IMP) Studio. The other recognizable face was Biograph Studios' Florence Lawrence, the "Biograph Girl." In 1910 Laemmle set about stealing her, too. She had been on stage since the age of three and made some of the first movies made in the U.S.— by Edison in 1906. Through 1909 she made 150 more, including the first versions of *Romeo and Juliet* (1906) and *Anthony and Cleopatra* (1908). The public clamored for her but she was known only as the Biograph Girl. Laemmle offered to identify her publicly in credits and advertising and when Biograph refused, Lawrence secretly joined IMP, where she would be "Florence Lawrence — The IMP Girl." Publicity people spirited her out of New York and planted stories about the "missing" star. Rumors floated that she was dying of a terminal illness, the victim of foul play, even kidnapped.[91]

The Lawrence story was a global phenomenon. Biograph was frantic, but like her fans was in the dark about her whereabouts. Laemmle planted a story in New York that she had been killed in a St. Louis streetcar accident, but brought the fiasco to an end by presenting Lawrence at a New York press conference.[92] She made 100 films for Laemmle in the next six years.

The Lawrence affair was an important event in movie history. Several tenets were etched in stone. The studios had to identify actors, and the balance of power was altered. The studios' vulnerability to having their assets stolen was evident, so ironclad contracts became the rule. It was also evident that publicity was a two-edged sword. A recognizable name had to be protected, and the actors had to be protected from themselves. With exposure came notoriety. With notoriety came problems. With problems came a need to conceal.

Geographic and communications challenges in the early 1900s were an important part of the equation. Simply put, it was hard for news to get out of L.A., and fans didn't question stories from the studios. Even if a story was reported in local trade papers it was difficult to get to the rest of the country. A cover-up mentality became the norm because it was easy to accomplish. In the early years damage control was more important locally than globally. The men with New York stage experience knew the importance of good press, and how to get it. *Photoplay* was the theater publication for the legitimate stage. Producers pushed its writers for better stories, and when the magazine began writing about the movies in 1914, circulation exploded from 10,000 copies to over 500,000 in a month. The press couldn't get enough of the movies, reporting even the most mundane items. On April 23, 1915, *Photoplay* informed readers that "Mabel Normand, Keystone comedy star, has returned from San Francisco." On June 24, "Mabel paid $45 for hospital service when her cat became ill."[93]

The most famous early publicity campaign was designed by Frank Powell at William Fox's Box Office Attractions Studio in 1915. Powell was finishing their first film, a horror version of the Kipling poem "The Vampire" titled *A Fool There Was*. Cleveland-born Theodosia Goodman offered comical, hammy overacting that was described with a word that Powell invented; "vamping."[94] "Kiss me, you fool" became famous overnight as Goodman was transformed into the mysterious "Theda Bara." At the time, people were obsessed with Egypt as archeologists were bringing artifacts out of the Valley of the Kings and filling museums and traveling shows with Egyptian relics. Powell used this interest to publicize Bara. Her name was said to be an anagram for "Arab Death," she the daughter of a French artist and an Arab mistress who grew up in the shadow of the Pyramids and the Sphinx. She had mysterious powers over men. Her movies were blockbusters for Fox.

Bara was forbidden to appear in daylight and when she did go out had to wear full costume. Interviews were conducted by candlelight in the bedroom of her Hollywood home, after set decorators transformed the ground floor into a desert tent hung with skulls and the smell of incense.[95] Eventually the public fascination faded, as did her career.

It wasn't the type of work that Howard Strickling was doing as a low-level publicity person at Metro. He would have been assigned a few films, making sure a flow of photographs and stories was released. Pictures were sent to newspapers and fan magazines. As early as 1915 Anita Loos noted, "Those P.R. cameras never ceased to function, recorded for posterity ... stars, scenarists, and directors."[96] Interviews with stars or directors were scheduled to boost the movie's prerelease popularity. His early work helped him develop press contacts he would use for 40 years. Lower-level publicists were also assigned to stars, taking care of their needs locally. If a vacation was planned for another city, publicists there would meet the star and make arrangements for the star's stay. Strickling's duties in the early years revolved around local studio activities.

Novice publicists also supplied "blind items" to newspapers and magazines. A blind item could be as mundane as the film's expected release date and how much the studio had spent on production. But the blind items also told the world who the stars were dating, marriage and divorce rumors, etc. Strickling's MGM bio indicated that his first job at Goldwyn was handling publicity for Rudolph Valentino. Truth or not, it was while working at Goldwyn that Strickling came to the attention of Pete Smith. Sometime around early 1923 Strickling left Metro and joined Smith's agency, handling director Rex Ingram.

When Howard Dietz refused to relocate from New York to California, Mayer hired Pete Smith within two days as West Coast publicity director, paying him the astronomical sum of $1,500 a week.[97] Smith wanted to bring Strickling but he was with Ingram's Victorine Studios in Nice on the French Riviera. Ingram had early success with Valentino's *The Four Horsemen of the Apocalypse* (1920) but wasn't a Mayer favorite. Strickling's fear of Mayer led him to take the European assignment in the first place, but it was Mayer who convinced Strickling to return to the U.S. to become Smith's top assistant in 1925.[98] Strickling was the de facto senior publicist at the new studio along with Frank Whitbeck, a former Barnum and Bailey circus barker who kept four elephants—from his circus days—as pets.

Strickling's rise to power came about for several reasons. First, his relationship with Smith made him the number-two man. Dietz's refusal to move to the West Coast and the size of the L.A. operation made L.A. publicity more important than New York. And Smith was more interested in writing screenplays than in publicity. Strickling technically reported to Smith but for day-to-day matters met directly with Mannix. Then Smith became seriously ill during MGM's first year, and Strickling was formally put in charge.

Physically, Strickling was unassuming although he was tall, over six feet. Owing maybe to his country roots, he didn't suffer fools gladly and sometimes appeared unsophisticated. He spoke loudly[99] and was blunt with people; as smooth as he was with reporters, in personal relationships he struggled. He had a quick temper, but strangely, he stuttered if he was angry or flustered. But he was a wonderful publicist, expert at ingratiating himself with the stars he worked with. He would use this talent throughout his career. The Strickling treatment began the day the new hire walked into MGM.

The first visit for a new hire was with Mayer, after which they were ushered down the hall to Strickling. As blunt as he could be, he was cordial and homespun with nervous new hires. They told Strickling their life stories so he knew what he had to work with as the base for the official studio bio. Every new hire was asked a series of questions and offered the same advice. Peter Lawford remembered meeting a genial Strickling in the 1940s. Strickling asked him, "Are you holding anything back? Is there anything embarrassing in your past that we should know about? If you tell me now, I can make sure that anything like that stays out of the press.... I don't want any surprises when I open my morning paper."[100] After the private meeting they were assigned one of his 35 publicists.

It wasn't surprising that higher-ups noticed Strickling from among 100 people in publicity. In addition to being a hard worker and his connection with Smith, Strickling relentlessly promoted himself. From his earliest days he was a ravenous self-promoter. He never missed an opportunity to get his name in front of executives he thought could help his career. According to Maurice Rapf, son of Harry Rapf and a friend, Strickling was the "biggest brown-nose I ever met in 30 years in the business." But he got noticed by everyone.[101]

Mayer was particularly susceptible to Strickling's flattery. Hollywood writer Col. Barney Oldfield echoed Rapf and told this writer, "Howard was always close to where Mayer might be. When Mayer went out for a function, when he emerged Howard would be standing at his limousine holding his coat." Coworkers called him "Mayer's coat-rack."[102] While Strickling was envied for his closeness to Mayer, he was ridiculed for his efforts, called "the taster," implying that he tasted Mayer's food to check for poison.[103] Not surprising, Mayer liked Strickling, but coworkers universally disliked the young man's constant kissing up to the bosses.

When he inherited Smith's job Strickling began an even more aggressive pursuit of Mayer's attention. Every morning he got up half an hour before Mayer in case Mayer wanted to call him first thing. Mayer never walked the hallways without Strickling at his side. Strickling also never publicly disagreed with Mayer. If Mayer liked you, Strickling liked you. If

Mayer liked a movie, Strickling liked a movie. If Mayer hated homosexuals, Strickling hated homosexuals. But Mayer never questioned Strickling's sincerity. When Mayer died only two employees were left money by him: one was Strickling; the other was Ida Koverman.[104]

Even so, Strickling was very good at his job. He designed the publicity model that was copied by every studio. He assigned publicists to individual stars or films, responsible for everything related to their assigned person or project. Junior publicists were assigned films, while senior publicists were assigned people. They could use unit reporters to provide stories for the press, and assign photographers to provide photos. He also instituted the requirement that publicists report to the studio on the daily lives of their assigned stars. In the beginning, there was a hands-off policy toward stars' transgressions, but Strickling said, "Early on I learned that people need help, and the secret of my job was learning how to help them. Help them and they help you." He also recognized that publicists were the linchpins of the system. "When I entered the business," he once said, "publicists were a joke, flunkies with a flask in one hand and a list of girls in the other. They got drunk and screwed around."[105] It was Strickling who was most responsible for the intrusiveness of the studio system that developed as the other studios copied MGM.

As Strickling became more visible, he and Mannix struck up an odd friendship, which lasted for decades. For over 40 years they were attached at the hip during the day and when problems arose. But interestingly, they didn't socialize at all. No dinners with their wives; neither joined the other's weekly card games. They never got together outside of the office, so different were their personalities.

An early Strickling tactic was actively soliciting relationships with the press. As early as the mid-1920s there were already 500 entertainment reporters in L.A.[106] Reporters, gossip writers, photo editors, or society writers, Strickling was in touch with them all. Getting photos in print was the most important part of the job. His small-town manner ingratiated Strickling with reporters. Judy Garland biographer Gerald Clarke described Strickling persuading "thirty magazines and newspapers to run feature stories that read like ads." He added, "Strickling [himself] couldn't have written more flattering copy." He probably did.

The gossip columns were also becoming popular, as public fascination with the stars' lives grew. By the mid-1920s entire sections of weekly papers were devoted to movies. There was a front page, a sports section, and a movie section. Strickling liked using the gossip writers. Simply put, they were easy. They didn't research anything to confirm what they were told, so planting items was effortless. A reader couldn't distinguish between truth and lies. Gossip columns were the perfect medium for Strickling's stories. The fan magazines started years earlier with *Photoplay* in 1911 and dozens of others followed, like *Screen Life, Movie Pictorial, Reel Life* and *Pictures and the Picture-goer*. Most of the early issues were little more than studio advertisements, with content supplied directly by the studios and more fiction than fact. They were little more than private public relations and advertising departments for studios. But it didn't take long for the magazines to take aim at the stars' private lives.

The first L.A. movie tabloid began in 1917 as an adult humor magazine, an early version of *Mad* magazine. By 1920 *Captain Billy's Whiz Bang* was dedicated entirely to the movies, with columns like "Movie Hot Stuff" and "Silver Screen Shrapnel." *Whiz Bang* promised readers "the more intimate life of the movie actors and actresses … and no 'press agent dope.'" Tame by modern standards, *Whiz Bang* took aim at the biggest stars like Pickford, Arbuckle, and Chaplin, with stories about drug use, parties full of illegal alcohol, fights, and affairs.

A later version was William Wilkerson's *Hollywood Reporter*. It began in an empty Hollywood clothing store that he had lost to bankruptcy, his sixth failed business. Wilkerson's weekly was banned from MGM premises though Mayer and Thalberg snuck copies inside their briefcases. If Mayer read an unkind piece about MGM he launched into an obscenity-laced tirade against Wilkerson. But strangely, Mayer socialized with Wilkerson, playing poker with him and Nick Schenck every Thursday night for 20 years—another Mayer contradiction.[107] Wilkerson and Strickling were also close friends.

Planting stories was a vocation for the studios. In the mid-1920s the best-known gossip writer was Louella Parsons, a bitchy fat doctor's wife who was the queen of the tabloids for 20 years. She was born Louella Oettinger and was married off to a family friend at age 17. Chronically unhappy, she wrote, "The only person I cared deeply and sincerely about was— me." She was a scenario writer for Essanay in Chicago and a movie writer for the *Chicago Herald,* but seemingly hated actors. She said she liked the work because, "no longer did I have to be nice to the spoiled little darlings of the set. They had to be nice to me."[108]

Parsons got her position as the chief movie writer for William Randolph Hearst's newspaper empire as reward for a story she *didn't* write. In 1924 she was in L.A. working for Hearst's papers and over Labor Day she was invited to join a small group aboard his 280-foot yacht *Oneida* for a trip from L.A. to San Diego. Hearst's Cosmopolitan Studios and his mistress Marion Davies worked for MGM. He first saw her when she was 14, dancing with her sister in a New York chorus line. The enchanted 40-ish

Hearst began an affair with the teenager that lasted until his death in 1951, but since his wife Millicent refused him a divorce he and Davies simply pretended they were married. He built her castles up and down the West Coast: Wyntoon, a 1000-acre forest estate in Oregon; Ocean House, a 100-room mansion on the Santa Monica beach; and the crown jewel, his castle on "Enchanted Hill," a hilltop in the middle of his 400,000-acre estate in San Simeon. His castle in the clouds held 200 rooms filled with European antiques and was visible from five miles away, in the middle of 52 miles of private coastline. His relationship with Davies never made the news, since he owned the ten largest papers in the U.S. and no other dared take him on. Money gushed also from his other inheritance — the largest gold, silver, and copper mines in the world.

In 1922 Hearst came to L.A. with Marion, buying her a mansion at 6697 Whitley Terrace in Whitley Heights in Hollywood, near neighbors Jean Harlow, Richard Barthelmess, Alma Rubens, and Rudolph Valentino. Hearst let his director Robert Vignola live in the home rent-free for decades, knowing Vignola was a homosexual and that he would watch — and ignore — his lovely roommate. Hearst was insanely jealous and worried that she was having affairs (she was). When he read in the *New York Daily Times* that Charlie Chaplin was paying "ardent attention" to Marion in Hollywood[109] he returned from San Francisco to Hollywood the next morning. They were indeed having a fling, and the Hearst jealousy erupted just weeks later during the Labor Day cruise. The only thing known for sure about what happened aboard the *Oneida* was that at the end of the weekend director Thomas Ince was dead.

Ince was extremely creative and the first director to lay out a specific shooting schedule for a story. Once he completed a scenario it was stamped PRODUCE THIS EXACTLY AS WRITTEN. By 1924 Ince was the most successful producer in the movies, working at his 20,000-acre "Inceville" where Sunset Boulevard met the Pacific Ocean. Ince was invited on the *Oneida* because Hearst was negotiating to rent Ince's studio to make Marion's movies. Hearst also invited Chaplin for some reason, along with actors Aileen Pringle, Seena Owen, Theodore Kosloff and Elinor Glyn, and several of Davies' sisters.[110] The *Oneida* left L.A. on Saturday but Ince boarded on Sunday because he had to attend a premier. What happened Sunday night is a mystery, but Chaplin telegraphed his longtime valet Toriachi Kono and ordered him to meet the boat the next morning back in San Diego. Kono was waiting dockside as the *Oneida* cruised into San Diego, next to an ambulance requested by the ship. Kono told friends that Ince was removed on a stretcher with a bullet wound visible in his head, and later stories mentioned wet clothes, as if he was fished out of the ocean.[111]

Ince was allegedly taken to a Del Mar hotel and treated by Dr. Daniel Carson Goodwin as the other guests scattered to their respective homes.

The morning bulldog editions of non-Hearst *Los Angeles Times* announced "PRODUCER SHOT ON HEARST YACHT!!!" Interestingly, later editions ignored the story without mention. Conversely, the Hearst-owned *Los Angeles Examiner* read "SPECIAL CAR RUSHES STRICKEN INCE HOME FROM RANCH." A Hearst ambulance did take Ince to his Benedict Canyon estate, but he was already dead. By that time, copies of the early papers had vanished forever and Ince's death was being attributed to stomach ulcers. Someone persuaded a local coroner to sign an incomplete death certificate and Ince's body was cremated before an autopsy could be performed or an inquest held. Both actions were against California law.

Rumors about Ince's death roared to life. The Japanese servants aboard ship said that Hearst shot Ince after catching him having sex with Davies on a private deck.[112] Marion reportedly told friends that Hearst thought he was shooting at Chaplin and was shocked to discover Ince. Circumstantial evidence indicates a massive Hearst-designed coverup that began before the ship returned to San Diego. Silence about the *Oneida* cruise didn't come cheap. Within a month, minor reporter Parsons was named the chief movie critic for the entire Hearst syndicate, ensuring a worldwide audience and immense power in Hollywood. Within a month, Hearst began building a huge apartment building on property near the Ince family's former Hollywood home on Franklin Avenue. When it was completed the luxurious Chateau Elysee Apartments were gifted to Ince's widow Elinor. The widow Ince lived there until her death in the early 1950s with tenants such as Clark Gable, Carole Lombard and Errol Flynn.

Associates of Hearst were prohibited from mentioning Ince's name. Mistakenly uttering the dead man's name resulted in permanent exile from the Hearst-Davies circle. Hollywood pioneer D.W. Griffith told friends, "All you have to do to make Hearst turn white as a ghost was [mention] Ince's name. There's plenty wrong there, but he's too big to touch."[113]

Parsons' introduction to MGM, an interview with Thalberg, was a disaster. Full of herself as always, she tramped past Thalberg's secretary into his office to meet MGM's Boy Wonder. When the diminutive executive walked in she growled, "What's the joke? Where is the new general manager?" Thalberg frostily replied, "I am the new general manager."[114] He never forgot the slight and encouraged Strickling to work with other writers. All of the stars kowtowed to Parsons. For years Lana Turner bought an expensive jewelry gift for Parsons at Christmas, hoping for nice stories. One year at Parsons' home she had a pile of hundreds of gifts so large that "You couldn't even walk into the room ... the floor was covered with hundreds of gifts … she'd be flashing some new emerald bracelet or some enormous diamond brooch."[115] Parsons never wrote kindly about Stan Laurel and Oliver Hardy because they refused to send Christmas gifts.

Strickling acted as a liaison between MGM and the gossip writers, convincing them not to print negative stories or planting positive ones. In return, he would promise them his next exclusive. Each thought he or she was his sole confidante. MGM gave Parsons a 48-hour scoop for exclusives because of Hearst. When no interesting exclusive was available, Strickling invented stories to watch the resulting frenzy. He concocted elaborate fictional exclusives for Parsons and later Hedda Hopper. One writer said, "it may have been a bit sleazy, but he took great pride in it." Strickling remained secretive about his work, refusing interview requests and lucrative offers for his memoirs. He never spoke a word to anyone.

Within 12 months of MGM's founding, Eddie Mannix and Howard Strickling had positions of incredible power. Eddie, at Schenck's direction, was the general manager reporting directly to Thalberg and Mayer. Strickling, because of Dietz's disinterest in the L.A. operation, Smith's illnesses, and his own self-promotion, was running the publicity department. Mayer liked both, the rough and tumble Mannix probably because they were so much alike. From hardscrabble backgrounds, both foulmouthed and street tough, Mannix was like his brother. Mayer liked Strickling because Strickling always agreed with him.

By the late 1920s Mannix sat in on every important meeting at MGM, with Strickling usually in attendance. All communication was signed by Mannix, who preferred green ink in a gesture to his Irish roots. Mannix and Strickling organized a system to control not only the information flow but the day to day activities of their stars. To keep track of the internal comings and goings they used spies liberally, people everywhere in the studio reporting back to them. Studio drivers, waiters at the studio dining room, even the lowliest janitors were routinely quizzed to see if they knew anything. They were rewarded in their paychecks.

Mannix and Mayer read every single telegram arriving at or leaving MGM and the Culver City Western Union offices. In the era before overnight delivery and email, telegrams were used for all important correspondence, and by reading the private letters Mannix and Mayer knew of affairs, financial problems, family issues, and disagreements affecting their stars. They knew everything about everyone. Mannix brought the telegrams home at night and read them in bed before retiring for the evening. He read them with his girlfriends, sharing the most private "secrets" of the biggest stars at MGM.[116]

The information flow was especially strong from within Strickling's department, since publicists and their assistants had day to day contact with the stars and handled the most intimate personal details. Many stars never knew their trusted assistants passed everything on to Strickling. One of the most treacherous was Betty Asher, a long-time mistress of Mannix, beautiful and bisexual and the daughter of a director. She worked with Lana Turner and Judy Garland, but unbeknownst to both was sleeping with Mannix and telling him everything. She also slept with Garland, allegedly at the suggestion of Mannix, who also thought Garland might be more forthcoming if she were drunk. So Asher encouraged the teenager to drink.[117]

Outside sources were also courted. Policemen were particularly good sources, as were reporters. Interestingly, during the 1930s and 1940s reporters hung around police stations looking for leads. It wasn't unusual for them to answer phones in busy squad-rooms and follow up on potential stories without telling their police pals.

Once Strickling and Mannix took care of a problem, they "owned" the actor. Strickling felt that once they did something for an actor they became important to the actor. The studio then could get them to do things. And they did what they were told: Get married if you were a homosexual. Stop sleeping with a married costar. Go back to your wife. Get an abortion. Almost anything.

Everyone in almost every position was a potential source for Strickling. His files contained the names, phone numbers, and personal information about virtually every doctor, nurse, psychiatrist, and pharmacist in L.A. They too were rewarded with cash, tickets to premiers, invitations to private parties with the stars, and, often, with women. The House of Francis was Hollywood's best known brothel, but too public for some of Strickling's police and lawyer types, so he often used MGM employees. Maurice Rapf described Strickling and Mannix as a "nothing but pimps for Mayer, getting women for them, their friends, and their business pals." There was a ready supply of female companions among MGM's six-month option girls.[118]

Thousands of beautiful women flocked to Hollywood to get into movies. Many were put under contract, normally for six months with an option for the studio to renew at the end of the time. Rarely did employment extend beyond. The option girls were often used for the benefit of management or their friends, a problem so well known that agents first had to represent the women as 18 so there wouldn't be any statutory rape problems.

The option girls were given just enough work to keep them occupied. If lucky, one might get a small role or an extra spot in a film. Their careers were only given middling attention by Strickling's publicity people. The phrase "casting couch" has become part of American lexicon, but in the first 25 years of Hollywood it was a harsh reality, particularly for the option girls. It wasn't a euphemism; it was a day to day reality and a humiliating price paid by thousands of beautiful young women. It would be difficult — maybe impossible — to find a studio executive who didn't take advantage of women. Harry Cohn, tyrannical head of Columbia, was said to have verbally or physically raped every woman that ever worked for his studio. He had a private passageway that connected his office with a private dressing room that was assigned to a string of Columbia starlets.[119]

Each and every new female hire had to visit Cohn's office. During that first meeting, he used a pencil to open the woman's mouth and check her teeth, and then used it to lift her skirt and look at her thighs.[120] After what normally turned into an obligatory sex session on his large white couch the girl was ushered out the back door and Cohn retreated to his all-marble bathroom for a shower. He was universally hated. At his crowded funeral Red Skelton said, "This is the type of crowd you get when you give people what they want."[121] Another scribe said, "Most of the people are here to make sure that he's dead."

Darryl Zanuck's abuses were legendary. Every single day the studio offices at his Twentieth Century Fox were basically closed between 4:00 and 4:30, because every single day some Fox actress, famous or anonymous, reported to Zanuck's office for a private "meeting." The large oak doors were locked, no calls were put through, and for 30 minutes no decision was made at Fox. Careers were undermined because of reputations forged during the mandatory call to Zanuck's office. Carole Landis was a gifted actress whose career suffered because Zanuck liked her; employees thought she was little more than a prostitute. Zanuck's behavior during his meetings was comically obscene. After locking the door and leading them to the inner office, he turned around to face his guest with an exposed erection. Few actresses were powerful enough to say no, but when he did it to Betty Grable, she simply said, "That's beautiful. You can put it away now," and walked out. Beautiful Linda Darnell was so often a target that a director friend once said he didn't "even think she knew who was on top of her" most of the time. Maurice Rapf suggested that Strickling took advantage of the opportunity, and it is known that Mayer and Mannix did.[122]

With all of the office sex and intrigue, MGM still ran as smoothly as any studio in Hollywood. Mayer demanded a structured work environment. The actor's daily schedule was dictated to the minute. Depending on status, the schedule was demanding. A typical day began with a 6:00

A.M. arrival. Bigger stars were picked up by studio limousines but newer stars drove themselves through the Washington Boulevard gates. By 7:00 A.M. they had to be in the makeup building for makeup and hair appointments, and to the set by 8:30 A.M. for rehearsals of that day's shooting.

Filming began in the late morning and continued until that day's schedule was completed. Unlike today, when actors demand and receive a schedule they want to follow, at MGM the filming day ended when everything was completed to the director's satisfaction. Filming almost never ended before 6:00 P.M., and it wasn't unusual for it to last past midnight.

Image was everything to a studio. From the earliest days, the public responded to specific stars for sometimes unknown reasons. But whatever the public wanted, the public got. If the public was clamoring for Clark Gable, the distributors would request "a Gable." And "a Gable" was what they got. Or "a Lombard." Or "a Harlow." The public had a preconceived notion of what and who Gable, or Lombard, or Harlow, were. It was a combination of their movie roles, the press that Strickling put out, and the non-studio publicity that might surface. Rarely were the notions based on truth. It was all image. According to Thalberg biographer Roland Flamini, Strickling forbade male stars to pose in fashion pictures because he thought it made them look too effeminate. Nor could they accept fashion awards for being well dressed, even though Strickling himself directed what they wore. It was all control. And it was necessary. There had been some early signs, some involving MGM and some outside the studio, that made it clear to everyone.

Three

Omens, and the Twenties End Roaring

In the early 1900s technology changed everything. The Wright Brothers flew, trains reached every state, and automobiles began taking control of American life. But technology got to the masses slowly. As 1910 approached, there were 8,000 cars in the U.S. but only ten miles of paved roads. The first cross-country auto trip in 1905 took 52 days. World War I mechanization made America the most industrialized country in the world. Henry Ford built the first assembly line in 1914 and within a year 1 million Model Ts rolled off. The $345 price was half the $750 the average family earned in a year but most could afford a car.

America became a global exporter of popular culture as people worldwide wore our clothes, copied our dances, listened to our music and watched our movies. Over 50 million people worldwide watched movies every week. During the early years between 1900 and 1920 the movie men learned as they went. Adolph Zukor's strategy of integrating the filmmaking process—he copied from European studios—controlled every aspect of the product from creation and distribution to marketing. Controlling employees would be as essential.

For the most part the first studio workers in Hollywood stayed out of trouble. They had their own problems with the local distaste for anything movie-related and tried to keep a low profile. They were really just day laborers. But actors were trouble. Almost all of them came from vaudeville and most were comedians. Serious actors were on the stage, and few wanted to do movies in the beginning. Movies were a vulgarity, and working there beneath them.

Vaudeville evolved during the 1800s as entertainment in large beer gardens and even larger dance halls. Its heyday was from 1900 to 1918; at its peak 10,000 people worked as actors, writers, stagehands, singers, dancers, comics, animal trainers, and magicians. A show was a dozen acts of all types, solo entertainers and groups. Vaudevillians were initially attracted to the movies because it offered stability.

Prohibition had also changed vaudeville. When the Eighteenth Amendment banned the manufacture and sale of alcoholic beverages, there were 15,000 saloons in New York and 5,000 in L.A. They went out of business overnight, along with all of the entertainers who worked in them. Hollywood looked even more appealing, and the new movie studios were flooded with potential employees. A large number came from bars, bringing with them freewheeling attitudes toward alcohol, sex — virtually everything. Few were from stable families; most were from broken homes. The family stories of the early stars were fraught with sadness and poverty.

Many of the female stars, such as Mae Marsh, Blanche Sweet, the Gish and Talmadge sisters and Mary Pickford, grew up without fathers. They all ended up dominated by overly involved stage mothers.[1] Clara Bow's grandmother died in an asylum when she was not yet two and her grandfather died pushing her on a swing at four. Her mother Sarah — who inherited mental illness from her own mother — attempted suicide several times and had bizarre fits. When Bow was just nine she awoke to find her mother holding a knife to her throat and threatening to kill her.[2] The poor woman never slept through the night during her entire life. Both Douglas Fairbanks' and Charlie Chaplin's fathers left after their births. There was an almost pervasive sadness among the acting community.

Most of the earliest movie studio owners and managers were from Jewish backgrounds, to a man driven by family and dominant fathers. They surrounded themselves with family and close friends among their staffs. This family influence extended to employees. It was not altruistic; it was survival. Screenwriter Anita Loos observed at the time, "To place in the limelight a great number of people who ordinarily would be chambermaids and chauffeurs, give them unlimited power and instant wealth is bound to produce a lively result."

Most of the studio heads and their stars were barely educated, lower middle-class working people before entering the business. They went from near poverty to immeasurable wealth overnight. While an average family might earn $1,000 a year, Mary Pickford earned $50,000 a week, Roscoe Arbuckle three times that. A 7 day cruise cost $100, milk 30¢ a gallon, whiskey $2 a gallon, a 15-room mansion $35,000 and a Rolls Royce less than $5,000.

The studios followed the lead of D.W. Griffith, who told Lillian Gish, "Not until your name becomes a household word in every family — not only in America but in the world, if the world feels it knows you and loves you — will you be a star." Even so, it's hard to overstate the adulation the stars received in the 1920s. During Mary Pickford and Douglas Fairbanks' 1921 European honeymoon the couple was mobbed everywhere.[3] Docking in Southampton two planes flew overhead, dropping thousands of rose petals onto the deck. Over 100,000 crowded the streets outside their London hotel, 200,000 in Paris, and 350,000 met their train in Moscow. Being driven through London, Pickford was literally dragged from her car by frenzied fans.[4] When Madge Kennedy traveled to Japan in 1922 the emperor asked for a private audience.

Mayer knew from his own mistakes that people needed protection from themselves. At a 1915 *Birth of a Nation* screening in Haverhill he got into a fight and fractured a man's skull. He wept when the man survived and paid a large settlement, but in 1920 he did it again in the crowded lobby of the Alexandria Hotel. Mayer had spent thousands of dollars promoting Charlie Chaplin's wife Mildred Harris, one of several pregnant teens married by Chaplin. Mayer promoted Mildred Harris Chaplin but Chaplin was divorcing her, making her useless to Mayer. When the two men met in the hotel lobby, Chaplin told Mayer not to use the Chaplin name and made an unkind remark about Mildred. Mayer knocked him out with one punch.[5]

In the period from 1915 to 1920 there were only a few publicized movie scandals, and the stories seldom found their way into newspapers in other areas. Telegraph service was unreliable at best. It took a train a week to deliver news cross-country. Coast-to-coast airmail service was not introduced until late 1924. Radio wasn't much help. First developed in 1879, early 1900s radios were big and had poor reception. The first public radio station didn't open until 1921. By 1924 there were 2.5 million radios in U.S. homes, but it was the late 1920s before they were practical on a large scale. The inability to get information out of Hollywood made it easy for the studios to quash stories. There were omens in the years between 1915 and 1925, omens that confirmed the need for studio intervention in their stars' lives.

Describing those years in 1960, Ramon Novarro said he had spent years writing an autobiography but couldn't publish it until after he died. His life was a secret. Everyone in Hollywood knew he was a homosexual alcoholic with a penchant for young male prostitutes. Nobody else knew, but Novarro was just the tip of the homosexual iceberg in the 1920s. It's hard to imagine the reaction had the public known the secret: the big three Latin lovers of the 1920s — Novarro, his friend Rudolph Valentino, and Antonio Moreno — were all homosexual.

Valentino's personal life was a contradiction. He was a fixture in the gay communities in Paris, New York and L.A., working as a gigolo and taxi dancer.[6] Writers June Mathis and Alla Nazimova found him in a New York dance hall and convinced Metro to cast him in *The Four Horsemen of the Apocalypse* (1923). It made him a star. He married Jean Acker in 1919 and Natacha Rambova in 1923, both lesbians and former lovers of Nazimova, the "queen" of Hollywood lesbians.[7] Acker and Rambova admitted that their marriages to Valentino were never consummated. After his November 1919 wedding to Acker, she publicly threw him out of their Hollywood Hotel suite on their wedding night. When she left two weeks later to film *The Round-up* in Northern California she sent him a telegram: "I cannot promise to visit at Christmas. Now be a good boy."[8] On May 12, 1922, Valentino and Nazimova were wed in Mexicali, Mexico. Unfortunately, when he returned Rudy was thrown in jail, since he had forgotten to divorce Acker. His wedding party collected $10,000 to bail him out.[9] Bigamy charges were dropped after Rambova told the court the marriage was never consummated. A friend said, "Rudy thought 'consummate' meant make soup."

Even so, he was portrayed as a great lover. Cameraman Paul Ivano (who was actually his boyfriend) described reviving Rambova after Valentino's lovemaking rendered her unconscious, and described Valentino's oversized erection. A year later Valentino was in New York when gastric ulcers led to peritonitis. Headlines screamed, VALENTINO DYING!!! and offered readers photos for 5¢. Over 500,000 sent nickels.

Novarro starred in *The Prisoner of Zenda* (1922) and *Ben Hur* (1926) and was described as "too beautiful to be taken seriously." He received 10,000 letters a week, but fans didn't know he was homosexual. Metro employees knew Novarro and Valentino were lovers.[10] His prized possession was an inscribed sterling silver replica of Valentino's enormous penis.

The third member of the "big three" was born Antonio Garride Monteagudo in 1887 in Madrid. Antonio Moreno debuted in 1912's *Voice of the Millions*, worked with D.W. Griffith in *Judith of Bethulia* (1914), and became a star in *The Temptress* (1926) with Garbo and in Clara Bow's classic *It* (1927). Author Elinor Glyn pronounced Moreno the "It" man. Twenty thousand women a week wrote, but Moreno never had a confirmed relationship with a woman. Dates were set up and "cast" by his studio with costars like Gloria Swanson or Pola Negri. In 1923 he built a 24-room mansion at the top of Micheltorena Drive and married L.A. heiress Daisy Canfield Danziger. Her father was a wealthy land speculator and she grew up on a 50-acre Stone Canyon estate with 15 servants.[11] She was a lesbian, and rumors abounded that the sham marriage was studio-arranged. On February 18, 1933, she filed for divorce; ten days later her car plunged 250 feet down a ravine at the top of Mulholland Drive, killing her. It was an accident — L.A. was blanketed by fog — but the death fueled rumors that she had been killed to keep her quiet.

Sexual preference was more of a studio issue with actresses than actors during the 1920s. A group of lesbians well-known as the Sewing Circle emerged in the 1920s. Many early stars emigrated from Europe, from cultures that accepted and encouraged sexual experimentation. Among the European salon crowd settling in Hollywood in the 1920s were Garbo, Marlene Dietrich, Alla Nazimova, and the writer Salka Viertel. Most believed that the lesbian affairs Garbo described as "exciting secrets" would help them become better actresses, and some felt they helped improve general health. The androgynous screen images of lesbian actresses like Garbo and Dietrich also mystified audiences.

Still, most studio problems in the 1920s were drug-related since drugs were cheap and abundant. As early as 1910 there was a flow of oriental drugs into L.A. Cocaine was an active ingredient in Coca-Cola and not even illegal until 1914. Many others weren't illegal either and long-term effects were still unknown, so heroin, cocaine, opium and morphine were easy to find.

The bigger drug dealers were in proximity of every studio. Each was serviced by its own dealer who used a network of low-level studio employees as paid couriers. Dealers like "Captain Spaulding," "Mr. Fix-it," and "the Man" arranged deliveries within minutes. The most famous was "The Count," who put heroin in peanut shells and sold them by the bag. He served the Sennett Studio and gave potential customers their first dose free. His clients included Mabel Normand and Wallace Reid. Director Eddie Sutherland said he was Keystone worker Hughie Faye.[12] "Mr. Fix-it" served Fox Studios and "the Man" Paramount. "Captain Spaulding" was at Lasky. He was arrested for selling drugs but when he threatened to name names, the charges were dropped.[13] As early as 1910 stars were using drugs to cure the hangovers caused by "bathtub gin" or fruit punch laced with 200-proof medicinal alcohol.

The first public casualty was violet-eyed Olive Thomas, an incredible beauty who was born in a Pennsylvania mining town, was a runaway bride at 14 and became a Ziegfeld Follies star by age 17. She was the first "Vargas Girl" painted by world-renowned portrait artist Alberto Vargas, who called her "the most beautiful woman in the world." She appeared in a number of films and in the fall of 1920 she married Mary Pickford's younger brother Jack.

During her September 1920 Paris honeymoon with Pickford, she died in the Royal Suite at luxurious Hotel Crillon. Maids found her lying nude atop a pile of some of her 150 furs, near an empty bottle of bichloride of mercury which she had swallowed, killing her slowly and painfully. Friends knew she was despondent over her and Jack's drug addictions. Adding to her despair, Pickford had infected her with syphilis, then considered untreatable. A sometime actor who lived off his sister's money, Jack was known to female studio workers as Mr. Syphilis.[14] The pathetic Pickford lived off of Thomas' $500,000 life insurance policy for three years before he died of a drug overdose in 1926.

Soon after Mary Pickford's 1921 wedding to Douglas Fairbanks, rumors erupted that their wedding had been preceded by an adulterous affair. The stories were true, and Fairbanks took the threats from Mary's husband Owen Moore — that he would kill him — seriously enough that he moved to Arizona for a month, and considered going to South America on an extended trip.[15] The public could never be allowed to know about the affair or that Pickford had paid Moore $100,000 ($2 million today) for a quiet divorce.

During the same 1920 weekend of the Olive Thomas tragedy, Robert Harron killed himself. Harron had juvenile roles in *Birth of a Nation* (1915), *Intolerance* (1916), and a dozen D.W. Griffith classics as he grew out of his teens. He signed a $5,000-a-week Metro contract in 1920 but only made one film. He battled depression, which worsened after his brother Charles died in a 1915 car accident and his sister Tessie died during the 1918 Spanish flu epidemic. His depression was worsened by drugs, and in September 1920 he was found in a New York hotel room with a self-inflicted bullet wound to the chest. Metro publicity told the press that before he died he told doctors it was an accident. The death was classified "accidental" but friends knew the truth. The next night *Way Down East* (1920) premiered; Harron had been devastated that Griffith gave the lead to Richard Barthelmess rather than him.

Within a year, Roscoe Arbuckle was in the middle of a scandal that ended his career. "Fatty" rocketed from $3-a-week extra in 1913 to $3 million-a-year star in 1921 ($150 million today). He had a mansion on West Adams and a custom-made Pierce-Arrow that cost over $250,000. It was four times the size of a normal car and had a toilet and bar. Adolph Zukor and Jesse Lasky made millions off of Arbuckle but were unhappy they had to pay him the biggest contract in movie history. They felt they had been extorted, and when Arbuckle got in trouble they got their chance to punish their star.

A year after the Thomas and Harron suicides, Arbuckle hosted a 1921 Labor Day party at the St. Francis Hotel in San Francisco. Uninvited guests showed up during the two-day affair, and Arbuckle never turned a guest away. One party-crasher was young actress Virginia Rappe, who became violently ill during the party, was rushed to a local hospital and died the next day of the effects of peritonitis. Her death bred rumors that are taken as fact to this day. An autopsy revealed that the peritonitis was caused by a seriously infected bladder, the likely result of a botched abortion that was her sixth. Coincidently, the doctor who probably performed the illegal procedure also cared for her in the hospital and later assisted in her autopsy. Arbuckle was somehow arrested and charged with her murder. His trial began in November 1921, and by then rumors were flying that he violated Rappe with a Coke bottle, a champagne bottle, or a piece of furniture. He was also said to have infected her with gonorrhea. All were patently untrue, although she did have gonorrhea when she died.[16]

He was convicted in the press. "TORTURE OF RAPPE CHARGED" screamed the *San Francisco Examiner* and "ARBUCKLE DRAGGED WOMEN TO ROOM" the *New York Times*.[17] Writer Adela Rogers St. Johns knew Rappe was a well-known whore. She knew that Mack Sennett had to have his studio fumigated twice after visits to clear out "crab" infestations Rappe left behind. Even so, Zukor and Lasky punished Arbuckle, using studio publicists to work against him. Not only did they refuse support, they encouraged stories and headlines that were untrue.

The witnesses all lied. A deputy coroner said he had bumped into an orderly with a bottle containing Rappe's internal organs, heading to the incinerator. Arbuckle's chief accuser was ugly, middle-aged Bambina Maude Delmont, who brought Rappe to the party. She had a record of over 50 arrests as a prostitute, bigamist, and conwoman who offered herself to lawyers as bait to trap married men in adulterous situations.[18] Delmont was the only one of 40 guests who implicated Arbuckle; the jury didn't know that Delmont wired her attorney, "WE HAVE ROSCOE ARBUCKLE IN A HOLE HERE. CHANCE TO MAKE MONEY OFF HIM."[19] The final witness was director Henry Lehrmann, who had become obsessed with Rappe after a few social dates and let her live in his home, pretending she was his fiancée. He visited her grave every Sunday and was buried next to her.[20] He was a prosecution witness, even though he wasn't at the party.

The first two juries hung due to single holdouts later found to be prosecutor plants. A third untainted jury acquitted him on April 22, 1922, after issuing the statement, "Acquittal is not enough for Roscoe Arbuckle. We feel a grave injustice has been done him and there was not the slightest proof to connect him in any way with the commission of any crime."[21] But Arbuckle's career was over. Zukor and Lasky pulled his films and stopped paying him, so he was reduced to working incognito using the name "Will B. Good." He died broke ten years later, only 42 years old. In a letter written just before her death, Minta Durfee said her "husband died of a broken heart over the persecution and prosecution he faced."[22]

Awaiting the Arbuckle verdict, the industry was rocked by another equally scandalous death. On the day Virginia Rappe was buried, the new head of the Motion Picture Directors Association said Hollywood was "cleaning house" and would only produce "the cleanest of films."[23] He was Vitagraph director William Desmond Taylor. But in early February 1922, he was found dead in his Hollywood bungalow court apartment. Most of the units at Lake Terrace Court, 404 South Alvarado, housed movie people. Charlie Chaplin's former leading lady and close friend Edna Purviance lived next door and actor Douglas MacLean on the other side. The MacLean and Taylor homes were separated by a dark, eight-foot-wide alley leading to the street. Police assumed Taylor had suffered a fatal heart attack since there was no obvious blood, but two hours later when detectives rolled the body over they discovered a pool of blood and a bullet hole in his back.

A policeman described Taylor as "a cultured, dignified gentleman with a charming personality and considerable magnetism," and his studio bio said he grew up in Kansas, prospected in the Klondike, served in the Canadian Army and earned medals for heroism at Dunkirk. He was one of the most respected directors in Hollywood. The story was a wonderful tale of a life well-lived but the truth was less romantic. In 1900 Taylor was known in New York as William Cunningham Deane-Tanner, owner of a small antique shop, married to actress Ethel Harrison and father of a daughter. In 1908 he simply disappeared, but in 1916 Ethel and his daughter saw him in a movie in New York. They found him at Vitagraph and he began paying her expenses.

Minutes after police arrived at Taylor's home his best friend Charles Eyton, a manager at Famous Players–Lasky, arrived and began removing personal items from Taylor's bedroom. The police had alerted the studio, who called on Taylor's friend to "clean up." He left the house with an armful of letters and paperwork, none of which was ever retrieved by police. Police had little except a statement from MacLean's wife that the evening previous she had heard what she thought was a gunshot. She saw someone walk out the alley between the units in a long coat with a high collar, a scarf and a hat, looking like a "man walking funny."[24] They had no evidence, but more suspects than they could use: the first wife; the chauffeur Dennis Sands, who may have been Taylor's brother Denis, a career criminal and thief; dozens of disgruntled drug dealers who hated Taylor for his public anti-drug posturing; actress Mabel Normand, the last person to see him alive; and most likely, actress Mary Miles Minter's mother Charlotte Shelby, who knew of the relationship between Taylor and her 16-year-old meal-ticket daughter.

Two pictures sat on the small piano above the body, one inscribed by

Left: It was this rarely seen photograph of Mary Miles Minter, inscribed to Taylor and prominently displayed on a piano just above his dead body, that brought the teenage star to the attention of the police. (Courtesy of the Cecil Jones Collection.) *Right:* One of the three photographs of Taylor inscribed to Minter that police found in the drawing room of her mansion. Another was inscribed "The most beautiful girl in the world!!"; all added to the suspicion surrounding Minter and her family. (Courtesy of the Cecil Jones Collection.)

Mary Pickford and the other by Minter, signed "For William Desmond Taylor, artist and gentleman, Mary Miles Minter." The real Mary Miles Minter soon arrived in her Cadillac roadster, painted her favorite robin's egg blue and emblazoned with her signature butterfly emblem in solid gold. She was the current leading child star and lived just a few blocks away in a 40-room mansion with a sister, a stepsister, several cousins, her grandmother, and her mother. She arrived hysterical, wailed over the body, and then disappeared upstairs. She was found rummaging through his desk. Police found a pink nightgown and a lace handkerchief, both monogrammed "M.M.M," and in the toe of his riding boot love letters written in a schoolyard code and signed "Mary."[25] All of the letters were on Minter's signature butterfly stationary. The schoolgirl scrawl betrayed the young age of the writer — Minter was barely 17 at the time. Taylor was 50. Police gathered physical evidence linked to Minter. Three strands of long blonde hair beneath the collar of Taylor's coat matched hair taken from a brush in Minter's dressing room.[26] Taylor's valet cleaned his suits daily, so police knew that Minter was with him the day of the murder.[27] District Attorney Thomas Lee Woolwine headed the case.

Budd Shulberg was the son of original Paramount Studio production head B.P. Shulberg, himself a successful producer. Speaking at a 1996 symposium at the University of Southern California, he confirmed the widespread corruption that allowed the studios free reign. "I always thought of Hollywood like a principality of its own, and the people who ran it really had that attitude.... Their power was absolutely enormous, and it wasn't only the power to make movies or to anoint someone or make someone a movie star or pick an unknown director and make him famous over night. They could cover up a murder. You could literally have somebody killed, and it wouldn't be in the papers." In the 1920s the D.A.s were for sale. Woolwine was paid to speak at dozens of movie functions, including a testimonial dinner for Roscoe Arbuckle just before his trial.[28] Woolwine was certainly not the first dishonest D.A., but his tenure from 1914 through 1923 coincided with the great growth of the industry.

Woolwine had the physical evidence moved into his cabinets and later moved to his house. When it was requested by the grand jury he said that it had been lost. Other evidence was destroyed by Eyton, who burned papers in the fireplace while police were there. What little evidence remained was kept in a briefcase and carried around by Woolwine's successor Asa Keyes. During a stay in Chicago in 1926, that too was stolen.[29]

The growing revelations about Minter were a bombshell, but Taylor's close friends had known about the friendship between the middle-aged director and the teenage ingénue. Within days police identified Charlotte Shelby as a prime suspect. She knew of the affair and that it would end her daughter's career, and her own livelihood. She told police that on the night of the murder she was playing cards with friends. Police remembered Faith MacLean's "funny looking" person, like a woman pretending to be a man. Even with dozens of suspects, physical evidence, motive and opportunity, Woolwine never publicly solved the Taylor case.

After he was run out of office in 1923, his close business and personal relationships with Shelby were publicized. Her card-playing alibi was Jim Smith, Woolwine's investigator. His alibi didn't come cheap. Shelby told her accountant that Woolwine's replacement "would require a lot more money than Woolwine."[30] Woolwine's successor was Asa Keyes, "Ace" to his pals. On the Wednesday before his death Taylor played golf with Antonio Moreno at the San Gabriel Country Club. Keyes, a golfer and friend of Taylor, shared dinner at the café there. Shelby was never questioned by police — ever. Nor was Minter. Shelby had testified before a grand jury but only one copy of her testimony was produced, and Woolwine "lost" that.

Minter's career was over, and her mother became a pariah shunned by anyone in the business. If Shelby did indeed kill Taylor, the unforeseen result was that Minter's career was over. For the remaining 50 years of her life, Minter lived in seclusion in a Santa Monica home overlooking the ocean, dying in 1984. Her mother lived — in the same house, with Mary — until her death in 1957.

As the Taylor fiasco was reaching a crescendo, the most popular male star in the world was quietly hospitalized with a fatal addiction to morphine. Handsome, dashing William Wallace Reid entered films for Vitagraph in 1910 and starred in over 100 films in three years. When he married actress Dorothy Davenport in 1913 he was the nation's favorite "boy next door." One young New York debutante fan gave a $25,000 emerald necklace to a security guard just to peek into his dressing room. Everyone loved Wally Reid, especially drug dealers.

The press was told that Reid was hurt in a train accident during the 1919 filming of *Valley of the Giants* (1920). His painful neck injury was known to fans, but they didn't know he had become hopelessly addicted to the morphine he was given for pain. In March 1922 he was bundled off to the Banksia Place sanitarium[31] where he died an agonizing death in a padded cell, tied to his bed. Davenport told friends she let doctors put the unfortunate man "to sleep."

Hollywood was spiraling out of control. Thomas, Arbuckle, Taylor, and Reid were just the start. Within a year of Reid's death over 30 movie stars were dead of drug overdoses. And sexual orientation was becoming an even bigger public embarrassment to the studios. Several 1924 *Photoplay* articles identified actress Nita Naldi's significant other as a woman, Mary Rinaldi, from whom Naldi also borrowed her surname. Valentino had been the target of similar stories. The result of the onslaught of sleaze took the studios off guard. For the first time, it seemed fans might not turn a blind eye to bad conduct. Behavior that had titillated fans was becoming abhorrent.

Cecil B. DeMille responded, "There's a sickness in Hollywood [caused by] crumbling standards." Gloria Swanson noted that scandal had "drawn down the lightning on us all." The studios were forced into a choreographed house-cleaning, beginning with the formation of the Motion Picture Producers and Distributors of America, Inc., quietly organized by Mayer, who stayed in the background. Morals clauses were inserted in contracts, an industry code of conduct was written, and an outsider was brought in to monitor everything. Indianan Will H. Hays was short and unimposing, a former postmaster general who was once accused of accepting bribes during the Teapot Dome scandal.[32] On January 14, 1922, the Hays Office opened and his committee designed a code to dictate acceptable behavior on and off screen that included 11 "don'ts" and 27 "be carefuls."[33]

New D.A. Asa Keyes' brief tenure was no different than his predecessor Woolwine's; just as corrupt and for sale to studios. He had few high-profile movie industry problems like the Taylor affair, and during his tenure 40 percent of the cases given to his office by police to prosecute were dropped. In the 1920s the studios feared neither department.

Mayer's new studio was pretty much able to navigate past any real scandals, but he was learning by watching the Arbuckle, Taylor, and other problems. They reinforced his opinion that no star was bigger than the studio, and all stars were expendable. He had dealt with a similar issue several years earlier with one of his first stars, Francis X. Bushman. Bushman was a fitness fanatic obsessed with his body, who raced bicycles, boxed, lifted weights and wrestled. His body was the model for dozens of statues. In New York, he can be seen as Nathan Hale in City Hall Park and George Washington in the financial district. In his hometown, Baltimore, there are a dozen, including Francis Scott Key near the harbor celebrating *The Star Spangled Banner*. The statue is a perfect likeness.[34] His physique led to roles in 100 movies for Essanay Pictures with established stars like Charlie Chaplin and the lovely Beverly Bayne. Bushman met 18-year-old Bayne in 1912's *A Good Catch*. Within a year they were the most popular couple in the movies, and off-screen lovers.

He was "the Handsomest Man in the World," wore a 20-carat violet amethyst ring and smoked handmade eight-inch, monogrammed, lavender cigarettes from a solid gold case. He passed out $100 tips to bellboys and coat-check girls and drove a 20-foot-long Marmon with solid-gold-monogrammed doors and a spotlight that illuminated his face when he drove at night. He received 20,000 letters a week and every letter got a personal reply. In 1915 Bushman and Bayne left Essanay for Metro, where Mayer argued with them from the start. He wanted them to do a movie serial, *The Great Secret*, but Bushman and Bayne didn't want to do serials. Mayer won out and they did several episodes, but as they had expected, serials didn't do as well as their romantic films. By 1918 they told writers they would leave the studio. Mayer was furious at a reported snub, when he tried to visit Bushman's dressing room and was rebuffed.[35]

Bushman owned a 300-acre estate outside Baltimore named Bushmanor, a dozen 100-year-old stone buildings including a 25-room mansion, servants' homes, barns, an aviary, a kennel for his prized dogs, garages and several mills. It was staffed by 22 full-time servants. His parents lived there with several brothers and an aunt, but also there out of the public view were a wife and five children kept hidden from his adoring female fans. When secret wife Josephine tired of Bushman's affair with Bayne and divorced him early in 1918, and within just days of his divorce Bushman wed Bayne, fans were aghast. Theaters around the world pulled his films, and Mayer directed Metro to release them from their contracts at the end of 1918. The long-forgotten idol died in 1966 after a fall in his Pacific Palisades home. The marker on his grave reads, "Francis X. Bushman, King of the Movies." Mayer let Bushman fall. It wouldn't be the last time he punished wayward employees.

MGM got off to a quick start. The first year they made 26 films, well ahead of the contract requiring 15 over two years. The second year they made 45. Everyone was getting rich. By 1927 Mayer was making $2,500 a week and Thalberg $2,000, in addition to the percentage agreement that paid them over $500,000. The first year's production included some movies produced prior to the merger at the original studios; Buster Keaton's *The Navigator* and *Sherlock, Jr.*; Valentino's *The Four Horsemen of the Apocalypse*; Blanche Sweet in *Tess of the d'Urbervilles*; and Norma Shearer in the first movie made entirely at the new studio, *He Who Gets Slapped*. The first year MGM made $5 million ($100 million today).

At the same time, MGM was hiring a young actress who would cause problems from the day she was hired. Harry Rapf first saw Lucille Fay LeSueur during a 1924 New York trip in the chorus line of the Broadway play *Innocent Eyes*. Rapf offered her a contract the day he saw her via telegram: "YOU ARE PUT UNDER A CONTRACT STARTING AT SEVENTY-FIVE DOLLARS A WEEK. LEAVE IMMEDIATELY FOR CULVER CITY, CALIFORNIA. CONTACT MGM KANSAS CITY OFFICE FOR TRAVEL EXPENSES."[36] She arrived in L.A. two days after New Years, 1925. Larry Barbier, one of Strickling's fellow publicity men, met her at the train station.

Rapf thought her name sounded like "sewer," and Pete Smith suggested allowing a fan to name her for a $500 prize. The winning entry was "Joan Arden" and for a month LeSueur was "Joan Arden" before Strickling discovered there already was a Joan Arden. The second place name: Joan Crawford. She was a workout for Mannix and Strickling due to her well-known bisexuality and voracious sexual appetite.[37] She told friends, "Sex is good for the complexion," and her reputation was so well known that stories about her were known as "Joan stories."[38] In fact, her reputation preceded the Rapf discovery. Early in her dancing career she was arrested in Detroit for prostitution but the matter was dropped (usually the club owners paid those bribes).[39]

In New York Crawford frequented Harlem's lesbian clubs, known for live sex shows called "buffet flats" and sex between audience members. The clubs were favorites of the 1920s lesbian crowd, which included Crawford, Bea Lillie, Tallulah Bankhead, Estelle Winwood, Barbara Stanwyck and Marjorie Main.[40] Rapf's support of his young protégée had more to do with sex than talent.[41] An inordinate amount of attention was show-ered on Crawford; MGM people assumed she was sleeping with Rapf. She saw sex with older male authority figures as normal; her second stepfa-ther slept with her for years. But she told friends that Rapf's big nose "hid his genitals."[42] Eyes rolled at MGM when a dancer with no experience received treatment reserved for stars. She had movie roles within weeks and was filmed having a costume fitting with renowned designer Erté. Smith and Barbier addressed Crawford rumors right away, telling writers that Crawford made morning visits to St. Augustine's catholic church for mass. But it would take more than publicity people to deal with the biggest "Joan story."

Like 1924, 1925 was a good year for MGM, still with a number of films left over from the previous studios. The biggest was *Ben Hur,* an enormous critical success. But the cost—$6 million—kept it from ever breaking even. Other 1925 hits included King Vidor's war drama *The Big Parade,* the Lon Chaney classics *The Unholy Three* and *The Blackbird,* John Gilbert in *La Boheme,* and Garbo's debut in *The Torrent* with Ricardo Cortez. Mayer faced another challenge that fall: Thalberg battled a weak heart and in November 1925 the 26-year-old had a heart attack at his desk. He spent several months convalescing before returning to the studio. Mayer was at least publicly distraught.

MGM's first official publicity problem was Barbara LaMarr, whom they inherited from Metro, who "spun" every aspect of her life from her arrival in L.A. to her death. The public knew almost nothing about her that was true, maybe because it was so sad. Reatha Dale Watson was a beautiful 13-year-old who moved to L.A. from Yakima, Washington. The day she arrived the physically mature teenager began performing in a bur-lesque show and working as a call girl. She was arrested; studio bios said it was for underaged dancing, but probably it was for prostitution. She was brought before a judge who said she was "too beautiful to be left alone unattended in the big city."[43] *L.A. Examiner* reporter Adela Rogers St. Johns happened to be in court and described a youngster so lovely "she took my breath away," and who "could stop traffic."

Reatha was hired by Metro, renamed Barbara LaMarr, and said to be the daughter of an Italian count and a descendent of Napoleon. Within a year she was a star, after *The Three Musketeers* (1921), *The Prisoner of Zenda* (1922) and *Thy Name Is Woman* (1923). Her bio was revised to suggest Watson had been a 12-year-old runaway rescued from the streets by a kindly judge and reporter St. Johns. The press learned LaMarr never slept more than two hours a day, because she "didn't want to waste a single minute of her wonderful life sleeping." But her wakefulness was due to her drug problem. LaMarr always had a healthy appetite for men and drugs. She was married to vaudevillian Ben Deeley, and actors Phillip Ainsworth and Jack Daugherty. *Photoplay* wrote, "even Barbara didn't know exactly how many husbands she had."[44] Her second husband was a young lawyer named Lawrence Converse, so smitten with LaMarr that he married her though he had a wife and three children at home. He was jailed the day after their 1914 wedding on bigamy charges, moaning her name, banging his head against the bars and knocking himself unconscious. He died three days later.[45]

MGM director Paul Bern also obsessed over her. LaMarr had already been married four times when she met Bern, but even though he asked her to marry him she decided to elope with a different fifth husband. She lived in a house in Whitley Heights, binging on cocaine she stored in a large, solid gold case shaped like a piano, and had a tunnel built between her garage and her bedroom to allow lovers access. By late 1924 she was more interested in drugs than men and was virtually unable to work. By the time she was found unconscious in her house that fall, everyone knew she was dying. Mannix and Strickling committed her to Banksia Place sanitarium and Strickling told the papers she was suffering from "exhaustion." It was the same hospital where Wally Reid had died barely a year earlier.

She had made 30 films between 1921 and 1924 but in the last two years she could only do three. In November 1925 she was arrested while carrying 40 cubes of morphine from a drug house, but prosecutors realized she wouldn't live through a trial, and at Mayer's request they let her go home. She moved to her father's house in Altadena, where she would die in January 1926. Mannix and Strickling kept her on a small salary and paid her bills in exchange for interviews about the dangers of drugs[46] that ran in all of the fan magazines. Her death was blamed on "vigorous dieting" and the coroner induced to ascribe death from "tuberculosis," at the time a common catchall for drug overdoses. Over 50,000 fans filed past LaMarr's closed coffin. Mayer described her as the most beautiful woman in the world and paid her homage by giving Czech starlet Hedwig Kiesler the name Hedy Lamarr.

Coincidentally, at the same time one of Lamarr's neighbors got in trouble with MGM. Joe Schenck called Mannix, worried as usual that his beautiful young wife Natalie Talmadge had another boyfriend. She always slept with her costars so Schenck usually asked that she be teamed with homosexuals.[47] One of private detectives told him she was having an affair with Richard Barthelmess. Schenck had been cuckolded by Norma dozens of times—her affair with Gilbert Roland lasted for years—but he disliked

Barthelmess. She was followed to Barthelmess' mansion just down the street from LaMarr's home several times. Barthelmess was a Griffith star, a wonderful natural actor and one of the most popular male stars of the 1920s, receiving 10,000 fan letters a week. He had begun a heated affair with Talmadge soon after she married the much older and decidedly unattractive Schenck. Schenck gave her gifts like Rolls Royces and a 10-carat diamond ring, and a movie career.[48] Longtime Hollywood writer Col. Barney Oldfield remembered the Barthelmess-Talmadge-Schenck story. Schenck was incensed about the affair and called Mannix, asking that Mannix contact his underworld friends. He demanded that Barthelmess be castrated and the excised body parts given to his wife.[49] Talmadge allegedly told friends that she convinced her husband to cancel the contract by promising to end the affair. Barthelmess' wife, actress Mary Hay, was not as forgiving. She divorced him.

During the first year after her 1925 arrival at MGM, Joan Crawford's career was workmanlike but not spectacular. However, her special treatment continued. She was given a starring role in the film *Sally, Irene, and Mary* and small roles in a dozen others. But even with a light résumé, publicity man Smith arranged for her to be named one of 1926's Wampas Baby Stars, the Western Association of Motion Picture Advertisers' list of the dozen most promising newcomers. Among the others were Mary Astor and Fay Wray. In 1926 Crawford also caught Paul Bern's eye. Like LaMarr before her, Crawford became a target of what John Gilbert called Bern's "Mary Magdalene complex; he does things for whores."[50] Bern sent her gifts like a $10,000 ermine coat and made sure Thalberg became aware of her. He got her bigger films in 1926 and 1927 and more money, raises from $75 to $500 a week. MGM people knew Crawford was sleeping with Bern. In late 1926 Mayer ordered an $18,000 loan for Crawford to purchase a house at 513 Roxbury Drive. Owning their stars' homes gave MGM even more leverage in disagreements, but it was unusual for the studio to do it for a young actress at such an early point in her career.

One of Crawford's closest friends was Billy Haines. In 1926 dashing William "Billy" Haines was becoming a star second only to John Gilbert in popularity. But he was also the first openly homosexual movie star, a fact kept from Mayer for three years. In the early 1920s Haines lived in New York, hanging with the theater crowd and, as he admitted, "kept by some of the best men and women in New York."[51] He was discovered in a Goldwyn "New Faces" contest in 1921 and came to Hollywood with female winner Eleanor Boardman. She went on to quick stardom but Haines had to learn acting. After two dozen forgettable roles between 1922 and 1925 he was still playing small parts and in 1925 almost got fired by Mayer.

Haines dabbled in heterosex- uality. He had an experimental sexual relationship in 1923 with Barbara LaMarr and a fling with Norma Shearer during the 1925 filming of *A Slave of Fashion*, but returned to men. During the Shearer experiment Haines spent evenings at a male brothel on Wil- shire Boulevard with his lover Ramon Novarro. Lou Cody — a pompous alcoholic who married Mabel Normand during a drunken party — got into an argument with Haines and retaliated by telling Mayer about Haines and Novarro.[52] At first Mayer refused to accept that Haines was a homosexual. He met with Haines and tried to use tears, putting an arm around Haines and begging him, "Oh, my son. I never had a son. I always wanted a son."[53] When Haines

Legendary comedienne Mabel Normand, whose addictions to parties and drugs ended in her death at the age of only 31. Her scandals helped force the industry to enact a strict morals code that would impact films for years to come.

didn't respond, Mayer was ready to fire both him and Novarro but Thal- berg convinced Mayer not to. Haines and Novarro were forbidden to see each other, an edict they ignored.

Experimentation aside, Haines was a confirmed homosexual. Although Dietz in New York and Strickling in L.A. tried to pair him with girlfriends, he annoyed the studio by refusing to play along with their attempts. When a reporter asked him about LaMarr, he responded that his one true love was actress Kate Price. His male friends howled; the interviewer, describ- ing Price, noted that of "all the women in Hollywood it's Kate Price, who's fat and fifty, that's his favorite."[54] He also said a girlfriend was horse-faced character actress Polly Moran. MGM was desperate to link Haines roman- tically with *any* woman, but never could.

From the moment of a first slight Mayer looked for ways to fire Haines, even though by 1926 he was the most popular male star on the lot. He had a string of hit movies like *Brown of Harvard* and *Tell it to the Marines* (both 1926); *Slide, Kelly, Slide* and *Spring Fever* (both 1927); and *West Point* (1928). He was receiving more fan mail than anyone at MGM, his films were moneymakers, and by 1927 he was earning the equivalent of $1 million a year. His popularity prevented Mayer from getting rid of him and emboldened Haines during meetings with Mayer. When a studio-hired voice coach described Haines' voice audition by saying he was "lip lazy," Haines replied, "I've never had any complaints."[55] Mayer was seething when he heard what Haines said.

In 1926 Haines met sailor Jimmy Shields at a New York bathhouse. He fell in love with Shields, brought him back to California and arranged that his new lover be hired as an extra. They moved into Haines' apartment and would stay together for the next 50 years. Even with his new lover, in late 1926 Haines was allegedly picked up in a vice squad sweep of Pershing Square. The square was a notorious homosexual hangout and "cruising the square" a popular way to pick up gay men. Strickling and Mannix took care of the problem but Mayer again tried to fire Haines. Thalberg interceded again on behalf of their huge star.

Elinor Glyn wrote a famous essay in the March 1927 issue of *Photoplay* describing who in Hollywood had "it" and who didn't. She noted the growing rumors about Haines by saying that he specifically didn't. Mayer was even more angry that Haines' sexuality was being openly questioned in the press and yet again told Thalberg they should fire Haines. Thalberg suggested an alternative: Haines could marry Joan Crawford. Thalberg knew that they were close friends and accepted each other's homosexuality or bisexuality. Most of Haines' friends at MGM were women but by 1927 his closest friend was Crawford. The two were inseparable pals. She considered the offer but Haines flatly refused.

In 1926 MGM's biggest male star was John Gilbert. Thalberg and Gilbert were close friends but Mayer hated Gilbert. Gilbert thought Mayer was a pompous prude and Mayer thought Gilbert a whoremonger with no respect for women.[56] Gilbert's pal Carey Wilson told Gilbert's daughter Leatrice Fountain that Mayer told him, "I hate the bastard because he doesn't love his mother." Carey told Leatrice, "I've never seen such hatred in my life. It was frightening." Strickling was perplexed by Mayer's feelings about Gilbert. He said, "It was very strange, this thing between Mayer and Jack. Like he'd made up his mind to hate the guy from the first time he saw him. As far as I was concerned Mayer was way off base, but you couldn't tell him that. Anything good about Jack Gilbert, he didn't want to know. It was strange because Jack was always one of the good guys. Not that he wasn't a little eccentric, and temperamental sometimes, but all great actors are. But people now say that Jack was crazy. It's the damnedest thing. He was one of the most interesting guys out here and one of the best liked."[57]

Gilbert was born in 1899 to Ida Adair, a vaudeville actress in a troupe run by her husband John Pringle. When she became pregnant during a tour he divorced her. She returned to a family farm in Logan, Utah, and after giving birth returned to the road. The travel was unglamorous; moving from boarding house to boarding house, stage to stage, week after week. It was even worse for little Jack, growing up backstage while his mother performed. It is little wonder that, as nice as he was, he had problems with women. At various times Ida left her son with friends, some whom she hardly knew. When he was seven, she left him for a year with a seamstress in New York, sharing a room in an Amsterdam Avenue apartment with the woman's daughter, a prostitute who told her customers to just ignore the little boy on the mat.

John Gilbert, at the height of his career, taken on the porch of his Tower Road mansion. Three years later he was dead.

He moved back with his mother after she married comedian Walter Gilbert, but Ida's infidelities ended the marriage and he was again lying on a matt listening to sex. But this time, his roommate was his mother.

Ida died of alcoholism and tuberculosis in 1913. Just minutes after the funeral, Walter Gilbert drove 14-year-old Jack from the cemetery to the train, gave him $10 and sent him to San Francisco to find work. He saw his first movie, a William S. Hart Western called *On the Night Stage* (1915), walked out of the theater and took a train to L.A. He made his way to Thomas Ince's Santa Monica studio and was hired as an extra. He had bit parts in 30 films between 1915 and 1919 and after signing with Fox starred in films like *Monte Cristo* (1921) and *The Madness of Youth* (1922). Just before the MGM merger in 1924 he signed with Metro. After *He Who Gets Slapped* (1924) with Norma Shearer, he became the new Valentino after the 1925 classics *The Merry Widow*, *The Big Parade*, and *La Boheme*. By 1926 he was MGM's biggest star, earning $10,000 a week and living in a mansion at the top of Tower Road in Beverly Hills.

In 1925 Greta Garbo entered his life. Mayer had found her during a 1924 trip to Europe. He was in Germany and saw plump blonde 19-year-old Greta Gustafson in Mauritz Stiller's *The Saga of Gosta Berling*. Stiller was a strange-looking homosexual with oversized hands and feet and a straying, watering eye, but Gustafson was having an affair with him. Over a drink in a hotel bar, Mayer offered her a job but warned her to lose weight, saying, "We don't like fat girls in America."[58] She and Stiller promised to arrive by April 15, 1925, but Stiller, having second thoughts, delayed the trip. By the time they arrived in New York aboard the SS *Drotningholm* on July 6, 1925, she had lost 30 pounds.

Howard Dietz asked his assistant, Hubert Voight, to take care of her. So unimpressed was Dietz that he booked her into the low-rent Commodore Hotel. Neither Dietz nor Voight even bothered to meet her boat; they paid a photographer $10 to greet her. He told Voight, "Do what you can but don't spend any money. Her name sounds too close to *garbage!*" None of the New York staff met with her during her short stay. Mayer was angry Stiller had delayed the trip, so he told his New York people to "let her sit." She and Stiller waited two months before being summoned to L.A. As angry as Mayer was, a fluke showed him her star quality. One of MGM's New York photographers, Arnold Genthe, met Garbo at a party and arranged for her to sit for a few photos the next morning at his shop. By the time he displayed the pictures in his studio windows, Garbo had been unceremoniously dispatched to L.A. While she and Stiller made the trip to L.A., a frantic hunt by New York agents had begun to find the women in Genthe's window. By the time she arrived in L.A. in September she was a celebrity, but even so, Mayer was still mad at Stiller and refused to assign her work for several more months. At Thalberg's suggestion he finally gave her tiny roles in *The Torrent* and *The Temptress* (both 1927).

Ignoring Mayer's anger toward Garbo and hatred of Gilbert, Thalberg assigned the two to *Flesh and the Devil*. There was an instant attraction; the chemistry was intense and obvious. Director Clarence Brown said it was "the damnedest thing you ever saw. When they got into that first love scene … well, nobody else was there. They were alone in a world of their own. It seemed like an intrusion to yell "cut" so I used to just motion the crew over to another part of the set and let them finish what they were doing. It was embarrassing."[59] It was a hit largely due to the love scenes, the first on-screen lovers filmed in a horizontal position and the first kiss with parted lips. They immediately became inseparable and would be assigned to Strickling himself. Within weeks of the *Flesh and the Devil* release they were the most popular couple in the movies. The relationship might have ended better had not Strickling so mercilessly capitalized on it.

Garbo moved into Gilbert's mansion, with its tennis court, pool, and privacy. He hired designer Harold Grieve to redo a bedroom suite for her and spent $15,000 ($300,000 today) to add a black marble bathtub with solid gold fixtures. When she told him that the marble was too shiny, he had craftsmen hack off the sheen with axes. He also had a small cabin built above the house and planted pine trees because she missed the smell of her Swedish home. A remote-controlled stream filled with trout bubbled over a waterfall in front of her cabin.

Gilbert loved Garbo—he asked her to marry him just weeks after they met—but she would never commit to the relationship. He was blind to the fact that she was self-centered, selfish, and rude. Four times she agreed to marry him, and four times begged off just before. He became an emotional wreck trying to figure out her strange moods. His daughter once said, "She loved him as much as Garbo could love anything." The Garbo relationship and the Mayer-Gilbert feud came to a head at the same moment on September 8, 1926, at a mansion across from the Beverly Hills Hotel at 1700 Lexington Drive. The Lexington House had been purchased by William Randolph Hearst for mistress Marion Davies' extended family.[60] Marion offered the house for the wedding of her pal Eleanor Boardman and director King Vidor. At a dinner with Vidor and Boardman a few weeks before, Garbo had inexplicably again agreed to marry Gilbert. Vidor suggested a double wedding and Garbo agreed. The morning of the wedding Gilbert awoke to see Garbo driving down Tower Road away from his mansion. Over 500 guests waited at the Lexington house, but as the morning wore on it was apparent Garbo was once again standing up Gilbert. Distraught, he escaped weeping into a bathroom. Mayer happened to be in there. The result was probably predictable.

Mayer slapped Gilbert on the back and laughed, "What's the matter with you, Gilbert? Don't marry her. Just fuck her and forget about her!"[61] Gilbert pounced on Mayer, a brawl ensued and Mayer's glasses went crashing to the floor. Mannix, never far from Mayer, jumped in between the two and broke up the battle with the help of several wedding guests. Mayer was apoplectic, screaming, "You're finished Gilbert! I'll destroy you if it costs me a million dollars!"[62] Over the next year and a half, it appears that he did.

Strangely, and frustratingly for Gilbert, he and Garbo remained somewhat of a couple after the wedding fiasco and did several successful films together, including *Love* (1927) and *A Woman of Affairs* (1928). Both made huge profits but Gilbert inexplicably started getting assignments to modest program vehicles. For decades writers have questioned whether Mayer would destroy his biggest asset. Mayer defenders suggest that studio interests would prevent him from doing so, but his personality suggests that he would, and the evidence suggests that he did. After all, he had "killed" before, with Francis X. Bushman and Beverly Bayne. Even though Thalberg had told Gilbert, "Don't worry, just keep your nose clean and he can't touch you,"[63] Mayer assigned him bombs like *The Show* and *Twelve Miles Out* (both 1927), *The Cossacks* (1928), and *Desert Nights* (1929). Mayer also limited the money spent on Gilbert films. The background sets for *The Show* were cheap hand-painted stage backdrops and even *Variety* wondered why Gilbert was given the roles he was getting. Gilbert critics suggest his performances were missing the spark present before. He was increasingly despondent, but Mayer was also destroying his career with bad assignments.

A year later, Mayer would finish Gilbert off, but in the meantime, Gilbert's off-screen behavior became more and more erratic. Career issues and Garbo's emotional torment pushed Gilbert further into an alcoholic haze. Most days he drank himself unconscious. One evening as he waited for Garbo at Tower Road a young couple parked below his front porch, enjoying the glorious view of L.A. Gilbert grabbed one of his guns and fired several shots at the car, hitting the car while the terrified couple cowered inside. Mannix took care of the police, and MGM purchased a brand new roadster for the young man.

Garbo usually escaped to an apartment at the Miramar Hotel in Santa Monica, just a few doors down the beach from former lover Stiller. In April 1927, a drunk Gilbert drove to the beach to confront Garbo. When she wouldn't answer her door he climbed to her second-floor balcony. But when he got to the railing Stiller was waiting and tossed the drunken actor down onto the beach. The police arrested Gilbert and dutifully informed Mannix that Gilbert was at the station, but Mayer reportedly instructed him not to help. He was charged with being drunk and disorderly.[64] Strickling let the press run the story without defending Gilbert. Gilbert was sentenced to ten days in jail.

Mayer forbade intercession, and Gilbert was booked into the L.A. Country Jail. It was clear to MGM that Mayer had allowed his star to go to jail, but the plan backfired when headlines blared "JOHN GILBERT IN JAIL CELL!" A public relations fiasco erupted as the jail filled with friends, drinking buddies, actresses looking for publicity, and thousands of fans. Mayer was forced to have Mannix and Strickling arrange for Gilbert's release just a day and a half later.[65]

On another occasion a drunken Gilbert grabbed his pistol and went looking for Stiller and Garbo, tearing through Beverly Hills toward the beach. Who knows what would have happened had a Beverly Hills policeman not seen Gilbert almost run off of Sunset Boulevard near UCLA. He stopped the drunken driver and had him taken to the station. Mannix and Strickling took care of the police and the press, and the story never appeared anywhere.

At the same time Gilbert's career was imploding, Mannix began an affair that, unlike the previous many, became serious. In 1927 he broke his own rule and instead of the normal one-hour stand with someone anonymous, got involved in a relationship. He was a sucker for a dancer. Mary Imogene Robertson was a former Ziegfeld dancer appearing professionally as Imogene "Bubbles" Wilson when they met. He was taken by Bubbles. He probably first met her in New York in 1923 or 1924, and it's unknown when the affair began, but they were a couple in 1927 when she was working for United Artists under the name Mary Nolan.

According to Nolan, she and Mannix began seeing each other in the summer of 1927, and within a week "were more than friends, we were in love."[66] Outsiders thought nothing of seeing a studio manager with an actress, but Hollywood knew all about the relationship, which would continue for several years. He tried to get her work at MGM, but when Thalberg tried to cast her in *Trader Horn* in 1928, she was so addicted to drugs she couldn't work.

As his affair with Nolan heated up, Mannix lost his line to D.A. Asa Keyes. C.C. Julian's Petroleum Company ran ads for investors aimed at "WIDOWS AND ORPHANS!!!" with folksy themes warning "ONLY DAYS LEFT!" In two years Julian stole millions from 40,000 investors. Keyes was forced to prosecute Julian but tried to fix the case. He gave the complicated case to a first-year lawyer, tried to reduce the charges, and even asked the judge to drop the case. He gave the closing argument himself and rebuked his own case, and ten defendants were found not guilty. Everyone knew "the fix was in." The bizarre final act of the Keyes-Julian scandal occurred in early 1930 when Frank Keaton, who had lost everything after Julian defendant Motley Flint convinced him to invest, quietly walked over to Flint during the trial and shot him three times.[67] Keaton had 10¢ in his pocket. Flint had $63,000. Keyes would be tried for accepting bribes when people learned that Keyes and the Julian group were drinking buddies and he had been gifted with a Lincoln convertible, furniture and over $150,000 in cash ($2 million today) to buy a Beverly Hills mansion. Mannix was busy with Nolan when Keyes went to jail. The studio waited patiently to see who would replace Keyes, knowing a new deal would have to be made.

The fall of 1927 was a busy time for the studio, on and off the screen, as a new technology took the movies by storm. That fall, Strickling moved from his rented room in the Sweeney house into his own home, a lovely Spanish hacienda above Sunset. Befitting a manager in the publicity department making $250 a week, the house at 1494 North Kings Road was the biggest home anyone in his family had ever owned.[68] He was also making more than any Strickling had ever made. He was busy making the studio introductions to the new D.A. at the time, and there were changes in the power structure at the studio as well.

Marcus Loew, president of the MGM's parent company, died suddenly over the Labor Day weekend, 1927. Loew was worth over $35 million ($500 million today) and his Long Island funeral was attended by 5,000 of the industry's titans, stars, and workers. Mayer bought a memorial page in *Variety* offering his thoughts (written by Strickling). "It would demand the pen of a great poet rather than my feeble capacity of expression in words to describe the real feelings that stir in my heart. In his memory I shall always find my finest inspiration." Loew's death changed the balance of power at MGM. The next morning, without bothering to inform the board of directors, Nick Schenck appointed himself president. Mayer was furious. Joe Schenck actively disliked Mayer and Nick could barely stand him. The enmity went back to the original merger, when Schenck wanted the new studio called Metro-Goldwyn-*Schenck*.

Just after Loew's funeral, Thalberg married actress Norma Shearer. He was the most eligible bachelor in Hollywood, even with his mother's constant presence. He hung around with a group of hard-drinking womanizers — Jack Conway, Victor Fleming, Jack Gilbert, and Howard Hawks — but he was an observer. The men were regular customers at Hollywood brothels, but while his friends were entertained he waited in the lobby reading his *L.A. Examiner.* Most of his dates with MGM actresses were for publicity purposes. He dated Bessie Love and Peggy Hopkins Joyce, but for years had been totally smitten with Constance Talmadge. "Dutch" Talmadge was the middle daughter of the three Talmadge girls — with Natalie (Mrs. Buster Keaton) and Norma (Mrs. Joe Schenck) — and was the most fun-loving and beautiful of the three. F. Scott Fitzgerald described her as a "princess of lingerie and love ... the flapper de luxe." She had a huge cocaine habit and liked to cruise gay bars with her best friend, homosexual star Billy Haines, and help him pick up men.[69] Thalberg was in love with her but by the fall of 1927 he had grown weary of spying on her from the bushes near her house, watching her return from her dates.

Thalberg's marriage to Shearer was more a merger than a romance. There was an obvious lack of passion and they talked mostly about her films. But while dancing one evening in August 1927, he casually asked,

"When are we going to be married?"[70] The next morning he summoned her to his office and offered a tray of rings. She chose the most expensive. She knew about his feelings for Talmadge, and called herself "Lotta Miles, Irving's Spare Tire" (a reference to one of her modeling assignments, for a tire company). The marriage took place on September 29, 1927, at Thalberg's rented Sunset Boulevard mansion in Beverly Hills. Mayer was the best man.

After a short honeymoon to Pebble Beach the couple settled into the Sunset Boulevard mansion, along with Thalberg's mother Henrietta, who retained her seat at the head of the table. Thalberg and Shearer slept at opposite ends of the huge house, and Henrietta still tucked Irving into bed every night.[71] Before Shearer set her sights on Thalberg there were rumors that she and Mayer had had an affair. It would make sense; Mayer slept with hundreds of his young starlets after telling them during their first meeting to think of him as their "friend and advisor." But he also told them, "Be nice to me and I'll be nice to you."[72] When Shearer first arrived at the studio, she was known as *Mayer's* protégée, not linked at all to Thalberg.[73]

In the two years before Loew's death, Warner Brothers—the smallest studio in Hollywood, run by brothers Jack, Harry, and Sam — was on a solo march to bring sound to theaters. Thomas Edison began experimenting with sound because of his growing deafness. In June 1925, a partnership was formed between Warners, Vitaphone, and Western Electric Company to develop a system to synchronize phonograph records with running film. The effect would be a "talking picture." Although in Hollywood lore, *The Jazz Singer* is known as the first sound film, the Vitaphone film *Don Juan* actually premiered earlier, on August 6, 1926. The crowd in the Warner Theater was astonished to hear the New York Philharmonic Orchestra playing the *Tannhäuser* overture and went

Norma during her marriage to Irving Thalberg; she was the "Queen of the MGM Lot." Even so, she still had to send pictures to the gossip writers, like this one sent to Hedda Hopper.

wild. William Fox, among a group of studio heads at the *Don Juan* premiere which included Mayer and Thalberg, purchased a German version of the technology for his Movietone newsreels. On May 21, 1927, Fox cameramen filmed Charles Lindberg taking off from Roosevelt Field on his way to France. His newsreel featured the sound of Lindberg's engines, evoking thunderous cheers from viewers.

People filled theaters showing four Warners sound films released in 1926 and 1927, but the early units were plagued by technical difficulties. A tiny slip in the film threw off the sound synchronization for the rest of the film. And the only sounds were background; there was still no *speaking*. Warners changed all of that on October 6, 1927, when the 89-minute *Jazz Singer* premiered in New York. There were five songs and a few lines of dialogue. Recording Gus Kahn's "Toot Toot Tootsie Goodbye," singer Al Jolson got so excited he blurted out, "Wait a minute. Wait a minute. You ain't heard nothin' yet. Wait a minute, I tell ya'. You ain't heard nothin.'"[74] Jolsen's ad-libbed lines drove audiences wild. Tragically, Sam Warner was not there; he had died the night before. Silent pictures died with him.

Thalberg was dismissive, saying, "It was a good gimmick, but that's all it was."[75] He gave brother-in-law Douglas Shearer the assignment of researching sound for MGM. Other studio executives agreed with him, and Louella Parsons wrote, "I have no fear that the screeching ... sound film will ever disturb our peaceful theaters."[76]

Sound presented numerous challenges. Most important, almost none of the 20,000 U.S. movie theaters were equipped for sound in 1928. The $15,000 cost for one theater was more than chains or independents could afford. MGM's 500 Loew theaters would cost millions to outfit. It took almost two years for the first 10,000 theaters to be readied.

Also, everyday filming was revamped. Filming a silent was simple: Cues and directions were given verbally while cameras rolled; there were no flubbed lines. That freedom was suddenly gone. Actors dreaded hearing, "Not good for sound," after a take. Recording was also a technical challenge, since early microphones were only sensitive toward one direction. Picking up dialogue from one side made it hard to control the sound level. Microphones were hidden in potted plants, floral arrangements, light fixtures, even hats. Also, the actors had to be stationary near microphones. Many wonderful camera techniques developed during the silent era were unusable in sound pictures. Sam Marx said, "Suddenly the movies stopped moving." The cameras were also a problem, so noisy they had to be encased in soundproof boxes. The contraptions were nicknamed Iron Mikes because they were so hot. Since air conditioning made noise it was banned, making sound stages even more sweltering.

Thalberg realized that foreign distribution would be a challenge, wondering aloud at a meeting with Mayer and Mannix if European audiences would want to hear English dialogue. MGM spent most of 1928 figuring out how to use sound and determining who could speak on film. Actor terror was palpable. Studios hired every available speech coach as Thalberg noted, "Audiences have formed their own idea of how each star sounds. They've heard the voices in their head in picture after picture, and what they hear may be disappointing. It's very risky."[77] Joan Crawford had a simpler assessment: "PANIC!"

Sound was a blessing to some, a curse to many, a threat to all. Hearing his voice for the first time, William Powell ran out of the room. None of her fans knew Marion Davies stuttered. Strickling's assistant Hubert Voight accompanied her to the premier of *The Jazz Singer*. On the drive home she said, "M ... M ... M ... Mr ... V ... Voight ... I ... I ... I ... ha ... ha ... have ... problem." Thankfully, she discovered that the affliction disappeared if she recited memorized words. Gloria Swanson hired Broadway star Laura Hope Crews as a private diction coach, paying her $1,000 a week to lose her New York accent. Hundreds of Broadway actors came to L.A. to sell their services as speech coaches.

Vilma Banky's Hungarian accent made her unusable. Just three months earlier, Samuel Goldwyn had spent $300,000 for her wedding to Rod La Roque, a wedding preceded by 22 showers and followed by a reception dominated by a 50-foot buffet table covered with paper-mâché food for the cameras. Banky retired to the Beverly Hills mansion she shared with La Roque for 40 years. Almost all of the New York stars were unsuitable. Constance, Norma, and Natalie Talmadge all had heavy Brooklyn accents inside their tiny voices. Constance said, "Leave them while you're looking good and thank God for the trust funds mom set up."[78] The sisters' marriages helped: Natalie's to Buster Keaton, Norma's to Joe Schenck. The first time Clara Bow heard her own nasal Brooklynese she screamed in anguish.[79] Alla Nazimova knew she would fail the test and just retired to the apartment hotel she had built around her Sunset Boulevard mansion.

"Failing the test" proved fatal for dozens of careers, but Karl Dane's case was perhaps the most tragic. He was born Rasmus Karl Thekelsen Gottlieb in Copenhagen, and starred in some of the biggest silent films, including *The Big Parade* (1925), *La Boheme* (1926), and *The Son of the Sheik* (1926). He was earning $5,000 a week and sharing his 622 Oakhurst Drive mansion with 13 servants and 5 Rolls Royces. But he could not speak any English, and his career foundered. Gone was the mansion, replaced by a small apartment in a seedy part of Hollywood. Gone were the Rolls Royces, replaced by L.A. transit buses. By 1933 he was selling hot dogs from a cart outside the studio gates. On April 15, 1934, he shot himself in the head in his apartment. When his body went unclaimed Buster Keaton appealed to Mannix, and MGM paid for a funeral.

MGM's cautious stance on "talkies" continued into early 1928. During that time MGM turned out some of its finest movies, such as Garbo's *Woman of Affairs,* Crawford's *Our Dancing Daughters,* and Lon Chaney horror films like *London after Midnight.* But Loew's theater managers were screaming for sound, since patrons were deserting them for theaters equipped with Thalberg's "fad." Even so, Thalberg was cautious. MGM's first try was the roaring of "Leo the Lion" during the beginning credits of *White Shadows of the South Seas.* Small bits of sound were added to movies in progress. Street noise and ringing phones were added to William Haines' *Excess Baggage.* The first dialogue was fitted to the Haines and Lionel Barrymore vehicle *Alias Jimmy Valentine.*

Behind Thalberg's back, Mannix himself hired college professor Vern Knudsen to design sound stages. He was paid $2,500 — more than his yearly teaching salary — for 10 days' work. Mannix supervised the construction of two massive buildings — 100 by 150 feet and 7 stories tall — with 10-inch concrete walls and soundproof camera booths connected to recorders in a separate building. The first sound movie filmed at MGM was *Broadway Melody,* which cost $275,000 and grossed $4 million. It won the studio's first Best Picture Academy Award.

Another of MGM's first uses of sound was in Mayer's plan to destroy John Gilbert. The dreaded tests were done by the end of 1928, and MGM unveiled voices in *The Hollywood Revue of 1929* on June 20, 1929. It was a compilation of sketches and dance numbers and Gilbert's voice fared fine. But Mayer apparently used the first Gilbert talkie to thrust a dagger into Gilbert's heart, weakened by Garbo's attitude and Mayer's bad movie assignments. Gilbert was assigned *His Glorious Night,* a minor film directed by a (usually) drunk Lionel Barrymore. The script was terrible, the photography bland, and Barrymore's alcohol-addled directing inept. The film was a bomb, but Gilbert's voice — normally smooth and masculine — was recorded as a high-pitched squeal. This could not have happened without the direction of Mayer, who, it was rumored, ordered all bass removed from Gilbert's dialogue.[80] At the September 28, 1929, premiere when Gilbert squeaked, "I love you. I love you. I love you," the viewers howled with laughter. Mayer heard a viewer yell, "Gilbert, your slip is showing," and dissolved with laughter. Gilbert walked out in tears. Mayer was said to have had Strickling leak stories that Gilbert's voice was unsuitable, and newspapers said Gilbert couldn't talk. He was soon awash in liquor.

Things had progressed steadily downward for Gilbert since the 1926 fight with Mayer. Garbo was still making his emotional life miserable. His low budget films were bombs. The voice alteration in *His Glorious Night* ruined his image. Strickling was also feeding the press stories about the Gilbert-Garbo relationship, worsening the fragile actor's torment. He cried when he read a *Photoplay* story—probably written by Strickling—that featured this poem:

> On again, off again, Greta and John again
> How they have stirred up the news for awhile
> Making the critics first sigh with them, die with them
> Making the cynical smile[81]

Through it all Gilbert still allowed Garbo to live with him on Tower Road. They often went days without speaking as she secluded herself in her cabin among the pine trees behind his house. Even as she spent entire afternoons sunbathing nude in front of Gilbert or his gardeners or guests, he clung hopelessly to the dream that she would someday marry him. Mayer would have finished him off in 1928, but Nick Schenck stopped him.

When Marcus Loew died the year before, his widow was left 400,000 shares of Loew's stock worth $30 million. It gave her control over MGM. Everyone wanted the stock and the studio that came with it. Paramount, Warners, and Fox all made plays, but William Fox went around Loew's widow and in June 1928 offered Nick Schenck a $10 million commission to arrange his purchase. Fox suggested that the merger would save the combined studios $20 million a year in redundancies and management, Mayer in particular. Schenck secretly met with the Loew family, who agreed as long as a deal was done quietly. They also required Schenck ensure that MGM's biggest stars—among them Gilbert—remained with the new entity. Without consulting Mayer, Schenck gave Gilbert a new contract worth $1 million a year. Mayer was furious; while he was trying to get rid of Gilbert, his bitter enemy Schenck extended Gilbert's contract. Mayer was so mad he didn't notice his own tenuous position, even after the November *Variety* headline "FOX WITH LOEW'S IN DEAL" and in December "LOUIS B. MAYER LEAVING MGM." He was in serious trouble.

Fortunately Ida Koverman's friend Herbert Hoover was being inaugurated as president, and Mayer was going (his family were Hoover's first overnight guests at the White House). While Mayer was in Washington, Thalberg learned of Schenck's plan. He was in a predicament; still loyal to Mayer, he rightly worried that Mayer was powerless in the new mix. For $250,000 he agreed not to say anything to Mayer. Mannix received the same amount. But several things conspired to thwart the Fox-Schenck MGM takeover. First, Mayer prevailed on Hoover and Attorney General William Mitchell to declare the merger a violation of antitrust laws. Mayer's favorite lawyer, Mabel Willebrandt, was an assistant attorney general, which helped. Second, on July 17, 1929, just after the *New York Times* confirmed Fox's purchase of the 400,000 Loew shares, Fox was seriously hurt in a car accident on the way to play golf. His driver was killed and his Rolls Royce demolished. Last, while Fox recuperated, the Black Thursday stock market crash reduced the Loew's stock value by half overnight. He was forced to sell of most of his holdings just to pay off bank debt.[82] The deal was dead. Incredibly, Mayer survived.

Although Schenck guaranteed Gilbert would at least make money for a few years, Mayer continued to assign him bad movies until the Schenck contract extension ended in 1933. His last role was a small part as a riveter in *Fast Workers*. Mayer's vindictiveness would never again be doubted. For years, MGM employees used Gilbert as a cautionary tale against crossing Mayer.[83] When alcoholism killed Gilbert in 1936, Mannix and Strickling received another late-night phone call.

By late 1929 Schenck's attempt to oust Mayer was a memory, but what had previously been distrust would become bitter hatred. For the rest of his life Mayer referred to Schenck — whose name was pronounced "skenk" — as the Skunk.[84] Also, Mayer learned of the $250,000 payment to Thalberg. Already upset that Thalberg had been demanding a raise, their relationship never recovered. Mayer was ready to disown the man he once treated like a son.

Joan Crawford momentarily grabbed everyone's attention when she surprisingly married Douglas Fairbanks, Jr. During the previous year she had risen from small roles to marquee status, and as stardom grew so did stories of Crawford and sex. There were rumors the studio "encouraged" the Fairbanks union. Her image needed scrubbing; she had been named in two divorce suits for alienation of affection. Fans thought the June 3, 1929, marriage made her part of Hollywood's royal family, but Fairbanks was on the outs with parents Doug and Mary, and was penniless. She paid for everything, so Mayer again lent her money for a house, a $40,000 mansion at 426 North Bristol in pricey Brentwood.

At the time an old rumor raged through Hollywood that Crawford had starred in a pornographic movie made in New York when she was called Billie Cassin. Rapf heard the story soon after he met her and it had enough credence that he engaged MGM's local offices to search for copies. Eddie Mannix took charge of the project, and according to Maurice Rapf, son of Harry, the studio later had to buy the negative.[85] Biographers are divided about the movie but there is enough circumstantial and anecdotal evidence to suggest it did exist. Some years later Mannix told friends he did arrange for the studio to purchase the negative, and Fairbanks told friends that during his Paris honeymoon he tried to find a copy. The Fairbanks story ran in *Confidential* magazine, an early tabloid. At the same time Crawford's Detroit prostitution arrest record somehow disappeared from Mayer's pal J. Edgar Hoover's offices. But her FBI file still includes a note that "a film of Crawford in compromising positions was circulated … to be used at smokers."[86] So a Crawford sex film did indeed exist, according to the FBI.

When Crawford eventually left MGM in 1943 she paid the studio $50,000, which was extremely unusual. She was obviously paying *back* something. The only real evidence that the film did *not* exist is that a copy never turned up publicly. Her sexual antics were a problem for Mannix and Strickling during her entire career. She had lovers of both sexes and slept with virtually all of her costars,[87] and had a long affair with Tallulah Bankhead that began in New York and lasted into the late 1930s, through marriages to Fairbanks and Franchot Tone. In an interesting coincidence, Bankhead also had affairs with Fairbanks and Tone.[88]

Mayer never liked Bankhead. When he called her into his office in 1932 to fire her, she told him she was "done with MGM. I slept with your six biggest stars."[89] She told a mortified Mayer that Crawford and Barbara Stanwyck were among the half dozen. During a dinner party later in her career Crawford told Mayer that Bankhead was telling the truth. Crawford's problems were not all sexual. In the summer of 1928 a drunken Crawford was driving down Hollywood Boulevard weaving in and out of traffic and onto and off of the sidewalk. She ran a red light and hit a woman in the crosswalk, tried to bribe the motorcycle policeman at the scene, and then drove away. Arrested later near her Brentwood home, she called Strickling, who reportedly went to the young girl's hospital room with $10,000 in new $100 bills (about $300,000 today). Nothing came of the problem.

Little changed in 1928 when D.A. Buron Fitts took over for the disgraced Asa Keyes. Fitts was more dishonest but was a sympathetic figure. He had a limp as the result of wounds received during World War I and was a director of the American Legion. Veterans kept him in office until 1940. Producer Budd Shulberg described Fitts as "completely in the pocket of the producers." Within six months he moved from a small house at 1217 West Second Street into a mansion at 8222 Marmont Avenue above Sunset.[90] It was a neighborhood of movie stars.

Fitts' first job was prosecuting his former boss Keyes for accepting bribes during the Julian Petroleum scandal. By November 1928, Keyes became the first sitting D.A. in California history to be tried during his tenure.[91] He was sentenced to 14 years in prison but was quietly pardoned after two and retired to his Beverly Hills home where he died a year later. Before he went into jail, Keyes kept Mayer out. Mayer was charged with a felony for providing funds to Julian's venture and receiving exorbitant returns, but Keyes convinced a judge to simply allow Mayer to repay the ill-gotten gains. Mayer repaid $53,000 ($750,000 today) and the charges disappeared. Fitts suggested he might reopen Mayer's case after Keyes went to jail, but Jerry Giesler and cash made it go away a final time.

At the same time Mannix had some personal problems of his own. By early 1929 he had been seeing actress Mary Nolan for two years. When she came to Hollywood in 1927 Nolan's sexual reputation from her Ziegfeld days forced the studio to change her name. Mannix arranged for her studio to loan her to MGM for the Lon Chaney film *West of Zanzibar* in 1928 (as a young girl becoming a prostitute) and then got her a role with Gilbert in *Desert Nights*. Mannix was helping Nolan get better work, but according to friends she had also undergone as many as three abortions arranged by Mannix and performed by a studio doctor. And she began arriving on the set with bruises and black eyes.

Mannix abruptly ended the relationship just after the *Desert Nights* release in the spring of 1929, expecting Nolan to quietly exit. But she threatened to confront him at home in front of Bernice. He beat her so badly she was taken unconscious to the hospital. It was not the first time Mannix injured a woman; he once broke Bernice's back. Nolan would eventually endure 15 abdominal surgeries for damage caused by his beating.[92] Instead of quieting Nolan, after six months in the hospital she sued Mannix for $500,000 ($5 million today). She filed a complaint against "Edward J. Mannix, V.P. and General Manager of Metro's Coast Studios." The affair, the lawsuit, and the beating became very public. *Variety* detailed Nolan's charges, and that he had allegedly beaten her on "numerous occasions."[93] Publicly, Mannix denied everything, while Strickling's publicity people described the lawsuit as a frivolous publicity stunt, at the same time leaking stories about Nolan's sexual past. Strangely, they even mentioned the abortions that Mannix himself had paid for. But Nolan was ready for court.

Mannix was incensed that Nolan brought him negative publicity. He first "suggested" that Universal fire Nolan, which they did in early 1930. Eddie then had some of his friends visit Nolan's home one night. He knew Nolan had become hooked on the morphine prescribed for the constant pain caused by the beating, so he had a detective intimate that she would be arrested for drug possession. With an MGM car waiting at the curb he

A grinning Eddie Mannix standing behind Marion Davies during a September 1927 visit by Charles Lindbergh (seated middle) to the set of *West Point*. Also there (from left) were MGM star Billy Haines, director Edward Sedgewick (seated in hat), MGM cameraman Ira Morgan (white shirt) and Harry Rapf (standing above Lindbergh). Haines and Davies were constant headaches for Eddie. (Courtesy of the Maurice Rapf Collection.)

told her she could stay and fight Mannix and face drug charges, or leave L.A. and the matter would be dropped. Within days she was back in New York.[94] She was back in L.A. ten years later and for the last years of her life managed a run-down bungalow court near downtown.

Mannix's treatment of Nolan is typical of a man deservedly nicknamed the Bulldog. Like Mayer, Mannix was a contradiction. He showed a different side to friends. Normally gruff and foulmouthed, Mannix was lovable to people he liked. He called Jack Larson "Junior" and treated him like a son. He helped Garbo and her lesbian lovers on numerous occasions and did so graciously. After writer Salka Viertel was introduced to Mannix by friend and lover Garbo in the 1920s, they remained friends for 30 years. Viertel told Larson that Mannix was wonderful to her and Garbo. Mannix always took her calls and when he heard her voice at the other end would sweetly ask, "What can I do for my Redhead today?" He never once refused a request from either Salka or Garbo.[95]

During the summer of 1929 Billy Haines was involved in yet another homosexual scandal when he was allegedly arrested in a raid on a homosexual bar in Hollywood. The story never made the newspapers but was detailed in several autobiographies, including Louella Parsons'. According to her, the only reason Haines was let off the hook was that he was with best friend Constance Talmadge. "Dutch" Talmadge was Joe Schenck's sister-in-law. What angered Mayer the most was that Haines never even half-heartedly tried to hide his homosexuality. Whether it meant refusing Mannix and Mayer's attempts to hide it or openly frequenting gay bars, Haines wouldn't yield. Jimmy's Backyard opened on New Year's Eve, 1929, the first openly gay bar in L.A. The gala opening was attended by 300 tuxedo-clad homosexuals. Haines attended the party with an entourage that included fellow actor Lowell Sherman and homosexual director Edmund Lowe and his lesbian wife, actress Lilyan Tashman.[96] Mayer hated him, but as 1929 turned into 1930 Haines was voted the number-one box office attraction in the annual Quigley polls. Money spoke to Mayer.

The 1930s is a decade widely recognized as the golden age of the movies. Some of the most famous movies in history were produced during that era but also some of the most heartbreaking scandals. And Eddie Mannix, Howard Strickling, and MGM were right in the middle of it.

Four

The 1930s: The Golden Age of Trouble

The end of the 1920s was difficult for the nation and the movie industry but MGM escaped relatively unscathed. March through September of 1929 was the Great Bull Market, as stock values doubled. But the inevitable occurred on October 24, the infamous Black Thursday when the market crashed. Fortunes were lost overnight. Many in Hollywood were affected including Thalberg, heavily invested in stocks. Mayer's investment in real estate left him untouched. The movies were affected less than most. Carl Laemmle boasted the industry would be "last to feel the pinch and the first to get over it."[1] Schenck told Mayer, "We could make money showing blank film"; remarkable thoughts given the 25 percent unemployment rate.

The Depression changed the way the most Americans viewed their lives. What had appeared as unlimited prosperity now seemed bleakness. Between 1929 and 1932 the income of the average family fell more than 40 percent to a low of $1,500 a year. The bedrock virtues of American life were in doubt. Americans doubted capitalism, democracy, indeed their way of life, and movies offered the best escape. Over 100 million people flocked to theaters weekly out of a population of 130 million.

Laemmle was right only to a point. Studios made money the first few years of the Depression but MGM, making $12 million in 1929 and in 1930 $15 million, and was the only one to pay dividends. RKO had to financially reorganize, Universal and Paramount almost went under and Paramount was forced into receivership. Fox merged with Twentieth Century to survive and United Artists stopped making movies. Mayer's cost-saving strategies could be cold-blooded. MGM's most popular character actor was Lon Chaney, but "the Man of a Thousand Faces" was unsure if his roles would translate to sound. For most of 1929 he procrastinated about committing to sound films. Mayer suspended Chaney for breaking his contract but finally offered a $50,000 bonus ($1 million today) and he returned in January 1930. Sadly, he was diagnosed with terminal cancer and died in August 1930. A week later Mayer tried to sue Chaney's estate to get the $50,000 back but Mannix suggested that the negative publicity wouldn't be worth the money.

During its first six years MGM had grown to 6,000 employees, including 61 stars or feature players, 17 directors and 51 writers under full-time contract. The 1930s would bring incredible change to the industry, to MGM, and to Eddie Mannix and Howard Strickling. By 1935 they would be known throughout Hollywood as MGM's "fixers." By 1930 Mannix was general manager below Mayer and Thalberg. He had friends in every arena. Sundays were spent in poker games at Sam Goldwyn's mansion with Joe Schenck, Sid Grauman, Eddie Cantor, and several Marx brothers. The games were expensive; it wasn't unusual to lose $150,000. Bernice kept up the Linden house and Eddie continued his affairs.

Mannix had cultivated powerful government friends, and underworld connections that he had developed on the streets of New Jersey remained strong. His friends included mobsters Mickey Cohen and Jack Dragna, and bootlegger-turned-agent Frank Orsatti. In 1930 he was put in charge of MGM's private police force, managed by Culver City police chief Whitey Hendry.

In 1929 Strickling shared his Kings Drive house with Ivan St. Johns. "Ike" was separated from writer Adela Rogers St. Johns. The daughter of famous criminal defense attorney Earl Rogers, Adela was a writer for the Hearst syndicate, a reporter for the *Los Angeles Examiner* and *Los Angeles Times* and a movie writer for *Photoplay*. She and Ike were married in 1914 when she was barely 18. She wanted to keep her maiden name — unheard of then — but her family talked her out of it; she became Rogers St. Johns.[2] Ike was the West Coast editor for *Photoplay*. By 1920 they had two children. It was an unconventional marriage and the couple separated often, but Strickling would use his relationship with Adela for years.

In late 1930 Strickling inherited the job that he so diligently lobbied for, the head of publicity. Production chief Harry Rapf wanted to produce comedy shorts and, needing a narrator, told Mayer he "had actors who can deliver a line but can't write and writers who can write but not deliver a line. I need someone who can do both."[3] Mayer suggested Rapf hire Pete Smith, who from 1930 to 1940 narrated or appeared in 150 shorts. When he was given this new assignment in October of 1930, Smith handed the publicity department to his 31-year-old assistant Strickling.

After his somewhat public battles with mistress Mary Nolan, Eddie went back to the anonymous affairs that were his preference prior to Nolan.

Sometime during early 1931 a rumor swept the studio that Eddie had awoken from a night of partying with one of his actresses in her small Hollywood apartment.[4] She was dead, probably from a combination of alcohol and drugs. Calls to Whitey Hendry and Strickling brought them to the apartment. Hendry called a police buddy to "investigate," but no police report was filed. Strickling told the press about the "suicide" of the unknown actress, and the story disappeared.

Of new D.A. Buron Fitts, Budd Shulberg said 60 years later, "Buron Fitts was completely in the pocket of the producers. You could literally have somebody killed, and it wouldn't be in the papers."[5] On May 31, 1930, his top assistant put that theory to the test. That afternoon, Dave Clark was in Charles Crawford's 6665 Sunset Boulevard office with Herbert Spencer, a writer for the political magazine *Critic of Critics*. Crawford was a lawyer and power broker who controlled L.A.'s bootleg liquor trade, dealing with corrupt lawyers, police, and the mob. His nondescript office had barred windows, bulletproof glass, and a fortified concrete bunker.

"Handsome Dave" Clark was running for a seat as a district court judge. When police arrived, Crawford and Spencer were dead. Clark was seen running from the office, but told the jury Crawford tried to recruit him to frame an honest policeman; when he refused, both men drew guns and he shot them. He was somehow acquitted but lost the election. Still, 60,000 L.A. voters cast their vote for the killer who was living in a $300,000 house while making $15,000. Several years later, he would die in prison after killing the wife of a friend.

Another challenge for Mannix and Strickling in the early 1930s was the proliferation of movie magazines, gossip sheets, and industry trade papers. They all wanted the latest story, the biggest scoop, and were increasingly able to ferret out what previously was easily hidden. As stars began getting into trouble it was more difficult to cover it up. In 1930 the trade paper *The Hollywood Reporter* was founded by William R. "Billy" Wilkerson, who hand-delivered the first edition on September 3, 1930. He was described by his last wife Tichi as "not a particularly pleasant man ... tough ... as stubborn as they come ... and ruthless."[6] Wilkerson's most popular writer was his first wife, former silent star Edith Gwinn. She rarely named names but readers always knew whom she was talking about. She told her stories in riddles. Addressing rumors of the homosexuality in Hollywood, Gwinn described a costume party where the guests included Marlene Dietrich as "Male and Female," Garbo as "the Son-Daughter," and Cary Grant was "One-Way Passage." She described Grant and his lover Randolph Scott as a "couple."

Mayer led a group that tried to shut down the new press. His Motion

Pictures Producers Association gave Wilkerson a check for $1 million to simply go away, but he figured that he must have a good idea if they wanted him out so badly. Eventually the studios would grudgingly accept Wilkerson's little paper. Strickling made use of Wilkerson's people for years, and the two became very good friends.

Strickling's first concern after taking over was MGM's biggest star, William Haines. By then Mayer, Mannix and Strickling knew Haines was a homosexual. They had fixed things when he and Ramon Novarro were found to be regulars at an L.A. gay brothel and when Haines was picked up in a vice sweep with a sailor in Pershing square. The public was unaware that his nickname in Hollywood was Lavender Lips, for his professed talents.

Haines had never been publicly linked with a single woman, and he was popular enough that he could ignore orders from Mayer and Mannix to do so. He made no attempt to hide his decidedly feminine persona and was openly living with Jimmy Shields.[7] Stories began to hint at homosexuality. Even a newspaper in hometown Staunton, Virginia, detailed a childhood devoid of male pursuits; his hobby was making clothes for his dolls. *Photoplay* ran dozens of articles between 1928 and 1930 hinting; his home was full of "lace pillows and pretty pictures," and one article noted Haines' guest was Roger Davis, a well-known homosexual.

MGM had tried to force Haines to marry several female friends, including Barbara LaMarr and Joan Crawford, but he had refused. More distressing, his movies were not doing well. It was impossible to maintain the success he had between 1926's *Brown of Harvard* and 1929's *Alias Jimmy Valentine*, but his popularity was indeed declining. All that mattered to Mayer was that his movies were not doing as well. His last two films in 1930 earned less than half of his 1929 films, but his close friend Thalberg prevented Mayer from firing him. At the worst possible time, Haines got in trouble again, arrested in the spring of 1931 at the Hollywood YMCA after reportedly being found having sex with a sailor. Mannix was called, Haines was released, no charges were ever filed, and indeed no record of the arrest exists anywhere.[8] But Haines admitted to the arrest in interviews during later years.

Mayer didn't fire Haines but punished him by slashing his salary from $3,000 a week to $1,250, a public, humiliating demotion. Haines was forced to endure a grueling public relations tour that fall, a requirement that most stars easily avoided. Jimmy Shields was also told that his daily lunches with Haines at the studio were forbidden. The Haines name, which previously had gone above the movie title, would now appear below. His days were clearly numbered, as if Mayer kept him around like a cat playing with a mouse before killing it.

Haines' 1931 arrest was at a bad time. The industry was abuzz over the death a week before of director F.W. Murnau. German-born Murnau came to Hollywood after directing the horror classic *Nosferatu* in 1922, and his few U.S. films were all groundbreaking. *The Last Laugh* (1924) starred Emil Jannings, *Sunrise* (1927) won an Academy Award for Janet Gaynor, and the South Seas documentary *Tabu* (1931) was completed a week before his death. On March 11, 1931, 42-year-old Murnau was killed in a bizarre car accident south of Santa Barbara when his Packard convertible plunged 30 feet over a cliff onto the beach. Also dead was his 14-year-old Filipino houseboy, Garcia Stevenson, who was driving. The position of the bodies and their state of undress indicated that homosexual Murnau was engaging in a sex act with the boy when the car went off the road.[9] Just 11 brave friends showed up at his funeral. The reclusive Garbo was one. She kept his death mask on her desk for the rest of her life.

In the summer of 1931 Thalberg decided that MGM would remake Edgar Rice Burroughs' *Tarzan the Ape Man*. First put on film in 1918 as *Tarzan of the Apes* (1917), other versions included *The Revenge of Tarzan* (1920) and *Tarzan the Mighty* (1928). MGM's would be the fifteenth. Rejecting Clark Gable's physique as to unathletic for the lead, Thalberg offered it to Johnny Weissmuller. The six-foot-three Weissmuller was educated at the University of Chicago and began swimming to improve his poor childhood health. In ten years he never lost a race, and won five Olympic gold medals in the 1924 and 1928 games. His acting debut was inauspicious. In *Glorifying the American Girl* (1929) he played a statue wearing a fig leaf. Writer Cyril Hume saw Weissmuller swimming laps in the Beverly Hills Hotel pool. He was under contract with BVD as an underwear model, but Thalberg arranged a release with a promise that MGM's female stars would model BVD swimsuits.

Thalberg chose his friend Woody Van Dyke to direct the film, and cast newcomer Maureen O'Sullivan as Jane. Van Dyke used authentic location footage from his movie *Trader Horn* filmed during his seven-month trip to African, the first such location trip for a U.S. studio. On the first day of filming, in 1931, Weissmuller arrived in costume, a large knife at his side. The first Cheetah bared its teeth, growled loudly and lunged at him. Weissmuller coolly took his knife out, slammed the chimp on the side of the head and then held it in front of its nose. Cheetah grinned at Weissmuller, and from that moment followed him around the set like a puppy.

The filming was delayed for almost three weeks because of the antics of two of the other animal actors. Van Dyke had imported three African hippos and dropped them in one of the studio's two large lakes. On the day they were needed, they disappeared, hiding in the lake for a month before trainers coaxed them out. *Tarzan the Ape Man* was a huge success financially and with the critics and Weissmuller an instant hit with female fans. People were enthralled with O'Sullivan's nudity and with Tarzan's trademark yell, which was recorded by sound director Douglas Shearer and played backwards.

In March 1932 Weissmuller was on a publicity visit to New York, when he strolled past Lupe Velez in his hotel. He didn't see her. Mexican-born Velez—née Guadeloupe Velez de Villalobos—was the feisty star of the *Mexican Spitfire* series. She was the daughter of a Mexican general and had come to Hollywood at age 18. Barely five feet tall, she had a 37–26–35 figure and had just ended a two-year affair with Gary Cooper and a short fling with John Gilbert. She lived down the street from Cooper and his parents in Hollywood, but to get away from their prying she and Cooper moved to Laurel Canyon. Writer St. Johns said, "Lupe Velez hit Gary Cooper like a Mexican thunderstorm."[10] All of her relationships were a series of fights and sex; her key to a successful relationship was physical violence, and she said that "the key to a happy marriage was to fight once a week, maybe more."[11] Her affair with Cooper was heated. She often beat up the timid Cooper, leaving bruises for makeup people to cover, and attacked him with knives, once opening a gash that required stitches.

Cooper's bisexuality was well known. He had close relationships with several men and his first 1929 serial in *Photoplay* featured a number of photos of the young Cooper sans women. A later issue had portraits of a very effeminate Cooper seated with his mother. When he was dating Clara Bow she said of his boyfriend, homosexual actor Anderson Lawler, "The whole thing makes me sick."[12] Cooper lived with Lawler several times and it was known that they were lovers; this was confirmed by Lawler's brother years later. When Velez was pressed about Cooper and Lawler, Velez told Hedda Hopper that when he came home after visiting Lawler she unzipped his pants and smelled for Lawler's cologne.[13] One thing he *was* known for was the largest organ in Hollywood and prodigious sexual skills.[14]

When Cooper ended the relationship with Velez in the summer of 1931 he had lost 40 of his 175 pounds, had jaundice and suffered a nervous breakdown. He was unable to function, so his studio had to give Cooper a six-month leave. He was sent to Europe to recuperate, but as he boarded the train Velez took a shot at him with a pistol.

The Weissmuller-Velez relationship began soon after and was equally intense. He hadn't seen Velez in the hotel but she saw him. She called his room and said, "This ees Lupe Velez. I am een the lobby. Will you come and have a drink weeth me?"[15] The two spent the next two days in her

The 1932 film *Devil and the Deep* featured four headliners with sexual appetites that MGM hid from fans: Tallulah Bankhead, Gary Cooper, Charles Laughton and Cary Grant.

room. The relationship offered complications for the studio. Six months before, he had married socialite and sometime actress Bobbe Arnst. Strickling learned of the affair from the New York publicity staff working with Weissmuller. He already was aware the Weissmuller-Arnst marriage was on the rocks, but knew that Weissmuller's image would be hurt if the public thought he was unfaithful. Conversely, the Weissmuller-Velez coupling would produce good copy, but Strickling knew that if the *Spitfire* star were branded a home-wrecker she would be damaged.

Strickling suggested to Weissmuller that he obtain a quick divorce. He agreed but Arnst hesitated, and the press hounded everyone. Velez said, "I don't want nobody's husband. I didn't even know Johnny like me. Then one day he say, 'Lupe, I love you. I just want to look at you.' I yell at Johnny, 'Go away.' Believe Lupe, she can't help it if handsome men say they love her, can she?" Arnst gave an interview with *Screen Book* titled

"Tarzan Seeks a Divorce."[16] She initially refused to agree to a divorce, but Strickling sensed that a Weissmuller-Velez affair would be better than an ugly Weissmuller divorce and paid Arnst $10,000 ($400,000 today) to quietly go away. He also got her small roles in a few films, after which she disappeared into obscurity. Velez and Weissmuller were married on October 8, 1933.

Even a married Velez was a challenge for Strickling. Just before the wedding she got into a fistfight with Lilyan Tashman in the bathroom of the Montemarte Café. Tashman made a comment about her family and Velez commented about Tashman's lesbianism, and in an instant they were wrestling across the floor. Velez threatened to "keel that beetch."[17] At a party at her mansion she showed guests stag films and let them watch cockfights on the meticulously manicured lawn. Velez invariably got drunk and danced at parties, twirling in circles until her dress floated over her head so everyone had a view of her without underwear. Over the years Strickling paid dozens of photographers to destroy hundreds of pictures that featured clear views of Velez's naked crotch. The battling Weissmullers were a long-term problem.

There were plenty of other relationship missteps to keep Mannix and Strickling busy. Part of the problem was the House of Francis. Lee Francis had worked at brothels in San Francisco and Reno before moving to L.A. before 1920 and owned several brothels before opening her biggest, at 8439 Sunset Boulevard. Francis had close ties with police and local officials, and hefty payoffs kept her business open. Over 40 percent of her net was paid to police and politicians. She allowed the vice squad to "raid" the business but they never arrested anyone. The police burst into the lavish lobby, picked up cash and treated themselves to Russian caviar and French champagne that she kept on hand just for them.

She also offered favors to reporters that kept her out of the papers, and by 1930 her large apartment building was the most famous brothel in California. She was known for beautiful girls and the ability to satisfy any request. For a visiting Middle-Eastern guest who preferred blondes, 100 women dyed their body hair blonde for his weekend stay. Most of the girls lived in small apartments in the large building, which also had private rooms, several bars, billiard rooms and a restaurant. The lobby resembled a that of a five-star hotel. Most of Lee's girls had come to Hollywood to get into the movies but ended up working as prostitutes. They were, however, highly paid, making $1,000 a week.

Actors—and actresses—frequented the house. A late 1920s regular was Jean Harlow, who hired prostitutes and asked Francis to deliver them to her home. She also visited the house and took male customers home, two or three at a time. Harlow paid Francis $500 for each customer she borrowed. Workers and customers alike complained about her rough sex.

During the 1930s Errol Flynn, John Gilbert and dozens of MGM stars were regulars. Thalberg's closest friends, "the Three Jacks"—Colton, Gilbert, and Conway—frequented Lee's house. Writer Colton was an alcoholic homosexual who came along to watch. Thalberg sat quietly in the lobby drinking coffee and reading his *Los Angeles Times* while waiting for his buddies. Clark Gable was a frequent visitor but Strickling had to warn him not to park his custom-made Duesenberg coupe outside. There were only two in the world, his and Gary Cooper's black one. Gable eventually had Francis deliver prostitutes to his dressing room. He told Adela Rogers St. Johns that he preferred prostitutes because, he said, "I can always send those girls home."[18]

Another weekly visitor was Spencer Tracy, a recurring headache for every studio he worked with. Tracy was a regular at Lee's house since his first days in Hollywood, but he was an alcoholic with an ugly temper that became uglier when he drank. After he signed with MGM in early 1935 Tracy's drunken bar-fights were Strickling's problem. But in 1930 he belonged to Fox. Just a few weeks after Tracy signed with Fox he got drunk at Lee's and as he was leaving hit a parked car in the alley. When police were called he became so belligerent that police restrained him with handcuffs and leg straps and carted him off to jail.

Like the other studios, MGM had a business charge account at Lee's under an assumed name. The bills were paid through Strickling, who was also responsible for arrangements for discreet visits by MGM distributors from all over the world during their visits to the U.S. studios. Eventually Mannix and Mayer decided that they should have a little more control so they opened a private location. Not to far from Lee Francis' business, "Mae's" was a large mansion estate high above Sunset. It was a Greek revival building with stately columns and wide porches. Inside, there were 14 lavish suites and a full-service restaurant and bar; the establishment was managed by a woman named Billie Bennett, who looked and spoke like Mae West.

Bennett's was a special house. The women were look-alikes of actresses from MGM and the other studios. For a hefty price customers chose between "Joan Crawford," "Barbara Stanwyck," "Alice Faye," "Carole Lombard," "Claudette Colbert," "Ginger Rogers," "Marlene Dietrich," or any other special request, except for Greta Garbo and Katharine Hepburn, who were never copied. Some of the women were surgically enhanced to ensure accuracy and each was an eerie replica of the original, versed in her life, movies, and interests. Clients felt like they were with the real stars. The studios lent Mae's actual costumes; if a particular outfit was not available an in-house wardrobe mistress in the basement made outfits by hand. Sharing the basement were hairdressers and makeup men.[19]

In his biography, Mickey Rooney described a similar site, but recalled the name as "the T&M Studio." Groucho Marx had taken him there and was a regular. Like the House of Francis, executives and actors from out of town used Bennett's girls as they pleased. Most were from among the rolls of the six–month option girls. Thalberg came with his friends, but waited in an overstuffed chair in front of the fire reading the paper or playing the grand piano.

In the late 1930s Francis began refusing bribes to policemen and lawyers. On January 16, 1940, police raided her house and arrested dozens of customers, prostitutes, and the grandmotherly Francis. The only arrest during a 40–year career put her out of business.

In 1931 Mayer found out about Joan Crawford's latest sexual peccadillo. She began a heated and — more troublesome to Strickling — public affair with another young MGM contract player, Clark Gable. Thalberg was championing him as the studio's next star, but while becoming one of Strikling's greatest friends he would be the biggest challenge. William Gable was born in 1901 at a family farmhouse is Cadiz, Ohio, a tiny river town. At 17 "Billy" quit school to work in Akron, where he first got interested in acting. He claimed to have spent several years around 1923 with a traveling tent show before ending up in Portland, Oregon's Red Lantern Players. His talents were not developed. He himself said, "They paid me next to nothing, and I was worth every cent of it."[20] He also worked in a lumberyard.

From his youth Gable was a relentless and amoral womanizer who used women to further his career. He promised to marry lovely actress Franz Dorfler, who got him his first job, but left her after he met acting teacher Josephine Dillon. He was 23 and Dillon 41 when he met her the night she opened her acting school in Portland. She was plain, sad-eyed, gray-haired and matronly, but within a week Gable moved into her home studio. Just a few months later in the summer of 1924, Dillon brought Gable to Hollywood. She taught acting and he looked for film jobs and worked at a gas station. Then the odd couple married in December 1924. They had their first fight when she caught him making passes at a guest at their wedding reception. Soon after, Dillon renamed Billy: He was Clark.

He was over six feet tall, perfect for military roles. During 1925 he was an extra in several big films and after Clara Bow's *The Plastic Age*, Gable joined a traveling West Coast stock company. In the 1920s there were over 400 such companies, employing 5,000 actors. He was chosen by

Jane Cowl; his primary job was "servicing" Ms. Cowl, but it got him lead roles.[21] From 1924 to 1926, while Gable toured and slept with Cowl, Dillon waited at home for the husband who only returned to have his cleaning done. In 1926 he took up with actress Pauline Frederick, who like Dillon was 20 years older but unlike Dillon was attractive and a nymphomaniac. He said of her, "That woman acts as though she'll never see another man."[22] He stayed at her Beverly Hills mansion without letting Dillon know he was in L.A. and Frederick gave him jobs, expensive gifts—including a $5,000 Roamer sports car—and paid for repairs to Gable's teeth. His rotted and stained teeth were replaced with gold ones.

In 1928 Gable and Frederick split and he left for the Laskin Brothers Stock Company in Houston. He was soon the most popular actor in town, with hundreds of women lined up for his performances. His most ardent fan was Maria Franklin Prentiss Lucas Langham, a wealthy 45-year-old divorcee with three children. "Ria" set her sights on him during a visit to California and arranged for his job without his knowledge. Like Dillon she was 20 years older and like Frederick could help his career. But she was reasonably pretty, and she was rich.

During 1928 and 1929 Gable juggled Dillon—his wife and de facto manager—and Langham—his wealthy girlfriend—while having other affairs unknown to both. Dillon arranged for leading Broadway agent Chamberlain Brown to represent her protégé and Brown got Gable a role in the play *Machinal.* Dillon "made" Gable; he responded by banning her from the theater and telling her via telephone that they were through. The day the disheartened Dillon left for L.A., Langham arrived in New York. Dillon divorced Gable in March 1930, as Langham was renting a Park Avenue brownstone. She said that they were married on March 31, 1930, but no record exists. They were listed as "Mr. & Mrs. Clark Gable" on the building directory. In May 1930 Langham financed an L.A. production of *The Last Mile,* a prison drama about a group of death-row inmates, giving Gable the lead as "Killer Mears." Mervyn LeRoy was casting a prison movie of his own, *The Public Enemy* with Edward G. Robinson, and wanted Gable, but his boss Darryl Zanuck saw Gable as "a big ape with big ears" and refused to hire him. Zanuck's error let Gable wind up at MGM. Langham, Gable, and her children took a large unit at the Ravenswood Apartments in Hollywood, just below Mae West, one apartment for them and a second for her children, who lived with a maid. He came to the attention of MGM in 1931.

Lionel Barrymore mentioned Gable to Thalberg, who first opposed hiring him; like Zanuck all he saw were ears. But Mannix convinced Thalberg to take another look.[23] Unbeknownst to Thalberg, Ida Koverman filled a Glendale theater test with female MGM employees who went agog at the new young actor. Gable biographer Warren Harris quoted Sam Marx: "The audience sat bolt upright whenever Gable appeared. He projected a tangible magic. Women asked ushers, 'Who's the handsome laundryman?'" The next day, December 4, 1930, Thalberg signed Gable to a contract, telling his staff to find scripts pairing him with Norma Shearer and Garbo. He also directed that Gable would appear in nine of MGM's 1931 films.

Strickling instructed Gable to ditch the expensive-looking New York "actor duds" that Langham bought him and replaced them with more manly wear. He added fishing, shotguns, hunting, and roadsters. He and Strickling became friends and he never questioned Strickling. "If it weren't for Howard," Gable said, "I'd be driving a truck."[24] Gable's other friend at MGM was Mannix.

During Gable's first year he starred with every female lead, with Garbo in *Susan Lenox: Her Rise and Fall*, Norma Shearer in *Strange Interlude*, and Joan Crawford in *Dance, Fools, Dance* and *Possessed*. *Motion Picture Herald* said "Newcomer Gable Shines!" *Film Daily* described his "magnetic personality." *The Hollywood Reporter* said, "A star in the making has been made, one that will outdraw every other star pictures have developed."

Thalberg had heard the most famous Gable rumor, about an incident during *Merry Widow* filming. It was well known among the gay community that Gable and Haines engaged in a brief relationship after Gable's arrival in 1925.[25] Friends confirmed that Gable and Haines had a brief sexual relationship. Different people saw the two together — some at the studio and some at the Beverly Wilshire Hotel during a party — engaging in a variety of sex acts.[26] It would not be surprising that struggling actor Gable would have allowed MGM star Haines to "service" him if he thought it would further his career. Haines' friends — including Joan Crawford — told friends later that the event did indeed occur. Gable and Haines did have sex.[27]

After signing Gable, Strickling realized his pal was a profligate womanizer. During the first month it was rumored he got writer Rogers St. Johns pregnant. She went on an extended vacation, and rumors survive that they had a child together. She would only say, "What women would deny that Clark Gable was the father of her child?"[28] A coworker described him as "the least selective lover in the hemisphere. He'd screw anything. She didn't have to be pretty, or clean." Myrna Loy said he was "always on the make at the studio, after everyone."[29] He once made a pass at Loy while the two were seated next to Ria Langham in a limousine. Passing through Strickling's office he paused to gaze at an array of publicity photos of dozens of MGM actresses. He smiled and said, "What an amazing group. I've had every one of them."[30]

The affair with the most potential damage to MGM was with Joan Crawford. St. Johns called it "the affair that almost burned Hollywood down."[31] They met on the set of *Dance, Fools, Dance*; the timing could not have been worse. Crawford's highly publicized marriage to Douglas Fairbanks, Jr., was a fan favorite. Gable was married to Langham and not yet divorced from Dillon. Neither was more unavailable in the public's eyes, but Crawford said, "The first time we met it was like an electric current went through my body ... my knees buckled ... if he hadn't held me by the shoulders, I'd have dropped."[32] Even much later in life, during an interview with David Frost, Crawford was bleeped a dozen times describing their relationship. They had a lot in common. Both were from working-class Midwestern backgrounds, both essentially parentless as children, both terrified that their career luck would disappear, and both in loveless marriages. They spent all their free time together.

Crawford was obsessed with control and choreographed her dalliances. Every detail was planned, and the ritual upon her arrival at home always the same. As soon as she walked in the front door she stripped and fell naked to the floor. The sex took place at that moment on the rug in the foyer. She would repeat the dance with dozens of men, from Gable to Spencer Tracy to Kirk Douglas, and with any number of women. Within days of their on-set clinch, Gable and Crawford were on the floor of her foyer. The affair was the talk of Hollywood by the spring of 1931. Fairbanks didn't care but Ria Langham was another matter: distraught, she approached Ida Koverman, who sent her to Strickling. Langham told Strickling that his new star was not legally married to her since his Dillon divorce was actually pending. Everyone had assumed they were married since they were living together with her children. She threatened to go screaming to the press unless Gable legally married her.

Strickling and Thalberg called Gable in and told him that he had to marry Langham and

Joan Crawford, ca. 1935, already known for a rugged sexual appetite for members of both sexes, though in the early 1930s her target was Clark Gable.

threatened to invoke the "moral turpitude" clause in his contract. Gable meekly complied, although he had told Crawford that he would divorce Ria and marry her. Strickling arranged a June 19, 1931, wedding at a small courthouse 100 miles from Hollywood. He ordered the couple to move out of the dual apartments at the Ravenswood and into a house since rumors were circulating that they were not sleeping together. They obediently bought a house on San Ysidro drive below Crawford's in-laws at Pickfair. Complicating matters, Crawford found herself pregnant. It is not known if it was indeed Gable's baby but Strickling arranged for an abortion. Fairbanks and Crawford were estranged at the time, and she told him that during the filming of *Rain* on Catalina Island, she slipped on the deck of a ship and lost the baby. Crawford told friends that she did have an abortion, [33] and that it was likely Gable's child.

Less than a month later, Josephine Dillon told Mayer that she would go public unless she were paid. Her blackmail worked. Thalberg ordered $200 of Gable's monthly earnings sent to Dillon as long as he worked there. He and Crawford made half hearted attempts to be discreet at the studio but workers knew they spent afternoons alone in her dressing room, a mobile room on wheels that was a gift from her husband Fairbanks, who was still paying for it.[34]

After friends caught Crawford and Gable in a passionate embrace behind the bandstand at the Coconut Grove as their respective spouses waited at their table, the story got back to Mayer. They were called to a meeting with Thalberg, Mannix and Strickling and were forbidden to see each other. Thalberg ordered that the two never be cast in the same film again. Gable told friends, "He would have ended my career in fifteen minutes. I had no interest in becoming a waiter." Crawford at first fought and demanded Gable be cast in her next picture, *Letty Lynton*. When Mayer persisted in his threat that he would fire them both, Crawford relented. Robert Montgomery got the part and the relationship at least publicly cooled.

Newspapers and movie magazines were already hinting at the Gable-Crawford affair, so simply ending it was not enough. After *Letty Lynton* was completed Mayer ordered Crawford and Fairbanks on a publicized and mandatory European vacation. He told Crawford, "I'm sending you and Doug to Europe. You will have a second honeymoon and forget all this foolishness with that roughneck Gable."[35] Strickling arranged a grand farewell as a phalanx of police cars escorted them to the pier and thousands waited for them to walk up the gangplank. But the month-long exile only convinced Crawford that her marriage was over. They would soon divorce, but the Gable-Crawford relationship would continue until the late 1950s.[36]

Mannix suggested the studio also send Ria Langham on a tour publicizing her as Mrs. Clark Gable. Strickling made those arrangements, putting Langham and her three children on a train for New York, with stops in Phoenix, Kansas City, Chicago, Cleveland, and Baltimore. The Gable family was met at each city by reporters and photographers—scrounged up by local MGM publicity agents—eager to describe Ria's loving husband to fans. Photos of the family soon flooded magazines and newspapers everywhere. The Gable-Crawford problem was forgotten as Mayer assigned Gable several forgettable films as punishment, one with Marion Davies in *Polly of the Circus.* On the *Polly* set it didn't take long for sparks to fly. Gable was in an unhappy marriage and MGM had temporarily ended his affair with Crawford. Davies' affair with Hearst, who was by then nearing 65, was not sexual. Within days Gable and Davies were sleeping together, escaping to Davies' bungalow. Before long, Strickling and Hearst both knew.

MGM had another reason to be displeased with the Gable-Davies relationship. His contract came up for renewal during filming and Mayer was angry about the Crawford affair and the Davies problem. Gable wanted an increase from $650 to $2,000 a week, which he deserved, but Mayer offered $1,250. Gable asked Davies for help and she asked Hearst to intervene. Hearst did so and Gable got $2,000. Mayer agreed but Strickling told Gable that a condition was that he stop sleeping with Davies.[37] His sexual escapades cost him; the new salary was less than he originally demanded ($5,000) or undoubtedly deserved ($10,000). By then Gable and Davies had settled into a friendship more than a sexual relationship, and remained close friends for the rest of their lives.

On June 6, 1931, MGM signed gifted eight-year-old child actor Jackie Cooper to star alongside Wallace Beery in *The Champ.* Beery was a loud and obnoxious drunk who raped his teenaged first wife Gloria Swanson on their honeymoon[38] (she divorced him less than two months later) and would later be involved in a murder. The same day, sound director Douglas Shearer's wife Marion, who was despondent after learning of his adulterous affairs, walked up to a Venice Pier amusement park shooting gallery, grabbed a loaded .22–caliber pistol off the table and shot herself between the eyes in front of hundreds of horrified onlookers. Strickling released press stories that Marion was suffering from depression, which was blatantly untrue.

Sexual issues were the biggest problem for the studios in the 1930s. There was an almost total lack of morality in Hollywood during the 1920s and early 1930s. It may have been a function of being a relatively small group with high visibility. Perhaps, as William Haines biographer William

J. Mann suggested, it was a function of what Fitzgerald described as "Flaming Youth, a generation of driven young people determined to make up for deprivations imposed by World War I." Perhaps it was an uneducated group with too much money.

What cannot be ignored was the influence of European expatriates through the late 1920s and early 1930s; not just the creativity of writers, directors, actors, and producers, but the social world as well. The industry was steaming ahead into a decade that would be known as "the Golden Age of the Movies." Most of the success of 1930s movies can be attributed to European influence. Every aspect of the industry was being influenced by European imports. During the early 1930s political unrest in Germany evolved into systematic persecution that was spreading though Europe. The avant-garde were labeled as degenerates by the Nazis, so artists of all types poured out of Europe by the thousands.

It wasn't easy to get to the U.S. Over 80 percent of Americans were against relaxing immigration laws, and foreign countries were granted a fixed number of visas. Petitioners had to prove they had either money in the U.S. or confirmed means of support. Without either, they needed a U.S. citizen to guarantee support. Even so, anti-Jewish sentiment in the U.S. left many European quotas unfilled in the early 1930s. A good number of exiled artists made their way to Hollywood and their influence was soon felt. Designer Rudolf Schindler worked for Frank Lloyd Wright, and German writers such as Berthold Brecht, Thomas Mann, Aldous Huxley, and Vicki Baum wrote screenplays for the studios. There were artists like Hans Burkhardt and Man Ray. Igor Stravinsky composed some of the greatest music of the twentieth century in California. Sergey Rachmaninoff, Arnold Schoenberg, and Ernst Toch came. Bruno Walter conducted the Columbia Symphony and Otto Klemperer the Los Angeles Symphony[39] (his son inherited a love of music but was better known as Colonel Klink in the 1970s television series *Hogan's Heroes*). The movies came under European influence even before the 1920s. The studio heads were immigrants, and dozens of directors of German and Austrian descent had already begun transforming the American film industry, beginning with Erich von Stroheim and Ernst Lubitsch. The early directors introduced production and visual elements drawn from German expressionism — using camera technique to focus on scene details, honest portrayals of poverty and sin, and eroticism — that were not part of the film landscape prior. Later directors like William Wyler, Billy Wilder, Fred Zinnemann, Otto Preminger, and Fritz Lang continued their influence over American films.

A group of English actors living in West Los Angeles started their own Hollywood Cricket Club in 1931. Founded by C. Aubrey Smith, members included Cary Grant, David Niven, Boris Karloff, Basil Rathbone, Nigel Bruce, and Ronald Colman. New Zealand–born Errol Flynn played for Sir Aubrey's team after his 1933 arrival in L.A., but his drinking and womanizing got him kicked off. Many Europeans didn't like the area or the movie business and quickly left. Those that remained lived mainly in the West Los Angeles area in the canyons of Santa Monica and Pacific Palisades, so many that the area was called The Weimar Colony.

Salka and Peter Viertel were the unofficial leaders of the community. Salka was a Viennese-born stage actress, and her husband a poet, writer and sometime actor. The couple had arrived in L.A. in 1928. He worked for Fox Studios and Salka was an independent writer. They rented a house at 165 Mabery from Irving Thalberg, who had built the house for his mother. The little house with the red door (unchanged to this day) became a gathering point for the Europeans. Everyone coveted an invitation to the "Viertel salon."[40] Writer Lion Feuchtwanger hosted similar meetings at his huge Villa Aurora at 530 Paseo Miramar in Pacific Palisades.

The Europeans had a pronounced effect on the social environment also, bringing a freewheeling sexual attitude that was quickly embraced by the film community. It is too easy to blame the Europeans for the explosion of sexual excess in Hollywood, but Europe was a breeding ground, particularly Germany. Writer Diane McClellan quoted writer Stefan Zweig describing post–World War I Germany: "Germans brought to perversion their vehemence ... the Rome of Suetonius had not known orgies like the Berlin transvestite balls.... Amid the general collapse of values, a kind of insanity took hold of those middle-class circles which had hitherto been unshakable.... Young ladies proudly boasted that they were perverted; to be a virgin at sixteen would have been considered a disgrace in every school in Berlin."[41]

European cities were full of transvestite clubs, lesbian and homosexual clubs and cabarets, and brothels, a fertile breeding ground for sexually adventurous Hollywood. Garbo said, "The thing I like best about Hollywood is that here is one place in the world where you can live as you like and nobody will say anything about it, no matter what you do."[42] Nothing in the arena of sexual experimentation was out of bounds. When German painter Eva Hermann arrived in the U.S., she moved in with Maria and Aldous Huxley, who shared their home and bed. During intimate gatherings at the home, Hermann lay naked on a mirrored coffee table in the middle of the guests, allowing those who wanted to photograph her or stroke her sexually.

The studios had to keep the social lives of their European transplants out of the papers, but none had as great a need as MGM. Irving Thalberg led the charge in recruiting European talent in the early 1920s at Universal, and he continued at MGM. Sexual issues plagued all of the studios in the 1930s. The lesbian and bisexual contingent living within the West Los Angeles Europeans, known as the Sewing Circle among the movie colony, included the biggest names in the movies. Greta Garbo, Marlene Dietrich, Mercedes de Acosta, Joan Crawford, Barbara Stanwyck, Agnes Moorehead, and dozens of other stars were part of the circle, but fans never knew. They were also ignorant to what were called lavender marriages, marriages of convenience between lesbian or bisexual women and their "beards," usually homosexual men. There were also arranged "white"— or sexless— marriages.

Garbo was the standard-bearer for European sexual attitudes in the 1930s. She spent the 1920s tormenting lover John Gilbert while engaging in affairs with dozens of women, including actresses Lilyan Tashman and Marlene Dietrich, and feminist writer Mercedes de Acosta. Garbo biographers insist it was Tashman who introduced Garbo to lesbianism, but there is evidence to suggest that she had an earlier affair with Marlene Dietrich while both filmed *The Joyless Street* in Germany in 1925.[43] It was certainly cruel irony that Gilbert introduced Garbo to Tashman at a Sunday afternoon tennis party in 1927. Their affair began that afternoon.

Lilyan Tashman was a former Ziegfeld Follies headliner who starred in a number of 1920s films including the original *No, No Nanette* (1930). She was one of the most popular actresses of the early 1930s. Her wardrobe cost $1 million ($20 million today) and nearly everything she wore was copied and sold all over the world. Women clamored to buy "Tashman hats, gowns and jewelry," but unknown to fans she was an ardent lesbian.

She was a free spirit. She ordered her servants to serve her cats high tea. She painted her dining room dark blue for an Easter brunch so that it would contrast with her blonde hair. She once asked guests to wear only red and white and painted the entire first floor of her Malibu mansion red and white, including dyed toilet paper. She was a throaty and abrasive lesbian a writer described by saying, "Calling Lilyan a lesbian is like calling Casanova a flirt."[44] She rarely passed up the opportunity to make passes at women and told friends she believed that she could seduce any woman alive. Even Mayer's family was not sacrosanct; Tashman made a blatant sexual request of married Irene Mayer in the bathroom during a Hollywood party.[45]

Her studio arranged a marriage between Tashman and leading man Edmund Lowe in 1930. The openly homosexual Lowe and his lesbian wife led separate lives, while being touted in *Photoplay* as having an "ideal marriage." Readers would have been shocked that the couple hosted weekly parties for her lesbian friends and his homosexual companions that routinely became full-scale orgies. An A-list of stars tried to wrangle invitations to the well-known parties.

Garbo was mesmerized by Tashman and Tashman reciprocated without limit. The two spent all of their time together soon after they met. Strickling soothed Mayer's concerns by telling him Tashman would at least teach Garbo how to be less manly, and he wrote stories for fan magazines downplaying the relationship aspect and touting the friendship as helping to polish Garbo's unfeminine image. They would continue as on-and-off lovers until 1930. When Garbo broke it off— she simply stopped taking Tashman's calls— the results were tragic.

Garbo took up with actress Fifi D'Orsay in 1930 while filming *Romance*. Mannix and Strickling and the rest of MGM knew of the affair and tried to keep Garbo from the open public displays that she so enjoyed. A February 1930 magazine described them as "inseparable since Garbo and Lilyan Tashman parted company," and wrote that "Hollywood is amused at the dalliance." Mayer instructed Mannix to act.[46] Knowing that Garbo jealously guarded her privacy, Mannix called Garbo in and told her that D'Orsay had told the press about their affair. He knew Garbo would end the affair over what she would consider a breach of trust. A heartbroken D'Orsay made denials in *Los Angeles Record* interviews but Garbo never spoke to her again.

She retreated into a secluded Santa Monica mansion at 1717 San Vicente Boulevard. Mannix and Strickling thought that by ending the D'Orsay affair Garbo would cease or at least hide her lesbian affairs. Mercedes de Acosta shattered the plan. If Garbo carried the flag for Hollywood lesbians, Mercedes Hede de Acosta was her loyal foot-soldier. She was a descendent of the Spanish dukes of Alba, born in 1893 into a New York theater family and raised on New York's ritzy upper east side. Her next-door neighbor was Teddy Roosevelt. She was a free spirit in a family plagued by tragedy. Her father and brother killed themselves, after which the young de Acosta carried a pistol with her at all times so at any moment she might "pop myself off this baffling planet."[47] John Barrymore arranged a 1917 meeting with writer poet Kahlil Gibran that forever changed de Acosta. She spent her life a committed spiritualist, believing herself to be a psychic. In her late teens she met Alla Nazimova in New York. It was de Acosta's first lesbian relationship and the two remained lovers on and off for the next 30 years.[48] To placate her mother in 1920 de Acosta married, but she brought her latest lover, heiress Hope Williams, on her European honeymoon and slept with her instead of her husband. She later took actress Eva Le Gallienne as a lover. Her best friends and

lovers came from the New York lesbian world, among them Libby Holman, young dancer Lucille Le Sueur in her pre–Joan Crawford days, and
Tallulah Bankhead, Barbara Stanwyck and Marjorie Main. De Acosta was
not unfamiliar with celebrity lovers; one of her first had been theatrical
legend Isadora Duncan. Duncan penned a poem to de Acosta during their
1920s love affair:

A slender body soft and white, is for the service of my delight.
Two sprouting breasts round & sweet invite my hungry mouth to eat
My kisses like a swarm of flies find their way between your thighs.[49]

In the middle of their affair in 1928, Duncan was killed visiting Paris.
In the back of a chauffeur-driven Bugatti convertible, her scarf wrapped
around the rear axle and her neck was broken. De Acosta was shattered,
but quickly targeted Garbo. She came to Hollywood with RKO in early
1931 with cowriter John Colton, a homosexual and a close friend of Irving Thalberg. Using Colton as her "beard," they rented a mansion at 12824
Sunset Boulevard in Brentwood. She chose the house because it was close
to Garbo's San Vicente house and during the next decade, she would move
14 times, each move near a Garbo house.

She struck up a friendship with Salka Viertel knowing she was Garbo's
close friend. Viertel never talked about Garbo, saying "I don't know anything about her," which gave Garbo comfort. De Acosta worked the Garbo-
Viertel relationship to get to Garbo and was introduced during a Sunday
afternoon brunch at the Mabery house. It was de Acosta's third day in
Hollywood. Less than a week later the two consummated their relationship at Garbo's mansion. The next morning Garbo's driver took the pair
to Silver Lake, a day's ride up in the Sierra Nevadas. She borrowed Wallace Beery's remote cabin, squatting on a small island in the middle of the
lake. De Acosta's pictures show a tanned and topless Garbo enjoying the
outdoors. She was exhilarated by the privacy, and in her memoirs de Acosta
described Garbo during their lakeside sojourn as "some radiant, elemen-
tal god and goddess melted into one." After six weeks alone at the cabin
the two returned as the talk of Hollywood.

Garbo and de Acosta were inseparable and within a week they rented
adjacent mansions on Rockingham. To the dismay of Mannix and Strickling the two were soon known publicly as the Garbos.[50] Even more troublesome, de Acosta began giving Garbo advice on roles, contracts, and
studio issues. She was Garbo's de facto agent. To keep an eye on them Thalberg hired de Acosta to write for MGM. When she suggested to a stunned
Mayer and Thalberg that Garbo play a character in male drag — she wanted

Hamlet or *Dorian Gray* — an incredulous Thalberg replied, "You must be out of your fucking mind."[51]

Strickling was soon hard at work writing and planting stories discounting his star's lesbian relationships. He linked her with a succession of actors, most of whom had never met the Swede. Strickling and his new assistant Eddie Lawrence tried to lecture her yet again about the negative publicity but Garbo refused any advice. Later, when Garbo returned from a Christmas trip in late 1931, Mannix forbade de Acosta to meet her train. Salka Viertel showed up and took her home to de Acosta. Strickling made sure several dozen photographers met her without de Acosta. Soon after, Garbo broke off her affair with de Acosta, who then moved in with Marlene Dietrich, newly arrived in the U.S. Feminist author Alice B. Toklas said of de Acosta, "Say what you want about Mercedes, but she had the three most important women of the twentieth century, including Garbo and Dietrich."[52] Speculation has been that the third conquest was either Gertrude Stein or Eleanor Roosevelt!

Not quite 30, Maria Magdalena Dietrich van Losch arrived from Germany in early 1930. Her bisexuality began with childhood fixations on women described in diaries. Her first experience with a man was at the age of 19 with a boarding school teacher, and was unpleasant. Dietrich told her daughter all she recalled was that "He groaned, panted, heaved … didn't take his pants off … very uncomfortable."[53] She returned to women, later saying, "In Europe it doesn't matter if you're a man or a woman. We make love to anyone we find attractive."[54]

In 1922 "Lena" joined the Rudolf Nelson Girls, a female troupe presenting risqué lesbian musicals. She also met Otto Katz, a stage manager and local Communist party leader. Katz somehow got her into the famed Max Reinhardt Acting Academy, but he was not mentioned in her autobiography. The two married in Czechoslovakia in the early 1920s but, oddly, at the same time she began a relationship with Rudolph Sieber. Circumstantial evidence suggests "Rudi" was Otto's brother; whatever the dynamics of the strange threesome, in 1923 or 1924 she and Rudi married.[55] Dietrich was pregnant and daughter Maria was born on December 13, 1924. Maria said that the couple was never sexual after the conception. Instead, they shared a deep platonic friendship. Strangely, Dietrich's support of Rudi ended the day Otto died shortly after World War II, executed as a spy. Intimates thought Otto was Maria's father, not Rudi.

Between 1926 and 1929 Lena performed on stage and in 17 movies, and at night she visited Berlin's lesbian and transvestite bars. Her stage and movie roles were nontraditional. In 1926 she starred with lesbian singer-comedienne Claire Waldof in *From Mouth to Mouth* (rumors of an affair made the papers), starred in the lesbian stage show *It's in the Air*, and in 1929 played a vamping slut in *Two Bow Ties*. Director Josef von Sternberg saw her in *Bow Ties* and gave her the lead in *The Blue Angel*, the first German talkie. Paramount offered the renamed Marlene a contract, so she left Maria and Rudi and went to America. She arrived in L.A. on April 15, 1930, and began working on *Morocco* (1930).[56] Paramount's first payment to Dietrich was $100,000 to von Sternberg's wife to quash an alienation of affection suit. Dietrich's preference was for female companionship and her first affairs were with Dorothy Arzner and Kay Francis.[57] MGM knew of the affairs and ordered Garbo to stay away from Dietrich, but Garbo was already avoiding her. MGM didn't know they had already been lovers.

In 1925 the two appeared in *The Joyless Street*. The affair was well known but Garbo was certain Dietrich would publicize their secret. The two pretended to have never met and Dietrich denied the affair until near the end of her life. Daughter Maria noted stories in the Berlin tabloid press describing the affair.[58] Dietrich eagerly jumped into the Hollywood lesbian and homosexual life. Her favorite club was BBB's Cellar in Hollywood, the first admittedly homosexual bar in L.A. Her club friends included Billy Haines and Tallulah Bankhead. (A BBB regular "couple" was Cary Grant and Howard Hughes.)

Garbo was in the headlines for her late 1930 film *Anna Christie*. Her fourteenth film was her first talkie, about a small-town girl turned prostitute. Headlines screamed "GARBO SPEAKS!!!" All she said was, "Gimme a viskey, ginger ale on the side … and don't be stingy baby," but audiences loved her alluring voice; Garbo hated it. One of her *Anna Christie* costars was an unusual challenge for Strickling. Marie Dressler was an unattractive, matronly spinster who had worked for MGM since 1927. Fans loved her but the studio was aware of her open lesbianism. The "ladies' nights" she hosted at her Alpine Drive mansion were well known, and well attended. Thalberg himself offered her a small role as a waterfront hag in *Anna Christie*, and even with Garbo finally speaking, Dressler stole the show and earned an Academy Award nomination. There was a rumored relationship between Garbo and Dressler, but Mannix, who described Dressler "a real bull-dyke," believed she was bragging to friends.

Garbo was obsessively reclusive but she had a strange friend in Harry Crocker, a Hollywood pioneer who had worked with Charlie Chaplin before becoming William Randolph Hearst's *Los Angeles Times* movie writer. The ties to Hearst and the studios made Crocker the toast of Hollywood and a frequent escort for Crawford and for Garbo, who became a close friend. When Garbo wanted to escape, Strickling invented phony travel plans, sent photographers to supposed train stops, and planted phony photos of Garbo allegedly taken during the trip. But Garbo would simply move to Crocker's mansion at 622 Bedford for weeks and months at a time.[59] Fans and reporters never knew of this hideaway. After Hearst's 1951 death, Crocker's party invitations vanished, and by his death in 1958 he was nearly forgotten. Six friends were at his funeral; among the six was Garbo.

Her MGM contract was set to expire during the summer of 1932, so Thalberg rushed her into *As You Desire Me*. As filming was ending, she told Cecil Beaton, "I want to get out of pictures," and left the country. She would not return until early 1933.[60] With Garbo gone, Dietrich took up with de Acosta after an introduction from Salka Viertel. Unknown to both, Viertel was actively working to keep Dietrich away from Garbo. De Acosta and Dietrich hit it off; describing their first night together, de Acosta wrote Dietrich, "Wonderful One, It is one week today since your naughty hand opened a white rose. Last night was more wonderful and each time I see you it grows more wonderful and exciting ... before you go to bed ring me so I can hear your voice."[61] The de Acosta–Dietrich affair continued into 1933 and they remained sometime lovers through the early 1940s. Unfortunately for MGM, the de Acosta–Garbo relationship would continue for another ten.

Dietrich also had an affair with Tallulah Bankhead. Like de Acosta, Bankhead was a free spirit, but Bankhead had no limits. Born in Alabama in 1902, the daughter of a future Speaker of the House, her mother died after giving birth to Tallulah. At 15, she ran away from a Catholic boarding school for the New York stage, and the beautiful teenager with the husky southern drawl was soon the darling of Broadway. She had a healthy appetite for sex of all types. Men were used solely for sex. Relationships were reserved for women. Her first sexual experience was being raped at the age of 11. Her father warned her to avoid men and alcohol in New York, but, as she told a friend, "he didn't say anything about women and cocaine." She had a voracious appetite for both.[62] She had many male lovers and got "abortions like other women got permanent waves."[63]

Her New York friends were lesbians. She was seduced by Eva Le Gallienne, shared an apartment with Estelle Winwood, and slept with Lilyan Tashman, Libby Holman and Blythe Daly. She appeared on stage on Broadway and in London and in 1930 was hired by Paramount. Sharing the late 1931 train to L.A. were newlyweds Joan Crawford and Douglas Fairbanks, Jr. Playing cards with the couple during the trip, she told Crawford, "You're divine. I've had an affair with your husband; you'll be next!"[64] Her New York reputation preceded her to Hollywood, but even so, during her first

weekend at George Cukor's Christmas party she stripped naked, grabbed
a bunch of grapes, and lay supine on a marble bench as guests arrived. She
was Goya's *Nude Maja*. Cukor later placed a bronze bust of her near the
spot.

Tallulah was known for her offhand remarks. Of sex she noted, "I've
tried everything. Going down on a woman gives me a stiff neck. Going
down on a man gives me lockjaw. Conventional sex gives me claustro-
phobia."[65] If she was bored, she would throw her arm around the least
attractive woman in the room and moan, "Surely by now you must know
that I'm mad about you." Touring Billy Haines' Stanley Drive mansion
before she rented it, she asked where "Billy Haines got it on with that
divine Clark Gable." But Tallulah was tiresome for her employers. Offered
a Dietrich role, she told the press, "I've always wanted to get into Marlene's pants."[66] New York publicity manager Howard Dietz told Mayer, "A
day away from Tallulah is like a month in the country."

Like de Acosta before her, Bankhead wanted Garbo and spent six
months stalking her. Again, Mannix and Strickling tried to head off a
Garbo-Bankhead relationship. They were already keeping the Garbo–
de Acosta affair quiet. Bankhead appeared in one MGM film and helped
write another, but it was her relationships with MGM actresses that concerned the studio. She was considered for an MGM contract to the horror
of Mannix and Strickling, who argued vehemently against it. Mayer was
furious when Bankhead told a writer that MGM's star quartet of Garbo,
Crawford, Harlow and Cary Grant were "Hollywood's most desirable
women."

Will Hays' committee presented each studio with a bound volume
called the Doom Book. Inside were the names of 150 performers deemed
unsuitable for the public. Jean Harlow was there simply for baring her
body. Bankhead was at the top of the list with a heading reserved for her:
"Verbal Moral Turpitude." She publicly called Hays "a little prick." Arriving on loan-out at MGM she asked Thalberg, "Dahling, how does one get
laid in this dreadful town?" He told her, "I'm sure you'll have no problem.
Just ask anyone."[67] Thalberg considered hiring her but Mayer hated her.
He threatened to expose her escapades to the press and she dared him to
do so, naming six top MGM actresses who had been lovers, including
Crawford, Garbo, Barbara Stanwyck and Jobyna Howland. She then simply walked away.

During the same week that Mayer was parting company with Bankhead, the MGM men became embroiled in the biggest scandal in the studio's history. It remains one of the great Hollywood mysteries, and the
finest example of the Mannix and Strickling's talent for controlling lives

and events. In the early morning hours of September 5, 1932, Strickling received a frantic phone call from Jean Harlow's mother. "Mama Jean" said something had happened at the home Jean shared with her husband of two months, MGM director Paul Bern. The remote site was less than a half-mile up Easton Drive off of Benedict Canyon Drive, which turned from pavement to gravel three miles down the canyon.

Strickling called Mannix and Thalberg, and they met MGM police chief Whitey Hendry and studio photographer Virgil Apger at the house. Called by Mannix, Mayer had already come and gone by the time writer Sam Marx arrived a little after nine. What they found sickened them all. Bern, one of Thalberg's closest friends and MGM's most creative director, lay naked, crumpled and bloody on the floor outside his bathroom under a full-length mirror. There was a pool of coagulated blood beneath the corpse. He had been shot in the head; blood and bits of Bern's brain dotted the wall and ceiling above.

Harlean Carpenter was born in Missouri on March 3, 1911. Her mother, Jean Harlow Carpenter, was from one of Kansas City's wealthiest families and owned a 20–room mansion, but secretly wanted to be a stage star. Becoming pregnant, she obsessed that she expected a baby with "spiritual, mental, and physical perfection." She christened herself "Mama Jean" and wrote, "There is nothing else in my life worth talking about. My life began with her."[68] She called Harlean "the Baby." She divorced her husband, and when Harlean was 11 took her to Hollywood to fulfill her dreams of stardom, arriving in the summer of 1923. Harlean enrolled in the Hollywood School for Girls with the daughters of movie titans like Francis X. Bushman, Cecil B. DeMille, and Louis B. Mayer. Her classmates were shocked by her short skirts and boyfriends, but loved her unpretentious manner. She was totally without conceit, though the prettiest girl there. Mama Jean's experiment ended after two years and they returned home.

During a visit to Chicago in 1926 Mama Jean met Marino Bello, a swarthy gold digger with a moustache and strong Italian accent. He was managing his wife's restaurant at the Sherman Hotel, but began sleeping with Mama Jean within days. In 1926 Harlean was sent to the Lake Forest School north of Chicago so that Mama Jean would have had an excuse to see Bello. In December 1926, Bello's wife divorced him, and he married his Kansas meal ticket on January 18, 1927. Harlean hated him, probably because he "dabbled incestuously with [her]."[69] To get away, 16–year-old Harlean eloped with wealthy 20–year-old Charles McGrew on September 21, 1927.[70] The newlyweds moved to L.A. to distance themselves from the in-laws and moved into a house at 618 Linden Drive. Neither worked; their diversions were drinking and picnicking.

Harlow's discovery is the stuff of legend. She gave a friend a ride to a Fox Studios audition, where three executives saw her in the parking lot leaning on her roadster. Hard to miss in her tight dress— she also never wore underwear of any kind — they suggested she go to the casting office herself. She declined, put their letter away and forgot about it. When Mama Jean heard about the offer she took a train to L.A. and dragged Harlean back to Fox. She signed in as "Jean Harlow," and went to work that day. For the next year she worked steadily in small roles but even as an uncredited extra stood out. *Why be Good?* director William Seiter said to Colleen Moore, "Look, you've never seen anything like it."[71] When Clara Bow saw her on the set of *The Saturday Night Kid* (1929) in a black, crocheted dress with nothing on underneath she demanded the director remove her, moaning, "Who's gonna see me in a scene with *her*?"[72] She was still only 17.

In a famous scene in the Laurel and Hardy short *Double Whoopee*, Jean emerges from a taxi and Stan Laurel closes the car door on her dress, which stays in the door as she walks away. Filming the first take, Harlow as usual without underwear — walked across the set essentially naked once her dress fell away. In seconds there was chaos. Shortly after, in June 1929, Mama Jean convinced her to divorce McGrew and abort McGrew's child. Her friend James Hall was working in the Howard Hughes epic *Hell's Angels* and arranged an audition. Hughes was dismissive and said her voice sounded like "a Missouri barmaid screaming for a keg,"[73] but she agreed to the minimum salary of $1,500 and got the role. She wasn't much of an actress but in her satin gowns and platinum hair, "Baby" was a bombshell.

For the May 27, 1930, premiere of Harlow's *Hell's Angels,* 200,000 people crammed the sidewalks outside Grauman's Chinese Theater. Hughes rented 200 searchlights (paying the equivalent of $350,000) to light up squadrons of bombers flying overhead. Hundreds of half-size planes hung from light poles and the biggest stars in Hollywood stepped from limousines. Fans showered her with 10,000 letters a week. She thought herself "the worst actress that was ever in pictures." She would later philosophically tell Thalberg, "people have been laughing at me my whole life,"[74] and of *Hell's Angels,* "the planes get better reviews than me." [75] But she had *potential*. Rumors, probably accurate, that Harlow was sleeping with Hughes were denied when she told reporters she was dating Paul Bern, who escorted her to the premiere. They were shocked; Bern was 45, short and bald. Irene Mayer Selznick said he was "the single most beloved person in Hollywood,"[76] but he was a tortured soul whose memory and legacy were tarnished by Eddie Mannix and Howard Strickling.

Like his close friend Thalberg, Bern had German roots; he was born Paul Levy in 1889, one of 17 children. That nine of them died before age one took a toll on his mother. Levy became Bern after his arrival in the U.S., and he worked for the Schenck theaters. Just before leaving for Hollywood, two women in his life were involved in related tragedies that affected Bern for the rest of his life. First, on September 15, 1920, his mother Henrietta drowned herself in a New Jersey canal. The second was caused by the first. In 1911 Bern met Dorothy Millette, a petite redheaded actress, and the couple lived together for a decade. Shortly after Henrietta's suicide, Millette suffered her own breakdown and was committed to a Connecticut sanitarium. Her breakdown was brought on by guilt at having caused Henrietta's, whose fragile emotional state was worsened by her son living with non-Jew Millette.[77] Unable to accompany Bern to Holly-

Jean Harlow, ca. late 1920s; a rare early still inscribed to her beloved grandfather, signed with her real name, Harlean. This was sent before her mother began signing all of her photographs.

wood, she moved into a small room at the Algonquin Hotel. For the next ten years she lived as a recluse, rarely going outside, while Bern sent monthly checks.

During those years Bern worked as a writer, director and producer. He shared a house on Kings Road with Jack Gilbert and director Carey Wilson and when MGM was founded, Thalberg hired Bern to head MGM's story department in 1924. Bern always tried to help his actresses, but usually fell in love with them. Al Lewin said, "He's got that goddamned Pygmalion complex; he's hellbent on finding someone to make over and fall in love with."[78] Jack Gilbert said, "He has a Magdalene complex. He does crazy things for whores."[79] In 1923 he became infatuated with Barbara LaMarr. He was living frugally while giving money to her, and though she knew he was in love with her, when she ran off with husband number five she asked him to wake up a friend who owned a jewelry store at two in the morning; he even bought the wedding ring. He was seldom invited to her parties, but provided LaMarr with bootleg liquor.

He was so distraught when she stood him up at a party that he threw a $15,000 diamond bracelet from the porch into the garden and fled in tears. Guests spent hours unsuccessfully searching for the bauble. When he finally asked her to marry him after her fifth marriage fell apart, she refused and Bern tried to drown himself in a toilet. While her drugs finally killed her, she asked for him on her deathbed.

It was Bern who first turned studio eyes toward Harlow, when in November 1930 he convinced Thalberg to bring her to MGM on loan-out. She appeared in *The Secret* Six and befriended her costar Gable, then went to Warner's for *Public Enemy*. Bern wanted MGM to buy her contract from Hughes but before they did, Harlow's boyfriend Abner Zwillman interceded on her behalf with another studio. "Longy" Zwillman and "Lucky" Luciano controlled bootlegging on the eastern seaboard. Marino Bello introduced Jean to Zwillman, who moved to L.A. and showered her with expensive gifts, from jewelry to Cadillacs. Bern hated Zwillman. He knew about the locket around Zwillman's neck that held strands of Jean's pubic hair, and all MGM knew that he also gave friends some of her hair.[80]

As Bern was trying to get her to MGM, Zwillman arranged that Harry Cohn would pay Hughes twice the normal loan-out rate for two pictures at Columbia. Zwillman also "lent" him $500,000 ($7.5 million today) interest-free and paid Harlow $750 a week out of his own pocket. His deal would catapult Harlow to stardom. Her first Columbia film was Frank Capra's *Gallagher*. He admitted he added Harlow "for sex."[81] It would have been a minor film, but publicity man Lincoln Quarberg coined a new nickname for Harlow — "The Platinum Blonde" — and designed a publicity campaign to promote it. Over 3,000 Platinum Blonde Clubs were formed across the U.S. Cohn and Capra changed the film's name from *Gallagher* to *The Platinum Blonde*; Harlow would forever be "the Platinum Blonde."

Even so, by 1932 her career was stagnant, but Bern persisted in his effort to bring her to MGM. Mayer objected because she had rejected his offer of a full-length mink coat to sleep with him.[82] Thalberg and Nick Schenck finally offered Hughes $30,000 for her contract, and she became MGM property on March 3, 1932. Bern got her $1,250 a week, up from $150 with Hughes, and an assignment in *Red-Headed Woman*. As usual she was playing a tramp.

Thalberg took advantage of Jean's sex appeal during *Red-Headed Woman* filming. A scene was added where Harlow's character asks a sales clerk if a dress can be seen through. When the clerk answers, "I'm afraid you can," Harlow replies, "Perfect, I'll wear it." Audiences loved the movie, and her.[83] Whenever she shot a scene dozens of non-working employees watched, knowing that powerful arc lights rendered her clothes transparent. Harlow biographer David Stenn interviewed William Bakewell, who watched one such event. "She made an entrance down the stairs, and as she did, everything under that dress kept coming out and going in! People were swarming from all over to see it." Among the viewers was Mama Jean, who looked on proudly as dozens of men gaped at her near-naked daughter.[84] Mama Jean was proud of Jean's body. When she filmed *Public Enemy,* costar James Cagney was so enthralled by her erect nipples that he finally asked her, "How do you make those things stand up?" She replied without the slightest embarrassment, "I ice 'em." Disgusted friends knew that it was actually Mama Jean who handled that chore.

She genuinely hated the image that was so different from her true personality. MGM workers loved her. She shared her coffee and food with her crew. When producer J.J. Cohn banned coffee breaks, Harlow said she wouldn't work if they weren't reinstated. People said she was "terribly sweet," "utterly guileless and naïve," and "a doll." She was Bern's perfect Mary Magdalene. His infatuation for his protégée was reciprocated and in May 1932, 45-year-old Bern and 20-year-old Harlow shocked friends by announcing they would marry. She told Zwillman they had not made love and told Jack Conway that Bern was nice to her, that he "explained things to me and lets me know I had a brain. He doesn't talk fuck, fuck, fuck all the time."[85]

At 8:30 P.M. on Saturday, July 2, 1932, the couple was married at Mama Jean's 1353 Club View Drive home, which Jean had bought. Attendees included best man Jack Gilbert, the Thalbergs, David O. and Irene Mayer Selznick, agent Arthur Landau and a few of Bern's relatives. Mama Jean's wedding gift was a picture of herself signed "My Baby — My Life — My Everything, Mommie." The newlyweds would live at Bern's secluded estate up in Benedict Canyon. A wedding reception was held there the next day. *Red-Headed Woman* was becoming a box-office hit and Harlow was ready to film *Red Dust.*

The relationship baffles researchers, suffering as it did from versions and variations told by people with reasons to devalue it. An oft-repeated incident took place at a USC football game. When Bern asked if she wanted anything, she pointed to one of the players and said, "Yes Daddy, get me that one."[86] What was a harmless joke has been transformed over the years into evidence that Harlow held Bern in contempt. The truth was clearly not that. Friends knew she adored him and she said, "Paul loves me for me."[87] Most stories that painted the opposite picture were part of the agenda that arose on a hot September morning.

The two months after the wedding were full of preparation for *Red Dust,* and filming with old friend Gable began in August 1932. They had filmed *The Secret Six* 18 months earlier and had had a brief affair, but by *Red Dust* the Gable was more of a "big brother." He hated Mama Jean but was friendly with Bello, who took him to speakeasies owned by Bello's

mob pals and hunted and fished with him. Leaving the studio on Saturday, September 3, 1932, Harlow had no inkling that her life would change
forever before breakfast the next morning. According to Strickling-
designed fiction, rather than drive the extra six miles to Easton, Harlow
stayed with Mama Jean so she could get up early for work on Sunday. Harlow would indeed arrive at Club View, but not until later that weekend.

The studio maintained that Mama Jean's first call on the morning of
September 5 was to Louis B. Mayer's Santa Monica beach house, but it is
much more likely she called Strickling. Within minutes the entire management of MGM was gathering at the remote Easton Drive estate.
Unchanged to this day, the house is surrounded by steep and heavily
wooded hills that rise almost straight up above the house. Narrow walking trails crisscrossed the hillsides around the house. All that is visible
from the street through the trees is the top of the tile roof. The garage and
a servant's apartment were on the street beneath the house. Between the
house and the garage is a pool surrounded by a flagstone patio.

As Strickling and Thalberg made their way over the cobblestones past
the pool, Mannix, studio photographer Virgil Apger and MGM police
chief Whitey Hendry were just arriving. They had been picked up by
Harold "Slickem" Garrison, studio bootblack and Thalberg's chauffeur.[88]
David O. Selznick and Sam Marx both heard the news from friends and
arrived about the same time. When Marx arrived, Thalberg was sitting by
the pool talking to Bern's gardener Clifton Davis.[89] Mannix denied being
there in later interviews, but he was there.

Walking past the pool, everyone noticed a half-empty bottle of champagne and a single expensive crystal glass. Lipstick remained on the rim. Scattered on the flagstones were the shattered pieces of a second glass. A still-wet
woman's bathing suit lay across a chair. It was visibly too large for Harlow.
The group was met by gardener Davis and led inside to John and Winifred
Carmichael, Bern's valet and cook. Carmichael had found the body and fainted
on the floor. When Davis had responded to Winifred's screams he thought
there were two dead people. They led the group to Bern's body. Apger took
several rolls of pictures of everything from the remnants of the poolside visit
to Bern's body and gave them to Strickling, wondering to himself why a police
photographer was not called instead of him. He never saw the film again.[90]

It was apparent to everyone that *someone* had visited by the pool with
Bern before he died. From his garage apartment just below, Davis said he
had listened late the night before as light conversation turned to a loud
argument punctuated by breaking glass. Bern obviously went into the
house to change out of the wet bathing suit found on the bathroom floor
and as he stood in his bedroom drying himself with the towel found tan-

gled around his body, was shot in the head. There were three pictures on the wall. They were all of Jean.

Standing around Bern's body, already showing signs of advanced rigor mortis, the group was facing a defining moment, a monumental scandal. They all knew who murdered Bern, and why. They had always known the truth. And that Harlow knew. They also understood that it would end her career and ruin the studio. They assumed Bern had been murdered by Dorothy Millette. They knew Millette was still his wife.

They had never wed, but they lived together for ten years in a New York common-law marriage. So Bern was *married* when he and Harlow wed. He was a bigamist.[91] They knew Bern's secretary Irene Harrison had sent monthly checks for a decade; along with every other outgoing MGM letter, Mannix had seen them. He even *signed* them. But they knew even more damaging information. They knew Millette had come to see Bern that weekend and that she was pestering his office with increasingly belligerent and demanding calls wanting her husband back. They knew that Bern finally agreed to meet with her at Easton on Sunday afternoon. The studio arranged for her transportation. There is no doubt Millette arrived late Sunday. Neighbors on the cramped street saw a veiled woman in black exit a limousine and enter the estate. MGM is tied to that limousine; incredibly, when Bern's estate was probated MGM presented a bill for the cost of bringing Millette to the house and taking her away later Sunday night.

They also might have known that Harlow was actually at the house at least part of Sunday. It is not clear exactly when she left. Gardener Davis said he had heard Bern and Harlow argue Sunday afternoon and that soon after, Jean left. He was sure that Jean was not part of the later poolside argument. Within minutes after the nighttime arguing stopped, the mysterious limousine vanished down the street in a cloud of gravel. Another neighbor, MGM special effects director Slavko Vorkapich, told Thalberg he had heard the same argument.

The men had to deflect attention away from MGM and Harlow. It was Strickling who first suggested suicide to direct the innuendo at Bern and away from grieving widow Harlow.[92] If Bern had committed suicide, Harlow wouldn't have been married to a bigamist whose common-law wife killed him in a fit of rage. She could be the victim of an unfeeling husband whom she mistakenly loved. That became the plan. The cornerstone came from an unlikely source; a green Moroccan-leather-bound guestbook Bern kept by the front door signed for him by friends. As Mayer absent-mindedly leafed through the book that morning he saw notes and sketches by Thalberg, Gary Cooper, Lupe Velez, and others. On page 13 he found a curious note that read,

Dearest Dear,
 Unfortuately (sic) this is the only way to make good the frightful
wrong I have done you and wipe out my abject humiliation. I love
you.
                                        Paul
 You understand that last night was "only a comedy [sic]⁹³

It was impossible to know what Bern meant or when the note was
written. When Mayer found it he first tore the page out and put it in his
pocket, afraid of what police might make of it. Strickling suggested they
use the note to imply that Bern killed himself, and told Mayer to put it
back.⁹⁴ The murder was becoming just another movie scenario written for
the public. The plot revolved around Bern, distraught over sexual problems and forlorn that he had beaten Jean, killing himself. The group
decided the script was believable but first had to take care of the scene and
the witnesses.

 The only gun in the house was on the bureau. Bern only owned one
pistol but police found two in the room. Knowing Millette's instability,
Bern would never have left *any* guns lying around, let alone two. An informant told Marx that Mayer had Hendry put a gun in Bern's hand.⁹⁵ The
surviving Apger photo of the nude body crumpled on the floor (which
didn't surface until 1990) shows both of Bern's hands visible *and empty*.
The picture was taken before Hendry placed the gun. The gun in Bern's
hand had so much oil on the handle that no fingerprints could be found.
Police also didn't know that the men turned Bern's body around so that it
was facing the room.

 Davis was sent to his garage apartment and told to speak to no one.
Police didn't hear about the argument between Bern and Harlow on Sunday afternoon or the argument by the pool between Bern and Millette.
Davis did not even talk to the police on the scene. The Carmichaels were
instructed to tell police they found the body at 11:30 A.M., explaining why
police weren't called until after lunch. Although they obviously arrived
before breakfast like every other morning, police would not notice this
inconsistency.

 By the time Thalberg called police at 2:30 P.M. Strickling had called
the newspapers. Even as police were first racing to Easton the *Los Angeles
Times* was printing special extra editions with the Bern story.⁹⁶ It was
Strickling's suicide version. Thalberg's call to police is the first weak link.
At the coroner's inquest he said, "I told them where I was [at the Easton
site] and what had happened."⁹⁷ Since he also said that it was he who told
Harlow, by the time police arrived he had already gone from the scene to
Westwood and then back up to Easton. Police ignored the obvious incon-

sistency. His trip to Club View is shrouded in controversy. His wife Norma Shearer said she waited in the car while Irving gave Harlow the news. Shearer said she could see "Jean's slippers and the hem of her negligee" in the light of the room.[98] But Thalberg said that he went Club View that morning, in daylight. How could she have seen into the room in daylight?

MGM writer Sam Marx said Thalberg took the strange note with him to Harlow to see if she could make anything of it. She could not. When Strickling allowed police to interview her two days later, she told them that she had already seen the note. Police ignored that too. Thalberg also no doubt told Harlow to deny being at Easton on Sunday, and provided her alibi: that she stayed with her mother because she had to be up early for work on Sunday. Police didn't notice, or ignored the fact, that no filming was scheduled for Sunday over Labor Day. Her *Red Dust* costar Gable was fishing that day, which would present itself as another problem later.

Mayer later claimed *he* went to Club View to tell Jean, that he grabbed her when she tried to leap from the balcony "to her death on the stones below" and slapped her to calm her down.[99] It is unlikely that a ten-foot drop would have killed her, as unlikely as that the visit ever took place. The MGM group had obviously arrived at Easton early in the morning. Gardener Davis told Marx that by 9:15 A.M. Mayer had already come and gone.

Strickling and Mayer then undertook a character assassination, portraying Bern as a sexual deviate unable to have sexual relations. They knew both to be untrue. He did have an under-developed penis (well-publicized by Mayer after the autopsy) but dated dozens of beautiful movie stars from Barbara LaMarr to Joan Crawford before marrying Jean. Thalberg first refused to be part of the plan, as close as he was to Bern, but a furious Mayer screamed and threatened to kill him if he didn't go along with the story, so Thalberg grudgingly agreed.[100]

Stories were planted and evidence altered to bolster the story. A dozen MGM employees were enlisted to offer "remembrances." Most barely knew Bern but nonetheless offered opinions released at the direction of Strickling. His best friend Gilbert was alleged to have said, "Paul once told me that should the time come, 'I would not hesitate to snuff out the candle.'" David O. Selznick offered, "A man should be ready to kill himself if he has outlived his usefulness."[101] Comments so totally out of character were probably written by Strickling.

Colleen Moore said she saw bruises on Harlow's back and that Harlow told her Bern beat her on their wedding night. Irving Shulman, Harlow's agent, wrote a ridiculous biography of Harlow describing Bern as a sadomasochist who beat Harlow bloody that night because he couldn't perform. However, there were no bruises on Harlow at her wedding reception the next day, and her studio dresser said she never saw a mark on Harlow. None of Bern's female friends ever mentioned sadomasochistic interests but, like much of the Bern legend, the stories have been passed on as fact. Moore also said she found a loaded gun in Bern's coat during a party, as did Strickling's pal, columnist Sydney Skolsky. Skolsky later said Strickling told him he found and kept a second suicide note from Bern, written for Thalberg. A second suicide note would surely have made the cover-up even easier and would have been used by Strickling had it existed.

Strickling recruited old friend Adela Rogers St. Johns to publicize that Bern was impotent due to his under-developed genitals. She said the "deformity" was the reason Barbara LaMarr never married him, and that Leatrice Joy told her she saw Bern naked and his penis was "smaller than my pinkie." She later told friends that Harlow was at the house when Bern died and was taken to Club View by Strickling. Had she indeed been there, Millette would probably have killed her too. Lastly, Harlow's maid Blanche Williams was recruited to say Bern told her the morning after the wedding, "Baby's still a virgin."[102] Bern would never offer that to Williams. Also, she was Harlow's maid and not even at the house that day, and Bern knew of Harlow's sexual reputation: abortions, boyfriends, Zwillman's locket of her pubic hair, etc.

Bern's alleged sexual problems were presented to the point of overkill. Books he was supposedly reading included Discourse on the Worship of Priapus, an eighteenth century story of a midget king with an oversized phallus, and The Glands Regulating Personality, about a variety of sexual problems that was allegedly open to a chapter about men with child-size sex organs. Strickling suggested Bern was a homosexual, another story he knew to be false. He recruited a studio doctor, Edward B. Jones, to say that Bern was depressed because of the lack of marital relations. Supposedly, Mayer happened to stop in Jones' office to pick up medicine and the good doctor volunteered information about Bern. But Jones had actually cabled from Hawaii when he heard the news. He offered to help, saying; "UNDERSTAND SUICIDE MOTIVE. WILL RETURN AT ONCE IF NEEDED."[103] Mayer bolstered Jones' comments, telling reporters that Bern was acting "strangely ... had a queerest look about his eyes ... had something preying on his mind."[104]

Mayer ordered Harlow to support the stories, but to her credit she refused to help slur her husband, even if it might mean saving her career. Her only comment about the affair was, "The 'frightful wrong' he apparently believed he had done me is all a mystery. I can't imagine what it means."[105] A day later the autopsy was leaked to the press noting "under-developed" sex organs. As Mayer and Strickling intended, the immediate Hollywood buzz was that Bern killed himself because he was impotent.

Police worked with the men from the first moments, when Mayer was seen directing investigators at the site. They were shown Bern's guest book opened to the note on page 13. Even though neighbors told police about the mystery woman in the limousine and the loud argument by the pool, neither was investigated. Many police statements were untrue. The first detective reported that the gun was "hidden from sight," and that he pried it from the dead man's hand. Apger's picture of Bern's body, taken before police arrived, shows his empty hands. On orders from Mayer, police did not interview Harlow for two days, and when they finally did meet with her she was drugged almost unconscious and seated with Mayer, Strickling, and two MGM lawyers. She told police nothing except "there was nothing between us that would cause him to do this."[106] Her silence about the awful rumors about Bern was deafening.

Bern's family immediately questioned the Strickling version. His brother Henry Bern angrily denied the rumors and noted that his brother had been "morally married" for over a decade before. But when he arrived in L.A. he was taken out of circulation by Strickling, who probably came to some financial arrangement with the family. In just a day, Henry Bern went from a vocal crusader saving his brother's good name to silence. After meeting with Strickling he refused to comment about the death.

Mannix and Buron Fitts choreographed the coroner's inquest just two days later. Held at the mortician's offices in Culver City, eight witnesses were called. Mayer kept Harlow out of the proceedings for "medical reasons." Henry Bern was never called to tell about Millette. None of the neighbors who saw Millette at the house the night of the murder were called. The witnesses who *were* called offered a lies and half-truths designed to sell the Strickling story.

Marino Bello testified that Bern was fraught with melancholia and had a house full of pills, and lied about where he was when he learned of the death. The Carmichaels both tried to offer sympathetic portraits of their boss and offered no motive for Bern to kill himself. But John Carmichael did admit that after finding the body — allegedly at 12:47 — he called "Mrs. Bello" first.[107] Gardener Clifton Davis testified but said there were no fights. "Slickem" Garrison — Thalberg's friend and driver — offered several new and interesting tidbits. He testified that Bern carried a gun at all times, spoke to him about suicide frequently, and took pills all the time.[108] It is unlikely that Bern would confess personal problems to the man who shined his shoes, but tell no one else. MGM accountant Martin Greenwood actually testified that he knew nothing about anything. But he did think the handwriting was Bern's, and his afterthought was taken as fact even though Bern's longtime secretary Harrison later stated that the writing was not Bern's. The prearranged verdict was death by suicide.

Bern's funeral at Grace Chapel at Inglewood Park Cemetery was a circus. Mayer arrived flanked by Mannix and Strickling. The casket was covered with $25,000 worth of flowers from Thalberg and MGM. Thousands of fans stood along the street and hundreds of reporters and photographers fought for spots near the chapel. After a short service, the funeral director asked that they take one last look at their old friend. A mechanical pulley attached to the casket slowly raised it to an almost vertical position, and the lid automatically slid open. Bern appeared to be standing in front of the horrified crowd, staring at them. Harlow burst into tears. So did Thalberg. Clark Gable scrambled out of the chapel as Jack Gilbert threw up.[109] After the bizarre finale to the service, Bern was cremated.

Unfortunately for the MGM cabal, reporters uncovered Dorothy Millette as they followed up on Henry Bern's comment about Bern being "morally married." They discovered a call from Henry's L.A. hotel room to "Miss D. Millette" at the Plaza Hotel in San Francisco (they didn't know that the call was made after his meeting with Strickling). At the Algonquin Hotel in New York they found records that "Mrs. Paul Bern" lived there for a decade. The hotel manager confirmed that Paul Bern visited his tenant twice a year.

The papers were having a field day. Stories like "BERN'S OTHER WIFE!" and "BERN RIDDLE INCREASES: 'OTHER WOMAN'" (*L.A. Times*) appeared and it was rumored that Harlow had met with Millette in San Francisco in the months before the death. But Millette had disappeared, last seen boarding the steamboat *Delta King* for a cruise up the Sacramento River from San Francisco to the state capital. The mystery would only deepen a week later when her body was found by a Japanese fisherman and his son floating in the muddy water along the riverbank. Millette's death removed a final obstacle for Strickling. The only person who knew the truth was dead, and there was a growing furor over Bern's past life and reported sexual problems. This was the result Strickling intended. He even used Millette's death to MGM's advantage. Informed that her body was unclaimed, Strickling paid for her burial and headstone, telling the press Harlow had "insisted on paying for everything herself." She probably had no idea.

D.A. Fitts approached Strickling, apparently with blackmail on his mind. Strickling was told that Clifton Davis, "Slickem" Garrison and the Carmichaels were ready to admit they lied at the inquest, at MGM's direction. He knew about neighbor Slapko Vorkapich, and knew that Millette had been at the house. He knew that Sacramento police found a bathing cap in Millette's *Delta King* cabin that matched the bathing suit found by Bern's pool. There were letters in her hotel room from Bern's office trying to postpone the in-person meeting. Fitts told Strickling that two days after her body was found a letter arrived at her hotel from Bern containing a check for $100 to Millette. It was undoubtedly Bern's normal monthly stipend, but Fitts could make the check appear to be a blackmail payment. He also told Strickling that police found a word scratched into a pad of paper in the hotel room, capitalized and underlined three times. Written by Millette, it said simply "JUSTIFICATION!!!"[110] Strickling was forced to make a new deal, and must have, because Fitts— even with a briefcase full of evidence — did not proceed.

An almost comic episode arose from Slickem's interview with Fitts. He told Fitts that he drove Bern to the Ambassador Hotel the night before the murder, where he had a drink with a couple before going home. He and Jean were supposed to go to a formal party but she was stuck at the studio and Bern said, "I won't go without my darling wife"[111] (hardly sounding suicidal just hours before his death). Instead he met the couple at the hotel; hotel guests saw Bern escort the woman into one of the hotel's secluded bungalows. Understandably, police wanted to know about the mystery woman.

The man turned out to be Thalberg's assistant and close Bern friend Bernie Hyman. The woman was his companion, actress Barbara Barondess. Hyman asked Bern to escort his mistress to their room so people would not see them together, and Bern obliged. Strickling prevented the newspapers from identifying the couple. William Randolph Hearst was called directly, and no Hearst paper ran the story. Barondess mentioned the problem to writer Sydney Skolsky, who told Strickling he would bury the story if his *Daily News* column were given access to the studio. Strickling got Thalberg to agree, and a few weeks later, Skolsky would tell his ridiculous story about finding Bern's gun in his coat.

Bern's death remains a mystery. The key to the crime has always been the cryptic note. It is clear that it was an apology. But a question that has never been asked is, "for what?" Because of Strickling, people have assumed that it was an apology for whatever went on at Easton between Bern and Jean the night before he was killed. What happened?

There are several theories. I don't believe any of them.

The vilest, first mentioned soon after the killing, was that Bern tried to have intercourse with Harlow wearing a large plastic dildo over his undersized penis. Humiliated when Harlow laughed at him, he beat her and killed himself. No mention is made of Millette in this silly theory, first mentioned by Irving Shulman. The men never found a dildo in the Bern house, which was searched rafter to basement after his death. If one had been found, Strickling would have used the fact. It fit his story perfectly. He knew it was untrue but he encouraged the rumor for years, as did writer St. Johns.

It has also been argued that Bern staged a fight with Jean to force her to flee to Club View so she would not see Millette. *Last night's comedy*. But given their relationship, he would simply have told her about the visit if he didn't want her there. Harlow knew of Millette and may have even met her. What we know of her personality leads me to believe she would not have wanted to be there.

Still others suggest that Harlow witnessed some portion of the visit and left either before Millette killed Bern or was taken from the house by Strickling, Mannix, or one of the other people who arrived after the shooting. But Harlow being at the house for even a portion of the visit is unlikely. If she had been, Millette probably would have killed her too.

There were only two champagne glasses at the pool. Harlow was a heavy drinker — liver problems would lead to her death — so if she were there a third glass should have been found. The same witnesses who saw Millette's limousine would have seen Harlow leave, but no other car was seen. I believe that Harlow went to Club View on her own, simply to be out of the way. She didn't "flee" there.

I don't believe that Bern or Harlow expected the Millette visit to turn violent. Perhaps neither did Millette. There was never any hint of discord in the relationship prior. Other than her reclusive lifestyle, little is known of her mental health in the ten years since her breakdown. It's hard to guess how disappointed or angry she might have gotten as she realized Bern was not returning. She did kill him that night, but I believe that it was on the spur of the moment, a crime of passion. The best evidence of this may have been her suicide just a day later. Millette would not have killed herself unless she knew that Bern was dead. If she wasn't there when he died, she would not have had any reason to kill herself. If she was there (and she was), the only reason for killing herself would have been that she killed Bern.

Bern and Millette enjoyed a pleasant poolside visit, at least for a time. They were both swimming, evidenced by the wet bathing suits found at the pool and in Bern's bathroom. They enjoyed a bottle of champagne. But an argument did erupt, a brief but very loud disagreement heard both by gardener Davis and neighbor Vorkapich. Bern went inside to change into dry clothes, and Millette followed him inside and shot him in the head. When he originally fell, he fell against the wall. If Bern had killed himself, he probably would not have stood naked facing a mirror and shot himself in the head. The evidence points to a much more likely scenario: that someone — Millette — walked up behind him and shot him.

There never been any evidence at all that Paul Bern was suicidal. His spirits seemed normal that week. He told writer Marcella Burke that he was "deliriously happy."[112] Just the day before, he had submitted a script outline for a movie he was producing titled *China Seas*. He was ebullient in his comments to Slickem about his "darling wife." He was charming as he shared drinks with Bernie Hyman and Barbara Barondess the evening before. Absolutely nothing suggests that Paul Bern was in the mood to kill himself that day. And why would he go swimming first?

Paul Bern did not kill himself, but the basis for my conclusion has not been suggested previously. A careful analysis of the circumstantial aspects of the note supports a contention that *the note had nothing to do with Bern's murder*. Like Harlow's innocent request that Bern buy her a football player, the note has been taken out of context to be woven into whatever story fabric Strickling produced about the murder. It is not a certainty that Bern wrote the note. His secretary said it was not his handwriting. In 1971, Howard Strickling told writer Charles Higham that even *he* thought that the note was a forgery.[113]

It was found on the thirteenth page of Bern's guest book on a table near the front door. Mayer found the book where Bern always left it, not even open to that page, and he innocently leafed through the interesting book with a Gary Cooper self-portrait and funny notes from friends like Lupe Velez. What he did next is interesting. He did not rush upstairs to show Strickling that he found a suicide note. He tore the page out and put it in his pocket and carried it around for over an hour. He thought it was strange and was going to destroy it — the reason why he removed it in the first place — but he never suggested it was a suicide note. It was not until he showed the crumpled page to Strickling that it became the linchpin to the suicide story. If it was a real suicide note Bern would have left it in the bedroom. It is laughable to suggest that Bern left a suicide note on the thirteenth page of a closed guest book by the front door.

Even the text of the note is imprecise. The final line, used to prove an asserted argument between Bern and Harlow, doesn't fit. It reads, "you understand that last night was only a comedy." *Last night*. Not *tonight*. *Last* night. If Bern did indeed mean this as a suicide note and it was written the night of his death, he would have described *tonight*, the night he supposedly did kill himself. Also, there are spelling and grammatical errors that would have been anathema to Bern. "Unfortunately" is spelled "unfortuately," the ending quotation marks are missing, and the syntax is jumbled. This from the person who was Irving Thalberg's most creative and intelligent manager?

Lastly, the note itself contradicts Strickling's own version of why Harlow was not at Easton. MGM always maintained that she was at Club View because she had an early call, which we now know was a lie. But if it were true, and she was gone for the early call, she would not have even been at Easton for "last night's" comedy.

I don't believe that the note had anything to do with Bern's death. Maurice Rapf told this writer that the people who knew Bern and Harlow never believed his death was a suicide. Asked for an opinion about this theory, Rapf said, "It makes more sense than what we were told." Harlow went back to work on *Red Dust* just a week after Bern's murder. The famous scene between Harlow — sitting totally nude in a barrel of water — and a dumbstruck Clark Gable (who did not know she would be nude) was filmed the day of her return.

Clark Gable accidentally fell into the middle of the Bern scandal. He had accepted an invitation from Bello that day to go fishing since no filming was scheduled. Strickling had to get Gable away from Bello before the press knew they were together the day Bern was killed. A studio limousine was dispatched to Long Beach to meet Gable's boat and whisk him into seclusion. Nobody ever heard about Gable's fishing trip with Bello. *Red Dust* was a hit for MGM. Public sympathy remained with Harlow for the rest of her short life.

Around the time of Bern's death, Greta Garbo was ending her four-year, on-and-off affair with Lilyan Tashman. By November 1932, Tashman's erratic behavior was beginning to wear on Garbo. Tashman was incredibly jealous and fiercely protective of all of her lovers, once getting into a screaming, hair-pulling fight with Constance Bennett at a Beverly Hills restaurant when she thought Bennett was coming on to her girlfriend. In 1931 she was arrested after beating up 23-year-old actress Alona Marlowe, whom she found her in her husband's dressing room.[114] It's hard to imagine why, since he was a homosexual, she a lesbian, and the marriage a studio-arranged sham. She was obsessed with Garbo, and when Garbo broke it off, Tashman was devastated. She suffered a fatal cerebral hemorrhage less than a year later, dead at 33. Several mourners were seriously injured when crowds trying to get a glimpse of her casket knocked a large grave-marker over.

Bernice Mannix knew about Eddie's frequent infidelities. They were the reason Bernice would have no children. But staunchly Irish Catholic Bernice refused a divorce, since it was forbidden by the Church.[115] While Eddie worked and carried on, Bernice hung around with her friends. They played cards, shopped or lounged by the pool, and ignored their husbands' infidelities together. They were an occupational hazard. During a trip back to New York that November, Mannix supposedly met Toni Lanier.

In 1932 it took five days on two trains to get to New York, but Eddie made the trip every two months to report to Nick Schenck. Toni Lanier told friends that Mannix introduced himself at a Ziegfeld performance in 1932 or early 1933, but his friends were told they met in 1934 in Culver City. However and whenever they met, when she arrived in Hollywood two years later, everything would change for Eddie Mannix.

As 1932 ended, one of Strickling's directors was in serious trouble. Edmund Goulding was a contemporary of Frank Capra and during the 1930s one of the most celebrated directors in Hollywood. "Eddie" was a frequent weekend guest of William Randolph Hearst and Marion Davies at San Simeon. Thalberg hired the 40–year-old Englishman in 1931 over Mayer's objections (Mayer hated him) and the two became close friends.[116] His first assignment was Thalberg's pet project *Grand Hotel*. His friends knew that Goulding was a sex addict and dedicated voyeur. He once paid Lee Francis $1,000 for a prostitute to have sex in front of a window across from his favorite service station, staging the elaborate scheme simply to see the reaction of the mentally handicapped boy who pumped gas.

Goulding hosted weekly orgies at his Beverly Hills mansion for his friends. His soirées were well attended, and he invited a cross-section of participants. In a 1978 interview with the movie journal *Focus on Film*, actress Louise Brooks mentioned that a typical party "guest list might pair Goulding's local baker with a movie star or major director. The call girls might be waitresses, or they might be movie stars." Eddie choreographed the sexual activities from a large chair in the massive dining room, which had a raised stage surrounded by studio-installed lighting and special furniture. But a party just before Christmas 1932 got out of hand, even for Eddie. A choreographed S&M session sent two women to the hospital, both seriously injured. One came close to death.[117] In a letter dated September 18 to her friend Cecil Beaton, writer Anita Loos said, "our friend Eddie Goulding is in a lot of trouble. He had a party that required two women to be hospitalized and apparently what happened is too filthy to print."[118]

Mayer wanted to fire Goulding, but Thalberg convinced him to keep him on. As usual, economic considerations outweighed Mayer's moral fiber. However, all agreed Goulding should get out of L.A. until things quieted down, so he was sent to England. Payoffs were made to the women, the D.A.s and police, and nothing ever came of the party.

Thalberg and his wife attended the annual MGM Christmas party on the afternoon of December 24. Thalberg drank more than usual — he rarely had more than one scotch — and stayed at the party until almost midnight. For several years Mannix had encouraged and allowed employees to drink as much liquor as they wanted and allowed them to have sex anywhere in the building during the party. It was an annual booze-soaked orgy with couples having sex everywhere — maybe one of the biggest secrets of the 1930s and 1940s[119] and perhaps why Thalberg stayed so late. The next morning he had a heart attack at his Santa Monica mansion.

Doctors ordered complete bed rest and allowed no work whatsoever for six months. Mayer took the opportunity to reorganize and effectively diminish Thalberg's power at MGM, since he and Thalberg had been in a protracted contract fight for most of 1932. First he hired his son-in-law David O. Selznick, who was given his own production unit reporting directly to Mayer and Schenck. Thalberg would have no input. It was a brutal rebuke, but Mayer wanted the mighty Thalberg out. Mayer gave Thalberg the news during a visit to his sickroom in late February 1933. Thalberg accused Mayer of betraying him and after a lengthy shouting match, Mayer stalked out. The argument was the death knell for their partnership. Mayer wrote Thalberg, saying he "felt an air of suspicion on your part towards me ... instead of appreciating the fact that I have cheerfully taken on your work, as well as my own, you chose to bitingly and sarcastically accuse me of many things." Thalberg's icy reply said he had "sustained a deep hurt...," but that there "are loyalties that are greater than the loyalties of friendship."

In March 1933, Mayer officially made Mannix responsible for all operations at MGM. His assistant was Benjamin Thau, formerly the casting director for the studio. Thau was gaunt and spoke in an almost silent whisper, and was addicted to sleeping with nubile actresses. His casting office was more of a brothel than an office. He was a good partner for Eddie.

While Edmund Goulding was serving his banishment to London, he was arrested when police raided one of his parties just two months later. He was convicted of lewd conduct, a minor crime for which he paid a fine, but it was still a felony conviction that meant he could never enter the U.S. Thalberg wanted him back, so MGM intervened. Mayer had placed former Assistant U.S. Attorney General Mabel Willebrandt on retainer, paying her $75,000 a year ($1 million today) and setting her up in plush Washington, D.C., offices. She set about getting Goulding back.

Willebrandt worked with the British and U.S. governments, writing, "Mr. Goulding's services are needed in this country. The matter represents an emergency to us, and it will be extremely helpful if you can expedite the inquiry." Even with his felony conviction, Goulding was allowed to return to Hollywood in 1934. Over the next two years Goulding would work on several MGM titles, including *Flesh* (1932), *Riptide* (1934), *The Flame Within* (1935), and *Hollywood Party* (1934). But Mayer never forgot — or forgave.

On March 25, 1933, just after Goulding's return, Thalberg left on an extended trip to Europe. Just afterward, Mayer completed his Thalberg putsch. On June 13 he sent a telegram to Thalberg, with friend Charles McArthur when it was delivered. Thalberg said to his friend, "They knifed me Charlie. They knifed me."[120] Mayer told his former partner that he had reorganized the studio and abolished the position of head of production. Thalberg was being removed. Mayer was self-serving as he betrayed his friend. In a telegram to Thalberg, he wrote "I'M DOING THIS FOR YOU."[121] Mayer offered every one of Thalberg's managers— Al Lewin, Hunt Stromberg, Bernie Hyman and the rest —contracts as independent producers with their own production groups. They each reported directly to him, so Thalberg had no department, no subordinates and, importantly, no allies. Their films were rushed into production during Thalberg's absence. When he returned, there were no stars left for any of his projects.

Thalberg returned in July. In New York he met with Nick Schenck and agreed to produce films for MGM. Schenck agreed to ensure Mayer did nothing further to damage Thalberg's standing, which infuriated Mayer. Thalberg returned to L.A. on August 19. Mayer had already moved his office into smaller space. Mayer's sacking of his old friend made Mannix even stronger at MGM. He was already running everything anyway, but Thalberg's ouster made him the official number-two man at the biggest studio in the world.

Now an independent producer, Thalberg set about several projects. His first was *The Barretts of Wimpole Street*. His wife Norma was to star and he wanted Charles Laughton to play the lead role, but Mayer and Mannix argued against him; Mayer because Laughton was a homosexual and Mannix because he knew Laughton had caused filming on George Cukor's *David Copperfield* to stop after suffering stage fright. W.C. Fields had been forced to replace the enigmatic Laughton. Interestingly, Mayer was less able to pressure Thalberg as an independent and given the deal Thalberg had made with Schenck, Laughton was hired.

Laughton came from the London stage into English comedy shorts. Though openly homosexual, in 1929 he married lesbian actress Elsa Lanchester. She thought their two-year courtship was sexless because of his manners. She was the only woman Laughton ever made love to, but the couple rarely slept together. Three years later, Lanchester walked in on a fight between Laughton and a homosexual male prostitute. Elsa very calmly said, "It's perfectly all right. It doesn't matter. I understand."[122] She then went psychosomatically deaf and remained so for several months! But the couple remained married. He appeared on Broadway in 1931 and was invited to MGM to star in the adaptation of the play he had been performing, *Payment Deferred*. He would star in dozens of films including *The Island of Lost Souls* (1932) as the infamous Dr. Moreau, *The Hunchback of Notre Dame* (1939) and *Mutiny on the Bounty* (1935). But Strickling would be kept busy keeping Laughton's private life out of the press.

The sham marriage to Lanchester supported Strickling's denials of Laughton rumors, and the couple was forced to endure numerous interviews and staged photo sessions. The strange couple actually stayed together for over 30 years, living in their mansion-turned-acting-school until the 1960s.

In the two years since Mayer, Mannix and Strickling had tried to put an end to her affair with Clark Gable, Joan Crawford's marriage to Douglas Fairbanks, Jr., had slowly disintegrated. Mayer's forced second honeymoon did nothing but confirm to the couple that their marriage was foundering. Knowing divorce was imminent, Strickling fed stories to a few select writers to protect Crawford. Strickling enlisted one of his favorites, Kathleen Albert, a writer with *Modern Screen Magazine*. Albert had been Pete Smith's assistant at MGM and had briefly worked for Strickling. She wrote several stories describing Crawford in glowing terms, calling her "a veritable hosfrau," who cooked, cleaned and ironed Fairbanks' shirts. Readers did not know of Albert's incestuous relationship with MGM, nor that she and Crawford were best friends. The "heartbroken Crawford" was "ever the loyal wife" according to Albert.

The truth was far from that. Crawford had been sleeping with Gable for two years. Bill Ferguson, an MGM employee, was taking a *Ladies Home Companion* writer on the tour of the studio, and as they passed Crawford's trailer, it began rocking rhythmically back and forth. Ferguson said, "You could hear these moans and groans coming from inside." Gable sauntered out of the trailer and walked past Ferguson and his astonished guest. But bisexual Crawford had other interests. To satisfy them she walked across the street to Barbara Stanwyck's house.

Stanwyck's lesbianism was an open secret as far back as her days as a New York chorus girl. She was orphaned as a child and reared by her older sister, a Broadway dancer. At 17 her sister got her a job as a dancer. She was a regular in the New York lesbian crowd, hanging out with Tallulah Bankhead, Marjorie Main, Blythe Daly, and another young dancer, Crawford.[123] In 1928, 21-year-old Stanwyck married comedian Frank Fay, an arrogant alcoholic but the most successful performer in vaudeville and reputedly homosexual although he married twice. He earned $17,500 a week performing around the world. He was 31 but looked 20 years older because of his drinking. Stanwyck had been approached by several studios, including MGM, but knew her lesbianism was a problem. Fay offered protection from the press and an entrée to Hollywood. Stanwyck and Fay were married in St. Louis on August 26, 1928. Immediately after the ceremony she left for Hollywood and he resumed a six-month tour.

Stanwyck signed with United Artists and six months later Fay signed at Warners. While Stanwyck's star rose quickly, Fay's stage talent did not translate to film. Warners' head Jack Warner decided the only roles Fay could do were character roles. He dyed his hair black, oiled it down, and cast him in small roles as Mexicans or Frenchmen. He was dropped in early 1931 after three years. The combination of his failures and Stanwyck's successes was too much for the egotistical Fay. He often beat her after she refused to quit movies and go back on the road with him. At the time, they were sharing a mansion at 441 North Rockingham across the street from Crawford's at 426. From 1932 to 1934 Stanwyck escaped Fay by crossing the street to stay with Crawford. The two remained on-and-off lovers for several years. Stanwyck and Fay divorced in 1935. The marriage became the basis for *A Star is Born* (1937). Stanwyck was not the only woman who slept with Crawford at the Rockingham house. Her children wrote that she slept openly with their nannies, and in the 1950s Marilyn Monroe told friends that Crawford made a blatant pass at her there, pawing at her breasts as she tried on Crawford's dresses.

Some Mannix and Strickling problems were laughable. In May 1933, Gable received a surprise visitor. He had become estranged from his father a dozen years earlier after angrily leaving home. His father wanted him to work the oil fields and was appalled that his son wanted to do something that "was for sissies."[124] But the old man showed up at Culver City like an image from *The Grapes of Wrath*. He drove up to the main gate at MGM with a group of Oklahoma dirt-farmers looking for work. He was in a caravan of cars piled with worn luggage and furniture. Years of alcohol and physical abuse had left Will Gable a shrunken 60-year-old who looked 80. Dressed in rags and reeking from a week without a bath, he walked up to the gate and asked to see his son, the star. Gable didn't know what to do, so he called Strickling. Strickling had the old man ushered in, arranged for a visit to the studio gym for a shower, the barbershop for a shave, and had a suit taken from the wardrobe department. When he emerged without shoes on, several pairs of those were requisitioned also.

Strickling arranged several staged photos of Gable showing his father around the studio. He also ordered Gable, in spite of his protests, to bring his father home. Gable moved his father into a spare bedroom in the Brentwood home he shared with Ria Langham. He had recently moved to the mansion, just a block from Joan Crawford's house.

Gable moved into the Bristol Drive house at the same time as Crawford's marriage to Douglas Fairbanks, Jr., was ending. Crawford did not even tell Fairbanks herself. In a routine repeated during each of her three divorces, she asked Fairbanks' agent Art Levee to drop by, handed him all of Fairbanks' clothes and told him to please inform Doug of the divorce. She then had the locks changed, and had Billy Haines replace the toilets and redecorate. Fairbanks went to Mayer and threatened to name Gable as a correspondent. Mayer had told Crawford and Gable they would be dismissed if they damaged the studio, and Fairbanks was threatening just that.

Mayer used his salesmanship during his Fairbanks meeting. Responding to Fairbanks' threats, he said if he tried to blame Gable he would look like a "schmuck." Mannix mentioned that the studio also knew of Fairbanks' affairs and they would be made public if Gable's name was mentioned. Putting his arm around Fairbanks' shoulder, Mayer also hinted that it would be assumed by fans that she was divorcing him because he couldn't satisfy her sexually.[125] Not only did Fairbanks keep Gable out of the press, he allowed *her* to divorce *him*! They were divorced on May 13, 1933.

On June 12, 1933, Gable was filming *Dancing Lady* with Crawford when his long-uncared-for teeth allegedly became infected. He was in so much pain that he called Strickling. Gable always called if he was ill; he was a hopeless hypochondriac. Though Crawford described him as "forever the ballsy folk hero," much of Gable was hidden from fans. Biographer Lynn Tornabene wrote of his obsessive behavior, "He won't take a bath because he won't sit in water he's been in. He only showers, and several times a day. He changes his bed linens at least twice a day. He shaves under his arms ... you could eat off him."[126] But this time, his panic was legitimate; he could have died.

Strickling brought in Dr. Edward B. Jones, who discovered Gable had an advanced case of pyorrhea that had become a life-threatening infection. Clark Gable was near death because of bad teeth. He was secretly rushed to a private hospital where it took three days for his health to stabilize before a studio dentist was able to remove almost all of Gable's teeth. They would be replaced with dentures.[127] *Dancing Lady* shooting had to be stopped and Gable was sent into seclusion. Strickling kept the longest production shutdown in MGM history a secret for ten weeks. He eventually had to admit that Gable had been hospitalized, but told the press it was for a gall bladder operation, an appendectomy and tonsillitis. No mention was made about teeth. Production was suspended until later in September, when Gable was finally able to appear in public.

The absence cost Gable. Mayer officially suspended him from June 20 to August 27, costing him $25,000 in salary. But it also cost him Crawford because during his lengthy absence he ignored his paramour. Fresh off of her divorce from Fairbanks, she needed a man. With Gable gone, she took up with another *Dancing Lady* star, Franchot Tone. Their affair would lead to marriage in 1935. When she refused to star in *Parnell* with Gable and the film failed, he blamed her and stopped talking to her. She responded by turning down a role in *Saratoga*, a role that went to Jean Harlow. Gable and Crawford would not reconcile until 1940, after Gable married Carole Lombard. After the death of Lombard in 1942, he turned to Crawford for support and sex. Their sexual relationship with Crawford would continue, according to Crawford, "a lot longer than anybody knows."[128]

It was rumored that fall that Crawford underwent an abortion in Connecticut. The press found her in a private hospital in late November under an assumed name, so Strickling had to address the story. On December 1 the *Los Angeles Post-Record* printed "ILLNESS DENIED BY JOAN CRAWFORD" with a short story that Crawford was "visiting" in New York and denied she was in a hospital.[129]

Johnny Weissmuller and Lupe Velez had to delay their wedding until the fall of 1933 because of his first wife's demands, but were married on October 8, 1933. He moved into her 732 Rodeo Drive mansion, where they battled almost daily and police visited several times a week. They fought in public too; when police broke up a fierce fracas in a Cleveland hotel room, he wouldn't leave the bathroom because she had beaten him up so badly. They were in the papers every week. Like Gary Cooper before him, Weissmuller's MGM makeup people covered up black eyes, cuts and bruises inflicted by Velez. More than once filming was canceled because of swollen and blackened eyes. Lovemaking was ferocious as well; *Tarzan* makeup people covered up large and bloody hickeys and bite marks covering his body.

When Velez came upon Weissmuller and a young actress having a quiet dinner at the El Mocambo she didn't say a word. She walked up, stabbed him in the hand with a fork, and walked out the door. Strickling knew he was powerless to force Velez keep things private, so he put a tongue-in-cheek spin on them and wrote stories describing their battles. One Strickling caption for a fan magazine photograph of the couple at a

Hollywood nightclub was, "What's wrong with this picture? Usually blows and angry words were flying between the movies' handsome Tarzan and his on-again off-again wife Lupe Velez."[130] In 1934 Thalberg would decide to cease doing movies aimed at the Spanish markets, and Spanish-speaking actresses at MGM lost their contracts. Velez would not work at MGM either. She took whatever roles she could get, worked in Europe, and in 1936 did vaudeville with Weissmuller.

In 1933 Nelson Eddy and Jeanette MacDonald joined the MGM family. Their bizarre relationship was a challenge for the studio for the next dozen years, during which they became the most popular musical duo in the history of the movies. Between 1935 and 1942 their films brought MGM millions, but their personal lives—individually and as a "couple"—were a disaster. Fans still believe that Eddy and MacDonald carried torches for each other, but for the sake of their careers never paired. Certainly it benefited MGM to present their most popular on-screen couple as an off-screen couple as well, and Strickling tried his best. But though they were close friends they never got together, and both were married at different times to different people (their individual marriages were each as bizarre as the relationship between the two). The true nature of the real Eddy-MacDonald relationship is as hard to decipher as the two people involved. Like quicksilver, you can see it, but you can never seem to grasp it.

Biographers can't agree on much about Eddy and MacDonald, and many historians cling helplessly to the obviously false MGM version. MacDonald was described as a "prude and a puritan" though it is widely accepted that she worked as a call girl in New York in the late 1920s (letters from Eddy to MacDonald discussing this survive). She wore such revealing clothes in so many publicity photos that her nickname was the Lingerie Queen. And she most certainly slept with Mayer to advance her career. For Eddy's part, one biographer described him as a serial womanizer and detailed many conquests, ignoring the fact that he was obviously either homosexual or bisexual and that his first marriage was engineered by Mayer to squelch the growing rumors in the newspapers about his sexuality. Listening to the people that knew them, what emerges is a portrait of two tortured souls who had less of an idea of their real personalities than perhaps we do.

Eddy was a product of his environment. He was born in Providence, Rhode Island, in 1901 to a father who abused both Eddy and his mother Isabel, to whom he became morbidly attached. His father was so worried about their relationship and that Eddy was a "sissy" that he made him dress up like a soldier and march back and forth across the front yard for hours at a time. To teach him to swim he took him far into Narragansett

Harbor and threw him into the water. He would live with his mother Isabel most of his life. He once said of her, "She strung along with me when I was struggling along, and now I'm sticking by her ... who's the loveliest woman in Hollywood? My mother."[131]

In the 1920s he worked as a newspaper advertising writer. Ida Koverman supposedly first saw him singing in an L.A. church. When he was discovered he was a 33-year-old boy who had never had a serious female relationship and lived with his mother. Koverman convinced Mayer to sign him, and despite the captivating voice, Eddy was described as cantankerous, pedantic, moody, overwrought, emotional, and immature. He was so bland that his nickname was the Singing Capon. His MGM debut was not auspicious; the test was reshot 58 times and was still unusable. But Mayer only wanted him to sing anyway, and women loved him.

In 1933 MacDonald was already an established musical talent, having appeared in almost a dozen musicals including *The Love Parade* (1930), *Monte Carlo* (1930) and *Love Me Tonight* (1932). She had wanted to be a star from the age of four. The opposite of the Eddy household, the MacDonalds were dominated by her shrewish mother Anna. Jeanette followed her sister Blossom, quitting school for Broadway stage (Blossom Rock's final role was Grandmama in the 1970s television show *The Addams Family*). MacDonald was willing to sacrifice almost anything to be a star, and in New York friends knew that she worked as a call girl. She would do the same thing for a time after her arrival in L.A. in 1929. According to a friend, "Jeanette did what she had to do to get to the top."[132] When she first signed with Paramount she supposedly slept with her director, Ernst Lubitsch, who adored her. He wanted to marry her.

MacDonald had lifelong problems interacting with men on a personal level. She was reportedly frigid and disinterested in sex, and early in her career her constant companion was her agent, Bob Ritchie. Friends felt she let Ritchie hang around just to keep other men away. It was just this type of unavailability and disinterest that appealed to Mayer. He tried for years to get her into his office. It was said that "MacDonald cooed her way to divadom upon Louis B. Mayer's lap."[133] He took a "personal" interest in the careers of dozens of his actresses but there was always a quid pro quo. He slept with hundreds of his actresses but fell in love with only two: Greer Garson and Jeanette MacDonald. MacDonald spent hours alone with Mayer in his office; it was an open secret that he and his protégée were sleeping together. She would later detail the sexual affair to Eddy. To keep Bob Ritchie out of the way, in 1935 Mayer hired him and sent him to London to work as an MGM talent scout. During his time there he would recruit Hedy Lamarr, Luise Ranier and Greer Garson.

In 1934 Eddy and MacDonald starred in the musical *Naughty Marietta*. During the early part of their relationship the two acted like they hated each other, forcing Strickling to plant stories about a "budding on-set romance." But they did have a relationship, even though it took Eddy over a year to try to consummate it. It appears that they were platonic friends from that point on. It's impossible to clearly define the Eddy-Mac-Donald relationship at any specific point. Whatever feelings they may have had for each other were distorted by MacDonald's ambivalence toward committed relationships and Eddy's ambivalence toward women. Friends describe him following her around in public like "a love-sick puppy."[134] The confusion has never been cleared up.

As the newlywed Weissmullers were battling and Eddy and Mac-Donald first meeting, Clark Gable came to Strickling for help. Exactly why has remained one of the great Hollywood mysteries, but during the fall of 1933 a rumor began circulating that has survived for over 65 years. The incident occurred during a bitter contract dispute between Mayer and Joan Crawford. It was already rumored at MGM that he had agreed to raise her salary to $4,000 a week. When Gable found out, he was furious. He was having a tough summer. He had only recently returned to work after his June 20–August 27 suspension and was in constant pain, which he tried to erase with liquor. According to MGM, it was the painful aftereffects of the gall-bladder surgery, but probably it was the replacement of all of his teeth. His personal life was in turmoil. He hadn't seen Crawford since June; she was seeing Franchot Tone. His father was still living in his mansion. His marriage to Ria Langham was loveless and had been sexless for four years. Professionally, he was angry to have been loaned out to Columbia, once the smallest and least respected of the old Poverty Row studios, to make a quickie titled *Overland Bus* that he thought would be disastrous for his career. But he was most upset that Crawford was making $4,000 versus his $2,500. For all these reasons, Gable was drinking even more than usual that summer and living in an apartment just above Sunset.

Seemingly nobody really knows what happened that fall, but *something* happened. Strickling allegedly received a call early one morning and was told by a drunken Gable that he had been in a car accident in Hollywood and he thought he had hit a pedestrian. A call to a police department friend confirmed that Gable's car had been identified as the car that hit a woman in a crosswalk. He had swerved into the crosswalk trying to turn west on Sunset as he careened down Sunset Plaza. Strickling and Mannix allegedly went to work immediately. Gable was driven to a secluded Palm Springs bungalow, where he was to remain for a month. At this point it becomes difficult to separate legend from truth.

The story that evolved over the years is that MGM paid off the police and D.A. and arranged for a middle-level MGM manager to take responsibility. According to Mayer biographer Charles Higham, it was Mayer who convinced the mystery employee to take the fall for Gable after reviewing a list of MGM employees who could be spared. Middle-level managers were targeted since Mayer felt they would be less apt to confess the plot than a lower-level wage earner. Mayer explained that the Gable incident could destroy MGM, and that the fall guy would be guaranteed lifetime employment and a trust fund set up for his heirs for taking responsibility for Gable's accident.[135] The dead woman's family was paid $125,000. D.A. Fitts was said to have made the arrangements and the manager spent ten months at an honor farm before quietly returning to work.

What makes the Gable accident story difficult to confirm is the number of similar *and* conflicting stories that could actually describe this specific event. I believe an accident did occur involving Gable, and over the years dozens of industry executives have confirmed the Gable story as true. Men at the highest studio levels, men with no ax to grind and no agenda, have said that Gable was indeed involved in a fatal car accident in the fall of 1933. B.P. Shulberg, head of Paramount Studios, swore the story was true. His son, also a Hollywood executive, confirmed his father's version. Col. Barney Oldfield also said the story was true.[136]

Confusing the issue at its core, Gable had several other car accidents that were well known, even though the worst details were kept out of the papers. He was hospitalized at least twice for injuries sustained in wrecks, as well as numerous times for more mundane ailments and cosmetic surgeries. Matching individual hospital stays to specific maladies is difficult. As the stories have been told and retold, incidents and dates have been duplicated or dates transposed. Gable was involved in a serious car accident in Brentwood. In various sources, that accident has been reported to have taken place in June, August, or September, of 1933, 1935, or 1937. One writer gave the date as June 20, 1933, and described Gable's Duesenberg. But he was not driving the Duesenberg, and the accident actually occurred in 1945. Interestingly, in June 1933 — exactly June 20, actually — Gable was being suspended by Mayer, allegedly because he couldn't work due to teeth problems.

No research has uncovered an MGM manager going to jail for a year for vehicular homicide. Neither the *Los Angeles Examiner* nor the *Los Angeles Times,* or trade papers such as *The Hollywood Reporter* or *Variety,* carried a story with those details. There are no newspaper stories of a fatal car accident involving any MGM employees that fall. With no MGM executive going to jail, no victim, and several other Gable accidents, the confusion has led some researchers to discount Gable's involvement in *any* accident. But he was.

What happened on Sunset in 1933? There is some secondary evidence that Gable was involved in a fatal accident. An eerily similar accident occurred at almost the same time as Gable's was supposed to have taken place. It happened at the same time. It had the same result. And it happened at exactly the same location. Everything about the accident is remarkably similar to the Gable story. I believe that the stories describe the same accident. Clark Gable killed a pedestrian, and walked away.

On September 22, 1933, the *Los Angeles Record* reported that 26-year-old John Huston ran over and killed Tosca Roulien on Sunset Blvd. She was the 25-year-old wife of Brazilian actor Raul Roulien, "the South American Valentino." Huston was allegedly with William Miller, a cameraman for a small Poverty Row studio called Excellent Pictures. Huston had allegedly borrowed the car from actress Greta Nissen. Interestingly, the first newspaper stories also mention that MGM was paying $400,000 ($5 million today) "to keep John out of trouble,"[137] and that the studio paid Raul Roulien $5,000 to settle a $250,525 claim.

On September 28, 1933, the *Evening Herald Express* described the accident, beginning, "One moment she was happy, a beautiful auburn-haired young woman of 25, trimly clad in slacks and tan jacket, and skipping merrily across a boulevard in Hollywood near her home. The next! Two great yellow eyes, followed by a hurtling mass of mechanical steel, bore down upon her, there was a crash and the beautiful girl lay crumpled and dying in the street."[138] After being struck by Huston's car, she was thrown 36 feet into the air and rolled another 25. Police reported she "got confused in the glare of the approaching headlights." Huston himself allegedly rushed the injured woman to the hospital.

The *Evening Herald* reported that Raul Roulien learned of the accident from a friend, concert violinist M. Maazal. Maazal said he was listening to "a police radio broadcast" at his home on Sutton Street in far away Encino "when he heard a description of the woman killed in the crash." Incredibly, he had "a hunch" that it might be his friend Raul's wife and drove the hour to Roulien's Hollywood apartment. It was never explained why he was listening to police radios or where his wild "hunch" came from.

Coroner and MGM friend Frank Nance held a brief inquest on September 30, ruling the death accidental and absolving Huston of blame. D.A. Fitts convened a grand jury on October 10, but told the press that "if there is no evidence it would be unfair and useless to file charges against this young man." On September 20, Fitts' grand jury refused to indict Huston and he walked away free. Why was he allowed to walk away from such a terrible accident? Huston was a writer whose only screen credits were minor dialogue additions to three movies, two of which starred his father, Walter Huston. Why would Mayer and MGM become involved in an accident that they had so little to do with? If Huston was driving the car, they had no reason to be involved. But if Gable were driving the car, that's another matter. There is circumstantial evidence that leads me to believe that the accident attributed to Huston was in fact Gable's accident, and that Mayer engineered a cover-up using Huston.

There are dozens of unanswered questions. Why did reports as early as September 22 describe MGM payoffs? Later stories put the date at September 27, though Huston always said the accident happened on September 25. Roulien was on her way to a "drugstore or market," but the accident happened well after midnight. Huston said he did not see her because she stepped from in front of a "motor bus" in a "flow of traffic,"[139] but buses didn't run on Sunset Boulevard at that hour. Also, Huston alleged that "there were no witnesses," which is why he took her to the hospital himself. But what of the large "flow of traffic" that he said caused the accident? And what of erstwhile Roulien pal Maazal: Why was he listening to police radios at midnight, and what made him think the unnamed victim was his friend's wife? And if the accident did indeed take place after midnight, it would have taken Maazal over an hour to get from Encino to Hollywood in 1933. He could not possible have been at Roulien's apartment anywhere near the time Roulien said he was told.

Just a few days later the "grief stricken" Roulien completed *Flying Down to Rio* with Dolores del Rio. A week later he sued Huston for $250,525 and some time later (reportedly June 6, 1935) was awarded just $5,000. But what of the September 22 newspaper stories detailing those amounts? Huston's attorney was an MGM staff lawyer. A much larger amount was probably paid; Roulien would never have accepted such a paltry amount.

When all of the little details and inconsistencies are added together, it begins to look like the Huston accident was actually the Gable accident. The first red flag is the level of MGM involvement, which makes no sense if Huston were driving but would be justified for Gable. There is the coincidence of the timing of Huston's accident and rumors about Gable first surfacing. And there is the similarity of the details of the two accidents.

Mayer would not have gone to the lengths that he did to protect a young writer who worked for another studio, even though his father worked for MGM. According to Huston biographers, Walter Huston himself approached Mayer and pleaded with him to call on William Randolph

Hearst to have his newspapers underplay the matter. But Mayer's involvement had nothing to do with protecting Huston's son. Huston was nowhere near the level of Gable. He quite simply would not carry that much weight with Mayer.

The circumstantial evidence leads me to believe that Mayer used Huston to cover for Gable. MGM staffers were aware of a rumor that Mayer spent in excess of $400,000 to suppress an "incident."[140] He would not have done so—that was the entire filming budget of a feature picture in 1933—for a young unknown writer. But he would have had to do it for a star. Hearst and his papers could not suppress a case that was so public that a grand jury was investigating it. But they could manipulate the Huston story to appear as a minor incident, which they did. Blame an accident on Huston; arrange for the coroner and the D.A. to find him blameless. I believe that Huston would become an "un-named MGM executive" taking the fall for Gable as the story evolved over time. Mayer could have convinced Huston to take the blame for the accident, since there was really no punishment involved. Almost immediately after the court proceedings, young Huston left for an extended vacation to Europe, a sojourn variously described as "abrupt" or "quickly-planned" in the newspapers. He remained in Europe and was virtually absent from Hollywood until 1938, when he quietly resumed working. He went to work for B.P. Shulberg at Paramount, which adds weight to Shulberg's opinions about Gable's accident.

Within a year, the inexperienced Huston was writing and directing major films such as *Jezebel* (1938), *High Sierra* (1941), *The Maltese Falcon* and *Sergeant York* (both 1941). His career would last 40 years and garner him several Academy Award nominations. Through the 1950s and 1960s he directed scores of films and acted in almost 50. He died in 1987. It is inconceivable that an unknown writer, even the son of a well-known actor, would receive the assistance that Huston received from MGM had he killed someone. The timing, the type of accident, the location of the accident, and the end result all smack of studio involvement at the highest levels, reserved for a star of Gable's stature. Over the years, the Gable story has been revised through repeated tellings. After Gable's initial seclusion in Palm Springs, he grudgingly went on loan-out to Columbia for *Overland Bus.* Renamed *It Happened One Night,* the movie he thought would ruin his career became a watershed event in Gable's career. Even though Gable's problems caused Strickling immeasurable grief, the two were fast friends. Beginning in the mid–1930s, the two shared lunch and in a back booth at Musso and Frank's Grill in Hollywood twice a week.

A number of MGM players were dropped in 1933. The first was William Haines. Not only was Haines living an openly homosexual life with

Jimmy Shields, he refused any studio-arranged relationships. He would not "play the game." Mayer's long-simmering dislike made firing him easy. He was called to Mayer's office and told, "Either give up that boyfriend of yours or I'll cancel your contract."[141] When he would not, he was sent to Mannix, who told him, "That last movie of yours didn't do too well," and fired him. Best friend Joan Crawford called Haines and Shields "the happiest married couple in Hollywood." Carole Lombard described Haines as "her closest girlfriend," and once stripped naked in front of him, saying, "I wouldn't do this if I thought you'd get aroused, Billy."[142] Their close friendship would disappear once Lombard began dating Clark Gable, due to Gable's dislike for his one-time sexual partner.

Haines remained in the Hollywood limelight for years, after turning a small antique business he had opened in 1930 into the most sought-after interior design firm in the U.S. Among the 400 celebrity homes he designed was that of his first client, Joan Crawford. Others included Carole Lombard's St. Cloud mansion in Bell Air, Marie Dresser's estate on Alpine Drive, and Wallace Beery's hacienda on Roxbury Drive. He and Shields remained one of Hollywood's most faithful couples, staying together for 50 years, sharing a house in Brentwood for the last 20. Haines lost a long battle with cancer just before Christmas 1973, and died in bed while a heart-broken Shields held his hand. Shields was utterly inconsolable and later committed suicide in the same bed.

After Haines, Niles Asther was next to go. Asther was one of MGM's top leading men in the 1920s. His movies, such as *Laugh, Clown, Laugh* (1926) and *The Single Standard* (1928) with Garbo, were enormously successful. Like Haines he was openly homosexual but unlike Haines he played the game. But he had a knack for getting in trouble, and worse for Strickling, he talked too much.

Asther was quoted in a 1928 *New York World* interview saying he "didn't like this love-making so much," and said he preferred roles that required him to grow a beard, because "you can't make love in a beard."[143] The obvious intimation was that he did not like making love to *women*. "Beard" was a veiled reference to the 1930s term for a man pretending to have a relationship with a woman. Strickling arranged dates and planted rumors, all to no avail. Mayer tried to fire him in 1930, but rather than be fired, Asther married Vivian Duncan, one of the dancing Duncan Sisters. Strickling engineered the union with Duncan; it took everyone in Hollywood by surprise. A daughter was born in Paris during a bogus "second honeymoon" also arranged by Strickling, but whether the child was Asther's or adopted was never confirmed. Duncan did not tell friends she was pregnant before the couple left, and Asther denied ever sleeping with her. Whatever the true parentage, Strickland released hundreds of photos of the couple and their baby. But when Asther returned to MGM his wife and daughter stayed in Paris. Asther and Duncan stayed married until early 1933, but never lived together. In 1933 Asther simply refused to play the game any longer, so Strickling allowed a sensational article to run in the April 1933 issue of *Screenland Magazine* under the title "The Strange Case of Niles Asther." The article criticized Asther for not living with his wife and child, and implied that his long absences were not because of other *women*. After the Asther-Duncan divorce was finalized in 1933, Mayer simply dismissed him.

Another casualty of the 1933 homosexual purge at MGM was Ramon Novarro. His popularity and his secrecy gave him an advantage for a while. Since Novarro was a loyal soldier, Strickling worked diligently to keep the secret. The publicity department sent thousands of Valentine's Day cards signed by Ramon to fans and to female MGM employees. Novarro was linked to virtually every actress at MGM, but the press still dropped hints. *Photoplay* spoke of his "loveless life." The *Philadelphia Register* noted that he is "never linked to any women." He grudgingly allowed Strickling to invent relationships with actresses; the first was with Myrna Loy. Loy was the subject of her own rumors but the fan magazines ran stories of Novarro and Loy and their "love at first sight." Loy first learned of her "love for Novarro" in the *Los Angeles Times*. Mayer and Strickling tried to force Novarro and Loy to wed, and Novarro seriously considered the request before fleeing for a nine-month trip to South America. While there, Mayer fired Novarro. He lived in quiet seclusion in a Laurel Canyon mansion over the mountain from Hollywood. It was decorated by Haines entirely in black fur and silver wallpaper. Novarro eventually lost his looks to alcohol, and in the 1950s was relying on young male prostitutes for sex. Two teenaged hustlers murdered him in his home in 1968.

The departure of Haines, Asther, and Novarro — three known homosexuals whose behavior had been disregarded for years — didn't really mark a drastic change in studio behavior. Mayer just hated homosexuals. And Strickling and Mannix just had to work harder to hide them.

In the 12 months since Paul Bern's murder, Jean Harlow had tried to return to normal life. She worked on several films after completing *Red Dust* within just days of Bern's death, followed by *Dinner at Eight* and *Hold Your Man*, which were filmed in early 1933, and *Bombshell*, filmed in August 1933. She buried herself in alcohol and anonymous sex and married *Red Dust* cameraman Hal Rosson in September 1933. The public was surprised, but it was understood at MGM that she married Rosson at MGM's direction to deflect attention from her affair with actor Max Baer, whose wife was divorcing him and threatening to name Harlow as a correspondent. A month later it was reported that Jean had undergone an appendectomy and, according to her mother, would spend a month recuperating at home. But on December 4, when it was reported that she was hospitalized in San Francisco for an "appendix vacation," it appeared that she had undergone yet another studio-arranged abortion.[144]

Mannix's life would be changed forever in 1934 by the beautiful Ziegfeld dancer he had met in New York years before. In 1934 MGM developed a movie based on the life of Broadway producer Florenz Ziegfeld, from his beginnings as a carnival barker to his rise to Broadway legend. The film would be a lavish feature with a dozen production numbers, hundreds of Ziegfeld dancers, and cameos by 40 MGM stars. Mannix visited the set daily. The film featured MGM stars such as William Powell, Myrna Loy, Fanny Brice and Luise Rainer, and dozens of Ziegfeld dancers brought to L.A. One of the Ziegfeld stars was Camille Lanier. Friends called Camille "Toni" and Ziegfeld called her the Girl with the Million Dollar Legs. Regulars simply called her Legs. She was a beautiful brunette with a stunning figure.

Soon after *Ziegfeld* filming began, Mannix stood watching a production number, staring at Lanier. He turned to an assistant and growled, "Give her $4,500 for the day's work and have her come to see me."[145] He was immediately smitten. It was not hard to see why. According to actor Jack Larson, a close friend of both Eddie and Toni, she was a "gorgeous Irish Catholic broad. She had an aire about her, and she spoke like Harlow. When she talked she used all long a's. It was wonderful."[146] She would not seem to be a good match for Mannix, once described as "a boxer with a cauliflower ear for a face."[147] Eddie was totally infatuated with Lanier, like every other man who met her. In addition to her beauty she was a "guy's woman" who loved a party. She was a feisty two-fisted drinker and enjoyed hanging out with men. Mobster Mickey Cohen once said she was the only person in L.A. with any balls, and she could swear like a sailor. In other words, she was the female Eddie.

Also, according to Larson the beautiful dancer was totally unaffected by glamour or Hollywood. In fact, she hated it. She never wanted to be a movie star and hated the laborious and boring work. She disliked all of the standing around between takes and thought the costumes—unlike the well-made originals she was used to wearing—were cheap.[148] One of the on-set accoutrements she particularly hated was the "slant board," a body-sized piece of wood that stood slanted back on an angle, equipped with arm- and head-rests. When actresses' long dresses made it impossible to sit down, they stood leaning back on a slant board. Lanier so hated the uncomfortable contraption that in the middle of filming she climbed down, walked off the set, and headed to Hawaii for a vacation.

When Mannix arrived at the set and was told that his new girlfriend left, he chased after her. When they returned from Hawaii a week later, they were a couple and he moved her into an apartment just off of Hollywood Boulevard. Mannix, still at least technically married to Bernice, had to be somewhat discrete in his travels with Lanier, though the two were seen regularly around Hollywood. She accompanied him on all of his MGM travels and the two socialized and vacationed with friends as if they were married. A favorite vacation spot was Tucson, Arizona, at the time hard for inquisitive reporters to find.

In the mid-1930s Roy Drachman worked part time at the Arizona Inn, a favorite hideaway for Hollywood stars. During the 1934 holidays Strickling called Drachman to arrange a two-week stay at the inn for Mannix and Lanier, but Strickling requested that Drachman come to L.A. and accompany the couple back to Arizona. Should a photographer be at the train station, Drachman would be Toni Lanier's unnamed new beau.[149] Mannix, Toni and Drachman were accompanied by Strickling and his girlfriend, Gail Greenstreet. Gail was a cute, blonde 21-year-old who came from Washington to Hollywood in the late 1920s. She worked for J. Walter Thompson Advertising and had frequent dealings with Strickling in her job duties. Howard and Gail would later marry at the Arizona Inn.[150]

Toni's free-spirited nature was visible — literally — the first afternoon at the inn, when according to Drachman, she "shocked the natives, the guests, and the management of the Inn when she sunbathed her first day at the hotel, stripped to the waist. The Inn would have none of that and told her so. At first Eddie was irate but I calmed him down, explaining that Tucson was not like Hollywood or even Palm Springs." During a second stay a month later, she invited guests to their bungalow for a private party. Lanier had the bathtub filled with crushed ice, caviar and champagne, and hired a group of Mexican troubadours to provide music. At three in the morning Lanier coaxed the band to the public pool and ordered them to serenade the other guests. Despite the vocal complaints from the angry guests, Mannix obviously relished the spontaneity of his young girlfriend. Unfortunately, after the boisterous Lanier parties the manager told Drachman to tell the Mannixes they were no longer welcome. Drachman, aware of Mannix's temper and reputation, was terrified so told Mannix he had to leave because the Inn didn't "take Jews." Instead of being irate — Mannix was Catholic — he laughed and quietly left the next morning. Mannix remained friendly with Drachman over the years and often asked his old friend to arrange accommodations for his movie and mob associates.

As Mannix's relationship with Toni grew stronger and more public, the marriage to Bernice faded. Sometime in late 1934 or early 1935 Bernice quietly moved to Palm Springs, supported with weekly checks from Eddie. But she still steadfastly refused Eddie a divorce.[151] Toni moved in with Eddie, and the two lived as a couple for the next 30 years.

Some of the issues faced by Strickling and Mannix were truly tragic. On April 15, 1934, Karl Dane, one of the greatest silent stars, sat in his tiny apartment on South Burnside and put a bullet into his head. Once a millionaire star with mansions and Rolls Royces, the advent of sound and a thick Danish accent ended his career. After an extra recognized him selling hot dogs from a cart near the Paramount Studio gates, he killed himself. When Strickling found out his body was unclaimed at the morgue and headed for an unmarked potter's grave he arranged for a funeral and headstone. On May 10, 1934, the *Los Angeles Evening Herald Examiner* ran a two-sentence article about Dane's estate: $255.[152]

On one same day, May 10, the newspaper reported that the body of a young woman had been found in her tiny Hollywood apartment. Police found 26-year-old Sigrun Solvason dead from a barbiturate overdose, discovered "amidst photographs of herself and Greta Garbo." The headline told the story: "GREAT GARBO'S DOUBLE KILLS SELF—LEAVES NOTE TELLING DESPAIR AT NOT BEING STAR." The prose was more Strickling than newspaper: "Beneath a mirror that told a bitter truth, Sigrun Solvason, the girl known in Hollywood as 'Garbo's double,' lay dead yesterday. She had taken poison. All about the room were photographs of herself and Garbo, mute evidence of the resemblance that raised her hopes so high she could not bear the pain when Hollywood dashed them to earth."[153]

What probably happened is that when police realized the victim was an MGM employee, they contacted the studio. At the time, Garbo was filming *Queen Christina,* and the tragic death would keep Garbo in the papers. Solvason's death would not normally have made the papers, and she wasn't even Garbo's stand-in, but a look-alike used for checking camera angles and lighting. Garbo's stand-in was Geraldine de Vorak; in the ten years she performed the function she never once met Garbo.[154] Portraying Solvason as a stand-in made her all the more tragic; a common Strickling ploy.

In late 1934 Strickling allegedly came to the aid of William Randolph Hearst and Marion Davies. Davies had apparently become pregnant by Hearst and refused to have an abortion. Keeping Davies out of the public view was easy, particularly with access to Hearst's remote estates. Explaining a baby was another matter. There are several unconfirmed theories of the baby's life. Interred with her in the Douras family crypt at Hollywood Forever Cemetery are Arthur Lake, star of the *Dagwood* movies, and his wife Patricia. Patricia Lake was said to be Marion's niece, but rumors have persisted for 35 years that she was indeed Davies' daughter by Hearst. Hearst declared in his will, "The only children I have ever had are my sons," but anecdotal evidence raises doubts. Davies supported Lake her entire life and she lived with Marion most of her life. When Davies died, she left Lake half of her $20 million estate. Late in life, Lake told her family that Hearst admitted he was her father.

Another child became part of Davies and Hearst lore several years later when Hedda Hopper described another child raised by Davies. When Hopper broke the story, Parsons was infuriated. Hopper scooped Parsons about Parsons' own boss! But if Hearst had asked for Strickling's help developing a biography for his love child, he would have used Hopper rather than Parsons. Parsons was part of the Hearst "family," and her story would have been immediately suspect.

According to Hopper's tragic tale, Marion's "long-time cook Mrs. Grace" died suddenly, but not before Marion promised—on her deathbed no less—to care for her young daughter "little Mary Grace." Marion would bring her up as if she were her own. There are rumors that little Mary was indeed her own. Mary Grace was a pretty blonde looking suspiciously like Marion—same smile, same cheeks, and the spitting image of a young Davies. Davies paid for her upbringing and she lived with her. On her bedside table was a photograph of Davies inscribed, "To my darling daughter."[155] When she broke her back in a car accident in college, she recuperated at Marion's home. Davies arranged for a date with William Curley, publisher of the *New York Journal American*. He was old enough to be her grandfather, had five children and a bunch of grandchildren. But they were married at San Simeon, with Davies and Doris Duke in the wedding party.

Marion Davies' daughter by William Randolph Hearst would have been a titanic story, and given his long-suffering wife Millicent's attitude toward Marion, probably an ugly one. But it still would have been moved to the back pages if another pregnancy fixed by Strickling and Mannix that summer had become public. Again, it was Gable called to the office.

In late 1934, Mayer banished Gable to Twentieth Century Studios to star in *The Call of the Wild* alongside young Loretta Young. Perhaps more than any other Hollywood actress, Young hid behind her self-designed image. A documentary described Young as "a symbol of beauty, serenity, and grace ... a woman of substance whose true beauty lies in her dedication to her family and her faith." One writer said, "Sweet, sweeter, sweetest. No combination of terms better describes the screen persona of lovely Loretta Young." But MGM people called her Attila the Nun.

Utah-born Gretchen Michaela Young came to L.A. in 1916 at age three when her mother opened a boarding house at Green Street and Ninth near downtown. She and her sisters Polly Ann and Elizabeth (later Sally Blane) were soon doing small silent-film roles. Actress Mae Murray was so taken with four-year-old Gretchen that she asked to adopt her. Mrs. Young declined the offer but allowed her daughter live with Murray for a year and a half. When Murray returned Gretchen at age six she was sent to a Catholic convent school where she lived until age 14. She was visiting home during a vacation when producers of the Colleen Moore film *Naughty but Nice* (1927) called, looking for her sister Polly Ann. But Gretchen went instead and with beautiful blue eyes and flawless complexion, got the role meant for her sister. She appeared in a dozen films over the next few years, including Lon Chaney's, *Laugh, Clown, Laugh* (1928) and Harlow's *Platinum Blonde* (1931). In 1930, the 16-year-old eloped to Arizona with her 26-year-older divorced costar Grant Withers, a union that was quickly annulled by her mother.

Young's studios spread what coworkers derisively called the Gospel of Loretta, story after story about her devout Catholicism. Marlene Dietrich told reporters, "Every time she sins she builds a church. That's why there are so many Catholic churches in Hollywood."[156] Young carried a rosary with her and forbade swearing on her sets. She carried a "Cuss Jar" and if she heard a profanity, the offender paid 25¢ "for the nuns." It is widely reported that after hearing Spencer Tracy say "damn" she walked up and demanded his quarter. He fumbled in his pocket, pulled out a $20 bill, tossed it at her and snarled, "Here's twenty, Sister. Go fuck yourself."[157]

In 1935 she was cast opposite Clark Gable in *The Call of the Wild*. Pairing the virginal Young and the profligate womanizer Gable was an open joke in Hollywood. The two reported to the set near Mount Baker in northern Washington in late November 1934. Even though Gable was in the middle of yet another affair — with English actress Elizabeth Allen — he set his sights on Young. She was a challenge for Gable. First, he saw her oft-proclaimed virtue a challenge to his faith that he could get any woman into bed. Second, their director was William Wellman, who had directed three Young films and bed his star during each, affairs everyone including Gable knew about. Wellman assumed that they would continue on the *Wild* set, so Gable saw stealing Young as a trophy. Lastly, he knew Young had just ended a yearlong affair with Spencer Tracy, who had broken her heart by refusing to divorce and marry her. He had moved out of his house, though, leaving his wife and two children behind. He lived apart from them for the rest of his life. Even so, Gable and Young were an unlikely pair. Why two such divergent personalities clicked is a mystery, but click they did.

Within days of checking into the Mount Baker Lodge the two were sleeping together.[158]

The shoot took over two months due to delays caused by frequent blizzards, so the crew were often stuck in the lodge for days and weeks at a time. Gable divided his time between Young's suite and drunken card games. When they could get through 60 miles of snow covered roads, Gable and Jack Oakie and a few others frequented the brothels in Bellingham, Washington. Rumors about a Gable-Young affair quickly reached Hollywood and Ria Langham. It reached a very public climax when an obviously peeved Wellman dressed down Gable in front of cast and crew, and the story made its way to the studio. There was little Mannix and Mayer could do but hope that the affair, like all of Gable's, would simply fade away. Reporters hounded everyone about an affair that everyone

Loretta Young during filming of *The Crusades* (1935) holding the rosary she carried every day off the set. At the time she was pregnant with a child conceived during an affair with Clark Gable on the *Call of the Wild* set. When *Crusades* filming ended she was secreted to Europe to hide the pregnancy.

denied. Things quieted down after filming ended in February 1935, but a few months later, Strickling would get a late-night phone call from Loretta.

In late 1934 MGM and William Randolph Hearst parted ways. Hearst was increasingly unhappy that MGM gave Thalberg's wife Norma Shearer roles he thought should go to Marion but Mayer realized Davies was not a box office draw. On November 1, Hearst had her bungalow carted away to Warners. Unfortunately for MGM, favored treatment from Louella Parsons and the Hearst papers went away as well.

There were several high-profile divorces in early 1935, some tragic, some funny. On March 26, Virginia Cherrill divorced Cary Grant on the grounds that he was "morose and quarrelsome."[159] She should have divorced him because he was gay. Soon after Cary Grant — then Archie Leach — came to Hollywood in 1932 he left his boyfriend Jack Orry-Kelly for another actor, Randolph Scott. Archie and Randy immediately became a couple and shared several houses together, forcing Paramount to describe them for papers as "room-mates." When they were called a "happy couple," they had to find girlfriends. Grant dated actress Cherrill — best known as the poor blind girl in the Chaplin classic *City Lights* — and the couple married in February 1934. Incredibly, she did not recognize that he was gay and paid no heed when Scott moved into the apartment next door at the La Rhonda Apartments. She finally figured it out about six months later and, in September, moved back in with her mother.

Just a week or so later, on October 5, 1934, Grant was rushed by ambulance to the hospital for a drug overdose originally described as a suicide attempt. His stomach was pumped but Paramount quickly issued a story; Grant had a bad reaction to liquor. Grant told reporters from his bed that he was under much stress, "all alone ... and my pal Randolph Scott is out of town."[160] Cherrill divorced him in March 1935 and Grant moved back in with Scott. Grant is credited for coining the term "gay" to refer to a homosexual; in the 1938 comedy *Bringing Up Baby*, when asked why he was wearing a dress, he replied, "I've gone gay."[161]

In the meantime, Strickling was given his greatest challenge when MGM signed Spencer Tracy on April 8, 1935. Tracy had been in Hollywood for five years working for Fox and adding to a reputation that began by getting thrown out of several *dozen* Milwaukee grammar schools. But he liked drama class and from Ripon College he and pal Pat O'Brien went to Broadway and eventually Hollywood. Tracy made his debut with Humphrey Bogart in 1930s *Up the River* and over the next few years became a major star for Fox. But he was also an awful human being, haunted by personal demons and alcohol. He suffered from depression, never slept, obsessed about death and was an ugly drunk with a hair-trigger temper. Within days of arriving at Fox he was arrested and hogtied by police outside the House of Francis brothel, and once knocked a Fox employee unconscious because the man took his parking spot. He disappeared on drunken benders for weeks at a time. During his benders, he sat naked in a hotel tub with two or three cases of whiskey. He drank himself unconscious, awoke and repeated the process until the whiskey ran out. He did not get out of the tub even to relieve himself, and when the whiskey ran out he returned to the studio.

Fox fired Tracy in April 1935. First, he got into a drunken fight with his wife in a Yuma, Arizona, hotel suite and broke everything except the bed. He returned to Hollywood two days later to film *Dante's Inferno*, but on March 25 assaulted director Harry Lachmann in a drunken rage. The fight ended when Tracy passed out on the floor. Studio chief Winfield Sheehan ordered the set evacuated and locked, hoping Tracy would awaken sober. But when Tracy did wake up he trashed the entire set, breaking everything including furniture, lights, and cameras. When he returned from a private sanitarium two weeks later, he was called into Sheehan's office and warned that he would be fired if he did not control his drinking. Without a word he walked to a bar across the street and got drunk, walked back to Sheehan's office and ransacked it. He was fired.

Thalberg knew Tracy meant box office and convinced Mayer to hire him, despite Mayer's concern that he didn't need "another drunken Wallace Beery."[162] The day of his firing at Fox, Thalberg met Tracy in a Hollywood bar and signed him to MGM. Tracy was still drunk. It was apparent to Strickling that Tracy would be what he called a "multi-problem person" so he organized a "Tracy Squad." He hired an ambulance team with a driver, a doctor, and four beefy security guards dressed as attendants. The squad's only job was to respond to "Tracy calls" and reported directly to MGM police chief Hendry and to Strickling. Every bar, tavern, restaurant and hotel within 25 miles of the studio was given a private phone number that rang directly to Strickling. He was called the moment Tracy *entered* the bar. The squad was dispatched directly to the location, where they waited for Tracy to get drunk. Then they physically wrestled him out of the bar, took him home and forced him to remain there under their guard.

Tracy was relatively quiet for the rest of 1935, other than having a fistfight with director William Wellman at the Trocadero Restaurant during the summer. The common denominator was Loretta Young. Young had a yearlong affair with Tracy and several flings with Wellman on movie shoots, but Wellman was still smarting from her rejection on the *Call of the Wild* set. Before the ambulance squad could react, Wellman punched the drunken Tracy and knocked him over another guest's table. Tracy was carted off by his handlers.

That same week Strickling got a call from Loretta Young's mother. After *Call of the Wild* filming ended and Gable earned an Academy Award for *It Happened One Night*, he signed the biggest contract at MGM and also of all time to that time. Gable was still having an affair with Elizabeth Allen, wife Ria Langham was still at home, and he was at work on *China Seas* with Jean Harlow. In May 1935, Young asked him to stop by the mansion she shared with her mother at 10935 Sunset Boulevard. Sitting in the living room, she told him she was pregnant. Gable was stunned, telling Young's mother, "I thought she knew how to take care of herself. She was married."[163] This had the makings of the biggest scandal in MGM history. Young was a fairly flexible Catholic but still went to daily mass; abortion was out of the question. She was going to have Gable's baby, but how?

Gable was older, married, and divorced. Young, a devout Catholic girl, was single. MGM knew their careers would be over if the news broke, and rumors were already starting. Gable called Strickling. Only Strickling and a few of Young's Twentieth Century bosses would know about the plan put into place that evening. The Young problem came on the heels of a studio payment of $2,000 — and arranging for the requisite abortion — after Gable got a young extra on *China Seas* pregnant.[164] Young was a much, much bigger problem. Strickling remembered a similar situation with Barbara LaMarr, who had gotten pregnant in 1922 and secretly given birth in Dallas. She briefly left her son in an orphanage before reclaiming him and bringing him back "adopted." Only her closest friends knew he was her real son. When drugs finally killed her in 1926, friend ZaSu Pitts and her husband raised young Don.[165] The same project was undertaken with Young.

They had to get Young out of Hollywood but she first had to shoot DeMille's *The Crusades,* her three-month pregnancy hidden by costumes and excuses. When filming was finished, the press was told she was "exhausted" and needed a "long rest cure." In late May she and her mother took a train to New York and boarded the *Il de France* for a six-month "rest." Reporters finally caught up with them literally as the gangway was being removed after they boarded ship. Industry people knew that no actor as popular as Young would be allowed a six-month break. Studios worked popular stars to exhaustion to take advantage of sometimes fleeting popularity. The story was taken as confirmation that she was pregnant.

Gable was assigned the Fletcher Christian role in Thalberg's *Mutiny on the Bounty* as Young was leaving for Europe. He hated the effeminate role and his costar Charles Laughton and originally refused to do it, but given the Young problem was forced to take a role he normally could have declined. He told reporters he did it as a favor to Thalberg. In October 1935, Gable was ordered on a publicity tour of the U.S. and South America to promote *Mutiny.* It was an unnecessary trip, since *The Call of the Wild* and *China Seas* were pulling in millions of dollars and *Mutiny* was a surefire hit. The studio didn't need publicity but they needed Gable out of the way, since Young was being secreted back to L.A. to give birth to his child.

It seems incongruous that Strickling would send Young away to hide her pregnancy but bring her back to have the baby. But Young wanted the child born in the U.S., and Strickling had to ensure proper medical care. If non-studio doctors and nurses attended the secret birth, the safety of their star, and their secret plan, would be at risk. Young was installed in a bungalow in the remote southern reaches of Venice Beach. Reporters on two continents had been searching for her for months after she dropped out of sight in England. They were camped out everywhere but the beach house that not a single press person knew existed. It was owned by Young's grandmother. (The neighborhood was later demolished to make way for the western runways at Los Angeles International Airport. What remains is an outline of cracked roadways and sidewalks arrayed on a hillside above the Coast Highway and the beach.) For the last two months of her pregnancy Young remained secluded inside the home with studio nurses.

There would be one trip outside the house, necessitated because of ever-growing press comments. Strickling simply couldn't hide her any longer. He had already told reporters that Young's rest was extended due to a mystery illness, but now people were guessing at other causes. Was she scarred in a terrible car accident? Did she have drug problems? Was she broke? For the moment the pregnancy rumors stopped, but when sister Sally Blane was married to Norman Foster at the Sunset Boulevard house neither Young nor her mother were there. UPI headlines screamed "COSTLY ILLNESS, FILMS DELAYED, YOUNG OUT FOR YEAR, FOUR FILMS CANCELLED." The papers speculated on theories but the Gable pregnancy rumor resurfaced with a vengeance.[166]

Ria Langham was also troubled, and by October was calling the Sunset house every day, asking to speak to Loretta and demanding that she renounce the rumors. Strickling knew something had to be done, and arranged for Dorothy Manners, an old friend and *Photoplay* writer, to meet with Young. Young was secreted from Venice to the Sunset house in a delivery van, and although she was entering her ninth month, was propped up in a bed overflowing with comforters and pillows covering all but her head. An intravenous bottle was rigged to drip into a pan under the bed. During the interview a studio nurse replaced the empty bottle several times. Young put on one of her finest performances, and after an hour, Manners was escorted out of the house. Later that evening Young was taken back to the beach.

Manner's article, "Fame, Fortune and Fatigue: The Real Truth about the Illness of Loretta Young," wouldn't run until January 1936, but Strickling arranged that snippets be released every week until then. "Hard work ... has aggravated an internal condition ... weakened her, sapped her strength; an eventual operation is the only remedy. In her present run-down condition she is not ready for that operation ... and may not be for a year!" Louella Parsons noted that Young had recovered from the "cough and cold that kept her in seclusion."[167]

Just before the baby was born, Gable arrived in New York aboard the liner *Pan America* from the South American tour. Langham had stayed home but also aboard for the week-long voyage was Lupe Velez, traveling without her spouse Johnny Weissmuller. Gable and Velez spent most of the cruise in her cabin. When Weissmuller saw his wife disembark in New York with Gable, MGM publicity men had to physically restrain their Tarzan from going after Gable, who quickly retreated to the protection of a waiting limousine.[168] MGM scheduled the *Mutiny* premiere in New York, far away from Hollywood, and scheduled it to occur as near Young's due date as could be estimated. On November 6, 1935, with Gable still in New York, doctors delivered a healthy baby girl. Young sent Gable a telegram telling him "BEAUTIFUL BLUE-EYED BLONDE BABY GIRL BORN 8:15 THIS MORNING." He tore it up and flushed the pieces down the toilet.[169] The premiere was the next night.

While Young was sequestered with her newborn in the Venice bungalow, the *Los Angeles Evening Herald Express* offered a short article hinting at the affair. Under a headline "THREE BEAUTIES LINKED IN CLARK GABLE ROMANCE," it is noted that "with cinema folks feeling that a spark of love sprang up during ... *Call of the Wild* ... [Young] is ill at home in Westwood." At the same time, Ria Langham, the erstwhile Mrs. Gable, who had financed his early career and endured a loveless marriage and a philandering husband, finally had had enough. On November 19, Louella Parsons announced the Gables were divorcing. Strickling made them wait until after his premiere and the birth of the Gable-Young child.

Young remained in Venice for three weeks recovering and was seen in public for the first time on November 30. The picture ran under the headline "LORETTA RECOVERS." Had reporters investigated birth records, they might have found the one filed on November 13 by MGM doctor Walter Holleran: Judith Young, born to mother Margaret Young and father "unknown." The mother was "22 yrs." old, born in "Salt Lake City, Utah," and in the "Motion Picture" industry. The record was apparently "misfiled" for several decades.

Fortunately for Strickling, a fresh scandal filled the papers at the same time, when comedienne Thelma Todd was found dead on December 18, sprawled across the front seat of her chocolate-colored 1934 Lincoln Phaeton parked in a hillside garage in the winding streets of Pacific Palisades above the beach. "Toddy" was a much-loved former school teacher who came to Hollywood after winning a Boston beauty pageant. Her nickname was "the Ice-Cream Blonde." Toddy had shared dinner on Saturday evening with Ida Lupino's family at the Trocadero. How she ended up dead in her car that cold Monday morning is still a mystery.

She began in the Laurel and Hardy shorts *Unaccustomed as We Are* (1929) and *Chickens Come Home* (1930) but a comedy serial with best friend ZaSu Pitts made her a star. Todd was also a Groucho Marx favorite; he featured her in *Monkee Business* (1931) and *Horse Feathers* (1932). She shared a duplex apartment with director Roland West in a building below the garage on Roosevelt Highway (now the Pacific Coast Highway) just north of Sunset Boulevard. Todd and West were once lovers but now lived in separate second-floor units above her popular Thelma Todd's Sidewalk Café and a small drugstore. Todd owned the building and West was a partner in the restaurant. The building remains unchanged today, as have the narrow, winding streets, named after towns on the island of Sicily, that meander across the hills above the café. The development was originally called Castellammare after the fishing port Castellammare del Golfo. The Sicilian village was the birthplace of the vendetta. A vendetta killed Todd.

At night she parked her car in a garage belonging to actress Jewel Carmen, Roland West's former wife, who lived in a large mansion above the garage. Between the garage and Todd's apartment below was a long—almost 300 steps—and very steep stairway. Her body was found by her maid, who brought Todd's car down to the café each morning. Todd was wedged under the steering wheel on the seat, blood spattered in the car, on her clothes, and on her face. She had an apparent broken nose (and broken ribs found later), deep bruises on her face and throat, and her front tooth was chipped. She had been severely beaten, but the official version was different. Eddie Mannix knew all the players.

Todd and Mannix were friends. She had been married to Pat DiCicco, one of Mannix's mobster friends. Pasquale DiCicco was a gangster, bootlegger and pimp who told women he was an agent. He was related to the Broccoli fortune, but was a lowlife, an amoral con artist. He worked for Charles Luciano, real name Salvatore Luciana, better known as Lucky. The New York killer came to Hollywood to gain a foothold in the lucrative L.A. drug business, but first organized a syndicate shakedown of the studios. Rival mobsters called him Charlie Lucifer. He was the devil. Todd met Luciano after she and DiCicco eloped to Arizona on July 18, 1932. The union was stormy and he often beat her, so on March 3, 1934, Thelma divorced him. Strangely, she then began dating Luciano, continuing an affair that began during her marriage and went on for the last year of her life.

Police behaved strangely from the moment they descended on the

Thelma Todd with Zeppo (left) and Harpo Marx during 1932 filming of *Horse Feathers*. She was murdered less than three years later.

garage at 17531 Posetano Road. Strangely, Chief Detective Bert Wallis and Chief Medical Examiner A.F. Wagner both came personally involved, unusual even for a high-profile death. They ordered police out of the garage, spent an hour investigating the crime scene alone, and emerged to tell the crowd that Todd had died from carbon monoxide poisoning. According to Wagner, when West locked her out after a quarrel she walked the 270 steps up the hill, climbed into her running car, passed out and died. But reporters asked about the visible injuries and blood-soaked body. Wallis suggested she broke her nose and tooth by hitting the steering wheel during her death throes. The broken piece of tooth was never found even after an exhaustive search of the car, though. Wagner would later suggest she broke two ribs the same way. His curious explanation for bruises on Todd's throat and neck? He said they were caused by "postmortem lividity." Such a determination is not supported by medical fact. He also inexplicably placed the time of death at 2:00 A.M. Sunday morning, more than 36 hours before. But Todd's body was just starting to show signs of rigor mortis when police arrived: She had been dead for no more than five or six hours. She was not killed late Saturday night; she was killed Sunday night. Wagner's comments made no sense.[170]

Strangely, Wallis and Wagner then let photographers enter the garage and posed for photos with Todd's body. For over an hour the crime scene was trampled by photographers and reporters. The death certificate indicated death due to carbon monoxide poisoning, but made no mention of the numerous physical injuries. There are dozens of problems with the official version. Todd was legally drunk but her blood alcohol level was only .13, barely above the legal limit. That would not be nearly enough to make Todd pass out. She would not have climbed up the steep concrete stairwell, a difficult and tiring trek, in the dark and cold. In the unlikely event she had, her shoes would have been scuffed; hers were pristine. Also, she would not have slept in the car. She would have driven somewhere to sleep, or awakened her accountant Charles Smith, who lived in the small apartment above the garage.

Todd was clearly beaten to death and placed in the car. D.A. Fitts probably knew that as well as the police and coroners, and probably would have let it die at Wallis and Wagner's hands had it not been for Todd's mother. Alice Todd warned him, "You know my daughter was murdered. I know my daughter was murdered. There's going to be an investigation. Either you solve this or I'll do some investigating of my own." Only after she slammed the door and stormed out did Fitts open even a halfhearted investigation.[171] Fitts did not want to tangle with Lucky Luciano. When Luciano had begun killing L.A. drug dealers earlier, he sent an emissary to Fitts' office with a five-word message: "Stay out of the way." Fitts never investigated Luciano, but to make sure, Luciano had two employees planted in Fitts' offices. He knew what Fitts was doing every minute. Even so, publicity forced Fitts to convene a grand jury.

A minor autopsy note threw the Todd investigation into a frenzy. There were traces of recently eaten peas and carrots in her stomach, but neither was served at the Lupino dinner Saturday night, supposedly her last meal. Todd's peas and carrots were eaten *within six hours of her death on Sunday night*. The entire Wallis-Wagner version crumbled under the vegetables and the question, "Where was Thelma Todd Sunday?"

Her relationship with Luciano led to rumors that he wanted her Sidewalk Café as a casino, and to an often-repeated legend that she refused Luciano's demands, so he had her killed. She allegedly said he would get her café "over my dead body," and he replied, "That can be arranged." That conversation probably never took place. Gambling was a low priority for Luciano. He was making millions from mob-controlled movie unions and even more selling drugs. Between 1929 and 1934 Luciano had taken over L.A. drug territories by bribing or murdering competing dealers. The studio dealers were replaced by Luciano's thugs, with access from DiCicco. Gambling was simply not important enough for Luciano to kill Todd.

As in any good murder mystery, there were a number of possible suspects. West was a suspect. He was obsessed with his former lover, upset that she would not marry him, and jealous of her relationships. Being separated from her by sliding doors must have been hard for him, but not enough to drive him to murder. On his deathbed he allegedly confessed to director Hal Roach that he had "killed Toddy." He may have felt responsible for her death by locking her out the night she was killed, but his near-death delirium is not supported by evidence.

Shadowy café accountant Charles Smith acted strangely in the days surrounding the murder. Todd did not trust Smith, whom she suspected of stealing from her on his own or of passing money to the mob. She had secretly arranged for an audit just after the holidays. Also, Smith was renting the apartment above the garage where Todd died. The apartment is directly above a garage, both carved into a hillside, yet he heard nothing; no screams, no scuffles, and no rumbling of Todd's truck-loud, 12-cylinder Phaeton as it filled the garage with smoke and fumes. Nor did he smell anything.

Todd's underworld connections led to her murder, but not because Luciano wanted to open a casino in her café. Luciano was indeed putting pressure to open a casino there, but he was directing the pressure at West, who was a partner in the restaurant. It was simply not important enough for Luciano to kill someone as well known as Todd. There was a casino of sorts already operating above the café before Luciano arrived, a fact not known by historians until now. Rudy Schafer's father was the manager of the Sidewalk Café. The name was often misspelled "Schaefer" in period reports; he was Jewel Carmen's brother. Rudy wrote, "Yes, there was a gambling casino in the floor above the restaurant." He remembered his father taking him to the "upstairs room and telling me that is where Thelma's friends play various games of chance. I'm not sure, but I believe there was a roulette wheel along with card tables of various kinds. There were slot machines, but they were downstairs. Nickel machines as I recall. This was no big deal for the time. You saw them all over ... the local drug store had them." He said that his "understanding was that the casino was an informal kind of thing for Thelma and her guests, but later on the 'baddies' wanted in. L.A. was notoriously corrupt in those days." Schafer said his stepmother, who was a waitress at the café, said "she and others were told that they would be killed if they revealed anything they knew. I tried several times to get her to talk about Thelma, her death, the café, but she would just freeze up and get this frightened look on her face. Even late in life she refused to talk about it at all."[172]

I believe Luciano did order Todd's death, but not over gambling. She was murdered because she knew too much about his involvement in the movie industry IATSE bribes. She was much more dangerous to Luciano as a federal witness to bribes than as a failed gambling partner. Her friends knew she and Luciano talked frequently about his problems with mobsters Frank Nitti, George Browne and Willie Bioff, who ran the largest movie studio employee union, the IATSE. Another possibility that has never been investigated is that perhaps it was a mob hit, ordered not *by* Luciano but a warning *to* Luciano. At the time of her murder, Todd's relationship with Luciano was not a secret. At the same time Luciano was involved in an escalating battle with Nitti, Capone's heir as head of the Chicago mob and the brains behind the movie industry IATSE bribes. Nitti was not only controlling movie union money but was slowly taking over Luciano's L.A. drug territory. Luciano was unable to stop Nitti; his power was rooted in New York while Nitti's ties to L.A. through Johnny Roselli were stronger. Luciano heard rumblings that Nitti wanted a piece of his L.A. gambling in addition to his drug territories. Luciano and Nitti hated each other, and Luciano was the sworn enemy of Nitti's boss Al Capone, but neither could afford a mob war in L.A. which would have stopped the money flow back to New York and Chicago.

From a mob angle it is just as likely that Nitti had Todd killed as a threat to Luciano as that Luciano killed her. Todd probably signed her own death warrant when she contacted Fitts' office on December 11 and made an appointment for Thursday, December 17, at 11:00 A.M. Luciano (and probably Nitti) would have found out immediately through their moles in the D.A.'s office. On Friday, December 13, just after Todd made her appointment, Luciano boarded a plane in New York and flew to L.A. for an unannounced visit. Both men stood to lose if Todd told the government what she knew about the mob dealings that had put Browne and Bioff at the head of the IATSE movie union. Nobody knows why Todd was going to meet with Fitts. She was smart enough to know that talking about Luciano would mean death. In the months before her death she received several death threats and ransom demands, but it isn't likely she wanted to talk about that. The Todd-Fitts meeting remains a mystery.

It appears from DeCicco's actions that weekend that he probably knew she was about to be killed. After their 1934 divorce, DiCicco rarely visited L.A. from New York. But for reasons never revealed, he showed up at the café the Wednesday before her death and later showed up uninvited at the Lupino Saturday dinner party attended by Todd. After fidgeting nervously through dinner, he excused himself from the table and made a phone call. After he returned he left the small party without saying goodnight to any of the dozen guests. Why was DiCicco watching Todd?

Todd got her private life intermingled with the underworld. Somewhere in that murky world lies the solution to her murder. The most likely scenario was that Luciano had Todd killed, not over failed intentions for her café but because she knew about his operations in L.A. She was killed to keep her quiet. Accountant Smith probably was funneling money to Luciano's mob friends. Every restaurant in L.A. was being shaken down, especially popular spots susceptible to mysterious fires or labor troubles. Friends said Todd was nervous and frightened about something the last weeks of her life. Was it Luciano? She was seen by literally dozens of people with a man said to be him, during the last day of her life, the day she was supposed to be dead: Sunday.

Activities by Todd on Sunday—after the time police said she had died—were revealed during an otherwise pointless grand jury convened by Fitts three days after the murder. His attempt to quietly sweep Todd's death under a rug was blown when witnesses having nothing to do with Todd came forward and testified to having seen her, in the company of an Italian-looking man resembling Luciano, during the day Sunday.

W.F. Persson owned a cigar shop at Figueroa and Eighth Streets in downtown L.A., and was shocked when a crying blonde in a mink coat stumbled into his store Sunday morning and asked to use the phone. Customer Robert E. Fischer recognized Todd, and the two men watched her leave in a brown convertible with an olive-skinned man. Both Luciano and Todd drove brown convertibles. At 4:00 P.M. several people saw Todd in a drugstore at Sunset and Laurel Canyon in Hollywood, making another phone call. That call was to Martha Ford, wife of actor Wallace Ford, who testified Todd called her at 4:00 P.M. on Sunday to confirm she would be at a party that evening. Next, a Santa Monica councilman testified that he and his family were shocked to see Thelma Todd in a brown convertible next to them at a Beverly Hills stoplight Sunday afternoon. In a final bizarre coincidence, Jewel Carmen herself testified that she saw Todd and Luciano in the brown convertible Sunday afternoon on Sunset Boulevard, heading west toward the beach. She was the seventh witness who saw Todd on Sunday.

Bob Anderson, a bartender at the café and also a mechanic who took care of cars for Todd, West, and Carmen, accidentally solved the riddle of the brown car when he testified. Called simply to confirm that Todd was gone all day Sunday, he said that Todd's car was empty and backed into the garage when he checked the garage for West early Sunday afternoon. When Todd's body was found the car was parked facing front, into the garage. It was driven Sunday.

Thelma Todd was murdered. It was almost certainly ordered by Lucky

Luciano to stop her from talking about what she knew about his operations in L.A. It is certain that she was alive Sunday in the company of a
man resembling Luciano. We don't know if Eddie helped with the publicity surrounding Todd's death. But DiCicco and Roselli were two of his oldest, closest friends, and he knew Luciano. Todd appeared in a number of
MGM films, so he obviously knew her well also. Her last film was MGM's
The Bohemian Girl (1935), filmed just before her murder. Fitts closed the
case. Luciano flew out of L.A. at 7:45 A.M. Monday morning before anyone even knew Todd had been murdered. He never returned. DiCicco left
at 9:00 A.M. He was back, and in the middle of another murder, just a few
years later.

To replace Todd, Hal Roach hired platinum blonde Lyda Roberti —
a 30-year-old former European circus performer — who came from vaudeville to Hollywood by 1932. She did comedies with stars like Eddie Cantor,
W.C. Fields, and Jack Oakie, and was a rising star. Roberti did three serial episodes with Todd's ex-partner Patsy Kelly, and a week after the last
one was released in 1937, she bent over to tie her shoelaces, suffered a massive heart attack and fell to the studio floor, dead.

After spending a year there, writer Raymond Chandler said of L.A.,
"Law is where you buy it in this town." That was nowhere more evident
than in the studios' relationship with Fitts. The influence the studios had
over him can be viewed in one of the few documents pertaining to Fitts
that survives. Before joining the D.A.'s office, Fitts was a defense attorney.
He earned his first courtroom victory defending his brother, a cement
contractor who murdered a business rival. His brother's company was tied
to L.A. mobsters, and government contracts were obtained by paying
bribes. He was acquitted and Fitts joined the D.A.'s office.

Buried in the UCLA political history archives is a yellowed copy of
Fitts' "1936 Primaries Listed Contribution" form, which was reported to
regulators. The carbon copy of the original listing included just over 70
names with contributions totaling $23,963.62 ($500,000 today). Incredibly, all but about $4,000 of the total came from studios. Sixty-five of the
70 donors were studio employees. No studio is absent from the fascinating list. Jack Warner donated $3,000 ($50,000 today), but the list is dominated by MGM. Mayer and Thalberg gave $2,000 each, Joe Schenck $1,000,
and Darryl Zanuck $1,000. Other MGM employees were forced by Mayer
to donate, including his son-in-law Bill Goetz, who "donated" $1,000,
twice his weekly salary.

Vic Orsatti, brother of mobster-turned-agent Frank Orsatti, gave
$1,000. Directors and producers such as Hunt Stromberg and Cecil B.
DeMille offered thousands. Actors such as Charles "Buddy" Rogers, Wal-

lace Beery, and Edmund Goulding were also included. Interestingly, both Beery and Goulding had recently avoided serious legal problems with studio help. In today's dollars the larger contributions are over $100,000. But these donations amount to a fraction of the total that studios gave Fitts.

During late 1935 Mannix finally got his hands on the original negative of the porn film made by a young Joan Crawford.[173] Mannix and Strickling were aware of that the film existed when they signed Crawford in 1925. During the intervening years Mannix had purchased several dozen copies, and was rumored to show it to his friends during their weekly card games. Regional MGM offices around the globe had standing orders to purchase any copies they came across, and Mannix was alleged to have arranged for a payment of just over $100,000 ($2 million today) for the negative of the lesbian porn film, which he promptly destroyed.[174]

In addition to crooked police and D.A.s, Mannix and Strickling and MGM had hundreds of crooked lawyers to turn to. The most famous and reliable during the 1930s and 1940s was Jerry Giesler. Strickling could dial CR6–6633 — the private line at Giesler's 522 Foothill mansion — at any time. "Get me Giesler" was the portly attorney's nom de guerre. He handled virtually every famous Hollywood case and seemingly always won. With studio clout on top of his legal expertise, he was unbeatable. Whenever a star walked out of court free, Giesler's smiling face was in the picture. One of his most famous cases during the 1930s involved noted choreographer and director Busby Berkeley.

Berkeley was the most successful choreographer in Hollywood history. He began in the army in World War I, conducting and directing large formal parades. After the war, he worked in New York for Flo Ziegfeld and came to Hollywood to work for Goldwyn and Warners. His signature production numbers were intricately choreographed and involved hundreds of dancers. By 1935 he was a legend, and a serious alcoholic.

Returning home from a party on the evening of September 8, 1935, a drunken Berkeley crossed the median on the Pacific Coast Highway just north of Sunset and slammed into two cars, killing three members of a family in one car and seriously injuring the two people in the other. He was charged with three counts of second degree murder. His first call was to Whitey Hendry at MGM. Hendry called Giesler. Over the course of two years Giesler navigated three trials, the first opening on the day Thelma Todd's body was discovered a half-mile from Berkeley's accident site. Giesler had Berkeley brought to court on a gurney covered with a sheet, his head and leg swathed in bandages. He arranged for dubious "experts" who testified that defective tires that were "cancerous" caused the accident. Even though witnesses claimed Berkeley was drunk,[175] Giesler and the studios arranged for a dozen Warners and MGM stars, led by Pat O'Brien, Frank McHugh, and director Mervyn LeRoy, to testify that Berkeley was sober when he left the party. McHugh testified that he didn't see one of the 200 party guests have a single drink. After two hung juries Berkeley was somehow acquitted. The studio paid $100,000 to settle civil suits. But as musicals lost their favor in the late 1930s, Berkeley's career stalled.

On January 11, 1936, Strickling received a late-night telephone call from John Gilbert's Tower Drive hacienda. Gilbert's downward spiral had come to an end on the floor of his living room. Who made the call has been the subject of speculation since that night. Mayer's vendetta against Gilbert rendered him almost unbankable as early as 1933. His final MGM role was a small role in the awful *Fast Workers* (1933). *The New York Evening Post* noted, "[that] such a story should be given to John Gilbert is regrettable."[176] Mayer piled on the indignities to the last. When filming was completed and his contract with MGM over, Gilbert went to his dressing room to find that Mayer was already having it remodeled.

Mayer ordered Strickling to tell the press that MGM might re-sign Gilbert. Everyone knew that would never happen, but no studio would invest in a contract that MGM had the power to invalidate. So Gilbert could not work anywhere, and from 1934 to 1936 hid out at his hilltop estate, moped about Garbo, and drank. Earlier, Garbo had tried to help Gilbert by forcing Mayer to replace Laurence Olivier with Gilbert on *Queen Christina*, but Mayer forced him to sign another long-term contract to get the job, effectively prolonging his inability to work, and then only paid him one tenth of his last contract.[177] On March 20, 1934, Gilbert took out a full-page ad on the back cover of the *Hollywood Reporter*:

> Metro-Goldwyn-Mayer
> will neither
> offer me work
> nor
> release me from
> my contract
> Jack Gilbert

It didn't matter; he remained desperately unemployed, telling *Movie Classic* magazine, "Four short years ago I had a contract calling for $250,000 a picture. Today I can't get a job for $25 a week." One of his old friends, director Walter Connelly, arranged for Columbia to hire him for *The Captain Hates the Sea,* but in his scenes Gilbert's drunken swaying was noticeable. This was the last view of John Gilbert, once the biggest star in Hollywood, on film. In 1934, Marlene Dietrich resumed a relationship with Gilbert and tried to stop his slide. She tried in vain to get him to stop drinking, and in December 1935 Gilbert suffered a complete nervous collapse due to his increased drinking. He barely survived, with Dietrich at his side day and night. He was bedridden into 1936, and during the predawn hours of January 9, 1936, a drunken Gilbert passed out and swallowed his tongue, dying in a pool of vomit. His face was distorted, his eyes open. Dietrich found him and tried to revive him, then called her doctor, Leo Masden, and Strickling. Masden rushed to Tower Drive, but it was too late.

Strickling ordered Dietrich out, so she gathered up everything of hers, stuffed it all into a pillowcase, and left.[178] Masden waited until the morning to call the fire department. Even though it was evident when they arrived that Gilbert had been dead for some time, the time of death was listed as 9:05 A.M. It was part of Strickling's plan to ensure nobody knew Dietrich was there when he died. The secret was kept for 40 years before her daughter admitted the truth. Mayer boycotted the funeral, a final snub. Dietrich passed out sobbing in the church. Gilbert's friend Cedric Gibbons said of Mayer and Thalberg, "Goddamn them, it didn't make any difference to them. Nobody cared."[179]

In May 1936, Jean Harlow called Strickling in a panic, pregnant. She was in a passionate relationship with William Powell, whom she wanted to marry. Powell would not marry, so she didn't tell him she was pregnant. Though she wanted with all her heart to have the baby, she called Strickling to arrange for an abortion, heartbroken. Strickling arranged for "Mrs. Jean Carpenter" to enter Good Shepherd Hospital, according to the hospital, "to get some rest." She was seen only by her own private doctors and nurses. She was given room 826, coincidently the same room occupied by her a year earlier when she underwent an "appendectomy." Three days later after undergoing the abortion she did not want, Harlow returned home. The final note in "Mrs. Carpenter's" record was her doctor's scrawled note, "Accomplished purpose."[180]

One of Harlow's first bosses was Howard Hughes, who hired her for *Hell's Angels* in 1927. He came from Texas in 1925 to get into the movies with no experience, but a trust fund paying him $10,000 every day ($300,000 today) from his father's mining patents (his drill bits are still used today). He was an adventurer and record-setting pilot and an active bisexual who dated Cary Grant when he first came to Hollywood. As Harlow was recuperating from her abortion, Hughes was involved in an automobile accident that showed again the corruptibility of the L.A. police and courts. On July 11, 1936, Hughes and a young woman left Trader Vic's with

Pat DiCicco—his "mourning" over Thelma Todd was over—and headed to the beach in Hughes' Duesenberg. At the corner of Third and Lorraine he struck and killed a man. Witnesses told police the victim was in the crosswalk and that Hughes hit him traveling at a high speed. Hughes was charged with vehicular homicide.

The victim, 59-year-old Gabe Meyer, lived a block away with his sister and her husband. Every night he walked home from his job selling furniture at the May Department Store. Just a few days later, L.A. County Coroner Frank Nance—who had recently signed off on the bogus Thelma Todd death certificate—held a brief inquest and pronounced Hughes not guilty of anything, even though there were 50 feet of skid marks and Mayer was hurled almost 100 feet.[181] Hughes paid Meyer's family $10,000 ($300,000 today) to help them "in their time of need."[182] No doubt that was not the only payment made by Hughes.

Through that winter of 1935 and 1936 Loretta Young's newborn daughter Judith stayed at the Venice beach house, cared for by studio nurses. Records at St. Paul the Apostle Church in Westwood show that "Mary Judith Clark, Child of William Clark and Margaret Clark," was baptized on December 27. According to Judy Lewis, in late January 1936, Gable came to see the baby after the couple was secreted into the Venice bungalow. In early July, Strickling arranged that the child be taken to St. Elizabeth's Infant Hospital in San Francisco, a home for unwed mothers run by nuns. Judy would stay there for a year, but regular checks from MGM continued to arrive at St. Elizabeth's for years afterward.

A young Howard Hughes at the time of his 1920s arrival in Hollywood, already dogged by rumors about his sexuality.

Strickling and Young always planned to get the child back to her. In the 1930s, actresses routinely gave up unwanted children and abortion was so common that Dietrich described it as "our birth control," [183] but in this case that was not possible. For fans to discover Loretta Young had given up Clark Gable's baby was absolutely unfathomable to the studio. The final part of the plan would not take place for another year.

There was another funeral that summer but unlike Gilbert's, Mayer couldn't ignore this one. He and Irving Thalberg had rarely spoken after Thalberg's public demotion. Thalberg hated Mayer, but Mayer still maintained that he had removed Thalberg because he was worried about his health, which finally caught up with him over the Labor Day weekend. Thalberg and Norma Shearer spent the weekend in Monterey with their friends Jack and Virginia Conway, Sam Wood, and Chico Marx. The group spent the evening of September 5 playing bridge on the balcony of their suite. Thalberg caught a cold that within a week would destroy his already frail body. The next weekend he was absent from the employee picnic at Clarence Brown's Encino ranch for the first time since MGM's founding. He sent a telegram that Mannix read to a somber crowd: "ONLY ILLNESS PREVENTS ME FROM BEING WITH YOU." Later that afternoon he told Bernie Hyman, "They don't know what they're doing. They're killing me. No, Bernie. This time I'm not going to make it."[184] Sunday night he slipped into a coma at his Santa Monica home and early Monday morning, September 15, he died from bronchial pneumonia.

Strickling wrote a fictionalized version of Thalberg's death for the press. Thalberg supposedly died surrounded by friends, reciting the Lord's Prayer, after bravely telling his wife, "Don't let the children forget me." When Mayer arrived at the house, he burst into tears. As studio workers found out about his death, MGM came to a halt. Employees at every level wept openly on the lot. The emotional public reactions were interesting, given his aversion to such displays and his aloofness, but they cried nonetheless. His funeral took place two days later as MGM closed for the first time before or since. Hendry's police force kept order at the funeral, as 10,000 fans crowded nearby sidewalks. Strickling's publicity staff directed the famous faces to the B'nai B'rith Temple on Wilshire Boulevard. Mayer sent a seven-foot-wide spray of flowers with a live dove inside a gilded cage. After the service, as Mayer sat in his limousine, he elbowed Mannix in the ribs, smiled and asked rhetorically, "Ain't God good to me?"[185]

He then returned directly to the studio and oversaw the dismantling of Thalberg's production unit and the emptying of his office. He ordered director Edmund Goulding removed from the lot. It was Goulding whose sexual peccadilloes had so offended Mayer; it was only Thalberg's support that kept him on the payroll. By the end of the day, almost all traces of his former partner and protégé had been excised.

MGM had an embarrassing problem with Norma Shearer in the months after her return. Thalberg had a weak appetite for sex and after his marriage it all but disappeared. When Thalberg died Shearer was beautiful, just 35, and apparently intent upon making up for lost time. MGM employees openly referred to her as the Merry Widow as she tore through affairs with David Niven, George Raft, James Stewart, and Clark Gable. During the *Marie Antoinette* filming just months after Thalberg died, Shearer stalked Tyrone Power, trying to get him into bed. Mannix called Shearer in when he learned she was having sex with Mickey Rooney, MGM's juvenile star of the *Andy Hardy* series. He was barely 16 when Shearer invited him to her trailer and seduced him. When Rooney's mother went to Strickling, she also asked if he could perhaps get Mickey to stop spending so much money on prostitutes! Mayer ordered Rooney away from Shearer, telling him, "You're Andy Hardy for chrissakes. Act like it."[186]

In early May 1937, Gable and Harlow began filming *Saratoga*. Even after 13 movies in five years at MGM, the star was still gracious to cast and crew and a hard worker. But unknown to the *Saratoga* crew, Harlow was gravely ill. Coworkers asked about her bloating and the unhealthy gray sheen to her normally perfect skin, but "the Baby" just said she was tired. On May 29, near the end of the three-week shoot, she was in obvious pain but insisted on completing a scene with Walter Pidgeon, telling a script man, "Please tell Walt to hold me lightly. My stomach is killing me."[187] Minutes later she stumbled off the set, doubled over in pain, and retreated to the 512 Palm Drive house she shared with her mother. A doctor called by her mother mistakenly diagnosed gall bladder trouble, while she was actually suffering from uremic poisoning caused by an infection from wisdom teeth surgery the month before. He prescribed liquids, which worsened the uremic poisoning. Worse, her mother's Christian Science beliefs forbade going to a hospital, where the condition would have been quickly recognized.

Instead, Harlow lay in her bed at home. Her mother refused to let any MGM friends visit during the week she lay slowly dying. Finally, on June 4 Gable and Frank Morgan angrily forced their way in past Mama Jean. What they saw sickened them. Harlow had bloated to twice her normal size and reeked of urine, a sure sign of uremic poisoning. Gable called Strickling, who rushed to the house with Mayer and Dr. Edward Jones. Mama Jean refused to let them in, recalling Jones' false statements about Jean's marriage to Paul Bern. When a different doctor saw Jean on June 6, he realized she was near death and rushed her to Good Shepherd Hospital. She was placed in room 826, the same room where she had undergone her abortions and the oral surgery that caused her death. By the time she arrived the illness was too advanced, the damage too severe. When her favorite aunt begged her to get better Harlow sighed through the pain, "I don't want to."[188] Her kidneys shut down and she died on the morning of June 7, 1937.

Harlow's death shocked the industry. Writer Harry Ruskin said, "On the day Baby died, there wasn't one sound in the MGM commissary for three hours. Not one goddamn sound."[189] Just crying. Harlow was buried next to Thalberg in a Forest Lawn crypt selected by Mama Jean, who told the press it was paid for "by William Powell." He knew nothing about it, but nonetheless, he paid. He was flabbergasted when he discovered the crypt cost $30,000 ($500,000 today).

Not everyone reacted to Harlow's death with tears. When a crew member on the set of *Captains Courageous* told Spencer Tracy, who adored Harlow, he simply walked off the set. He went back to his sixth-floor suite at the Beverly Wilshire Hotel where the next day he got into a drunken fight with his brother Carroll. The hotel alerted Strickling, and Hendry and his crew were dispatched there. When he was let into the locked room, Hendry sprinted to the balcony just in time to stop Tracy from throwing his brother over the railing to his death.[190] His attendants carted Tracy off to a sanitarium and Strickling told the press that *Courageous* filming was suspended while Tracy recovered from pneumonia. A week later, Tracy escaped from the private hospital and was seen by a reporter in a Hollywood bar. When he approached Tracy in the bathroom, Tracy punched him and shoved him into a urinal. His ambulance crew ushered him back to the sanitarium and shooting was delayed for two months while he dried out.

In the few weeks before and after Harlow's death Mannix and Strickling were dealing with two events, each with potentially immeasurable impact to MGM. The first was played out in front of millions of fans. The second was kept a secret for 50 years.

Ten days after Harlow's death, a wedding took place that shocked movie fans and studio people alike. In the three years since their MGM debuts, Jeanette MacDonald and Nelson Eddy—she, the most talented diva to ever appear in movies and he, a singer who couldn't act—had become the biggest musical duo in the history of the movies. From their 1935 debut, *Naughty Marietta*, to *Rose Marie* and *San Francisco* in 1936, they shared an on-screen chemistry rivaling that of Gilbert and Garbo. But their personal relationship was a mess. Strickling led millions of fans to believe there was romance between the two, hiding Eddy's sexual ambiguity, MacDonald's promiscuity, and the bizarre and contradictory relationship between them. By the summer of 1937 everyone everywhere believed that Eddy and MacDonald would marry. But in 1935 she began dating Gene Raymond, who was an odd choice to say the least. He worked for Paramount and RKO and as early as 1932 was featured in a magazine article titled "Indifferent to Girls." RKO kept him until the parents of a teenaged boy threatened to sue after they learned Raymond was dating their son. The studio paid the family and fired Raymond, whom MGM hired soon after for reasons still unknown.

For some reason — jealousy perhaps, since he was bedding MacDonald in his office and felt that Eddy was unacceptable for her — Mayer tried to torpedo the Eddy-MacDonald pairing. He encouraged her to marry Raymond and posted studio security guards outside her dressing room to keep Eddy away. When MacDonald surprisingly announced her marriage to Raymond, Mayer forced Eddy to sing at the ceremony. On June 16, 1937, MacDonald married Raymond. Outside the church 15,000 fans lined the streets; inside the church Eddy's loud sobs almost drowned out the vows. During the first days of the planned two-month Hawaiian honeymoon, MacDonald learned of Raymond's bisexuality or homosexuality. She returned to L.A. the next day, six weeks early. Eddy was still distraught, for whatever reason. The Raymonds settled into a tumultuous relationship, marked by pitched public battles and affairs of all kinds.

Eddy's heartbreak is hard to figure. He was bisexual but at many times during his life had experimental affairs with women. Although he always returned to men, there were at least three confirmed aborted pregnancies attributed to him, and at least one illegitimate child. The child, a boy, was the result of an affair with married Philadelphia socialite Maybelle Marston in 1934. Probably due to the intervention of Strickling, no record of birth survives. The son, named Jon, survives. Earlier in 1935 MacDonald found herself pregnant. Eddy assumed that he was the father, but Raymond — or perhaps even Mayer — may have been responsible. Mayer told her to "get rid of the problem ... and that chowder head."[191] The chowder head was Eddy. She told her friends, who knew she was pregnant, that she had a sudden miscarriage, but Strickling and MGM arranged for an abortion.

Eddy's sexuality became an issue when a 1937 *Motion Picture* magazine article titled "Who's Whose" listed literally hundreds of stars and their respective mates or girlfriends. But Eddy's picture had none next to it, just a Strickling statement, "M-G-M is still looking for romance for him." Louella Parsons, long since gone from the MGM lot with Hearst and Davies and turning into a vocal critic of anything MGM, wrote "The big laugh in Hollywood these days is Nelson Eddy's feminine pursuers. Strange that Clark Gable, Gary Cooper, Dick Powell, or the other handsome male heroes have never suffered the embarrassment of having so many girls ready to die at their feet. Come on, Mr. Eddy, think up a new one. Even the hinterlands are wise to you." A furious Mayer demanded Strickling find a woman for Eddy. But MGM had more important and more dangerous concerns during those very busy weeks in June 1937.

Everyone knew about Harlow's tragic death, MacDonald's wedding, and Eddy's personal problems. But no one knew that just a few weeks earlier, at MGM's annual sales convention, a young extra was brutally raped by an MGM employee. It could have closed the studio, which is why Mayer, Mannix and Strickling made sure the story stayed buried. It stayed that way for 65 years, uncovered by David Stenn, writer of celebrated biographies of Clara Bow and Jean Harlow, who brought it to light in a 2003 *Vanity Fair* article.[192]

The 1936–1937 year was phenomenally successful for MGM. With films like *Mutiny on the Bounty, China Seas, The Great Ziegfeld* and *Romeo and Juliet*, MGM would earn $12 million in profits ($150 million today). The Annual Sales Convention would be a raucous celebration of the studio's success and for the first time in the studio's history, Mayer held the five-day meeting in Culver City. It began on Sunday, June 1, 1937. A private train started in New York City and picked conventioneers up in various cities along the way before proceeding on to L.A. By the time the Sante Fe train arrived, the 282 conventioneers had been on a three-day, transcontinental binge. In Pasadena, young starlets hired to pin carnations on their lapels were kissed and groped by men crawling off the train.

Mayer welcomed the men at the station, saying, "Our fine Chief of Police Davis remarked to me a moment ago that we must think a lot of these men to have sent the beauty that he sees before him," referring to the dozens of young women arrayed before the men. He continued, "These lovely girls, and you have the finest of them, greet you, and that's to show you how we feel about you, and the kind of a good time that's ahead of you. Anything you want." The implication was clear: the women were there to show the 282 men a good time. The meeting began with a loud Sunday evening dinner at the Ambassador Hotel and continued the next day at the Culver City lot, where 4,000 confetti-throwing employees lined "the Alley" while the chosen 282 marched past a band playing "The Gang's All Here." The men shared lunch at the commissary with all of MGM's biggest stars including Gable and Crawford.

By Wednesday the delegates had been drinking for a week. Activities culminated at a huge Western barbeque described in the convention bulletin: "YIPPEE! GET SET FOR WILD WEST SHOW AT ROACH'S. WEDNESDAY, JUNE 5, 1937. IT WILL BE A STAG AFFAIR, OUT IN THE WILD AND WOOLLY WEST WHERE 'MEN ARE MEN.'" The gathering was at an outdoor lot farther south in Culver City owned by MGM-affiliated producer Hal Roach. It was known as Rancho Roachero. Waiting for the 300 conventioneers were 120 female MGM dancers and girls who had answered a small newspaper ad for MGM party hostesses. For $7.50 and a hot lunch they were told they would work at a studio function. They were fitted with short suedette skirts, tight bolero jackets, leather-studded cuffs and black boots, and were layered in makeup. At 4:00 they were herded to Rancho Roachero and told to wait — two to a table — inside a huge tent. Also waiting were 500 cases of scotch and champagne — for 300 men.

Mannix, Roach and the 282 conventioneers arrived after 7:00 P.M. At first, the event appeared to the women to be uneventful. Everyone enjoyed a barbecue dinner served cafeteria-style in the large mess tent, there were exhibition boxing matches in an adjacent arena, and Stan Laurel and Oliver Hardy appeared. The Dancing Dandridge Sisters featured a talented 13-year-old named Dorothy. But by mid-evening the liquor-stoked salesmen started to take the "stag affair" seriously and the 130 women became targets. As Stenn described, "They had been promised a stag affair ... delegates mistook the professional dancers for party favors and treated them accordingly; without telephones or transportation, the young women had no means of escape."

One of the women was Patricia Douglas, a chestnut-haired 20-year-old with a movie star smile. She lived in Hollywood with her mother, who interestingly made clothes for high-end call girls (and may have worked at "Mae's"). Patricia attended a convent school until age 14 and as a teenager became friendly with a group that included Bing Crosby, Dick Powell, and Jimmy Durante. She took the hostess job thinking it would be a fun party. Among the 300 drunk men was David Ross, a 36-year-old Chicago bachelor whom Douglas described as "repulsive ... slimy, with eyes that bulged out like a frog." After a perfunctory dance with Ross, Douglas escaped to a ladies' room. By then, the party was becoming unsafe for the women. Waiters later described a sexually-charged scene completely out of hand. One said it "was the worst, the wildest, and the rottenest I have ever seen." In a rare display of manners, Wallace Beery actually helped one of the women, dancer Ginger Wyatt, after she begged him to save her. As he herded her away he "socked a couple of men" to get her out.

But Ross and a friend grabbed Douglas as she exited the bathroom, and while one held her down and pinched her nose closed, the other poured a bottle of scotch down her throat. As she stumbled away to throw up, Ross snuck up behind her, covered her mouth with his hand and told her, "Make a sound, and you'll never breath again." Then he raped her in the back of a nearby car. When she passed out, he slapped her across the face and yelled, "Cooperate! I want you awake!" When he was done raping Douglas he staggered away, walking past parking lot attendant Clement Soth, who helped a hysterical and battered Douglas to a studio car.

Accompanied by a Culver City policeman, Douglas was taken to the Culver City Community Hospital, which sat across the street from MGM. Edward Lindquist, who treated Douglas, was one of the owners, described by an MGM employee as "our family doctor." After Lindquist cleaned her up, she was taken home. She naively expected something to be done and mentioned the assault to a payroll clerk when she picked up her $7.50 a few days later. But no one at the studio responded, and she got mad. She didn't try to blackmail the studio; had she done so, they certainly would have paid handsomely. Douglas went to D.A. Fitts and swore out a complaint against David Ross for rape. She picked Ross' photo out of two dozen photographs of MGM employees. On June 4, the *Los Angeles Examiner*'s front page screamed "PROBE OF WILD FILM PARTY PRESSED," along with a picture of Douglas and her home address. MGM was never mentioned. Unsuccessful in pushing aside the Douglas story with other headlines— on June 11, the *Los Angeles Evening Herald Express* trumpeted, "LORETTA YOUNG ADOPTS TWO BABIES!"— the still-unidentified MGM released a statement saying, "We have read with astonishment the alleged charges of the girl. It is difficult to make any real comment as to a situation which appears so impossible and as to which we know nothing."

MGM would be decimated if the public knew it had sponsored a liquor-fueled orgy with teenaged party-favors, that cost the equivalent of $500,000. But the extent to which they covered up the Douglas affair is nothing less than spectacular. The Pinkerton Detective Agency was hired to dig up dirt on Douglas, but when they reported that she was a virgin who never drank, they were redirected to interview every single girl at the party and make sure they went along with the story. As expected, they came up with several girls—one of whom was a friend of Fitts'—who described "good clean fun" but remembered Douglas swilling scotch "from a quart bottle all night."

Wallace Beery suddenly remembered nothing of his encounter with the young girl being assaulted, and parking lot attendant Soth now said the man walking away from Douglas wasn't Ross. Soth's family told writer Stenn that in exchange for changing his story, MGM offered him a job for life, "anywhere he wanted." He worked as a driver for the rest of his life. Hal Roach himself tried to get Douglas' gynecologist to testify falsely that she had a venereal disease, and the good Dr. Lindquist from MGM's private Culver City Community Hospital claimed he believed there had been no intercourse (but could not explain the black eyes and the cuts). Even though there had been a dozen police officers at the party and a Culver City motorcycle patrolman took Douglas to the hospital, no crime scene report was written or filed.

Because of the newspaper coverage, Fitts scheduled a grand jury hearing for June 16 and summoned Ross back to L.A. Before he met with police or Fitts he met with Mayer's personal attorney, Mendel Silberberg. The hearing at the Hall of Justice went as scripted by MGM. Only two of the 120 dancers tried to help Douglas. One, Ginger Wyatt, recounted her rescue by Wallace Beery, but he denied it happened. When Douglas herself testified, Silberberg's partner pointed at her and asked rapist Ross, "Look at her. Who would want her?" The charade complete, the grand jury refused to indict Ross and he returned to Chicago.

But Douglas still tried to clear her name, filing suit against Ross, Mannix, Roach and others for "unlawful conspiracy to defile, debauch, and seduce" her and asking for $500,000. When that avenue closed due to a technicality, she became the first woman ever to take a rape case to federal court as a violation of civil rights issue. Interoffice MGM memos uncovered by Stenn reflect that Douglas, "our girlfriend" in the notes, was a problem. One, from Roach attorney Victor Collins, was clear: referring to one of the perjured witnesses developed by MGM and Roach, he "hopes that somebody could phone Mr. Mannix direct about getting a few days at M-G-M ... it is highly imperative that we keep these people in good humor, and get them work. May I say again — it is really important!" The case would drag on into 1938 before Douglas lost due to a series of MGM-engineered technicalities and the fact that Douglas' lawyer had decided to run for district attorney against Fitts. He knew he needed MGM's help to win so began skipping court appearances until the judge dismissed the case.

Interestingly, the notorious Wild West Party completely disappeared from the history books. There is not a single mention anywhere in any archives. This writer could also find no mention anywhere. Before he died, someone asked Mannix whatever happed to "that girlie" who stood up to MGM. He responded, "We had her killed." He was metaphoric rather than literal, but MGM did indeed "kill" Patricia Douglas. After they raped her.

Strickling tried to use the final act of the Loretta Young baby saga to deflect attention from the Douglas story when he planted the June 11 story in the *Times*, "LORETTA YOUNG ADOPTS TWO BABIES." He also knew that the papers were full of Harlow's tragic death, so there would be less attention to Loretta Young's story. Louella Parsons wrote, "Loretta Young, film star, admitted to me today that she is a mother — by adoption. Two little girls, Jane age three, and Judy, twenty-three and a half months, have been adopted by Loretta."[193] Judy was her daughter with Gable. Strickling had to falsify every record having to do with the child, since it was illegal for a single person to adopt in California, and illegal for a person to adopt their own child.

Like the birth and baptismal records, nobody every looked. The depth of the process is borne out with the choreographed adoption of not just her own child, but a second as well. The second little girl was a prop. Just three weeks later headlines said "LORETTA YOUNG RELINQUISHES TOT TO MOTHER." According to the story, a heartbroken Young returned the baby to her biological mother, who had changed her mind about the adoption.

The plot arranged by Strickling was almost Machiavellian, with payoffs to dozens of people — reporters, doctors, nurses, police, county records staff, priests, nuns, steamship employees, railroad workers. Rumors dogged the child for years. Photographs of the child with her ears uncovered either by hats, earmuffs, or hair were forbidden — ears just like Gable's. She always dressed in outfits with hats or bonnets. Young denied the rumors to everyone, even her subsequent husbands. After she married Tom Lewis in the late 1940s she told him that the resemblance to Gable was because the child was the result of an affair between Gable and her sister, actress Sally Blane.[194] Incredibly, he believed her. Young denied the rumors publicly until her death in 2000, but told Judy the truth earlier. She only publicly confirmed that Gable fathered her adopted child in the autobiography she would not allow published until after her death.

As the tempestuous Velez-Weissmuller marriage was coming apart in late 1937, Velez turned to an unlikely ally for support, and sex: Eddie Mannix. It was not unusual for studio executives to appear in public with actresses, so the public barely noticed. Like most of Eddie's affairs, it was brief, but Eddie was cheating on his wife and his mistress. It was impossible for Strickling to put a positive face on the Velez-Weissmuller split. The public confirmation came from Weissmuller during their last dinner, at Ciro's in January 1938. After loudly arguing in front of other patrons, Weissmuller dumped his food onto Velez's head and stalked out. The story was too juicy for the tabloids to ignore, so Strickling simply let the story run, and they were divorced a few months later. Velez's career was over, and Weissmuller's would end in the early 1940s when the public tired of *Tarzan*. But Strickling would offer one last courtesy for Velez in 1944.

Eddie's relationship with Bernice reached a controversial end in November 1937. For several years Bernice had lived quietly in Palm Springs, but for some reason she decided to very publicly sue Eddie for divorce rather than quietly working something out. She accused him of "cruelty and infidelity," and "kicking and beating her so violently" that he broke her back. She also took a jab at mistress Toni Lanier, accusing Eddie of "associating with other women." She asked for $4,000 a month ($50,000 today) in alimony and property worth $1 million ($10 million today). Eddie was stunned.

In an amazing coincidence, just before Bernice's divorce petition came to court she died in a mysterious car accident in the desert near Palm Springs. According to newspaper reports Bernice spent the night of November 18, 1937, at a small casino outside of Palm Springs. As she was being driven home in the early morning hours by Al Wertheimer, the owner of the casino, his car ran off the road and she was killed. He was left paralyzed. Rumors arose immediately that Bernice's death was no accident. Police noted two sets of tire prints in the sand off the road, and the Wertheimer car was scraped front to back along the side. It appeared that the car was run off the road, but as might be expected, no charges arose from the mysterious death. Bernice was quietly laid to rest in a Palm Springs cemetery and another problem with Eddie's women went away.

One of Mannix's close friends at MGM was actor Wallace Beery. The two were actually very similar men, both hard-drinking womanizers with no morals. But Beery was out of control from his youth and didn't improve with age. Beery and Mannix also had another similarity: They both allegedly killed someone. Beery was born in Kansas City, Missouri. At age 17 he joined the Ringling Brothers circus as an assistant elephant trainer, leaving two years later after being mauled by a leopard. He worked in vaudeville until 1913, winding up in Hollywood in the Essanay "Sweedie"

Wallace Beery (seated; shown with Lewis Stone) at about the time that he and two mob pals beat vaudeville legend Ted Healy to death.

comedy serials. His costar in 1915's *Sweedie Goes to College* was beautiful teenaged ingénue Gloria Swanson, and the two were married a few months later. According to Swanson, the marriage was over after the wedding night when a drunken Beery brutally raped her. During their two-month marriage Beery also regularly beat her black and blue.

He left the comedy serials in the 1920s to play heavies in dozens of films including *The Wanderer* (1925). Thalberg himself hired Beery away from Paramount in 1930. He earned an Academy Award nomination for his first MGM film, *The Big House* (1930), and became one of the top MGM stars in hit films such as *Min and Bill* (1930), *The Champ* (1931), *Grand Hotel* (1932), *Dinner at Eight* (1933) and *Treasure Island* (1934). He was a star, but he was always battling the studio. Beery wanted off of the Catalina Island set of *Treasure Island*; telling Mannix he had severe cramps, he left for the mainland. Mannix had an MGM cameraman follow Beery for several days, filming him fishing and barhopping. Beery was fined $5,000. He appeared easygoing but was as tough as nails, and a drunk—a mean drunk.

On the morning of December 21, 1937, Mannix received a call, allegedly from Beery.[195] He said that he had been in a fight outside the Trocadero Restaurant and with Pat DiCicco and Albert Broccoli and had beaten Ted Healy badly. Mannix called the club and was told there had been an altercation, but Strickling found no hospital admittance for Healy and there was a collective sigh of relief. Like Beery, Healy was an obnoxious drunk and a jerk. Moe Howard described him as a "Dr. Jeckel when he's sober, and Mr. Hyde when he's drunk."[196] He was the most successful vaudeville comic in the world but lost it all because he was stubborn.

Healy was born Ernest Lea Nash in Brooklyn, and became the top vaudeville star, earning $8,500 (over $100,000 today) a week, around the world. During a 1922 show at Brooklyn's Prospect Theater three childhood friends showed up — the Horwitz brothers, Moe, Shemp and Jerome. They were soon clowning with Healy and by the end of the night Healy hired the boys he dubbed "Ted Healy's Stooges." Originally there were four: Moe and Shemp Horwitz (their mother forbade young Jerome from going), Healy's valet Ken Lackey, and Pansy Sanborn. Sanborn left after a few months and Lackey left in 1928, replaced by Louis Fineberg. To avoid anti-Semitism Healy changed the Horwitzes to "Howard" and Fineberg to "Fine." The group changed regularly as members moved around. Shemp left in 1925 to form his own team, and Moe left for a while in 1926 when his wife became pregnant. He disliked selling real estate and returned in 1928. Shemp returned for a short time in 1927 when Moe and Larry left to star in the musical *A Night in Spain*, returning with Shemp in 1929.

Healy went into films in 1930, debuting in *Soup to Nuts*. From the beginning Shemp did not want to do films with Healy; he never trusted him, didn't like his drunken outbursts, and was upset that Healy made $10,000 a week and still paid the Stooges $500 each. He left for good in 1932 and was replaced by younger brother Jerome. Before leaving, Shemp suggested Jerry shave his head and become "Curly." Curly filled some void in the already-popular group; his impact was immediate. He had trouble remembering lines and if stuck ad-libbed with his famous "n-yuk, n-yuk, n-yuk" and "woo woo woo" lines. At the time Larry was the most prominent Stooge; he slapped around Moe and Curly.

In 1934 the group filmed MGM's *Hollywood Party* but were feuding because Healy was still paying them less than $500 a week. By the time filming was completed the Horowitz brothers and Fine quit to go on their own as the "Three Lost Souls." They were soon selling out theaters without their former boss. Healy's replacement "Superstooges" never caught on, and his career floundered. Columbia's Harry Cohn loved the new Stooges. In 1934 he offered them a contract as "The Three Stooges" and agreed to the first of 30, one-year contracts. They made 97 shorts in the next dozen years and become international stars.

Healy's career was over, his money gone, and in 1935 he was living in a small house in Westwood with his wife, UCLA coed Betty Hickman. He spent every night at one of the Sunset Boulevard bars. On December 21, 1937, he was celebrating the birth of his first child at the Trocadero, sitting by himself, when he picked a fight with three drunks down the bar. Nearby were two men Healy hated. Pat DiCicco and Healy had been at odds since Healy dated Thelma Todd, DiCicco's murdered ex-wife. Healy, like everyone else, knew DiCicco was involved in Todd's murder and that DiCicco had beaten her. Sitting with DiCicco was Beery. Beery and Healy openly disliked each other, for no reason other than that they vied for many of the same roles. With those two was Albert "Cubby" Broccoli, DiCicco's cousin and a fringe mobster.

After words were exchanged at the bar, Beery punched Healy in the head in front of the other patrons and was challenged by Healy to "step outside," where he said he'd beat each man "one at a time." But Broccoli had snuck outside, and when Healy walked through the door jumped him and held him while the other two beat Healy. They left him unconscious, sprawled in a pool of blood, and returned to the bar loudly toasting their victory. Healy was allegedly taken to his nearby home at 10749 Weyburn Road in a cab. The following morning, Healy died of very apparent head injuries. He was only 41. Police called to Healy's house called Strickling and Mannix. To his horror, Strickling discovered that as he lay dying in his bed during the night, Healy had spoken with a number of friends over the phone, including Shemp Howard, and described the beating by Beery and DiCicco. On December 23, the *Los Angeles Daily News* reported that even though Healy fought with "Albert Broccoli, 29, a wealthy New Yorker ... police said the case was closed and would not question Broccoli ... rumors that Healy had engaged in a terrific fight at the Trocadero ... were spiked by manager H.W. Hoffman." Even more strange, the article indicated Healy died of "natural causes," the result of his alcoholism.[197] The funeral was at St. Augustine Catholic Church in Culver City, and among the pallbearers were Harry Rapf and "E.J. Mannix." Since Mannix did not know Healy well, he was no doubt inserted into the mix to show that MGM and Healy were friendly.

Strickling obviously got to the coroners as well, since the severe head injuries seen by his wife were ignored in the autopsy.[198] Surviving photographs of the body clearly show at least a half dozen serious head injuries. The documents were so patently fraudulent that Healy's physician refused to sign any of them. Lastly, at the direction of county coroner Frank Nance the body was embalmed, making any further autopsy pointless.

Strickling was obviously responsible for much of the fiction in the *Daily News* article, but he had to get Beery out of town, so Beery and his family left on a hastily arranged month-long trip to Europe. They left for New York later the next day. Studio photographers recorded their departure, smiling and waving as MGM's biggest star left for a holiday vacation.

Beery was also separated from mention with DiCicco or Broccoli, since both were known mobsters. The Trocadero staff would be no problem. Most of them were already on Strickling's payroll anyway. Waiters, busboys, and maître di's were paid to keep on eye on partying stars, reporting back to Strickling and Mannix any problems. But Mannix nonetheless made sure that nobody remembered Healy arguing with DiCicco, Broccoli, or Beery. Just in case someone remembered Healy in a fight that night, Strickling planted a story that survives to this day. It was noted that perhaps Healy had indeed been in a fight with three drunken fraternity boys who had been arguing with him that evening. The "drunk college boys" were obviously never located. To throw a little mud, Strickling revived a story of a minor paternity suit against Healy filed by unknown actress Gloria Schumm. She would not have prevailed, but the story got plenty of press in the weeks after Healy's death.

A minor problem arose when Healy's first wife called the papers. Betty Brown (or "Betty Browne" or "Betty Braun") was married to Healy for ten years until 1932, and was an MGM contract actress. She complained to the press that the police were not investigating the right people. Just after the funeral Mannix terminated her contract and had her blackballed from the other studios, and she never worked again. Just a months later, Broccoli—who had no movie experience—was made an assistant director, and his wife Gloria Blondell (sister of Joan)—who had never acted—was given costarring roles with stars such as Ronald Reagan and Errol Flynn. Beery was never publicly mentioned in stories of Healy's death, which "Curly"

Howard noted, "can't be on the level."[199] He returned from his European vacation in February 1938 to a Hollywood that had already forgotten about Healy. Mannix's studio connections and DiCicco's mob friends were enough to keep people quiet.

The last few months of 1937 had been challenging for MGM and for Mannix particularly, and early 1938 would give him little respite. On January 11 his father John died, and less than two months later, on March 7, his mother Elizabeth passed away, both back home in New Jersey. Mannix was tough and probably involved in the death of his first wife Bernice, but it must have been difficult to lose a wife and both parents in the space of four months.

As 1938 unfolded, amid all of the carnage an unlikely ally appeared in the form of a new gossip columnist, Hedda Hopper, rival to the throne held by Hearst's Louella Parsons. Since Parsons' loyalties to MGM had departed with Hearst and Davies, Hopper would become a Strickling favorite and challenge Parsons for every scoop, every tidbit of studio news. For the first time Strickling had leverage with Parsons, since she was no longer the only game in town.

Edna Furry was the daughter of an Altoona, Pennsylvania, butcher. In 1913 she married traveling vaudevillian William DeWolfe Hopper. He was 25 years older than his teenaged bride. They moved to Hollywood, where she paid a numerologist $10 to conjure up "Hedda." The Hoppers appeared in dozens of films but as he became a star she toiled in small roles, and though her 100 films included classics like *Virtuous Wives* (1918) and *Wings* (1927), her roles were lousy. In 1935 she began a weekly radio show featuring interviews with movie stars, which turned into a studio gossip column for the *Washington Times-Herald*. Her column, spiced with her acerbic wit, soon challenged Parsons. Strickling saw Hopper as an opportunity to lessen Parsons' strength. He arranged for Hopper to appear in the *Esquire* syndicate, and made sure the *Los Angeles Times* ran it as well.

Hopper was successful due to the universal dislike for Parsons. Hearst's support let Parsons operate like a queen, with impunity, demanding and receiving slavish devotion from the biggest and the smallest. She was spiteful and petty, lavishing undeserved praise on those who paid her homage and spiteful punishment on those who did not. Hopper was not as vindictive, and was likeable, and also (unlike Parsons) actively cultivated other sources outside of the movies. She was also very friendly with Hearst. At his behest, she would later work with Parsons to torpedo Orson Welles' *Citizen Kane*, an obvious but veiled view of the Hearst-Davies affair. The Hopper-Parsons rivalry dominated the gossip business for the next 20 years.

Just before he died, Irving Thalberg suggested that Mervyn LeRoy be brought into MGM, and just after his death Mayer did so. LeRoy was the nephew of Jesse Lasky but began his career at Warners after Lasky refused him a job. As a director he hit it big with his first assignment, *Little Caesar* (1930) with Edward G. Robinson. Coming to MGM he brought along a teenager he had found in Hollywood. Lana Turner's career and image are examples of how a Strickling creation overpowered even the people and the movies they made. Turner made her film debut in LeRoy's 1937 Warners film *They Won't Forget*. The movie had a provocative theme. She played a Southern woman who was raped and murdered. The movie was about an innocent teacher unfairly charged with the crime, who was eventually lynched before his trial. Turner's screen time was brief, and she was listed sixth in the credits. It was a minor role but all anyone noticed was the teenager in the formfitting sweater. Director LeRoy showcased 16-year-old Turner's figure and it swept her into stardom. In February 1938, LeRoy brought Turner with him to MGM and Strickling formally dubbed her the "Sweater Girl," flooding the press with suggestive photos of the teenager.

Strickling also personally revised the story of Turner's "discovery," a fiction that remains today. He wrote the famous story that Turner was first seen by a Hollywood agent — wearing her signature sweater — eating ice cream at the counter of Schwab's Drugstore. Turner had never even been to Schwab's. It was actually *Hollywood Reporter* chief William Wilkerson who first saw Turner, not at Schwab's but at the run-down Top Hat Café, a grimy grill across the street from Hollywood High School, which Julia Jean Mildred Turner was attending after her arrival from Idaho. Her mother moved Lana and her sisters to Hollywood after Lana's father — a gambler and bootlegger — was murdered during a card game. Wilkerson asked her if she'd like to be in the movies, to which she replied, "I don't know. I'll have to ask my mother."[200] He gave her the phone number of agent Zeppo Marx and told her to call him. But Strickling's other story remains a Hollywood legend.

While the new teenager in the sweater was turning heads, the press was told Spencer Tracy was recovering from a hernia operation. Friends assumed he was drying out again. On March 10 he won an Academy Award for *Captains Courageous* and Strickling arranged for his wife Louise to accept the award as a public show of the marriage. When she walked on stage, the crowd, who knew of her trials with her philandering husband, gave her a prolonged standing ovation. Fittingly, the Oscar statue was inscribed incorrectly to "*Dick* Tracy."

Just after the Academy Awards, Strickling married Gail Greenstreet on March 28, 1938, at the Arizona Inn in Tucson. The first year of their marriage would be a busy one for him. MGM had begun filming two movies that would cement the studio's reputation as the biggest and best in Hollywood. The casts of *The Wizard of Oz* and *Gone with the Wind* were a Who's Who from Gable to Garland. But the personal lives of Jeanette MacDonald and Nelson Eddy intruded regularly.

MacDonald's June 1937 marriage to Gene Raymond had quickly dissolved into physical abuse and his resumption of homosexual relationships. By the spring of 1938 Raymond was sharing a small house with a 19-year-old Universal actor. According to friends the homosexual relationship "was commonly known around town."[201] Worse, in January 1938 Raymond was arrested for "a morals charge" during a vice raid on a Hollywood homosexual club. MacDonald herself paid a $1,000 bribe to get Raymond out. It never made the papers but an arrest record still exists in Los Angeles Municipal Court files. But "Gene Raymond's" arrest form was crudely tampered to reflect "Miss Gene Raymond's" arrest for prostitution.[202]

At the time MacDonald and Eddy were filming *Sweethearts,* she arrived at a Woody Van Dyke party sporting bruises from a beating by Raymond. Eddy rushed to the MacDonald-Raymond home in Bel Air with Van Dyke in pursuit, but by the time Van Dyke arrived, Eddy had beaten Raymond unconscious in the driveway. Van Dyke's intervention saved Eddy from killing him. Newspapers said Raymond injured himself falling down a flight of stairs.

At the same time, MacDonald discovered she was pregnant. Biographers credit either Eddy or Raymond depending upon their own preference, but whoever the father was, on July 26 she was in the hospital for an "ear infection." Biographers halfheartedly claim MacDonald lost the baby after falling down a flight of stairs, but probably the studio arranged an abortion. At the same time the studio was trying to quell rumors that MacDonald and Eddy were somehow getting back together. Knowing nothing of their various problems, fans believed she was happily newlywed to Raymond, and Eddy was "still looking." But gossip writers were already mentioning the MacDonald-Raymond tiffs, and even national *Look* magazine noted "Jeanette's will be the first Hollywood divorce of 1939." Mayer was so angry he went unannounced to the MacDonald-Raymond home. Raymond was summoned there from the house he was sharing with his young boyfriend, and when he arrived Mayer told the two they not only were *not* going to divorce, but that Raymond was moving home and they "were going to constantly let the world know how happy you are." Knowing that their careers and financial futures were in Mayer's shaking hands, they reluctantly agreed.

Next, Mayer directed Strickling find Eddy a woman. In the 18 months since MacDonald's wedding, he had not been linked to any other woman. To the contrary, rumors of his homosexuality resurfaced. Eddy was ordered to take a bride, and according to actor Noel Coward, "Eddy agreed, but didn't want some virgin bride or insatiable creature." Instead Mayer arranged for Eddy to wed Ann Denmitz Franklin, the older, matronly ex–wife of director Sydney Franklin. The Franklins had split up in 1933 after spouse-swapping dates with the Conrad Nagels led to mutual divorces; Sydney married the ex–Mrs. Nagel but Conrad declined to marry Ann. Eddy noted, "Marriage is the tax of stardom."[203] He told his mother, "I HAVE to marry Ann, mother, it's a duty." According to Coward, "She was wise to the ways of Tinseltown ... not sexually demanding ... and pleased to live the comfortable life of a movie star's wife."[204]

Eddy and Franklin eloped to Las Vegas on January 20, 1939. Everyone at MGM was stunned except Mayer. Perhaps the most surprised was MacDonald, who, according to Woody Van Dyke, tried to overdose on sleeping pills in her dressing room when she heard. The strange duo would both leave MGM in 1942. The entire history of the MacDonald-Eddy relationship was so full of contradiction it's impossible to determine with any certainty exactly who loved whom.

Gone with the Wind was one of the few confirmed mistakes made by Irving Thalberg. When David O. Selznick approached MGM about doing the story in 1936, Thalberg told Mayer, "Pass on it Louie, no Civil War picture ever made a dime."[205] Selznick purchased the rights to Margaret Mitchell's novel for just $50,000, but knew it was a steal and felt so guilty that a few weeks later he sent her another $50,000. He wanted to make the film himself but no studio would make the film without Clark Gable as Rhett Butler, so he had to go to Mayer, who gave him Gable for distribution rights and half the profits. Strickling immediately undertook the most massive and intense publicity campaign in the history of the movies. Hundreds of thousands of preproduction photos were taken and tens of thousands of press releases were sent out. The casting of Scarlett O'Hara would include 1,500 screen tests, and was not completed until January 1939 when Vivien Leigh became Scarlett opposite Gable's Rhett and filming commenced. It had taken over three years of preproduction research, casting, prop-building, etc., before the first foot of film was shot.

Mayer lent Selznick every type of talent, from director George Cukor to cameramen and actors. Over 4,000 MGM employees worked on the film. He even lent Selznick his old sets. On the first day of filming— December 10, 1938 —for the burning of Atlanta, Mayer torched 100 old sets dating back to the silent era. Filming lasted eight months, but the film

would win ten Academy Awards and set ticket records. It was Strickling's
most ambitious and successful publicity campaign. By the time the film
premiered on December 14, 1939, millions of people already knew almost
everything about it.

One thing they did not know was that just two weeks into filming,
Clark Gable had director George Cukor fired. Cukor was a homosexual who
was widely liked and respected, but Gable hated him. He was openly con-
temptuous of most homosexuals, but his homophobia probably resulted
from his own earlier experiences, one of which was with Billy Haines. Joan
Crawford — who slept with Gable for years but was a close friend of
Haines'— talked about the affair. In an interview with this writer, writer
Barney Oldfield also confirmed the story. As his career grew Gable worried that the Haines story would become public, and he knew that Cukor
knew, since Cukor and Haines were good friends. Gable was uncomfortable from the moment Cukor was signed to direct. Cukor made matters
worse by inviting Haines to the set. In fact, the vintage paintings on the
walls of "Tara" belonged to Haines, and had been borrowed by Cukor for
the film. He also angered Gable by calling him "dear" and "darling" on the
set, which was a habit rather than a dig at Gable's alleged relationship with
Haines.[206]

There are various versions of Gable's actions in getting Cukor fired.
Homosexual actor Andy Lawler allegedly joked at a party that "George is
directing one of Billy's old tricks," and the comment found its way back
to a furious Gable. Gable later erupted at Cukor during a difficult scene
and in front of cast and crew, screaming, "I can't go on with this picture.
I won't be directed by this *fairy*! I have to work with a *real man*!"[207] He
stormed off the set. Strickling admitted only that "Gable personally complained about George Cukor,"[208] and Cukor was fired on February 12.
Strickling's *GWTW* publicist, Russell Birdwell, told the press Cukor paid
too much attention to the actresses and not enough to the actors, an excuse
that lives on today. But insiders knew that Gable's homophobia and personal revulsion at his own past was the reason for Cukor's firing. Mannix
replaced him with Victor Fleming, a close friend of Gable's. Many of the
actors, including Vivien Leigh and Olivia de Havilland, continued to meet
secretly with Cukor for directorial advice during filming.

Barbara Stanwyck had been a challenge since her arrival in Hollywood. Her marriage to alcoholic vaudevillian Frank Fay was a sham; his
attacks led her to flee across the street into the arms of neighbor Joan
Crawford. In 1934, a drunken Fay approached Mannix at the Brown Derby
and when Eddie mentioned Fay's "dyke wife," tried to hit him. Mannix
sent him crashing over another table with one punch. After the Fays

divorced in 1935 she was loaned by RKO to MGM for *His Brother's Wife*. Her costar was MGM matinee idol Robert Taylor. He was born Spangler Arlington Brugh in Filley, Nebraska, in 1911. "Arly" Brugh was an only child raised by a coddling mother, who grew into a spineless mama's boy. He came to California to attend Pomona College, following his music teacher there from Nebraska. He said the day teacher Hubert Gray left, his "world fell apart," but in California moved in with Gray.

After he graduated from Pomona, his recently widowed mother moved to L.A. and in with him. He began performing at the Pasadena Playhouse, an avant-garde repertory company directed by homosexual Gilmor Brown. Every year Brown chose a student protégé; in 1934 he picked Brugh. Other Playhouse actors "all knew what it meant to be his protégé. The next year it was Tyrone Power." The "perk" was overnight private rehearsals at Brown's house.[209]

MGM hired Brugh in 1934 for $35 a week, and Ida Koverman renamed him Robert Taylor. He was still living with his mother. By the time he was cast with Stanwyck in *His Brother's Wife*, he had already become a star in *A Wicked Woman* (1934) and *Magnificent Obsession* (1935). He was also an immediate project for Strickling, who tried everything to hide Taylor's sexuality. His studio bio described growing up in rugged Montana surrounded by guns and hunting trips. He ate lunch at the commissary's notoriously macho Director's Table. He was paired in studio romances with Virginia Bruce and Hedy Lamarr. But Taylor never tried to hide his sexuality. Strickling publicist Rick Ingersoll said, "Taylor was careless because he thought he had the cleanest image of any of Metro's male stars. Whispers that his intense virility was a sham never went away."[210] In fact, he was lusted after by male moviegoers as often as female.

Strickling then paired Taylor and Stanwyck during *His Brother's Wife* filming. They were sent on arranged dates and stories of a heated affair were planted. Taylor allegedly sent her a dozen roses every day. The two became fast friends, because in part they were so alike and in part so opposite. Taylor was an impressionable mama's boy who craved approval; Stanwyck a domineering mother figure. He wanted to be led; she wanted to lead. He was so timid he could not say no to anyone, so afraid he rarely answered his phone for fear someone would request something of him; she was tough as nails. And they were both certainly not heterosexual. When the couple met Ernest Hemingway some years later, he hated the effeminate Taylor but loved Stanwyck. He described her "nice with a good tough Mick intelligence."[211]

After the 1936 release of *His Brother's Wife* the careers of both Taylor and Stanwyck continued to rise. He starred in *Camille* (1937) and *Stand*

Up and Fight (1939) while she did *Stella Dallas* (1937) and *Golden Boy* (1939). They steadfastly maintained a public relationship, but the truth about it is hard to divine. It was obvious they did love each other on some level, but it was not emotional male-female love. They rarely if ever had sex. She called him Junior and he called her the Queen. She was living on her ranch in Chatsworth surrounded by her horses, and he was still living with his mother in a Hollywood apartment.

An infamous article in the December 1938 *Photoplay* magazine forced MGM to do something about the odd couple — about several MGM "couples," actually. "Hollywood's Unmarried Husbands and Wives" was written under a pseudonym by Sheila Graham. "Unwed couples they might be termed ... but they go everywhere together and do everything in pairs ... build houses near each other ... mother and father each other's kids ... to the world their official status is 'just friends.' No more."[212] The article caused shock waves through the studios, exposing the private lives of Gable and Lombard, Taylor and Stanwyck, Chaplin and Paulette Goddard, and Constance Bennett and Gilbert Roland.

To the horror of the studios the couples were described as all but married. Chaplin's girlfriend was much younger, like his other child brides. Gable was not yet divorced from his second wife Langham, but was in an adulterous relationship with Lombard. Taylor's purchase of a ranch next to Stanwyck while she was not yet divorced from Fay was also labeled adulterous behavior. In 1939, such stories could ruin careers and studios. The public reaction was staggering; the edition sold out within a day of hitting the newsstands, and four extra editions were printed. Excerpts were printed in every major newspaper in the country. The Hays Commission office was bombarded with thousands of complaints from outraged moviegoers, and Hays contacted Mayer personally to tell him to take care of Gable and Taylor. An enraged Mayer ordered Strickling obtain a retraction. Proof of his power, *Photoplay* inserted a written apology in the next issue even though everything they had printed was true. Next, Strickling set about "correcting" the relationships.

The Gable-Lombard coupling was public, although Strickling did his best to downplay the seriousness. Fans did not know that Gable had lived apart from Langham for several years, spending almost every night at the Bel Air mansion Lombard rented from Alfred Hitchcock. Gable had to sneak in and out in the dead of night to avoid Langham's hired detectives. The biggest star in the world crawled on his stomach across the back yard to get to his girlfriend. Mayer ordered Gable to do whatever was necessary to jettison Langham and marry Lombard. Strickling negotiated the divorce with Langham, who ended several years of refusals and sped to

Las Vegas for a quickie divorce on March 8, 1939. The trip and the legal-ities—the proceedings took four minutes—were arranged by Strickling. Langham received the equivalent of $2.5 million to divorce him, most of it paid by MGM as an advance against Gable's earnings.

Otto Winkler was Gable's MGM publicist. When Gable met Win-kler, he was a reporter for the *Herald-Examiner* covering a bogus pater-nity case filed against Gable. Gable liked Winkler's stories and asked Strickling to hire him as Gable's press agent. Gable asked Winkler to arrange a secret wedding for him and Lombard. A date had been tenta-tively set, but the studio wanted to be sure that the couple could get in and out of Kingman, Arizona, unseen. Winkler drove his own fiancée there and married her in a mid-March test run.[213] Two weeks later, on March 29, Winkler drove Gable and Lombard the 357 miles to Kingman in his blue DeSoto coupe with a rumble seat in the back. They were wed at the home of a very surprised Protestant minister, then turned around and drove right back to L.A., stopping only at a Western Union telegraph office in Arizona so Winkler could send details of the wedding to the MGM pub-licity office. Gable called Lombard's mother, saying, "Hey Ma, this is your new son-in-law."[214] Strickling arranged a press conference at Lombard's Bel Air home for 9 A.M. the next morning.

Just before the wedding they purchased a San Fernando Valley ranch from director Raoul Walsh. A whitewashed brick house sat in the middle of 20 secluded acres away from the prying eyes of fans and press, sur-rounded by hundreds of eucalyptus, avocado, fig and peach trees, and groves of orange, lemon and grapefruit. There were pastures to graze horses, barns and a stable. The Petit Avenue ranch was paid for by Lom-bard since Gable was broke after the Langham divorce. Hollywood's most popular couple called each other Pappy and Ma and settled into quiet domesticity on their secluded ranch. When Gable offered to buy his wife an expensive present, she told him, "To tell you the truth, Pa, I could use a couple of loads of horseshit to spread around the rose bushes."[215]

Mayer then turned Strickling's attention to Taylor and Stanwyck, ordering they too marry. The ever-compliant Taylor agreed, to save his job, and Stanwyck agreed because she knew better than to anger Mayer. Strickling's publicists drove them to San Diego on May 13, 1939, and Mayer made Ida Koverman go along to make sure Taylor didn't back out. The couple responded to married life differently from the Gables. After the wedding Taylor refused to kiss his bride for Strickling's photographers.[216] Stanwyck went back to her ranch and Taylor went home to his mother. When he told his mother he was married, she had to be sedated. Even a marriage couldn't stop rumors Taylor was gay. The couple were rarely together, they proudly showed reporters their separate bedrooms, and on his weekends off Taylor flew planes with his homosexual copilot and longtime buddy. Within six months the tabloids were describing the marriage as over, but Stanwyck and Taylor knew better than to separate. Clifton Webb described Stanwyck as his "favorite Hollywood lesbian" and even the crusty Stanwyck rarely denied the stories during her later years. She and Taylor experimented with the opposite sex, and during a later 1941 experiment Stanwyck would not react well.

It is incomprehensible today that a studio could force a marriage, but such was the control that MGM exercised through Mannix and Strickling. There were dozens, maybe hundreds, of "lavender" marriages orchestrated by studios as late as the 1950s. In the 1930s, when homosexuality was technically illegal in all 50 states, they were commonplace. Another compromise relationship at the time was that of Laurence Olivier and Vivien Leigh. Olivier was a lifelong bisexual. His first marriage to lesbian actress Jill Esmond was never consummated and ended in a year, after he met Leigh during the 1936 filming of *Fire over England*. Olivier was initially not interested, but Leigh pushed hard for a relationship; he was a star, and she, as friends noted, was "intensely ambitious." Unlike his marriage, the Leigh relationship was consummated, though it was over a year before he would have sex. She described it as passionate; he said it was "rapturous torment."[217]

During 1939 she filmed *Gone with the Wind* and he worked on *Wuthering Heights*, and because both were married Strickling arranged for a rental house for her at 520 Crescent Drive and Olivier shared Leslie Howard's house at 606 Camden. Olivier also resumed a sporadic 15-year-long relationship with comedian Danny Kaye. Kaye was living at 1103 San Ysidro Drive, so Olivier uprooted Leigh shortly after *GWTW* filming ended and moved into next door to Kaye. Leigh was convinced that she could keep Olivier interested in heterosexuality, but confronted with the Kaye relationship, she exhibited the beginnings of a breakdown. During the next decade the Olivier-Leigh relationship would dissolve amidst a string of sexual identity and mental problems.

Through the 1930s all of the studios had to carefully watch the personal lives of their actors and actresses. One studio head took it a step further. Howard Hughes had been able to extricate himself from a vehicular manslaughter charge in 1936, but not because he worked for a powerful studio. He did it with cash, paying off the family, the coroner, police, and witnesses. Living from a large inheritance, Hughes arrived in Hollywood and bought a mansion at 211 Muirfield Road in Hancock Park. He looked for women, and men. His first Hollywood friend was Randolph Scott, who came to him looking for a job. Hughes instead moved him into his house.[218] Hughes took up with Cary Grant, with whom he regularly visited the homosexual bars like BBB's Cellar. Neither relationship was a secret among the Hollywood gay community.[219]

Hughes' first female obsession was actress Billie Dove, a flawlessly beautiful Ziegfeld star introduced to Hughes by Marion Davies in 1928. Her husband, producer Irving Willat, found out about the affair and demanded $325,000 ($3 million today) from Hughes to divorce Dove. Willat demanded payment in brand new, unused $1,000 bills, which Hughes arranged. He gave her $20,000 pieces of jewelry monthly, but for two years avoided a wedding date. In 1933 she moved out; he never spoke to her or ever uttered her name again.

Over the years, Hughes pursued hundreds of gorgeous Hollywood starlets. It's difficult to find a woman Hughes *didn't* date, but among those he *did* were Jean Harlow, Ava Gardner, Bette Davis, Gloria Vanderbilt, Katharine Hepburn, and Ginger Rogers. Every one of them broke it off as soon as they discovered Hughes was not serious, and was barely sexual. He collected women like stamps, and kept them in apartments like pets. He was obsessed with actresses from name stars to newcomers. They were recruited by a network of talent agents and photographers paid by Hughes, including well-known Hollywood portrait photographers John Engstead, Christy Shepard, and Paul S. Hesse. Hesse was a pioneer in the use of color portrait photography, working out of a well-appointed shop at 8484 Sunset Boulevard. Living in an apartment above Hesse's shop was Walter Kane, a talent agent. Kane and Hesse — along with Engstead and Shepard — allowed Hughes to install two-way mirrors in their portrait studios so Hughes could watch the women having their portraits taken. Hughes had each pose in skin-tight sweaters profiled to expose their breasts. If Hughes liked a particular girl she was given a contract right there. Only a select few actually met Hughes. He just watched.

Hughes kept them in one of almost 100 apartments, hotel rooms, and houses that he owned in Hollywood and Beverly Hills. The better the girl, the better the lodgings. They were paid more than a typical studio hopeful — $175 a week instead of $50 — and were given acting or singing lessons and sent to auditions. But they were not allowed to date or go out. A cadre of 100 company detectives followed the girls 24 hours a day, seven days a week. He did the same to famous girlfriends; Ava Gardner knew her pursuers so well she often asked them in for drinks.

To keep track of the women Hughes kept an elaborate index card system in his private office. The detailed notes included the girl's vital statistics, including breast size (most important to Hughes), height, weight, shoe and dress size, likes and dislikes in food, personal habits, and her mother's name. It also indicated when on his weekly schedule he was to see the woman. Eventually the women would realize that nothing was going to come from the experience except weird visits from Hughes, and they invariably gave up and left Hollywood.

The decade of the 1930s had been a tumultuous one for the industry, for MGM, and for Howard Strickling and Eddie Mannix. It had ended with a blockbuster year for MGM. In 1939 the studio released *Gone with the Wind, The Wizard of Oz,* Garbo's *Ninotchka, Babes in Arms, The Marx Brothers at the Circus,* and *The Women.* As MGM headed into the 1940s the studio was the largest and must successful movie plant in Hollywood. It was then employing over 10,000 people.

Five

The 1940s:
War Inside and Out

As the 1940s began, MGM was the top studio in Hollywood. It was living up to its nickname; at Culver City there were "more stars than there were in the heavens." Given the financial troubles some studios endured in the 1930s, MGM's solid financial standing made it even more attractive to the talent. MGM's roster heading into the 1940s was impressive. Their stars were Lionel Barrymore, Wallace Beery, Joan Crawford, Clark Gable, Garbo, the Marx Brothers, Norma Shearer, and Robert Taylor. Featured players included Melvyn Douglas, Reginald Gardner, Judy Garland, Hedy Lamarr, Mickey Rooney and Rosalind Russell. The leads were Walter Pidgeon, George Murphy, and Robert Young. There were also thousands of ingénues, character actors, comics and child actors on the MGM payroll at the time. The studio also had the best writers, directors, producers and technical support.

As the war in Europe raged, American films were prohibited in a dozen European countries. Studio revenues began to fall in 1939, and by 1940 only a few studios were able to eke out profits. MGM made money because of its titles. Almost every MGM film featured some uplifting theme, most playing into the increasing need for escapist entertainment among a population occupied with war fears.

The political climate in L.A. hadn't changed; it was still a studio town. Studio-friendly D.A. Fitts tried to use the Red Scare to get reelected, and it cost him his job. In early 1940 Martin Dies brought his special committee to Hollywood to root out communist influences. Fitts persuaded a dopey local party member to lie and testify that some famous actors were communists, including Fredric March, Franchot Tone, Melvyn Douglas, James Cagney, and Humphrey Bogart. Most were MGM employees. Bogart faced down Dies by yelling, "I was born an American.... I have great love for my country.... I resent the intrusion and insinuation that I am anything else," and walking out. His obvious contempt put an end to the proceedings, and just after, Fitts faced a 1940 reelection challenge from John Dockweiler, a three-time U.S. congressman with an impeccable record. In what the *Los Angeles Times* described in four–inch headlines as "THE BIGGEST UPSET IN THE HISTORY OF THE D.A.'S OffICE!!!," Fitts lost in a landslide. Fitts couldn't find work as a lawyer and went back to the military and retired to the California desert town of Tulare. On March 29, 1973, the 78-year-old sat in a worn lawn chair inside his garage and put a .38 caliber bullet into his temple.

It seemed that Dockweiler might be a reformer, but beneath the public veneer, he was no different from his predecessors. Just a few months after the election, on August 16, 1940, Ben "Bugsy" Siegel was arrested for the Hollywood murder of mob turncoat Ralph Greenberg. He was placed in the L.A. County Jail, but local chefs prepared meals, he had two telephones, and he was allowed unlimited visitors day or night. On December 11, Dockweiler dismissed the indictment and Siegel walked away free. The same day, writer Florabelle Muir uncovered a $50,000 contribution ($750,000 today) from Siegel to Dockweiler. A year later, as Dockweiler began an investigation into the L.A. police, he died at his desk of pneumonia. Strangely, he wasn't reportedly ill at the time.

Through different administrations and personalities, MGM could still prevail upon D.A.s and police, as when child star Mickey Rooney's stepfather, Fred Pankey, ran over a woman in a Glendale crosswalk on January 24, 1941. Pankey was working in the accounting department of MGM and from the moment of the accident the "investigation" was handled by Strickling's good friend, Chief of Police Arthur Hohmann, a very unusual occurrence for a simple car accident. Pankey left the scene without a formal interview, and no charges were ever filed.[1]

During 1940, Spencer Tracy was one of MGM's biggest stars, and worst problems. He was still living apart from his wife Louise, staying at the Beverly Wilshire and pursuing every woman that crossed his path. Producer Joseph Mankiewicz said of him, "Nobody at MGM gets more sex than Spencer Tracy," adding, "except Joan Crawford." Tracy seemingly lived in bars. In 1940 Strickling had to deny Tracy relationships with Olivia de Havilland and Judy Garland. Tracy was forty and Garland was 17. Mannix ordered Tracy away from the teenager, but Mannix and Strickling both knew the vile secret about Tracy and Garland, one of the few they knowingly kept from Mayer: They knew he had begun sleeping with Garland when she was just 14. She was one of his first MGM conquests.

Leonard Maltin described Judy Garland as a "furious, excessive talent and a true 'victim' of the Hollywood studio system." Even though Strickling loved the youngster and no doubt felt sorry for her, MGM would eventually consume and kill Garland. Strickling tried to get her help almost from the moment she arrived at MGM in 1935. She was a tortured soul even as a child. Frances Ethel Gumm was born on June 10, 1922, in Minnesota. Her father was a bisexual actor and her mother originally planned to abort her. For some reason her mother told her. It tormented her for her entire life.[2] Frances had two sisters and was nicknamed Baby. When she was two the Gumm Sisters were already appearing together. In 1926 the family came to California, settling first in a rented house at 3154 Glen Manor in Hollywood and then moving to far-out Lancaster, 30 miles north of L.A.

Their father opened a theater, and mother Ethel acted as manager and agent, finding jobs for the sisters at theaters all over the West Coast. They were given a few small roles in several short films in 1928 and 1929, and in 1934 appeared at the Chicago World's Fair with comic George Jessel. He suggested changing their name to Garland, and at the same time Frances took the name Judy because she liked the Hoagy Carmichael song of the same name.

Ida Koverman found Garland after an L.A. music agent, one of Koverman's many moles, brought the 12-year-old singer to her in 1935. Halfway through an audition for Koverman, she called Mayer. He told Koverman, "If you like her, sign her."[3] On September 27, 1935, Garland signed a seven-year contract starting at $100 a week. Just a month later she suffered the first of the personal setbacks that haunted her at MGM, when her father died suddenly. Garland was distraught, but went right back to work. She would always go right back to work.

Garland got a break when MGM allowed the contract of their top child star, Deanna Durbin, to accidentally lapse. Garland was then MGM's only ingénue. She appeared in a half dozen films before Clark Gable's birthday on February 1, 1937, made her famous. The 14-year-old Garland sang the birthday song, "Dear Mr. Gable." In 1937 she endured the sexual affair with Spencer Tracy. To the 37-year-old drunkard it was just another conquest, but it was jarring to a 14 or 15 year old.

Strickling tried to balance the studio's needs with the needs of his charge, but she was worked to exhaustion. The studio was rarely sympathetic about personal problems. For example, on May 24, 1938, Garland was in a serious automobile accident during the filming of *Love Finds Andy Hardy*, suffering severe cuts, three broken ribs, a sprained back and a punctured lung. She recuperated for only eight days and went back to work.

By the time *The Wizard of Oz* began filming in 1938, 16-year-old Garland was already hooked on drugs. The studio that made her a star made her a drug addict. Garland's contract included clauses about maintaining physical appearance. When she first arrived, she was a 12-year-old singer round with baby fat. As she grew into a teenager and her body began changing, she had a tendency to gain weight but had to remain thin. Strickling ordered the commissary to feed her only soup and cottage cheese, and he fed her drugs. To an insecure teenager plagued by normal weight problems and mounting personal anxieties, her contract was terrifying. If her physical appearance changed or she lost her voice, she could be fired. Developing breasts as she filmed *The Wizard of Oz*, she was forced to wear a painful truss to maintain the flat appearance of a preteen for the role.

Strickling's ever-present Dr. Edward Jones prescribed Benzedrine, Phenobarbital, and Seconal, among others, to keep Garland working.[4] Fifteen-hour days meant she had trouble sleeping, so she took dozens of different sleeping pills. Also, Garland began taking a new class of drugs— amphetamines—before anyone knew their addictive powers. Garland described MGM as, "working days and nights on end. They'd give us pep-up pills to keep us on our feet long after we were exhausted, and they'd take us to the studio hospital and knock us cold with sleeping pills when we were done. Then after four hours they'd wake us up and give us the pep-up pills again so we could work another seventy-two hours in a row." MGM didn't know how dangerous these drugs were, particularly in the cocktail that Garland was forced to take. Nor did they know of the side effects. By 1940, the 18-year-old was a hopeless addict, taking pills to sleep, to wake up, to work, and to stay calm. As early as 1940 Garland's family approached Strickling about the side effects already visible. As her drug intake increased, her youthful insecurities began affecting her psyche, so Strickling arranged for her to see psychiatrists. She would be permanently damaged by the visits. She met with studio psychiatrists five mornings a week for 20 years.

By 16, Garland began to exhibit the erratic emotional behavior that would plague her years at MGM, mostly caused by Strickling's regimen of drugs and therapy. Her drugs caused psychotic episodes and insomnia, headaches, fatigue and behavior changes. Some caused awful hallucinations and shortness of breath, and are now known to cause suicidal tendencies. She was a time bomb. Her addictive personality was exacerbated by Strickling's medical protocol and studio demands. The problems extended to relationships with men, and women. She couldn't live without a man in her life, and her affairs were numerous, beginning when she barely 16. Most of her men were older, like Tracy. If men were not available, she slept with women.

In early 1939, 17-year-old Garland was obsessed with bandleader Artie Shaw, twice-divorced and a wife-beater. She snuck around with him for months. In desperation her mother asked Strickling for help. He first assigned publicist Betty Asher to keep an eye on her. Betty's father was Universal producer Ephraim "E.M." Asher and her brother would become a famous director. She grew up a privileged child in a Beverly Hills mansion next to Edmund Lowe and Lilyan Tashman. She was a petite, attractive, curly-haired blonde who fit in perfectly at UCLA. Unfortunately, in 1937, as she was starting her junior year, her father died and she had to quit school to help her alcoholic mother Lillian survive. Family friend Strickling gave her a job.

She worked with Lana Turner before being moved to the unstable Garland. Asher was 22 and Garland 18; friends were shocked by how quickly Garland and Asher became inseparable. Garland was so attached that Mannix ordered that no one was to interrupt conversations between the two even if it meant delaying shooting. Mannix's memo instructed, "Mr. Mayer wants them left alone."[5] For most of 1940 Garland pursued her affair with Shaw, with Asher doing what she could to temper the lustful wanderings. But Asher also encouraged Garland to drink and made sure she continued taking the dangerous mixture of drugs prescribed by MGM.[6]

Publicists ingratiated themselves into the lives of their assignees so as to become indispensable. Most MGM actors wouldn't think of doing *anything* without their publicists. Mickey Rooney described his as "vice president in charge of Mickey Rooney."[7] He was smart enough to know that his publicist, Les Peterson, wasn't a true friend or a real confidante. He knew Peterson was a company man looking out for MGM first, a spy, and a threat to Rooney. Rooney was one of Garland's only real true friends and warned her about Asher, but Garland still would not keep Asher at arm's length. Asher was a confidante, best friend, personal valet and private fixer, and a lover. Garland didn't know until years later, but Asher told Strickling and Mannix everything. At the time she was working with Garland, she was sleeping with Mannix himself.[8] When she found out years later, Garland was devastated, saying Asher "gave a report to the studio office every week on the people I saw, what I ate, what time I came in at night and what time I got up in the morning." She told friends, "I can remember crying for days after I found out what she was doing to me."[9] By then the damage had been done, but in 1939 Asher was Garland's new best friend.

Garland's competition for Shaw was Lana Turner. She was a year older than Garland. From the moment she arrived at MGM in 1938, Strickling shaped an image that endured 40 years. Turner loved men. A former MGM executive described her as "amoral. If she saw a stagehand with tight pants and a muscular build, she'd invite him into her dressing room." Choreographer Jack Cole was more blunt, saying, "Well, Lana Turner's a little different because she really liked men a lot, she just liked to fuck a lot."[10]

She partied with fellow young stars Ann Rutherford, Mickey Rooney and Jackie Cooper, and lost her virginity at 17 to lawyer Greg Bautzer. When her frolics made the papers Mayer summoned Turner. He gave an emotional speech, leaving the frightened youngster in tears. When she looked up, Mayer was crying, too. But the performance failed. Soon after, in February 1940, 18-year-old Turner flew to Las Vegas and married 28-year-old Shaw. She knew so little about him that it was two months before she discovered he had been married twice before.

Garland was heartbroken when Shaw married Turner, and went into one of her funks. She once told Hedda Hopper, "Sometimes I'd think I couldn't live through the day. I'd have my driver circle the block because I so hated going through those gates." She was living with her mother and sisters in a mansion she paid for. She was kept in younger roles that she hated, and she was hopelessly addicted to the MGM-prescribed drugs. The day after the Turner-Shaw marriage, Garland began dating David Rose, whom she met on *The Bob Hope Show*. English-born and raised in Chicago, the serious-minded 31-year-old was a bandleader in Hollywood. He briefly married lesbian comedienne Martha Raye in 1938, and, strangely, was Artie Shaw's best friend.

Garland was elated when the Turner-Shaw marriage fell apart after just three months, but Strickling wasn't. Turner returned from her honeymoon to work on *We Who Are Young*, and threw Shaw out when she finished. She then found herself pregnant. Mayer was still furious she had married Shaw, but Mannix stopped him from firing her and Strickling arranged an abortion. Stickling arranged a publicity tour to Hawaii with her mother, her agent Johnny Hyde, and Betty Asher. The abortion took place without anesthesia on her hotel bed. Her mother covered her mouth with her hand to stifle her cries.[11] It was performed by a studio doctor, who was paid $500 that Mannix then deducted from Turner's paycheck. Within days of her return from her week-long trip, Mannix had her back at work on *Ziegfeld Girl*.

The Turner-Shaw divorce offered some interesting tidbits to people who noticed. Mickey Rooney tried to warn Garland about Asher and her affair with Mannix. But Asher was also sleeping with Artie Shaw, also allegedly at the direction of Mannix. Like Garland, Turner thought Asher was a friend and didn't find out about the affair until Shaw testified during a divorce hearing that he answered the door and Asher invited herself inside. According to Shaw, "The next thing I knew we were in bed together. She paid me a little visit and stayed three days."[12]

In late 1940, Strickling was called in to keep dozens of stars out of the press or jail. One big problem was Lionel Atwill's parties. He was born in England and came to the U.S. in 1932, building a career portraying suave villains in horror films such as *Dr. X* (1932), *Mystery of the Wax Museum* (1933), and *Son of Frankenstein* (1939). During his loan-outs to MGM, Atwill became friendly with many actors and executives. He lived in a lovely Spanish hacienda in Pacific Palisades at 13515 d'Este Drive and cultivated an image as an erudite country gentleman surrounded by English master paintings and antiques. But his dark side was obsessed with murder trials and his weekly sex parties. The parties were by invitation only, and guests had to bring a doctor's letter certifying a clean bill of health. After a formal dinner, guests retired to the living room and ceremoniously removed everything but jewelry. Atwill assigned partners according to personal preferences and visited different rooms during the weekend-long party.[13]

Strickling knew dozens of MGM stars visited the parties, including Gable, Crawford, Stanwyck, Dietrich, and allegedly Mannix. Atwill's soirées remained a Hollywood secret until early 1941. His 1940 Christmas party included several underage girls, and one 16-year-old Minnesota runaway named Sylvia claimed she became pregnant there. Atwill was found innocent at trial but subsequent court proceedings led to a conviction for perjury. Strickling prevailed upon the police and the prosecutors not to investigate his parties any further, and Sylvia was sent home from L.A. with a cash settlement.

In February of 1941, as the Atwill party stories filled front pages, a Hollywood legend was dying in a small bungalow in Beachwood Canyon. For 25 years, Larry Edmunds' cramped Hollywood Boulevard bookstore was a favorite of the movie elite like W.C. Fields, the Barrymores, Basil Rathbone, and every beautiful actress in Hollywood. Edmunds had a voracious sexual appetite and affairs that included Mary Astor, Marlene Dietrich, Paulette Goddard, and dozens of others. He also slept with men. But by February 1941 he had drifted into alcoholism and mental illness and was living in a garage apartment at 2470 Beachwood Drive, consumed with alcoholic delusions. Police found his head wedged into the stove, dead from gas fumes, near a suicide note describing little men he saw crawling through the walls trying to kill him. Of more concern to Strickling, after he received the call from police, was the house full of mementoes from MGM stars, both male and female. His men rushed to the house to remove hundreds of notes and gifts from lovers of both sexes.

In the early months of 1941, MGM began filming *Dr. Jekyll and Mr.*

Hyde, with Spencer Tracy as the crazed doctor. He threatened to walk out unless Ingrid Bergman was given the sexy role of Ivy, the doctor's love interest, rather than Victor Fleming's choice, Lana Turner. The studio bowed and Bergman got the part. She was married to a Swedish doctor and had an infant daughter, but once filming began she slept with Fleming and Tracy, who stole the 26-year-old from his old friend. The fight over Bergman led to frequent arguments between the normally close friends. The fling lasted for several months until her husband heard about it and approached Mayer. Mannix ordered Tracy to end the affair or be fired, while Strickling told writers that Tracy was just "mentoring" the young actress and arranged photos of the two at a Beverly Hills ice cream shop sharing milk shakes.

Tracy's next fling would last 30 years. When Katharine Hepburn first came to Hollywood, one of her RKO bosses described her as "a cross between a monkey and a horse."[14] She wasn't the typical Hollywood ingénue; she was covered with freckles. David O. Selznick found her "sexually repellent,"[15] and described her as a "boa constrictor on a fast." Writer Dorothy Parker described her acting talent as "running a gamut of emotions from A to B." But fans loved her. Born into a wealthy Connecticut family, she moved to Hollywood in 1932. She left her husband behind, refusing to let him come along. But she did bring best friend Laura Harding, an heiress to the American Express fortune. The two were inseparable. Even Hepburn's marriage, forced upon her by her family, didn't end the strange relationship. She and Harding lived in a Coldwater Canyon house that had once belonged to Boris Karloff. By the time she met Tracy in early 1941, she was an established star with a résumé that included *A Bill of Divorcement* (1932), *Bringing Up Baby* (1938), and *The Philadelphia Story* (1940).

She had relationships with men and women. Her men included Leland Hayward and Charles Boyer (both were married), and she lived with Howard Hughes. She called them her beaus but continued to share the house with Harding. The couple's weird arrangement was often discussed, since they acted as a couple and Harding described herself at RKO as "Kate's husband." Hepburn described her actual husband as being "swell about everything," and he stayed in Connecticut until she divorced him in 1936. Harding accompanied her to Mexico for the quickie divorce. In early 1941 Tracy and Hepburn were cast in *Woman of the Year*. The sexual tension between the two was evident from the first day. It's hard to explain why they got together. Tracy was an absentee married man and Hepburn had an aversion to marriage, whether from her earlier failure, her sexual preferences or, as she told writers, because "actors should never marry." For Tracy's part, perhaps at 41 (to her 34) he wanted to trade affairs for a more permanent — but still illicit — relationship. Hepburn knew that Tracy was an alcoholic; mothering the recalcitrant drunk fulfilled some need for her. Whatever the reason, by the time shooting ceased in October 1941, the two were a couple.

Strickling had an odd challenge with the Tracy-Hepburn pairing. For the most part, Tracy's indiscretions went unpunished in the press. He was so unfaithful that he appeared faithful. Louise lived in their Encino ranch and Tracy lived in hotels, but they spoke daily, and on most weekends he visited his children. Louise founded the John Tracy Clinic, named for their son (who was born deaf), using a sizeable portion of her own wealth. She raised millions to found research and treatment centers for deaf children. She also served on a variety of charity boards and was a sympathetic figure and a press favorite. Somehow his relationship with Hepburn went uncommented-on.

At the same time in early October 1941, Strickling received a frantic phone call from Robert Taylor. His arranged marriage to Barbara Stanwyck was bizarre. It wasn't sexual other than experimentally, and he sometimes tested the waters with other women if the mood suited him. Stanwyck bullied Taylor in front of his friends. She once strode into their family room while Taylor had a drink with John Wayne and said, "Send your friends home. It's time for bed."[16] He meekly complied, shrugging his shoulders.

During that summer, 1941, Taylor had filmed *Johnny Eager* with Lana Turner. She made plays for most of her leading men and, Taylor's sexual identity and marital status aside, she went after him. In her memoirs Turner suggested she walked away from the affair because she didn't want to "break up a marriage." More likely, she walked away when Taylor told Stanwyck of his interest in the younger star. Even though his was a marriage of convenience between friends arranged by their studio, Stanwyck reacted strangely. She tried to kill herself.

On October 7, 1941, Taylor found her in the bathroom bleeding profusely from gashes in her arms. She had severed arteries in her wrist and forearms and would have bled to death had Taylor not stumbled upon her. Strickling had her quietly taken to Cedars of Lebanon Hospital, the favorite for the MGM doctors. The press was told that Stanwyck was trying to open a jammed window and had accidentally cut herself. In an odd coincidence, Strickling would use the same excuse after a 1952 suicide attempt by Lana Turner.

The Taylor-Stanwyck marriage wasn't the only strange coupling at MGM during the early 1940s. Nelson Eddy and Jeanette MacDonald kept Strickling busy, as did Judy Garland and David Rose. Garland and Rose had been dating since early 1940 and as the relationship bloomed in 1941, Mayer called them in and warned them against marrying. Garland responded by hosting an elaborate engagement party for 600 and a few weeks later on July 28, 1941, eloping to Las Vegas. Garland brought along Asher. Mayer could do nothing because Garland was by then a proven star, but to keep a closer eye on the actress Mannix hired Rose in the music department. The couple moved into a mansion in Bel Air, but just a few months later she decided to end the marriage. Unfortunately, she also discovered she was pregnant. Mannix and Strickling convinced her to get an abortion and keep it from Rose. The procedure was done at a private medical office by studio doctors and nurses[17] and Rose apparently never knew.

As 1941 drew to a close and people came to grips with the coming of World War II, MGM was dealing with Mickey Rooney. Growing up during the 1930s, Rooney and pal Garland led a rowdy group of young stars who partied and rebelled against studio controls. Rooney was valuable; a dozen Andy Hardy movies between 1938 and 1940 made him the most popular young actor in the world, but Mickey loved women. He tried to bed almost every woman he met at MGM, and even had a fling with Norma Shearer after Thalberg's death. In late 1941, Rooney fell in love with beautiful southern belle Ava Gardner. MGM's control over the relationship is an example of the pervasiveness of studio presence in actor's lives by the 1940s.

Mayer at first tried to stop the romance, but on Christmas Eve, 1941, Rooney convinced Gardner to marry him. During a drunken party, he called Hedda Hopper to give her the news. Hopper called Strickling at home to let him know before she wrote an article. Strickling called Rooney and told him, "Mr. Mayer isn't going to be happy about this"[18] and tried to talk him out of it. Then Mayer called Gardner and Rooney into his office and tried. He warned Gardner, "He just wants to get in your pants," and told Rooney, "You're so hot for her you can't think straight ... I warned Judy Garland ... I warned Lana Turner ... You kids don't think." Then he cried, telling them, "You're breaking my heart, Mickey."[19] But nothing worked.

Mayer realized he couldn't stop them, but he could control everything else. As soon as the couple left his office, Mayer called Strickling and Les Peterson. He told Peterson, "I want no publicity until it's over. Find a church out of town and see to it the local press gets an exclusive after the wedding. We don't want snoopers or reporters getting wind of it beforehand. Strickling will take care of the rest. Under no circumstances is anyone to know where they will be spending their honeymoon. Find a hotel nearby. Stay with them every minute they're not in the room. Mickey will be very busy filming in the meantime so I want you to get the wedding ring. Ask him about the inscription, but it's important no one knows who's buying it. Then there's the matter of a place for Mickey and Ava to live. Make sure it's off the beaten path. Bel Air and Beverly Hills are out! A two-bedroom apartment in a nice building. Not too expensive because Mickey's paying off the mortgage on his Encino house. When you think you've found a suitable place ... take care of the lease."[20]

Like Otto Winkler with Gable and Lombard, press agent Peterson accompanied Gardner and Rooney on their wedding trip to Santa Barbara and stayed for the Carmel honeymoon. The news was spread by Hopper — given the scoop over rival Parsons because she had warned Strickling when she heard from Rooney. MGM orchestrated everything even as Rooney and Gardner divorced two years later. During the divorce Mayer promised Gardner starring roles if she wouldn't demand too much of Rooney's money.

The weekend after the premiere of the Tracy-Hepburn film *Woman of the Year,* the United States was thrown into World War II by the Japanese attack on Pearl Harbor on December 7, 1941. Studio life changed from the moment the first bomb fell. The studios would be an important part of the war effort at every level. Like the rest of America, Hollywood people were glued to their radios during the days after the attack. Popular weekly radio shows were replaced by emergency broadcasts confirming that the U.S. would be at war with Japan in days.

Employees at every level joined the services, including many stars. Cameramen and technicians were inducted to produce training and propaganda films. Stars sold war bonds. Everyone in Hollywood would be involved in the war effort for the next four years. A blackout was enforced in L.A., and bomb shelters were everywhere — in backyards, under businesses. Sandbagged bunkers were thrown up all over the studios. People along the coast lived in fear of an invasion, in fear that L.A. was a primary target given the numerous aerospace facilities. Near the tangle of Burbank studios stood Lockheed Aircraft's camouflaged hangars, runways and office buildings. From the air the property looked like the surrounding homes and fields.

Next door was Warner Brothers and eccentric studio chief Jack Warner, whose first response was something less than patriotic. Worried his large sound stages would look like the nearby aircraft hangers he had workers paint the name "LOCKHEED" in 50–foot-tall letters on the roof of his biggest soundstage, along with a 100–foot arrow pointing in Lockheed's direction. When a Civil Air Patrol pilot saw the sign and it made the papers, Warner painted over it.

Mayer was desperate to hold onto as many stars as he could. Some enlisted before the Japanese attack. Jimmy Stewart and Robert Montgomery had already finished basic training and were in Europe, and Mayer was terrified he would lose Clark Gable. In the two years since he had married Carole Lombard, Gable had become the most popular star in the world, but he wanted to enlist. Mayer pleaded with him to stay and had him appointed head of the Hollywood Victory Committee, and without his knowledge, lobbied Washington friends to keep him out of harm's way. Lombard fought even harder to get him in. When she learned they were arranging a noncombat position for him, Lombard told Strickling, "The last thing I want for Pappy is one of those phony commissions." In the midst of the wrangling, Gable's Victory Committee needed someone to headline a bond rally ending in Indiana. Gable suggested his wife, an Indiana native, and in early January 1942, Lombard, her mother Bessie Peters, and Otto Winkler prepared to leave for a week of rallies.

It was a difficult time for Lombard. She had retired from moviemaking to become pregnant but suffered two miscarriages and made numerous trips to fertility specialists. There was no public sympathy or support; the trips had to be kept a secret since MGM didn't want Clark Gable known as infertile. When the couple went to the renowned fertility clinic at Johns Hopkins in Baltimore, the press was told Gable was receiving treatment for a back injury that occurred when he was thrown from a horse in 1933. Strickling also reminded Lombard not to keep telling her friends, "Pa ain't much of a lay."[21]

At the same time, the Gables were fighting about his *Somewhere I'll Find You* costar Lana Turner. Gable and Turner had worked together in 1941's *Honky Tonk,* and Lombard knew about Turner's reputation as an oversexed star-climber. Lombard and everyone had waited for sparks between Turner and Gable. During *Honky Tonk* filming Strickling had fed stories about the "on-screen fireworks" between the "two powerful sex symbols." Lombard and Gable had had fierce battles over Turner, and she had threatened to come to the set "and kick them both in the ass." She told Gable, "I'll have her fired!" When he told her she couldn't do that, she yelled, "Then I'll have you fired!"[22] She began making surprise visits to the set, forcing Gable to ask her to stay away, allegedly because "the kid was nervous," and MGM banned her from the set. Gable and Turner both denied they were lovers, but Gable often bragged that he "had them all." He probably had her.

Somewhere I'll Find You filming began as Lombard was leaving for her bond-rally trip. The Sunday evening before her departure, she and Gable had a furious fight about Turner, after which Gable stormed out and spent the night elsewhere.[23] The press took note that Gable wasn't at the train station when Lombard boarded the City of Los Angeles for the first leg of the trip. But by the time she arrived in Salt Lake City, the couple had made up via telegram and for the rest of the trip they spoke twice a day and he sent dozens of roses to every hotel where she stayed.[24]

In Indianapolis on January 15, Lombard sat at a large desk in the rotunda of the Indiana statehouse for over eight hours, selling bonds and visiting with fans. The committee hoped to raise $500,000 but she sold $2,017,513 ($30 million today). That evening she headlined a dinner and was scheduled to depart the next morning by train for final stops in Kansas City and Albuquerque. Instead of waiting for the train, Lombard decided to return to L.A. immediately. As strong as the relationship was with Gable, as much as they were in love, the thought of the love scenes with Turner was driving Lombard crazy. She wanted to go home and make sure nothing was happening, even though it meant skipping the two remaining bond rallies.

Otto Winkler tried to talk her out of it, using as his excuse avoiding canceling the remaining bond stops. More likely, he just didn't want to fly; he was terrified. The only other flight he had taken was a charter flight carrying an MGM contingent to Atlanta for the 1939 premiere of *Gone with the Wind*. Seeing him shaking with fear, Lombard had taken the seat next to him and tried to calm him during takeoff, saying, "If we're going to crash, we might as well go together." It was a tragic premonition.

Like Winkler, Bessie Peters was terrified. She had never flown and begged her daughter not to fly. She was a lifelong believer in numerology and there were too many bad signs for her. The flight was on January 16; 16 is a harbinger of death. Peters' unlucky number was three. The plane was a DC-3, there were four 3s in the craft's registration number, the flight was no. 3, they were a party of 3, and her daughter was 32 years and 3 months old. To pacify her companions, Lombard agreed to decide between plane and train with a coin flip. Winkler flipped a nickel, Lombard called tails. Tails it was, so the group boarded the plane in Indianapolis at 4:00 A.M. and took off into the night. With seven fuel stops scheduled, the flight wouldn't get to L.A. until late the next afternoon. Lombard would only miss one day of the filming with her husband and Turner.

The sixth and final refueling stop was to take place on a leg from Albuquerque to Boulder, Colorado, but at the last minute the flight was diverted to Las Vegas. The plane landed at 6:30 P.M. to take on fuel and was to depart on the final leg to L.A. at 7:07 P.M. Aboard were the crew of three (another bad sign for Peters), the Lombard group and 15 servicemen. Servicemen were allowed by wartime regulations to "bump" nonmilitary passengers and tried to take Lombard's seats, but she appealed that her travels were war-related and she stayed.

As the plane took off, a crowd of almost 50 photographers and reporters orchestrated by Strickling had already gathered in Burbank to await the expected arrival at 8:45 P.M. At that moment, miners working a remote site in the hills outside Vegas saw a bright orange flash near the summit of Mount Potosi. Fifteen minutes after takeoff and just 32 miles from the airport, the TWA Skysweeper carrying Lombard flew directly into a sheer cliff on the side of what locals called Table Rock Mountain. They were seven miles off course and 750 feet below the summit when they slammed into a ridge called Double or Nothing Peak. A few hundred yards in either direction and the plane would have missed the mountain. Carole Lombard was Hollywood's first victim in WWII.

One of Strickling's publicity assistants was at the Burbank airport with the press throng when an airport official told him privately that the plane had gone down. He called Strickling, who called Mannix and Mayer. Mannix called Gable. His phone call came just after Gable had told his household staff, "It'll sure be nice having Ma back. Life without her ain't hardly worth living."[25] Mannix kept Gable in the dark about what he already knew, that Lombard was dead. Strickling chartered a plane to fly everyone to Las Vegas, and dozens of friends and coworkers raced to the scene by car. Sitting with Gable during the flight, Strickling felt that Gable already "sensed what had happened."[26] They converged on the Rancho Las Vegas Hotel even as search operations had already started. When the group checked in, the side of Table Rock Mountain facing their hotel was glowing red from the fires still burning at the site.

Searchers were led to the remote site by 73-year-old Indian guide Tweed Wilson. Mannix himself went on the 12-hour trek through knee-deep snow. The snow was covered with blood and body parts and pieces of the disintegrated, still-smoldering plane. What little was left of the bodies was charred. A decapitated female body was Lombard's. Incredibly, Mannix found a battered ruby earring, one of a pair Gable had given Lombard for Christmas the month before. Never one to lose an opportunity, Strickling told the press that a matching heart-shaped pendant had been embedded in Lombard's own heart by the force of the crash.

Gable waited the night in his bungalow with Strickling. Early the next morning, Mannix sent a telegram from a miners' station near the peak: "NO SURVIVORS. ALL KILLED INSTANTLY." Gable sat inconsolable. All he could say was, "God damn it, why Ma?"[27] It would take two or three days to bring the remains of the 22 victims down the mountain. Gable wouldn't leave Las Vegas without the remains of Lombard, her mother, and Winkler.

Waiting in a tent with a group of searchers, he noticed a toothless old cowboy trying to eat a piece of steak. He handed a deputy $100 and said, "For God's sake, get him some teeth."[28]

President Franklin Roosevelt sent a condolence telegram to Gable and awarded Lombard a presidential medal, as "the first woman to be killed in action in defense of her country in its war against the Axis powers." It was later determined that the pilot erred by changing course to make up for lost time. After a private funeral for 50 friends, Lombard was laid to rest at Forest Lawn next to her mother and an open crypt Gable purchased for himself. Strickling took full-page ads out in the L.A. newspapers. Juxtaposed with a Clarence Bull glamour photo of Lombard was MGM's trademark Leo the Lion, dressed in mourning clothes and holding a wreath in an outstretched paw. Gable was never the same.

Not all of the relationship issues were as tragic as the Gable-Lombard love story, nor were they limited to MGM couples. Publicity people at other studios faced the same challenges as Strickling. The antics of Humphrey Bogart and his feisty wife Mayo Methot were a constant headache for Warners. Their mansion at Horn and Shoreham was the battlefield for "the Battling Bogarts." She was a drunk with a temper described as a "blend of Zelda Fitzgerald and Tugboat Annie." The tone was set at their 1938 wedding, when a drunken Bogie stalked out of the reception after a fight with Methot and spent the night drinking with friends.

The two enjoyed two things: drinking and sex. Bogart said, "The whole world is three drinks behind; everybody should take three drinks and we'd be fine." He said of her, "I love a good fight. So does Mayo. We have some first-rate battles."[29] Their house was named Sluggy Hollow, their dog Sluggy, and his sailboat the *Sluggy*. A private telephone connected the house to Warners. A carpenter was on call 24 hours a day. A dozen extra doors were kept in the garage, replaced at a rate of two a month after Methot blasted them with her .45 pistol.

While stepping off their boat, Methot once tossed Bogart off a dock. At Thanksgiving dinner she hit him over the head with the turkey. Friends leaving a Hollywood restaurant found her sitting on Bogart's back, rhythmically pounding his head on the sidewalk. After a full drink thrown by Methot whistled past his head at a party he said to a friend, "It's a good thing she's a lousy shot."[30] When a drunk approached them in La Maze restaurant on Sunset, she beat him with a shoe and a brawl erupted. David Niven and his wife dove beneath a table for safety and were surprised when Bogart crawled in with them, saying, "Don't worry, Mayo's handling it."[31]

They always followed their fights with furious sex; Howard Hawks asked Bogart if "he could get an erection without first fighting Mayo."[32]

When she heard rumors Bogart and Ingrid Bergman were having sex during *Casablanca*, she stabbed him in the back with a knife. Bogart took ten stitches and told the studio doctor "ain't she a pistol?" In 1944 he left Methot for 20-year-old actress "Betty" Bacall. Methot was found dead in an Oregon motel room in 1949.

During the war Strickling had a steady problem with Lana Turner. Her short marriage to Artie Shaw and subsequent abortion didn't slow her down. In early 1942 she met John Crane through a friend and eloped to Las Vegas three weeks later. But five months later, Turner was pregnant again and discovered that Crane had not divorced his first wife. She was becoming one of MGM's most popular actresses; being branded a bigamist would be a disaster. Through friends in the Catholic church Strickling arranged for an annulment, and crafted headlines for the L.A. papers: "LANA TURNER WANTS DIVORCE, DIDN'T KNOW CRANE'S DIVORCE DECREE WASN'T FINAL!"[33] He then arranged another abortion, but at the last minute Turner refused to comply. Strickling had to orchestrate a quick remarriage to Crane on Valentine's Day, 1943. Eventually, she gave birth to daughter Cheryl Crane. As a teenager Cheryl would play a prominent role in Turner's life.

On May 29, 1942, the legendary John Barrymore died. A few days later, several of his MGM friends—part of a group that had partied together for decades—played a macabre prank on Errol Flynn. The rakish Flynn had openly adored Barrymore and deliberately started a rumor that persists to this day: that he was Barrymore's illegitimate son. Barrymore had spent months at a time staying at Flynn's Torreyson Drive mansion until the last six months of his life. Owing to his prodigious alcoholism, during his final years Barrymore was incontinent, and during a visit to Flynn's estate six months before he died, had had an accident while seated on a 200-year-old settee in Flynn's living room. Flynn had somewhat sadly banished Barrymore.[34]

According to MGM director Raoul Walsh, on the night Barrymore died he and Flynn and some friends were toasting Barrymore's passing at the Cock and Bull on Sunset. Walsh excused himself, met three other friends and went to Malloy Brothers Mortuary, which he had arranged to receive Barrymore's body before it was being sent to Pierce Brothers. According to Walsh, Dick Malloy, a former actor and friend, allowed him to borrow Barrymore's body for an hour. The group loaded the body into Walsh's station wagon and drove up to Flynn's house. Mulholland House was legendary, with several amenities designed by Flynn himself. The entryway was dominated by a floor-to-ceiling fish tank backed by a carving of tropical sea life; closer scrutiny showed the carved fish all were endowed with oversized male genitalia. A huge mahogany liquor cabinet was fronted by an ornate hand-carved bullfighting scene; to open the cabinet one had to squeeze the bull's testicles. The cushions on several of the carved dining-room chairs hid hydraulic dildos, which were controlled from a panel beneath the table by Flynn's chair. Flynn, a notorious voyeur, installed bugs in the ladies' bathrooms, peepholes in walls, and a mirror above the main guest bed. Above the (two-way) mirror was a game room with a glass-bottomed card table, through which players could view the bed directly below.

Walsh and his friends propped Barrymore's body up in an overstuffed chair in the living room and sat quietly in the dark waiting for Flynn. According to Flynn, he arrived drunk, walked in and saw Barrymore in his favorite chair. He let out an earsplitting scream and ran from the room. The group had one final toast and then returned the body to the funeral home.

Some Barrymore friends deny the kidnapping took place. Flynn described it in his *My Wicked, Wicked Ways* and Walsh in his *Each Man in His Time*. But Barrymore friend Gene Fowler said he and his son sat through the entire night at Malloy Brothers and, according to Fowler, the only visitor was a local prostitute, who knelt before the body in prayer and then quietly left.[35] Any or all of the accounts may be apocryphal, but all have become part of Hollywood legend.

By the fall of 1942, Judy Garland moved out of the mansion she shared with David Rose and into an apartment in Westwood with Betty Asher. The two were never apart and were still lovers.[36] They were photographed all over L.A. shopping, dining, and walking hand in hand. The couple was so obvious that MGM workers questioned Garland's actual sexual preferences. Asher and Garland were on-again off-again lovers for years, though Garland wasn't a lesbian. By then she preferred oral sex to intercourse and preferred women to men.[37] Sexual experimentation was rampant in the permissive movie colony of the 1940s, so Garland wasn't the exception.

During the last week of October 1942, both Asher and Garland attended a party in Brentwood where she was introduced to Tyrone Power, son of the legendary Tyrone Power, Sr. The 28-year-old actor was a major star and Garland was transfixed. He had just seen her performance in *Me and My Gal*, which had just been released, and remembered for her the exact date that he had seen her movie: October 16. She was smitten and fell in love with Power. His wife, the gorgeous but androgynous bisexual French actress Annabella, was on an extended vacation. According to Power's best friend Watson Webb, "There was an immediate attraction between them, and by the time Annabella got back ... he was crazy about her." Power began secretly visiting Garland's duplex at 152 Glenroy Avenue, near UCLA.

Tyrone Power was an enigma. He was handsome, intelligent, athletic, and talented, and had an almost mystical power over women even though he was bisexual or homosexual. But strangely, he seemed as interested in Garland as she was in him. Their intense sexual chemistry somehow quieted Power's sexual confusion. His studio planted hundreds of articles describing his power over women. The July 1937 *Hollywood Magazine* listed 40 actresses supposedly in love with him under the title, "They Carry a Torch for Tyrone." The November 1937 *Movie Mirror Magazine* offered "Tyrone Power's Bachelor Guide to Hollywood." When a studio pairing with Janet Gaynor fizzled, she married her own "beard," homosexual MGM costumer Gilbert Adrian. Of the Gaynor-Adrian wedding, Bob Cummings said "Janet Gaynor's husband was Adrian, but her wife was Mary Martin."[38]

On April 23, 1939, Power had married the bisexual actress Annabella, 20 years his senior. It was in the context of their open marriage that he had the affair with Garland, who didn't know Power's proclivities. The two appeared in public arm in arm, clearly a couple, which no doubt alarmed Mayer and Mannix. Obviously, Mannix knew about the affair, since Garland was still sharing her Westwood house with Asher, and Asher reported everything to Mannix. Rumors about the relationship between Asher and Garland aside, a public relationship between Garland and Power, two married stars, was a bigger problem given that his studio's campaign to hide Power's homosexuality relentlessly bombarded fans with articles about his marriage.

To further complicate matters, Power was enlisting in the Marines. Mannix and Strickling knew the unstable Garland wouldn't react well when her lover went to war, so they enlisted Asher as a double agent to help end the relationship. In January 1943, as Power was leaving for basic training, Garland asked him to divorce Annabella and marry her but he was noncommittal. He told Annabella he was in love with Garland, but she told him she didn't care. It was a stalemate; Power wouldn't ask for a divorce and his wife wouldn't offer one.

Garland began filming *Girl Crazy* with best friend Rooney. She missed Power, and director Busby Berkeley's frantic filming pace and badgering sent her over the edge. She was "just a wreck"; only Rooney saved her from a nervous breakdown. Just a few weeks later she was confined to a hospital and found out she was pregnant with Power's child.[39] The baby was the wedge Mannix and Strickling needed as they plotted with Asher. They sent Garland to New York to visit Power in May 1943, and she waited in a hotel room with Asher. She tried to get Power on the phone, while Asher bad-mouthed him and kept calls he *did* make from getting to her. Asher told Garland that Annabella was pregnant (a lie) and that MGM had discovered Power entertaining his bunkmates by reading Garland's private love letters to them. This last deception was the final blow. A heartbroken Garland returned with Asher and never spoke to Power again. Garland would say of the relationship, "It really was different between Tyrone and me. It was no small affair."

Strickling arranged an abortion, and Garland and Asher settled back into their Westwood duplex. Over the next two years Garland ground out an incredible nine films. Musicals require more preparation and physical exertion than other film genres. Doing two musicals a year would be hard work; Garland more than doubled that. For several years Asher continued in her role as a mole for Mannix, still Garland's lover. Asher, as unstable as Garland, would eventually commit suicide, but would first serve as maid of honor at Garland's later wedding to Vincente Minnelli.

During the war the studio faced challenges of all types, from family and personal to military. Strickling and Mannix made sure that some stars received deferments from military service, while publicizing the wartime exploits of those who did serve. Lew Ayres didn't fit into either category. Minnesota-born Ayres was discovered in the Coconut Grove nightclub in 1927 and starred in dozens of films through the 1930s, from Garbo's *The Kiss* to *All Quiet on the Western Front* (both 1930) to eight *Dr. Kildare* pictures. But he was profoundly impacted by the antiwar theme of *Quiet* and became active in a variety of social causes. When he was drafted in 1942, he informed Selective Service that he was claiming conscientious objector status, refusing to carry a weapon. He volunteered to serve in the medical corps at the front, but the public backlash was loud.

Strickling suggested the studio publicize Ayres' accomplishments, but Mayer demanded that he be fired. Nick Schenck defended Ayres but his efforts backfired when he told reporters, "He's been a vegetarian as long as I've known him." Ayres served as a front-line medic in dozens of South Pacific battles, served in New Guinea, and won several awards for bravery. Even so, he could find little work for five years after the war. He never fully returned to public favor until a role as a sympathetic physician in *Johnny Belinda* (1948), but Mayer forbade him from working for the studio as long as he was there.

One MGM star who wanted to carry a gun was Gable. In the six months since his wife's death he couldn't work, overwhelmed with guilt for offering her for the ill-fated bond-selling trip. When ex-lover Joan Crawford offered her shoulder he took her up on her offer; four times a week he sat with her until almost sunrise.[40] Gable told his closest friends— Strickling, Mannix, racing driver Al Monesco, and his favorite hunting companion Harry Fleishman — that he could never face a camera again. He told Fleishman he hoped he would be killed in combat.

Strickling convinced Mannix and Mayer that Gable should be allowed to go. Several years later when he renegotiated his MGM contract, Gable included a clause that if Strickling ever left MGM, Gable himself would handle his own publicity. Strickling was the only person that Gable trusted. In May 1942, Mannix convinced Mayer it would be better for MGM if his friend was allowed to go. His emotional state since Lombard's death made him unusable on film anyway, so that August Gable enlisted in the air force. On the day he left for basic training he rode his motorcycle to Jill Winkler's North Hollywood home. Otto's widow was surprised to see him ride up, more so when he gave her a gold I.D. bracelet. He told her, "I'm going in and I don't expect to come back, and I don't really give a hoot if I do or not."[41]

Gable was sworn into the air corps on August 11, 1942. The chain that held his dog tag also held a gold locket that enclosed the remnant of the earring Mannix found near Lombard's body. The only soldier allowed to redesign his dog tag, Gable remade a box to hold Lombard's picture.[42] Mannix arranged for him to serve with Andrew McIntyre, an MGM cameraman who wouldn't leave Gable's side for two years. Strickling also arranged that the Air Force would not to release photos of Gable with his crew cut or without a hat. Those ears must remain hidden, even during the war. In October 1942, Gable was commissioned a second lieutenant and assigned to produce a propaganda film about aerial gunners. It was one of the most dangerous assignments in the corps, and it was thought Gable's movie might help. In early 1943 Gable and McIntyre headed for England with the 351st Heavy Bombardment Group.

Gable's friends and superiors all thought he wanted to die in action, and he almost did during a year's worth of B-17 bombing raids over Europe. He returned from sorties in planes riddled with bullet holes. One exploding shell ripped through one of his boots, and one barely missed his head. Hitler offered a bounty to the pilot who shot down Gable's plane, and several came close. Strickling made sure that Gable's exploits were well publicized back home.

His fellow airmen loved him. He refused any special treatment and volunteered for dangerous missions. As he stood by the bed of a wounded comrade, a doctor walked up and told Gable the boy would be dead soon, thinking he couldn't hear what was said. Gable noticed a tear on the doomed flyer's face and exploded, grabbing the doctor by the throat and saying, "If you ever do that again, I'll kill you."[43] He also resumed womanizing, reigniting an affair with ex-girlfriend Elizabeth Allen, an English actress he had met at MGM. And he drank himself unconscious with his pals. Gable manned the extremely dangerous turret guns during dozens of real dogfights, and continued flying for the rest of 1943, gathering 50,000 feet of film for his project. He went home in 1943 with a Distinguished Flying Cross and the Air Medal.

Gable wasn't the only brave MGM employee. Director John Ford flew aboard one of the 16 B-25 bombers in Lt. Col. Jimmy Doolittle's raid on Tokyo. Filming from the nose of one of the bombers, Ford

Jean Harlow and Clark Gable during the 1937 filming of *Saratoga*. Harlow would be dead two weeks later, ending a romance and friendship. Gable began dating Carole Lombard soon afterward.

screamed for the pilot to fly lower! He was seriously wounded by Japanese machine-gun fire while filming during the Battle of Midway. Another man's man at MGM was prolific director Woodbridge "Woody" Strong II. After serving in World War I he fought as a mercenary in Africa, and was a lumberjack in Canada and a prospector in Alaska. He got a job with director Charles Brabin in 1915 and starred in D.W. Griffith's *Intolerance* (1916), adding "Van Dyke" for affect. His nickname was "One-Take Van Dyke." He felt the first take was usually the best, and the studio loved him for bringing films in on time and under budget. Van Dyke finished William Powell's *The Thin Man* (1934) in 18 days.

He personally chose Johnny Weissmuller for the lead in his *Tarzan, the Ape Man* (1932), and was known for *Manhattan Melodrama* (1935) and the popular Jeanette MacDonald–Nelson Eddy musicals of the 1930s and 1940s. He was just the second director honored in the fabled Forecourt of the Stars at Hollywood's Grauman's Chinese Theater, when he and his friend Gable left their handprints side by side after 1936's *Love on the Run*. He was a close friend to Gable, Mayer, Strickling and Mannix. They hunted and drank together and chased women, and in 1935 Van Dyke and Mannix became family when 45-year-old Woody married Eddie's niece, who was only 20. Ruth Mannix came to L.A. with Eddie and Bernice and lived with them until her marriage to Van Dyke.

During the 1940s Van Dyke fought a losing battle with cancer, and in 1943 the feisty 52–year-old decided to take his own life. Over the last month he hosted farewell dinners at the Brentwood home at 334 South Bundy Drive that he shared with Ruth. He invited his friends over for what most guests didn't know were in fact goodbye dinners. Only a very few of his closest friends knew the secret.[44] On February 3, 1943, Van Dyke put on a favorite army uniform and had dinner with Mayer and Strickling. The next day he was found dead in the same chair, dead of an overdose of barbiturates. The world would never know that Van Dyke committed suicide; the word never appeared in a single obituary, nor on his death certificate. Strickling arranged that Van Dyke's death certificate indicate death caused by the vaguely-described "primarily cancer of the lung."[45]

Beginning in January 1943, most newspapers were full of Errol Flynn's statutory rape trial. Perhaps the most notorious womanizer in Hollywood, his lifestyle was described as "a total affront to good taste." The first assault allegedly took place at a September 27, 1942, party at a Bel Air mansion rented by Flynn's friend, wealthy playboy Freddie McAvoy, and actors Bruce Cabot and Stephen Raphael. Fifteen-year-old Nebraska runaway Betty Hanson said she went to the party with friends from Warners, and after watching Flynn play tennis had sex with the star in an upstairs bedroom. The second accusation was made by 16–year-old Peggy Lee Satterly, who alleged that Flynn attacked her aboard his yacht *Sirocco* during a cruise off Catalina in August 1941. Satterly actually did date Flynn, but her case was lost when it was shown that if she been beneath Flynn, as she claimed, she couldn't have seen the "beautiful full moon" through the porthole that she testified to seeing.

After the month-long trial, dueling headlines yelled, "'SEND HIM TO SAN QUENTIN' STATE URGES ERROL FLYNN JURY!"[46] and "DEFENSE HITS CHARMER VIEW OF ERROL FLYNN."[47] After the jury deliberated for nine hours, a final headline read, "VERDICT GIVEN UP—ERROL FLYNN CLEARED! CAREER SAVED!"[48] During the media frenzy a *Los Angeles Times* reporter invented the phrase "in like Flynn" to describe his success with women.

Incredibly, during Flynn's trial he took an interest in teenager Nora Eddington, who tended the cigar stand at the courthouse. His pal and stunt double Buster Wiles said Flynn's lawyers ordered him *not* to sleep with her until the trial was over, and just a month later Flynn and Eddington began dating. When she hesitated to have a first sexual encounter with Flynn, he got high on cocaine and alcohol and brutally raped her.[49] They were married in Mexico in August 1943, and the teenager gave birth to a daughter four months later. Flynn died October 14, 1959, in Canada, where the 50–year-old was living openly with a 16-year-old. His life is best summed up by his autopsy, which noted, "blood-alcohol level of 0.35 percent [four times the legal limit] appears not unusual for the deceased to have been able to handle without difficulty."

During the Flynn trial, young English actor Peter Lawford arrived at MGM and debuted in Greer Garson's *Mrs. Miniver*. Over the years Strickling linked Lawford with dozens of actresses including Lana Turner, Ava Gardner, Dorothy Dandridge, Lee Remick, Kim Novak, and June Allyson. He would also marry four times and father four children by Patricia Kennedy, but even his reputation as a ladies' man and membership in the "Rat Pack" with Dean Martin, Sammy Davis, Jr., and Joey Bishop didn't stop questions about his bisexuality. Lawford had bit parts in dozens of World War II films such as *A Yank at Eton* (1942) and *London Blackout Murders* (1943), and as World War II wound down was on the verge of stardom.

But MGM was worried about his growing reputation. From his earliest days at MGM, Lawford hung around with a strange group: bisexual Keenan Wynn, homosexual Van Johnson, and emotionally unstable Robert Walker. The foursome rode motorcycles, socialized nightly, and were a problem for Strickling. Lawford's mother approached Mayer in 1944 and asked for help, saying "There's no use to beat about the bush. I'm concerned my son is a homosexual."[50] He called young Lawford in and offered the latest MGM "cure" for homosexuality: injections of extracts from monkey glands that Mayer said were working for several MGM homosexuals. Lawford offered a relationship with Lana Turner as proof he was heterosexual. Wynn, Lawford, Walker and Johnson stayed together, but a few years later Mayer would step in with a radical strategy to stop the stories.

Strickling cleaned up after another suicide in 1944, but Lupe Velez's tragic death wasn't as well planned as Woody Van Dyke's. Divorced from Johnnie Weissmuller since 1938, her South American–themed *Mexican Spitfire* had dropped in popularity, and she was reduced to low-budget spin-offs such as *Mexican Spitfire Sees a Ghost*, *Mexican Spitfire's Elephant*, and *Mexican Spitfire's Blessed Event* (1943). *Blessed Event* was a madcap comedy about a mistaken pregnancy; it pushed Velez into an emotional tailspin.

Velez's failures with men were legend. Her relationships were as volatile as she, and though she longed to be married and have children she could never sustain a relationship. Being childless was a source of constant sorrow, and *Blessed Event* made her feel even worse. In 1944 she was living alone inside the 732 Rodeo Drive mansion that she named Casa Felicitas; the home that never was a "Happy House." She was in love with Austrian playboy-actor Harald Ramond. On November 27, Velez discovered she was pregnant and announced that the couple were engaged. Ramond first promised to marry her but abruptly changed his mind and left her. The devoutly Catholic Velez wouldn't have an abortion.

She wrote a pathetic note imploring, "How could you, Harald, fake such a great love for me and our baby when all the time you didn't want us?" On December 14, 1944, Velez sat alone to a huge Mexican dinner and for dessert took 80 Seconals. She expected to quietly die in her 30–foot bedroom, but the combination of liquor, dinner, and drugs made her violently ill, and as she ran into the bathroom she tripped on a rug. She sprawled headlong into the commode and broke her neck; she was found with her head in the toilet. Velez had not been an MGM employee since the 1930s but remained friendly with Mannix and Strickling. She and Mannix were lovers in 1937, but even Strickling was unable to arrange a Van Dyke–style revision of the death.

The press already knew she killed herself, but he was at least able to cleanse the publicized version. He didn't want Velez remembered for breaking her neck on a toilet, so he enlisted old friend Adela Rogers St. Johns to offer a more serene scene. She wrote of a quiet dinner, 100 glowing candles filling her all-white bedroom, and soft music playing in the background. Velez, in a beautiful white nightgown, swallowed pills and lay on her all-white bed, where she died peacefully with her hands folded on her chest clutching the rosary that St. Johns said had been used every day by the tragic actress. She described her as "the epitome of joyous, uninhibited lust for life." Louella Parsons wrote "Lupe was never lovelier as she lay there, as if slumbering ... like a child taking nappy."[51] Both writers also publicly condemned Ramond. Strickling and Mannix reported Austrian citizen Ramond to immigration authorities who conveniently "lost" his paperwork, making him an illegal alien. Then they made sure Ramond was blackballed from every studio in Hollywood. He had to wait until the war in Europe was over before returning to Austria and until the day of his 1952 departure didn't work a minute.

The mid-1940s continued to be emotionally trying for Judy Garland, and it was difficult for Strickling and Mannix to keep her stable enough to work. She went through a long divorce from David Rose (they separated in 1943 but weren't divorced for a year) and was tortured by her doomed relationship with Tyrone Power and the resulting abortion, but somehow managed to stay on the MGM treadmill. During the war years Garland did hit movies like *Girl Crazy* (1943), *Meet Me in St. Louis* (1944), and *Ziegfeld Follies* (filmed in 1945). Barely 20, her popularity skyrocketed as her personal life spiraled downward.

She had sexual liaisons with dozens of MGM employees, most for sport. She tried to seduce her homosexual friends and seduced one man simply because he was ultra-faithful to his wife. She gave a friend the thumbs-up sign to indicate she had been successful. Her heated affair with married Joseph Mankiewicz cost him his MGM job when he refused Mayer's demand that he end the affair. She also slept with Orson Welles while he was married to Rita Hayworth. In his autobiog-

Fiesty and sexy Lupe Velez when she was Mrs. Johnny Weissmuller.

raphy, actor Charles Bickford described the young actress as a "sex-driven, drug-crazed wreck," blaming Asher, who he said was a "spy ... drug addict sex pervert."[52]

The studio made halfhearted attempts to help Garland, all the while feeding her drugs. Earlier in 1944 rumors of Garland's use of illegal drugs led to an investigation by federal drug agents. When Mannix learned a female drug dealer associated with gangster Lucky Luciano was indeed selling drugs to Garland, he arranged for an old New Jersey gangster acquaintance to take the drug dealer to the Palisades Amusement Park for a ride on the park's huge Ferris wheel. With the car stopped at the top of the ride, she was told that she would either stop selling drugs to Garland or she would be thrown off. She disappeared from the lot.

Adela Rogers St. Johns described rumors that Garland and Asher were giving lesbian displays for an unnamed studio executive. The only executive with that power was Mannix, and his relationship with Asher was well known. But it was only a rumor.[53] In March 1944, Garland was cast in *Meet Me in St. Louis* with director Vincente Minnelli. Lester Anthony Minnelli had worked as a costume designer, a photographer's assistant and an art director when Arthur Freed hired him at MGM in 1940. MGM knew Minnelli was a homosexual; Freed's unit had so many gay men they were called "Freed's Fairy Unit."[54] During *St. Louis* filming Garland and the 19–years-older Minnelli became friends, and a romantic relationship of *some* kind blossomed. She apparently ignored Minnelli's relationship with his live-in Japanese valet. The fact that they had a relationship of any kind shocked everyone; their sole attraction was probably mutual neurosis.

Her costar on the follow-up *The Clock* was Robert Walker, perhaps the only person at MGM more emotionally unstable than Garland. His gorgeous wife Phyllis had been selected by David O. Selznick to play the lead role in *The Song of Bernadette*; unfortunately for Walker, during filming Selznick fell in love with his wife — whom Selznick had renamed Jennifer Jones — and stole her away from him. Walker spent most of the filming in a drunken stupor. Just six months later, Selznick divorced his wife, Mayer's daughter Irene, and married Jones.

On June 15, 1945, Garland married Minnelli. Garland researchers guess that by marrying a homosexual she could continue her sexual affairs without guilt. She told St. Johns he was "the most interesting man I've ever known."[55] And he was nice to her. Mayer hoped marriage might cure Minnelli's homosexuality and that the care Minnelli showed Garland would translate into a happier employee. Betty Asher was the maid of honor. At Strickling's suggestion Asher hinted to Garland a child would be good, and during her New York honeymoon Garland and Minnelli discovered she was already pregnant. She would have a baby in early 1946.

In late 1943 Clark Gable sadly returned to the Encino ranch he had shared with Carole Lombard. Officially still in the Air Force, he was still receiving $7,500 a week from MGM even though he told Mayer he would film nothing until the war ended. The publicity Strickling milked from their patriotic star was worth much more than what they were paying him. He had time to date, and drink. He was drunk most of the time, downing over a quart of scotch every day.[56] Even so, friends said the only way to tell that Gable was drunk was that when he walked through doorways drunk, he turned sideways.

At about four in the morning on March 24, 1945, Strickling received a call from MCA talent agent Harry Friedman, who lived next to the Bristol Drive traffic circle at Sunset. He was awakened by a loud crash in the trees in the middle of the circle. Lying next to the still-smoking wreckage he found a drunken and bloody Clark Gable, who had driven into the circle. He had been at a party at the home of Paulette Goddard celebrating the U.S. victory at Iwo Jima, and was probably heading to Joan Crawford's house up the block for his almost nightly visit. Friedman said to Strickling, "Geez Howard, your friend is bleeding, what do you want me to do?"[57] Strickling, living out in the valley in Encino, called Ralph Wheelright, one of his publicity men, and MGM police chief Whitey Hendry. Both arrived before police, and Hendry brought an MGM doctor. Police roped off the area, keeping inquisitive bystanders and reporters a block away.

The MGM doctor took Gable to Cedars of Lebanon Hospital, where he received ten stitches to his head and shoulder. He was signed into a private wing for observation. Even several hours later, Gable was still in a drunken stupor, loudly threatening to walk out of the hospital, so Strickling ordered that all of his clothes be taken and he be confined to his bed. He spent the next three days locked in isolation, naked, drying out. Had Gable been uninjured in the accident, it would never have surfaced. No evidence remained at the scene except for a few scarred trees, and no witness saw anything. But Gable had been hospitalized and the press had paid informants at Cedars, so within minutes of his arrival, they knew Gable had been in an accident. Strickling had to go public, so he released a statement the next morning, blaming a drunk driver:

> Clark Gable, the motion-picture actor, was in Cedars of Lebanon yesterday recovering from injuries he received in a freak accident late Saturday [24 March] on the traffic circle at Sunset Blvd. and Bristol Ave., Brentwood. Gable was driving east on Sunset Blvd. and, in accordance with traffic regulations, proceeded around the south half of the traffic circle. He was confronted with another car, the driver of which apparently had become confused and was proceeding west on the same arc of the circle. To avoid colliding with the other car Gable drove his automobile over a curb and struck a tree, throwing him against the steering wheel. The actor received a laceration of the right leg which required several stitches, and a bruised chest, the studio reported. The driver of the other car apparently didn't realize there had been an accident and didn't stop.[58]

Strickling said Gable was on the way to visit *him*. Why Gable would visit him at 4:00 A.M. was never explained. But the Brentwood accident has become part of Gable lore for different reasons. What should have been just another drunken bender has evolved into legend, partly because of the confusion it spawned. The 1945 accident is confused with the 1933 Hollywood accident when Gable allegedly killed a pedestrian.

Gable wasn't chastened. He didn't let up on his drinking, nor his womanizing. Returning from the war, he had affairs with Virginia Grey, Marilyn Maxwell, Kay Williams (he liked her from the first when he said,

"Why don't we go upstairs and get undressed?" and she responded, "Why don't you shit in your hat?"),[59] socialite gold-digger Dolly O'Brien, gorgeous model Anita Colby, who was known as "the Face," and dozens if not hundreds of actresses, script girls, extras, etc. He would marry twice more. His last wife, Kay Spreckels, was pregnant with a son when he died in 1960. She buried him next to his one great love, Carole Lombard.

MGM was shocked when Judy Garland found herself pregnant during her honeymoon with Vincente Minnelli. As summer turned to fall pregnancy caused her mental and physical health to deteriorate, so in October she took a leave to await the spring birth. She was living a strange life. She was married to a homosexual who spent no time with her, living in his house with his longtime staff who didn't like the wife they viewed as an intruder. She was temporarily off the studio drug cocktail due to her pregnancy, but the withdrawal resulted in huge mood swings. But on March 12, 1946, she gave birth to daughter Liza and plunged into motherhood and a rapid decline back into a morass of drugs and depression.

Former MGM director Busby Berkeley's career had fizzled after his drunken car accident in Santa Monica killed three people in 1937. Jerry Giesler solved his court problems, but his once-popular choreographed musicals went out of fashion by 1940. Gone was his 25–room mansion; by 1946 he was living in a small apartment at 1583 Altivo Way in Hollywood. On the morning of July 17, 1946, Berkeley got drunk and tried to kill himself by slashing his wrists and throat. His houseboy called police, who rushed him to the hospital.[60] He survived and lived in obscurity in Palm Springs until his 1976 death at the age of 81.

Early in 1947, Mayer ordered perhaps his most bizarre arranged marriage. Through the 1940s Keenan Wynn, Van Johnson and Peter Lawford were almost never apart, and everyone thought they were homosexuals. Mayer finally stepped in early in 1947. Blonde, blue-eyed and covered with freckles, Van Johnson had come to Hollywood in 1939 after a stint as a New York chorus boy. He had reportedly been caught in vice problems reminiscent of William Haines' incidents a decade earlier, but he had a huge following of young bobby-soxers.[61] He was MGM's top leading man after movies like *Murder in the Big House* (1942) and *Thirty Seconds over Tokyo* (1944). Keenan Wynn had been married since 1938 to Eve Abbott and was from an old theater family; son of comic Ed Wynn and grandson of actor Frank Keenan. MGM inexplicably signed him in 1942 and he met Johnson during his first movie, *Somewhere I'll Find You* (1942). The two became inseparable and would pair in other films over the next four years including *Without Love, Weekend at the Waldorf* (1945) and *Ziegfeld Follies* (1946). During those years an affair with Johnson was well known at

MGM, but marriage to Abbott kept the public in the dark. The third member of the group was heartthrob Lawford.

The wartime shortage of male stars made Wynn and Johnson two of MGM's most popular, but rumors at MGM were rampant that Eve and Keenan Wynn, Van Johnson, and Peter Lawford were a sexual foursome, a strange *ménage a quatre*.[62] Mayer assumed that anyone who hung around with Johnson was gay. He frequent escorted Garland, who preferred gay friends accompany her to parties since her gay husband didn't like to go out.

By late 1946 Mayer was increasingly concerned about the Johnson-Wynn relationship and, to a lesser extent, Lawford. The perception among fans was that Johnson was gay. Mayer ordered an unusual solution when Eve, who was her husband's manager, met with Mannix and Mayer to negotiate Wynn's contract in December 1946. She was told that unless she divorced Wynn and married Johnson, Wynn's contract wouldn't be renewed and she would never represent anyone at MGM again.[63] According to *Van Johnson: MGM'S Golden Boy*, Abbott said, "I was young and stupid enough to let Mayer manipulate me. They needed their 'big star' to be married.... I divorced Keenan, married Van and became one of L.B.'s victims."

Strickling made the arrangements; on January 25, 1947, the Wynns were driven to El Paso and crossed the border to be divorced. Four hours later, Abbott and Johnson were married back in El Paso. Gay writer Arthur Laurents noted in his L.A. column, "A sunny male star caught performing in public urinals once too often was ordered by his studio to get married. His best friends, a young comedian and his wife, divorced so he could marry the wife." MGM people knew also that Lawford and Johnson were lovers; the question around the studio after the bizarre divorce-marriage was, "Who gets custody of Peter?"[64] Johnson worked for MGM for another dozen years but Mayer's forced marriage did more harm than good; young girls found him markedly less attractive as a married man. The strange marriage lasted until 1968 but Eve said he left her in 1961 for a young male dancer. Wynn married twice more, briefly to Betty Butler in 1949 and to Sharlay Hudson in 1954.

Lawford was never able to shake his reputation, and it appears that despite his multiple marriages and numerous affairs he was a healthy bisexual. Sal Mineo admitted to a sexual affair with him and Johnson told friends that Lawford and Wynn were lovers. Lawford also had a reputation among his Malibu neighbors for hanging around Will Rogers State Beach and picking up homosexuals for sex in the public restrooms. His neighbors called him "that screaming faggot from State Beach."[65] When he dated Marilyn Monroe in the 1950s she asked friends, "What's the deal with him. Do you think he's gay?" He never made a pass at her.

The late 1940s were turbulent for Lana Turner, Lawford's first Hollywood fling. In just five years she endured a studio-arranged abortion, an annulment and two marriages, one of which prevented a second abortion. Promiscuity didn't affect her work, though. Between 1942 and 1946 Turner starred in films like *Somewhere I'll Find You* (1942) and *The Postman Always Rings Twice* (1946). She was one of the most popular wartime pinups in the world. In 1946 she found out she had been infected with syphilis. Venereal diseases were anathema due to the stigma attached. Turner's promiscuity was legendary; she had recently had sex with Howard Hughes on the cockpit floor in his huge Sikorsky while they cruised over California on autopilot at 12,000 feet. She called Hughes to inform him and suggest he seek treatment. She told him actor Turhan Bey had infected her. Hughes told friends the Bey story. Strickling had to arrange for studio doctors to provide the treatment, but it didn't slow Turner down.

In late 1947 she began a torrid affair with Tyrone Power. Power was still a vain and narcissistic committed bisexual who counted among his conquests Cesar Romero and Hughes.[66] He was still in a sham marriage with Annabella. The Turner-Power affair reached a crescendo during the Christmas holidays in 1947, when Power was filming *Captain from Castile* and living in a villa in the Mexican mountain village of Morelia. Turner traveled there and walked unrecognized in dark glasses and wide-brimmed hat. She went to Mexico with Cesar Romero, not knowing he and Power had been lovers. At week's end Turner was pregnant.

Turner informed Strickling. Power and Annabella were divorcing but he refused to marry Turner, so Strickling made arrangements for another abortion.[67] Strickling's counterpart at Fox was Harry Brand, and the two had worked together many times before, including on the Power–Judy Garland problem, so Strickling asked Brand to get rid of Power for a while to keep him away from Turner. Brand complied, sending him to Europe. Brand added Linda Christian to Power's traveling party to keep him occupied; the two would later marry.

Sometimes the public affection for a star was enough by itself to take care of problems. The voluminous FBI files on Bing Crosby contain an amusing story of such. In early 1946 the FBI learned of an illegal casino operating at the Dancara Stock Farm in Burbank. When police raided the operation on March 16, 1947, dozens of gamblers were arrested and thousands of dollars confiscated, but the FBI file noted that "some patrons, among them Bob Hope and Bing Crosby, were permitted to leave."

Studios often had to make trade-offs, usually between a star's earning power and the negative publicity acceptable; between protecting the studio and protecting the employee; even basic trade-offs between right and wrong. The story of Lila Leeds and Robert Mitchum was a story of trade-offs, two studios trading a just-starting career for an established star.

Robert Charles Durman Mitchum's life story would make good movie. His father was killed in an accident when he was two. As a teenager, he hopped trains, crisscrossing the country with a band of hobo pals. Arrested at age 15, he spent a summer on a Georgia chain gang for being a "suspicious character with no means of support." One afternoon he walked away and headed for California to live on a beach and soak up sun. He settled in Long Beach, attended high school on his own and worked a variety of jobs, including ghostwriting for astrologist Carroll Righter. He married his high school sweetheart in 1940 and when World War II began, worked at Lockheed and joined a local theater group. He drifted into movies in 1942 in *Hoppy Serves a Writ* (1942), replacing an actor who had been killed in an accident. When he was handed his costume, the dead man's blood and brains were staining the hat and shirt. He appeared in two dozen wartime films and several Hopalong Cassidy movies, usually cast as a heavy.

Mitchum signed with RKO in 1944 and became a star. He did several MGM films, *Undercurrent* with Katharine Hepburn, *Desire Me* (both 1946), and *Thirty Seconds Over Tokyo* (1944). He once said that "the only difference between me and my fellow actors is that I've spent more time in jail." In 1948 Mitchum separated from his wife Dorothy and became a Hollywood party fixture and a regular marijuana user; unknown to him, he had been under police surveillance since late 1947. During the fall of 1948 he was dating Lila Leeds, a 19-year-old actress at MGM and Warners. She also enjoyed smoking and was also being watched by the police. She was beautiful; writer James Bacon described her as "one of the most beautiful women who ever landed in Hollywood ... like Lana Turner, only cuter." Jack Elam was more emphatic, saying, "You just stood there with your fucking mouth hanging open."[68]

On September 1, 1948, Mitchum and Leeds were at Leeds' bungalow on Ridpath Drive, surrounded by trees and hills at the end of a narrow, winding road. At about midnight police burst in and caught the couple and two friends smoking marijuana. It sounds ridiculous today, but the confiscation of three marijuana cigarettes was a scandal in 1948. They were branded "dope fiends"; one headline read, "A MAN IN THE GRIP OF DEMON DRUGS!" Mitchum was so certain the arrest would end his career that he wrote "former actor" when asked his occupation. RKO boss Howard Hughes said, "Well, who do we pay to kill this thing ... and for Pete's sake someone call Jerry Giesler."[69] Leeds had recently left MGM for Warners, but there was concern about spillover from negative publicity so with Mayer's approval, Leeds was sacrificed for Mitchum.

Jerry Giesler decided the best strategy was for Mitchum to admit his mistake and take his medicine like a man. Leeds had to do the same. Given her value to the studio versus Mitchum's, she had no choice. Her lawyer's prophetic comment was, "She had a promising career and was headed for success if only she had behaved differently. It looks like she's blown her chances sky high." After a non-jury trial, quick and with fewer headlines, they were sentenced to two years with all but 60 days suspended. Photographers followed both through the courthouse and during their stays in jail. Pictures of Mitchum at an honor farm east of L.A. ran in every fan magazine. After his release the unrepentant Mitchum said, "Prison was like Palm Springs without the riff-raff." He starred in almost 200 movies while Leeds was ruined, vanishing with nary a trace.

Carole Landis' life was a cautionary tale of the pitfalls of Hollywood. She was beautiful, a remarkable talent, and one of the first independent women in Hollywood. It was perhaps the latter that made her life so difficult. Landis wasn't an MGM employee; she worked at Twentieth Century Fox. She was born Frances Lillian Mary Ridste in 1919 on a Wisconsin farm. After her father abandoned the family when Lillian was born, her mother moved with her four children first to Montana and then in 1922 to San Bernardino.

Young Francis was a feminist before it was fashionable, and rebelled at a young age. During her first year of high school she tried to form a women's football team but was rebuffed by school administrators who felt such activity "unwomanly." Francis tired of life in the desert, hours from L.A. During her sophomore year she eloped to Yuma, Arizona, and married a 19-year-old aspiring writer she had only just met. The marriage lasted a month. A year later she gathered $16.82 in tips from her waitress job and bought a bus ticket to San Francisco, intent on becoming a lounge singer. Sitting in her rooming house she became Carole Landis; Carole from Carole Lombard and Landis after baseball commissioner Kennesaw Mountain Landis (she loved baseball). She had a lovely singing voice and was soon working regularly at lounges and bringing in a large following. In 1936 she decided to go to Hollywood.

Her introduction to Hollywood was her first audition, with notorious skirt-chaser Busby Berkeley, interviewing actresses for *Varsity Show*. For his movies Berkeley chose a group of his "old girls," actresses who had worked for him before. He then gathered 250 to 300 unknowns, all barely legal, beautiful, and desperate for work. From among that group he chose another dozen new faces. Landis received the typical Berkeley audition treatment. She stood in front of him and was told, "Raise your skirt," so he could check her legs for the dance numbers. Then he said, "Oh, I need to see more than that," and the little charade continued until her skirt was over her head. Than Berkeley informed the humiliated woman that she already had the job; it was all just a joke. He hired Landis as a new girl and even gave her a line of dialogue, though it didn't make the final print. That was another Berkeley ploy; offer women throwaway dialogue knowing it would be excised from the final print. Landis had to play the game and probably slept with Berkeley for that one line.

In July of 1937 Berkeley arranged a Warners contract for his protégée. Unlike most option girls, Landis worked—a lot. From July 1937 to August

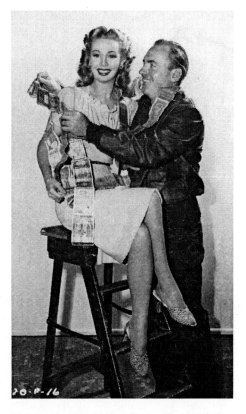

The lovely Carole Landis in 1944 with her *Having Wonderful Crime* co-star Pat O'Brien.

1938, Landis appeared in 19 films including *A Star is Born* (1937), *Broadway Melody of 1938*, and *Boy Meets Girl* (1938). A dozen were at Warners and three on loan-out to MGM. It was a lot of work for an option girl even though the roles were small, so rumors that Landis was earning work in bed arose. Worse, she was targeted by a powerful group, the studio wives. Married to actors, directors, or studio executives, the wives feared the beautiful women willing to offer their spouses sex for work. They were a more catty, vindictive clique than other employees. Landis was even more visible when she became a target of the wives. They were the most hypocritical, since most of them earned *their* husbands by trading sex.

Adding to their jealousy was Landis' personality. She was genuinely nice, was pleasant to crews, and her tomboy personality was appealing to everyone. Few in Hollywood worked more tirelessly during World War II. Her first trip in late 1942 to the European theater lasted four months and

25,000 miles. Many visits were near front-line positions. In June 1944, she logged 100,000 miles touring the South Pacific theater. Unfortunately, she returned to the U.S. with pneumonia, malaria and amoebic dysentery, which led to severe ulcers that plagued her for the rest of her life.

During her first year at Warners a rumor circulated that Landis had worked as a call girl in San Francisco. There is no proof, but friends from her café days who ended up in Hollywood years later perpetuated the story as fact.[70] Landis probably did trade sex for work. An oft-quoted Landis comment—"I have no intentions of ending my career in a rooming house, with full scrapbooks and an empty stomach"—offered some insight. She was also independent and feisty enough to be less bothered by the unseemly nature of affairs. In any event, Landis continued to get B-roles and continued having affairs she viewed as a requirement.

She would marry four times, and wore all four wedding bands on her thumb as a reminder "never to marry again."[71] Her first marriage to Albert Wheeler at age 15 had lasted only a month, as did a remarriage, but trying to get money from her, Wheeler named Berkeley as a correspondent, saying that Berkeley "carried on a campaign to win the affections of Miss Landis, finally succeeding in destroying the actress' love for her husband." The judge ruled against Wheeler but it cemented her reputation. Landis' lawyer was Greg Bautzer, a Hollywood attorney who bedded his all-female client list, which included Paulette Goddard, Dorothy Lamour, and Joan Crawford. Everyone, even her lawyer, took advantage of Landis. In 1940, Hal Roach's publicity man gave Landis the nickname the Ping Girl. She had earlier been called the Sweater Girl and the Garter Girl, so it's a mystery why Roach used "Ping." In the 1940s it was slang for a male erection.

In June 1941, Fox head Darryl Zanuck included Landis as one of three actresses (with Anne Baxter and Gene Tierney) as "new faces singled out for special attention."[72] But his attention was sexual; she was his favorite and was so often called into his office for one of his daily "4:00 meetings" that she was known as his personal mistress or by the more insulting moniker, "studio hooker." Sadly, Landis' reputation prohibited her from becoming the star that she should have become.

Landis' beauty was always noticed before her acting ability, but she was much smarter than people thought. She wrote a book about her first wartime USO tour which was made into the film *Four Jills in a Jeep* (1944). Watching that film, her talent and natural beauty are evident. After the war she settled into a mansion on Capri Drive in Bel Air and did a half dozen films in 1946 and early 1947. She also began a tragic affair with British actor Rex Harrison. She thought she had found love with Harrison, but he was an amoral womanizer who was living with his wife Lilli Palmer just two miles away. The affair was all over the tabloids. Edith Gwinn's *Hollywood Reporter* column offered weekly updates on "the carryings-on of the English star whose name begins with 'H' and the local glamour girl whose name begins with 'L.'"

The attention had more to do with the universal dislike for the egocentric Englishman than with Landis. Nobody except for Landis wanted anything to do with him; her punishment was by association. When Walter Winchell reported that "Carole Landis' next and fifth husband, when she becomes available, will be Rex Harrison," the gig was up. Amid the public condemnation, Landis became more depressed at Harrison's unfulfilled promises to marry.

By the Fourth of July holidays, 1948, Landis knew Harrison was using her. Her career was in neutral, she was haunted by the disdain of the studio wives, and she was fighting a growing addiction to the Seconal she was taking for sleep problems. On Sunday afternoon Landis hosted a large picnic and then had a private dinner with Harrison. After Harrison left, Landis sat in her living room and went through every one of her personal photo albums and every letter from Harrison. She filled a small case with the papers, drove to their mutual friend Roland Culver's Napoli Drive home, and left them next to the front gate. She returned home and took a handful of Seconals.

She was found the next morning by her maid, curled up on the bathroom floor. Her pathetic suicide note to her mother read, "Dearest Mommie, I'm sorry, really sorry to put you through this. But there is no way to avoid it. I love you darling. You have been the most wonderful Mom ever. Everything goes to you. Look in the files, and there is a will that decrees everything. Good bye my angel. Pray for me. Your Baby." She left a second note for her maid, reminding her to take her kitten to the vet for a sore paw.[73]

It was her fourth suicide attempt, but in the three others Landis had followed a pattern that was known to her friends. She left messages that she was going to take sleeping pills and was invariably saved by friends. She might have forgotten that nobody was home for the holiday weekend so her messages got no response. The picture of the dead 29-year-old lying by the toilet was on every front page in the country. Harrison allegedly was there when the body was found, but rumors were that he was there when she died and that Zanuck's people made sure he was gone when police were called. Zanuck arranged for Harrison to speak to police and testify before the coroner's inquest in private.

Harrison's indifference to Landis' death doomed his U.S. career. The

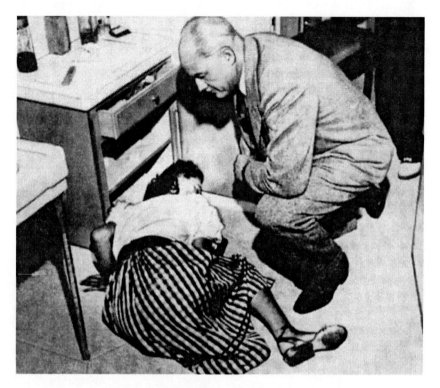

A Los Angeles police detective and the body of Carole Landis.

Hollywood Reporter spoke for all of Landis' friends when Gwinn wrote, "We don't remember an actor … who has breached so many rules of good taste … the wonder of the whole thing is that he hasn't had his face smashed by now." Persona non grata, he returned to England. A minor career that reemerged in the 1970s was tarnished by a similar suicide of his fourth wife, Rachel Roberts, in 1980.

The Landis tragedy underscored the price of fame in Hollywood, especially for women, and the incredible sexual double standard at work. It highlighted the inequities of the studio system, the preferential treatment given actors over actresses, and the almost impassable road to stardom faced by the "six-month option girls." Because she was forced to submit to the sexual bribery in order to work, her career stalled. She is all but forgotten.

Through the 1940s the relationship between Spencer Tracy and Katharine Hepburn was an open secret. Tracy still refused to divorce his long-suffering wife Louse; the logistics of the odd relationship between the two and Hepburn had remained unchanged. He and Hepburn were as close as husband and wife. Tracy described the relationship to Joan Fontaine, trying to get her to sleep with him, saying, "I can get a divorce any time I want to, but my wife and Kate both like things just as they are." He called Hepburn unattractive nicknames like Olive Oyl, Carrie Nation, Miss America, or Kathy. When she called him "Spen*suh*," he would ask, "Why do you always have to sound like you have a broomstick up your ass?"

Neither suffered any negative effects from the affair. That was strange since both hated the press. Tracy's battles were legendary, breaking cameras and assaulting reporters. Strickling spent tens of thousands of dollars replacing broken photographic equipment. Hepburn too had a love-hate relationship with the press. Her background made her feel superior to reporters and photographers, and running from photographers at New York's Idlewild Airfield in 1934 she had been almost decapitated by a whirling propeller.

Strickling worked almost full time to keep Tracy afloat. The problems were endless. In 1942 a young fan approached him at a New York bar; unprovoked, he whirled around, knocked the man unconscious and then returned to his drink. Strickling kept the story out of the papers and quietly paid the man off. During the mid-1940s Tracy was living at the Beverly Hills Hotel and Hepburn in John Gilbert's old estate on top of Tower Road. The essentially platonic relationship evolved into something like that of a mother and wandering son. Hepburn took care of Tracy. When Strickling's ambulance crew received a call about Tracy, Hepburn was also notified, and was always available to assist the drying-out, no matter how ugly.

She often cleaned up after him. Arriving at his hotel she cleaned him, took care of his clothes, and got him into bed. He would frequently lock her out, so she sometimes sat quietly in the hallway for hours. If he passed out she tied him to the bedposts so he wouldn't fall out of bed. It wasn't a typical glamorous movie-star life. Between 1942 and 1949 her efforts were at the expense of her own career. During that time she made only eight films, a low number for an actress as popular as Hepburn. Six of those films were with Tracy. One of Strickling's publicists, Esme Chandlee, said, "Tracy wouldn't have lived very long — he would have died long before he did — had it not been for Hepburn."[74]

If Tracy and Hepburn were apart he went back to the bottle. In 1946, while she filmed *Undercurrent*, he went to New York. Without telling Tracy, Strickling had Whitey Hendry tail him there. The first evening he and some friends went to Lamb's restaurant and got drunk before the "Tracy Squad" responded. It was Tracy's worst bender and would nearly kill him. He was forced into a straitjacket and dragged from the popular bar.

Strickling's New York office arranged that he be installed in Doctor's Hospital under a female alias, hidden in a private room on the gynecological floor, which was for women only. After a friend smuggled in a bottle of scotch and Tracy guzzled it without pause, he suffered alcohol-induced delirium tremens so severe that he was forced to stay — in restraints—for over a week.

In a bizarre coincidence, MGM actor Don Taylor's wife was at the same hospital at the same time, and as Taylor was leaving her room he came upon Whitey Hendry and his squad pushing a gurney into a nearby room. Tracy was strapped to the gurney, bound, gagged and straitjacketed. Hendry told Taylor, "You didn't see anything. If you open your mouth and say one thing about this, I'll have your ass."[75]

Strickling's attempts to improve Tracy's image were often thankless. Tracy had long ignored his son John, privately embarrassed at the bright young man's deafness. He never spoke of his son's condition publicly, even after his wife Louise founded the John Tracy Clinic. Louise arranged with Strickling to have the 1946 premier of Tracy's film *Cass Timberline* shown as a benefit for the clinic named after their son. Tracy only grudgingly attended and offered a one-minute speech thanking supporters. He was so angry that his family had been publicized that he wouldn't speak to anyone in Strickling's department for months.

On November 12, 1948, a malnourished and morphine-addicted actress died of liver disease at Cedars of Lebanon. Just 43 years old, she looked 60 and weighed barely 70 pounds. Former dancer Imogene "Bubbles" Wilson, known as Mary Nolan when she was Eddie Mannix's mistress, died alone as "Mary Wilson." Her protracted battles with Mannix; fights that left her with broken bones, a dozen surgeries and a morphine addiction; and suing him for $500,000 had left her a Hollywood pariah. There were three people at her funeral. Her ashes at Hollywood Memorial are behind a simple marker: "Mary Nolan 1948."

During the years between 1940 and 1945 Judy Garland starred in over a dozen films, made 100 radio appearances, attended 500 benefits, appeared at bond drives, and recorded 40 albums. Everything was done at the command of MGM. The birth of daughter Liza in March 1946 worsened her mental health, racked with postpartum depression and feelings of ambivalence toward her homosexual husband. She was to start *The Pirate* with Gene Kelly in November 1946, directed by Minnelli. When filming finally began in February 1947 she was a wreck. Seriously addicted to Benzedrine and clinically paranoid, her emotional state was so fragile that she was meeting with a studio psychiatrist for an hour every day. When Hedda Hopper visited Garland on the *Pirate* set, she was "shaking like an aspen leaf ... and went into a frenzy of hysteria."[76] By June, her unpredictable behavior and chronic absences left the film months late and $2.5 million ($30 million today) over budget. Of the 135 days of filming, she was absent for 99. Interestingly, when Koverman and Mayer viewed the daily rushes of a scene between Garland and Kelly they both thought it so erotic that the entire negative was burned.

Soon after filming was completed in August 1947, Garland made a third attempt to kill herself, slashing her wrist with a broken water glass after an argument with Minnelli. Her mother, who was helping care for infant Liza, bandaged her up, and Strickling and Mayer had her committed to a sanitarium near Compton. At the hospital she later described as "the first of my nuthouses,"[77] doctors tried to cure her addiction to pills and restore some mental health. After a month she was moved to a sanitarium in Stockbridge, Massachusetts, that had treated Mayer's wife some years earlier. She was away from the studio for several months and seemed to be making progress when she returned in early September, but the box office failure of *The Pirate* hurt her recovery and her marriage.

She was rushed back to work in *Easter Parade*, again with Minnelli. Garland's studio psychiatrist suggested she wanted Minnelli removed; he was replaced with Charles Walters. When filming was done in late 1947 Garland was again hooked on pills and for the first half of 1948 was unable to work. Strickling made discreet inquires with the Bureau of Narcotics and was told that they knew she was addicted to the drugs given her by MGM and also to morphine purchased elsewhere.

By July 1948, the studio was desperate; as Mayer reminded everyone, "We have $14,000,000 tied up in her."[78] She *had* to work, so they got her to work the only way they knew: propped up with drugs. But even that didn't work, so she was suspended, via a letter through her agent. Garland's life was at a crossroads. Her career and livelihood were in jeopardy. She was in a loveless marriage with a homosexual, but neither was willing to initiate a divorce. She had a child she wasn't sure she wanted, and was a hopeless drug addict.

By some miracle, she rallied temporarily in late 1948, recording some music and filming *In the Good Old Summertime*. During the spring of 1949 she was surprisingly assigned to Busby Berkeley's *Annie Get Your Gun*, a play that MGM had spent millions wresting from Broadway. Assigning the unstable Garland to a high-budget film with a frenetic director they knew Garland hated was a terrible idea. She once said of him, "I used to feel as if he had a huge black bullwhip, and he was lashing me with it."[79] Her hair was falling out in clumps, she couldn't sleep, and she was plagued by migraines. She was also exhibiting the euphoria-to-depression swings of a drug addict. On May 8 she was suspended again.

A terse memo was distributed around the studio, saying "For your information, Judy Garland's contract has been suspended as of May 11, 1949. She is not to be called … unless the matter is cleared with Mr. Mannix." Garland spent the rest of 1949 at Boston's Peter Bent Brigham Hospital. She personally begged Mayer for money to pay the hospital. To his credit, he agreed, and even visited her during her three-month stay in Boston. Doctors were shocked to discover the 27-year-old star was malnourished, exhausted, and on the verge of a complete breakdown. She suffered from chronic sleeplessness, ever-worsening migraines, unexplained tantrums, and constant thoughts of suicide. She had a life-threatening addiction to amphetamines. She endured electro-shock therapy, at the time an untested and dangerous procedure thought to alleviate mental problems. Garland's tragic downward spiral wouldn't end in Boston, though.

After three months she returned to Hollywood. She was doing better, and although MGM told her to take a year off if she needed (she undoubtedly did), they put her back to work as soon as she returned. The next week she was assigned *Summer Stock* with Gene Kelly. Within days she was hustling friends for drugs, showing up late or not at all; in short, killing herself with MGM. But she managed to complete the film. It would be her last at MGM.

As the postwar era was giving way to the 1950s, changes were underway that would change the way the industry worked. Not only that, the value of the studio publicity department and its inherent power would be greatly reduced. With the growing strength of the press and improvements in communications, it was increasingly more difficult to keep secrets. Money was less valuable and secrecy harder to obtain as the 1940s ended.

In May 1948, the U.S. Supreme Court forever altered the industry. From the earliest years, the studios had had several tools that helped them maintain an iron-fisted control over the product and the industry. Among the oldest was the Title Registration Bureau, which since 1925 had been maintained by the Motion Picture Producers and Distributors of America (the Hays Office). Under these rules, any studio could control a specific film title, whether or not it was actually even planning to produce a film under the name, for a long period of time.

Originally enacted to prevent one studio from releasing a film with the same title as one already done or in production, the result was that smaller independent filmmakers were prevented from using almost any title. An individual studio could only control 250 titles, but the rule was circumvented by reserving titles through related production companies. Small firms couldn't afford the charges that larger firms demanded for use of titles they controlled. Even Charlie Chaplin's successful studio balked at paying Paramount $25,000 ($500,000 today) for the title "The Dictator," which Paramount owned though they had no intention of ever using it. Chaplin revised his famous antiwar film title to *The Great Dictator*. (The system is still in force today but only 100 titles may be owned.)

The larger studios also managed their markets with the practice of "block booking." The clearly monopolistic practice was developed by European studios in the early 1900s. It was brought to Hollywood by Adolph Zukor, who made exhibitors buy several inferior movies in exchange for the right to show premier titles. Block booking lowered competition, since exhibitors had no alternative but to submit to the blackmail. Block booking was still openly enforced in the 1940s. Not only were theaters and chains forced to pay for low-quality films, they were also forced to purchase newsreels, cartoons, and studio public relations pieces. By the mid-1940s, block booking was called "full-line forcing," with exhibitors forced to take almost anything a studio offered. Worse, the chains were forced to agree to a booking mix without knowing what films would be included. In effect, the studios dictated an exhibitor's films for up to 12 months at a time. Obviously, since the bigger studios were also owners of large theater chains, their own outlets were not shackled with these requirements.

The courts had attempted to stop the monopolistic studio practices as early as the 1920s, and in a number of cases the studios were found guilty of monopolistic practices. However, a controversial back-room deal made with the Roosevelt administration — negotiated by Mayer's Washington, D.C., lawyer Mabel Willebrandt — voided the decisions. But in 1948 the Supreme Court would effectively put an end to the practice in a decision in the case *U.S. vs. Paramount Pictures, et al.* The court declared that the studio control over film distribution via their ownership of first-run theaters violated federal antitrust law. The studios had to abolish block booking, and worse, had to divest themselves of their theater holdings. The industry was truly a free-market enterprise from that moment on.

A second influence that helped dissolve the studio control was the emergence of television. It was first introduced in the early 1940s but wasn't available technically to the mass markets. However, by 1949 over 1 million Americans owned sets. In the postwar years marked by suburbanization the larger city movie theaters were harder to fill. It was the first of the baby booms that the movie industry had to adjust to. The collapse of the studio system paralleled a collapse in ticket sales. During the war, movies accounted for 25 percent of recreational spending. By the end of the decade, that percentage was below 10 percent. It was becoming a challenge to sell tickets. Falling revenues also meant a decrease in the number of films.

The end of the 1940s made it clear to the studios that the world was changing. From the postwar euphoria that resulted in almost 80 million movie-viewers, by 1949 that number dropped to below 60 million. In 1948 MGM—for the first time in history—laid off almost a quarter of its employees. Profits were down. MGM quality also fell; 1947 was the first year the studio didn't receive a nomination for a Best Picture Academy Award since the inception of the prize. The public was deserting MGM formulas. Successful serials like *Andy Hardy*, *The Thin Man* and *Lassie* were not selling tickets. Big Technicolor musicals were not making money at all.

Worse, movie viewers seemed to prefer genres that MGM was ill equipped to provide. Westerns, film noir products, and movie types better suited to smaller, more flexible studios were drawing growing crowds. From 1930 to 1945 Hollywood averaged almost 600 films a year. During the first half of 1949, less than 50 films were made. MGM, which had risen to the summit by promising a classic movie a week, was laboring to produce one a month.

The industry problems led to internal squabbles at MGM. For years Mayer enjoyed a free-wheeling, despotic management style. Irving Thalberg controlled the production decisions but after his death that process shifted to Mayer's middle-managers; the heads of production units Mayer had put in place when he deposed Thalberg. In the decade and a half that followed, as long as the films did well, individual mistakes were forgiven. In the more competitive environment of the late 1940s, Nick Schenck looked at Mayer as a dinosaur.

On June 1, 1948, Schenck placed Dore Schary in a spot just beneath Mayer in a position reminiscent of Irving Thalberg's as head of production. Schary technically reported to Mayer, but Mayer's role had clearly been diminished. Mayer was then 63, and Schenck felt that he was more interested in bedding his starlets than adjusting to the changing viewer profile. Schenck felt that Schary, only 43, had a better idea of what people wanted to see in the movies.

Beyond the internal machinations, the outside climate continued to change. The five large studios (MGM, Warner Brothers, Paramount, RKO, and Twentieth Century Fox) were less than a year from the court-imposed deadline to dispose of studio-owned theater chains. Schenck thought Mayer incapable of running a studio in the newly competitive environment. The development of television, which had been slowed by the war, was now surging. Since the war MGM's profits and reputation for excellence had fallen steadily.

On the personnel side, fans continued to be interested in the private foibles of the stars. Indeed, tabloid journals were erupting almost weekly, filling a seemingly insatiable interest for information about the stars' personal problems. But rather than pushing them away, the problems had begun to make them *more* interesting. The roles of Strickling and Mannix would continue to be important to MGM heading into the 1950s, but they had clearly changed.

Their roles were significantly different, as different as the industry. By 1949 Strickling was as likely to arrange a wedding as cover up a death. As the 1950s dawned, things had changed forever. But there would be one last, big secret.

Six

The 1950s: Relics and the Last Big Secret

The 1950s marked the end of the studio system, dismantled by the courts in the 1940s and the stars themselves in the 1950s. As the 1950s dawned there was less need for the amount of studio protection required in the earlier years. With the exception of the most popular stars, studios were gradually lessening involvement in personal problems. Heading into the 1950s, Mayer was technically in charge but Dore Schary was running the studio. Mayer still had Kay Koverman outside his office. In her 70s and earning the same $250 a week she was making when she was hired in 1924, she still lorded it over the office sitting silver-haired and ramrod straight. She was still the eyes and ears of Strickling and Mannix, but it seemed there was less for them to talk about.

It was clear that under Schary things would be different at MGM. As Spencer Tracy said to Clark Gable, "Since Schary took over, nobody gets laid at MGM."[1] Schary wanted to have his hand in everything in the studio like Thalberg but "he didn't know how to run a studio ... and didn't know what sex was like."[2] He did not understand actresses, so he would lose out on Marilyn Monroe and Grace Kelly, among others. He was also less willing to put up with problems caused by problem stars. Not that Strickling and Mannix were dinosaurs; there were still challenges, but now they only dealt with big problems with major stars. Strickling's work was evolving to almost mundane publicity and Mannix was for the most part an absentee manager, spending most of his time at home as his health deteriorated.

Mayer and Schary had an acceptable relationship when Schary first arrived in 1948, but by 1950 they rarely spoke. Schary found Mayer's verbal tirades unprofessional and avoided him. The two argued over films, assignments, everything. It was clear one of them would have to go, but there were more pressing issues.

During the 1950s, unless MGM itself could be tainted by a scandal the studio simply washed its hands of problems. Judy Garland was the first example, when her tortured relationship with MGM came to an end in 1950. Increasingly erratic after years of drug use for everything from weight loss to depression, she had been suspended countless times. By 1950 her once-dedicated work ethic had dissolved into unreliability. Her late 1940s films were all successful but 1950s *Summer Stock* would be her last. The studio pushed the exhausted actress directly from *Summer Stock* into rehearsals for *Royal Wedding* with Fred Astaire, but she was too emotionally drained to work and was suspended for the last time.

Her emotional problems had been in headlines for the previous 12 months. By the summer of 1950, MGM decided they could no longer deal with her increasingly erratic behavior. Schary had the final say and on June 17, Garland was fired from the only place she had ever worked. The studio didn't anticipate the public sympathy for Garland. They also didn't anticipate her reaction. She had joined MGM as a plump 12-year-old singer and her films had earned $36 million ($500 million today), but when she was fired she was an emotionally exhausted, drug-addled 28-year-old.

She was struggling financially and separated from Minnelli. However, he was always available to help her and again tried to help her through her firing. She had rented a house on Evanview Drive in Hollywood. Three days after her firing, Minnelli, her manager Carelton Alsop, and her secretary Mrytle Tully were discussing her options—from Broadway to concerts to other studios—but Garland was unresponsive. During the visit, Garland wordlessly went into the bathroom.

Hearing the sound of breaking glass, Minnelli rushed to the bathroom where he found Garland on the floor, blood pouring from a gash in her neck. She had sliced her own neck with a piece of the broken mirror. It was her sixth or seventh attempt, and as she lay there she screamed, "Leave me alone. I want to die."[3] Minnelli called Strickling or Mannix; even though she was technically no longer an employee, MGM was going to look bad.

Garland was rushed to Cedars and admitted under a fictitious name but the *Los Angeles Mirror* headline the next morning was "JUDY GARLAND FAILS IN SUICIDE ATTEMPT."[4] Strickling moved her back into the mansion at 10000 Sunset and tried to downplay the seriousness. He recruited Hedda Hopper, who wrote that the wound was a "scratch [that] could have been made with a pin."[5] She would remain secluded at the Sunset estate for nearly a year with a staff of studio-hired doctors, psychiatrists, and nurses. The growing public sympathy forced Mannix to wait several months before formally discharging Garland.

Garland would not work again for almost three years before being hired by Jack Warner for *A Star Is Born* in 1953. She was given the role only because she agreed to sing at Warner's daughter's birthday party in exchange.[6] The movie flopped, and Garland would not work for another four years. Bing Crosby said of Garland, "There wasn't a thing that gal couldn't do, except look after herself." She was found dead on the toilet in a rented London apartment in 1969, only 47 but looking 67. The day she died there was a tornado in Kansas.

Later in 1950 and early 1951 several random events would conspire to drag Strickling and Mannix into their final, and perhaps biggest, secret. The studio system was disintegrating while television was growing. In 1945 there were less than 7,000 television sets in the U.S. but by 1950 there were over 5 million. Casting and initial filming was starting for the first three weekly television shows. *I Love Lucy* was being developed for Lucille Ball and her bandleader husband Desi Arnaz. Jackie Gleason was filming *Life with Riley*, though by the time it was released a year later Gleason would be replaced by William Bendix. A third serial based on the *Superman* comics was also being developed. Over 250 actors auditioned for the lead role of Clark Kent and his alter ego, Superman. One was George Brewer Bessolo Reeves.

Helen and Don Brewer, a Woodstock, Iowa, druggist, married in 1913 only after Helen became pregnant. Just a few months after their son George was born in January 1914, Helen divorced Brewer and took her newborn cross-country in a car by herself. The pair settled in Pasadena where she married bank auditor Frank Bessolo, who adopted young George. He grew into a six-foot-two, 190-pound junior college boxer, but Helen made him give up boxing and begin acting at the Pasadena Playhouse. Fellow Playhouse actor Jack Larson remembered those days: "Eugene O'Neill directed the likes of Robert Mitchum, Bill Holden, and George, who all began there."[7] It was a popular haunt for studio talent scouts.

Bessolo was renamed George Reeves, and at the Playhouse he met Ellanora Needles. He was signed by Warner Brothers and then the two married on September 21, 1940. He had minor roles in five films but was better known for roles he lost. Ronald Reagan beat him out for *Smashing the Money Ring* and James Cagney took the *Fighting 69th* lead. He was so upset that he quit Warners and signed with Twentieth Century Fox. He earned a sizable role as Stuart Tarleton in *Gone with the Wind* but it didn't lead anywhere, and during 1940 he appeared in 20 movies like *Knute Rockne All-American* and *Calling All Husbands.* But he was still not getting prime roles, so he left Twentieth Century for Paramount. Other than having a torrid affair with Veronica Lake, he didn't do much there, either. Between 1942 and 1949 he appeared in another 25 movies, still in mediocre roles, and by 1950 was so disenchanted that he headed to New York and television. He had only been in New York for a few months when the L.A. casting call for *The Adventures of Superman* was announced.

In 1934 Cleveland high school student Jerry Siegel had woken up during the night with the inspiration for "Superman," and his best friend Joe Schuster drew the characters the next day. *Detective Comics* paid the boys $130 for the rights and *Action Comics* introduced *Superman* in 1938.[8] When television called, the character was already internationally known. On May 16, 1951, Flamingo Films purchased the television rights from National Comics and five days later a production company was formed to produce a television serial titled *The New Adventures of Superman*. A movie would be produced to help introduce the television serial, entitled *Superman and the Mole-Men*. Actor Kirk Alyn was already starring in a movie serial based on *Superman* but he turned the role down, later sheepishly remembering that "they were only offering a few hundred dollars a week for four months of work." Few actors in the early television projects wanted to become television stars, nor did they think the medium would offer that. It was believed to be just a fad and, although they liked steady work, television was considered a step down for serious actors—like the early movies for stage performers.

Jack Larson had that opinion. He was also discovered at the Pasadena Playhouse. The son of a milk-truck driver and a telegraph clerk, he grew up in Montebello, California, and was a good enough bowler at age 14 to become state champion. At Pasadena City College in the mid-1940s he was discovered by a talent scout for Twentieth Century Fox. In May 1948, Warners signed Larson and his best friend Frannie Reynolds. Jack and "Debbie" would appear together in musicals; Larson's first role was in a comedy, *Scudda Hoo Scudda Hay*. At the last minute the director switched the role from male to female and gave it to a third newcomer. Her name was Marilyn Monroe.[9] Larson auditioned for the role of Jimmy Olsen in the Superman series.

Over 250 actors auditioned for the lead but on June 25, 1951, it was given to George Reeves. He had an advantage with good looks and a very athletic six-foot-two-inch, 200-pound frame. Even so, there were whispers that he had "outside help" getting the role.

Through early July 1951, the other main character roles were cast as Reeves began filming *Mole-Men* at the Culver City lot. One of his costars was Phyllis Coates, who would bring the Lois Lane character to television with Reeves for the first season. Filming the entire movie took just 11 days and ended on July 21. Around July 19, Jack Larson was signed to play Jimmy Olsen. He is foggy on the date but remembered meeting Reeves and Coates while they filmed *Mole-Men*. Larson said he took the role because, "My friends told me, 'Don't worry, nobody will ever see the show. Just take the money and run.'"[10] He was paid $250 a show for the first 26 episodes. He had just turned 18.

Within a few days of the *Mole-Men* wrap the series casting was complete. John Hamilton would play *Daily Planet* editor Perry White and Robert Shayne became police inspector Bill Henderson. Phyllis Coates would be replaced by Noel Neill as Lois Lane after the first season. Willard "Bill" Kennedy provided the announcer's voice that would be recognized worldwide. Filming began days later.

Reeves was disgusted by his hand-me-down costume, which was poorly made and included shoes worn previously by Kirk Alyn. His contempt was palpable; he welcomed Phyllis Coates to the set the first day by holding up his drink and saying, "Here's to the bottom of the barrel, babe."[11] But not everyone shared the misgivings. Even before filming began, the cereal company Kellogg's signed on as a sponsor, assuming the tie-in between the children's cereal sales and the youthful viewers. Downtown L.A.'s Parker Center was used for exterior shots of the *Daily Planet* offices. Most of the exteriors were filmed on the "Forty Acres" back lot at RKO Studios in Culver City. *The Adventures of Superman* filming began on July 23, 1951, and between then and October 13, 26 episodes with titles like "The Case of the Talkative Dummy," "The Monkey Mystery," "The Mind Machine," and "The Runaway Robot" were filmed. Every 12 days five episodes were completed.

The schedule meant that individual scenes for different episodes were filmed at the same time and out of sequence, which made it very difficult for the actors to keep track of where they were in the stories. Also, episodes with common themes were filmed together. For example, all of the episodes with caves were shot together. Watching episodes filmed at the same time, it is often evident that costumes were not changed.

According to Larson, Reeves and Toni Lanier met during the early days of filming and may have met during the *Mole Men* filming. In either case they became close as soon as they met. Everyone on the set could see that the two "clicked." It was the beginning of an affair that would last until Reeves' mysterious death some eight years later. There were rumors that Toni and Reeves were already an item when filming began and that he had been given the role at the "suggestion" of Eddie Mannix. Some say that Reeves and Toni met during his earlier visit to New York City, but this has never been substantiated.

Reeves won the role on his own. Reeves was perfect for the part physically. Secondly, the Toni-George affair would only have been in its infancy, even if they had met by that time. Jack Larson confirmed to this writer that "George met Toni just after 'Superman' filming began." But to call the George Reeves–Toni Lanier pairing an "affair" is inaccurate. Reeves and his first wife Ellanora were divorced by the time filming began.

When Reeves and Lanier met, he was 35 and she a very attractive 46. From the day they met she called him "the boy." Like her faux English accent described by Larson, a little nickname for her "boy" seemed to her very upper crust. He called her "Mama" or "Mama

George Reeves in the 1930s before *Superman* made him famous.

Toni." [12] Like everyone else, Reeves assumed she was married to Eddie Mannix. Everyone on the lot believed Eddie and Toni were married, but it was probably a common-law marriage. They shared the same house for almost 30 years, they owned millions of dollars of MGM stock jointly, and they certainly appeared to be man and wife. But it is unknown if they ever legally married.

Few but their close friends knew that Eddie and Toni weren't "legal." Everyone at MGM knew her as Toni Mannix and she referred to herself as Mrs. Mannix. Everyone also knew Mannix's reputation, his New York mob ties dating back decades, his toughness, and his ability to "make things happen." By the 1950s more people knew him as the Bulldog than knew him as Eddie, or the E.J. that only close pals used.

According to some sources, on May 31, 1951, the same day that Superman, Inc., was moving to Culver City to begin filming, Eddie and Toni were married. Reeves researcher Jim Nolt told this writer he had seen a marriage certificate, but that it was dated August 1951.[13] He does not know if the copy still exists. There is no formal or even informal record of a wedding taking place. No friends remembered attending a ceremony, nor has documentation been found. Another unsubstantiated story had them marrying on Eddie's death bed. But for all intents and purposes they lived as if they were married.

For all those reasons Reeves' coworkers were shocked at how quickly he and Toni became a couple. When Lanier met Reeves in 1951, Eddie was a barrel-chested 60 years old. He and the 14-years-younger Toni had been together for almost 20 years. Theirs had always been an odd relationship. Both were chronically unfaithful to each other and knew the other's infidelities. By the time Toni and Reeves met, Eddie's health problems had limited him to just one mistress, a young Japanese woman who had been taking care of Eddie since after World War II and lived with the couple.

Toni had no such limits and was known at MGM for her promiscuity. In his autobiography *Sparks Fly Upward*, actor Stewart Granger devotes several pages to his first meeting with Toni, starting with her reaching into his pants under the table during dinner and ending with her barging into his bungalow at the Beverly Hills Hotel demanding sex.

Toni came by the set almost every day during the 1951 *Superman* filming, bringing Reeves his lunch in a brown paper bag. Both were heavy drinkers so lunch was usually liquor shared in the privacy of his dressing room. She was possessive and jealous even early in their relationship. She did not want him alone with any other women, and let Phyllis Coates know without being told that she was to keep her hands off.

Almost immediately Reeves and Toni began appearing in public. To a casual movie or television fan, nothing untoward was read into a television star escorting the wife of a studio executive to a concert or to dinner. But Hollywood and MGM were agog at the openness of the affair. What they did not know — what nobody knew — was that Eddie Mannix knew all about it. In fact, he encouraged it. While everyone around them wondered aloud about the affair, Eddie, Toni and Reeves were perfectly comfortable in what they called "the arrangement." All three implicitly agreed that when Eddie died — his heart disease was so advanced that he could drop dead any moment — Toni and Reeves would marry.[14]

There were probably several reasons Mannix was so understanding. He had had hundreds or thousands of affairs during his time at MGM, lasting from five minutes to five years. But affairs by themselves were not the answer. Their ages and his health probably had more to do with it. When Mannix and Toni began their affair in the 1930s he was in his early 40s and she was in her early 20s. By the time Toni met Reeves, Eddie was approaching 60 and she her mid-40s. He couldn't keep up with her any more and was also spending time with his Japanese girlfriend. They had always ignored each other's affairs, but for some reason he took a liking to Reeves. He enjoyed his company and liked him as a person.

Just after Toni and Reeves began dating, Eddie himself quietly paid $12,000 for a small Cape Cod–style house for Reeves at 1579 Benedict Canyon in Beverly Hills, just two miles north of Sunset. At the time he was living in an apartment in Hollywood. Eddie and Toni were still at Buster Keaton's old Linden Drive house. Toni took charge of decorating Reeves' new home and filled the cupboards with excess silver and china from her own house just down the street. Eddie and his Japanese friend were among the guests at the housewarming party. At the same time Toni gave George a brand new Alvis convertible, an expensive English sports car.

It was not unusual for Mannix to find Reeves at his own kitchen table, reading the paper and having coffee with Toni, when he came down for breakfast. According to Reeves researcher Nolt, Noel Neill was often at the Mannix house when George would walk in, say hello, and head for the refrigerator or bar as though he lived there. The three also attended mass together every Sunday.

In 1953, Eddie built a new home at 1120 El Retiro Way. The modern white mansion was on a quiet cul-de-sac adjacent to the Greystone Mansion and Park, just three miles from Reeves' Benedict Canyon house. Jack Larson has a photograph from the 1953 groundbreaking. Standing in front of the bulldozer is an interesting threesome. Toni Mannix is in the middle, flanked by Eddie on one side and Reeves on the other. The three — usually accompanied by Eddie's young Japanese consort — also vacationed together. Eddie and Toni traveled in one section and Reeves and Eddie's girlfriend in another. When they reached their destination the women switched partners. It was just one of the many strange variations to the whole Mannix-Reeves scenario that was playing out around the *Superman* set.

The arrangement was very clearly defined. It was understood between the three that when Eddie died, Reeves and Toni would share the El Retiro house. Reeves took an active part in the construction along with Eddie and Toni. According to Larson, Toni was totally devoted to both men but very much in love with her "boy." A few years later that love would be tested, and according to some Toni flunked the test.

As filming was getting underway on the initial *Superman* episodes, another odd relationship reached a sad ending. By 1951, William Randolph Hearst and Marion Davies had been together for almost 40 years. The real Mrs. Hearst had steadfastly refused offers as high as $10 million (probably $250 million today) to divorce her husband.[15] So Hearst and Davies went on as if they were married. In 1946 he left his beloved San Simeon estate to be closer to his L.A. doctors. Marion found a 30-room gated estate at 1011 Beverly Drive, and they moved in with his nurses and Marion's dogs. For five years they remained secluded in the mansion, with the heat kept at a stifling 82 degrees. On the night of August 13, 1951, the frail tycoon was near death in his massive second-floor suite with Davies and doctors nearby. Also at the death watch were his sons Bill and David, and Richard Berlin, president of Hearst Corporation. Mrs. Hearst declined Davies' invitation to come.

Even though they knew death was imminent, Hearst's sons convinced Marion to take a sedative. She was given a shot and went to bed. While Davies slept Hearst died, not holding the hand of Davies but of his valet Henry Monohan. When she awakened the next morning to the barking of her dogs, the house was empty.[16] During the night Hearst's body had been removed and put on a train for his San Francisco funeral. The next morning, a dozen friends for whom Marion had gotten jobs at Hearst's L.A. papers were fired, and the complimentary delivery of two newspapers to her house was cancelled.

But Marion got the last word. In an angry interview with *Life* magazine, she said, "Do you realize what they did? They stole him ... he belonged to me. I loved him for thirty-two years, and now he was gone. I didn't even get to say good-bye."[17] Then she told a Hearst family member via telephone, "You can have him now; he's dead. I had him when he was alive." When he died, she also had almost $8 million in the bank, and owned three skyscrapers in New York, the Desert Inn in Palm Springs, and a dozen mansions in Beverly Hills. Davies spent her last unhappy years at Beverly Drive before succumbing to cancer in 1961.

Just a few weeks after Hearst's death, there was another "death" at MGM, one much more startling. On August 31, 1951, Louis B. Mayer resigned his position as the head of the studio that he had created. The resignation was not entirely of his choosing. The wheels had been put in motion when Nick Schenck inserted Dore Schary above Mayer in 1948. When Mayer told Schenck in August 1951, "It's either me or Schary," Schenck chose Schary.

In the fall of 1952, Lana Turner's marriage to alcoholic businessman Bob Topping was falling apart, the IRS was after her, and she had to borrow money from her agent for a mansion at 120 South Mapleton in Bel Air. As she battled the onset of clinical depression while her life fell apart around her, she tried to kill herself in the first floor bathroom of the Mapleton house.

Turner's mother had asked friend Ben Cole to check on her. In a scene eerily reminiscent of Judy Garland, Turner quietly excused herself and locked herself in the bathroom where she swallowed a bottle of sleeping pills and slashed her left wrist to the bone. By the time Cole kicked the door in, Turner had nearly bled to death. He called the studio; fortunately a studio doctor lived nearby and rushed to the house to secrete Turner to a private sanitarium where she awoke several days later.[18] The press was told Turner had fainted in the shower and cut her arm when she broke through the glass shower door, the same story Howard had invented for Barbara Stanwyck a decade before. MGM rushed her back to work to complete *The Merry Widow*, where filming was done so as to hide her bandages. Her left arm is never visible on camera unless covered by either a long glove or a wide bracelet.

At the same time Clark Gable and 23-year-old, green-eyed, blonde beauty Grace Kelly filmed *Mogambo* in Nairobi. Filming was tense; the British governor of Kenya ordered troops to guard the film crew against the Mau Mau warriors murdering white settlers. MGM paid Mau Mau leader Jomo Kenyatta $50,000 for safety, and every member of the cast carried a weapon. Even so, amid the filming and the jungle war Gable and Kelly managed to forge a heated affair.

Kelly's reputation for sleeping with *any* man who might further her career was deserved, since she had countless affairs with men married and unmarried. She slept with Bing Crosby while his wife was dying of cancer, meeting for sex at the pool house of his next door neighbor Alan Ladd. Her affair with Ray Milland, Hollywood's most-married man, was a major scandal. William Holden was also married when she slept with him, and Gene Lyon tried to have his marriage annulled during their affair. She slept with Spencer Tracy while he was married to his wife Louise *and* having his affair with Katharine Hepburn. She slept with Aly Khan and Howard Hughes and allegedly had affairs with directors Fred Zinnemann and Alfred Hitchcock. *Confidential* magazine described her as "the most dangerous dame in the movies today."[19] Her father and brother were so upset about the magazine's coverage that they stalked into the offices and beat up two of the editors. The *Mogambo* crew escaped Kenya unscathed except for Gable's costar Ava Gardner, who discovered that she was pregnant during the African shoot. When the crew moved on to London an abortion was arranged for Gardner.[20]

At the time Gable was completing *Mogambo*, his *Never Let Me Go* was such a flop that Dore Schary thought about not re-signing him. Gable wanted not only an extension but for the first time wanted a percentage of his films' profits. Common now, percentage deals were never done in the 1950s. Schary and Nick Schenck were adamant that no MGM actor would set that precedent, knowing the studio system in place since the 1920s would be gone. Schary offered Gable a two-year extension, banking on *Never Let Me Go*'s failure to sway Gable, but Gable told them they "could take their money, their studio, their cameras and lighting equipment and shove it up their asses."[21] When *Mogambo* earned raves Schary increased his offer, but Gable refused to re-sign. He left MGM in March 1954 after 51 films, but Schary was comforted that no actor had a percentage deal. Everything MGM was removed from Gable's life, except Grace Kelly. He rekindled his affair with Kelly, meeting at her Bel Air Hotel bungalow. She was also sleeping with Bing Crosby and William Holden at the time.

By the early 1950s Spencer Tracy's alcoholism and worsening depression had turned him into a shell of a man, but Katharine Hepburn stayed by his side. She was about to leave for a prolonged 1951 shoot of *The African Queen* and was worried Tracy would not survive her absence; his benders worsened when she was gone. She asked close friend George Cukor to put him up in a guest house on his estate and Tracy grudgingly moved into 1919 St. Ives Drive in the fall of 1951 after Cukor wrote, "I have taken it upon myself to send you the plans of the Tracy Residence in the new Cukor Development ('THE-LAST-STOP-BEFORE-THE-MOTION-PICTURE-RELIEF-HOME'). To satisfy a certain Touring Actress we are draining the malarial swamp on which this residence is to be constructed."

The tiny house had two bedrooms, a kitchen, a living room, and a large dressing room. She had telephones installed in every room of her own mansion so she could answer Tracy's calls on the first or second ring in case he was in trouble.[22] Since 1943 MGM doctors had been giving Tracy large quantities of the powerful amphetamine Dexedrine to combat depression, but the drug led to insomnia that tortured him, and gave him a greater opportunity to drink for days at a time. He had heart problems, liver and kidney ailments, digestive problems, insomnia, and was impotent.

Tracy's box-office success forced MGM to save Tracy from himself, but by 1954 Strickling no longer staffed a "Tracy squad"; police would handle Tracy's problems. Through almost two decades of work at MGM Tracy's on-screen successes in films such as *Boy's Town* (1938), *Dr. Jekyll and Mr. Hyde* (1941), *State of the Union* (1948), and *Father of the Bride* (1950) made up for his off-screen problems. His worsening physical condition left his work uneven. His early 1950s films were for the most unremarkable, the only exception being *Pat and Mike* (1952), successful because he was paired with Hepburn. As he started *Bad Day at Black Rock* during the summer of 1954, the studio had had enough.

Tracy went through the same process at the start of every film. At first he was supportive of projects but as filming approached became glum and disagreeable as his insecurities fed self-doubt. He would threaten to quit and go on a bender. This time, anticipating Tracy's desertion, Schary told him that he would be sued if he delayed filming, an unprecedented threat.

There were no Tracy problems, and filming was completed with a new Tracy strategy implemented. His work was exemplary and he earned a fifth Academy Award nomination (he would lose to Ernest Borgnine's *Marty*). *Bad Day at Black Rock* would be his MGM swan song.

As he was starting another Western, *Jeremy Rodock*, a series of events sent him over the edge and forced the studio to drop their most successful actor. Just before *Black Rock* filming began, Tracy had a brief dalliance with Grace Kelly. At the time she was feuding with Schary and had rebounded from her Gable affair into a new one with 40-year-old Oleg Cassini. Hedda Hopper mused in her column why Kelly would go out with Cassini; "It must be his moustache." He responded with a telegram, "Hedda, I'll shave mine if you shave yours."[23] After 1954's *To Catch a Thief* she declined every role MGM offered. After Tracy committed to *Jeremy Rodock*, Kelly was offered the costarring role. Over a month she "met" with Tracy to discuss the film she had no intention of doing. A close friend noted, "I don't know what happened between her and Tracy but she didn't go all the way out there to sit at a conference table to talk about a movie she wasn't going to do."[24] Hepburn was not pleased about the relationship.

Then, two months after Kelly left Hollywood, in April 1955, Constance Collier, Tracy's 77-year-old surrogate mother, died. Ignoring Tracy's pleadings to stay with him after the funeral Hepburn left for Australia, leaving him to grieve alone. Feeling she was punishing him for the Kelly affair, he went on a bender. Adding his typical last-minute phobias to the mix was a disaster. *Jeremy Rodock*, renamed *Tribute to a Bad Man*, was to begin filming on June 2 at an elaborate set director Robert Wise spent three months building high up in the Colorado mountains. Tracy did not arrive until June 11; he had lunch with the crew and retired to his hotel. The next morning Wise discovered Tracy had disappeared. When he had been missing eight days Wise and Strickling contacted Hepburn in Australia and had her talk Tracy back to the set. When he arrived back on the set on June 19, he insisted that he only work half days, that meals be prepared in his hotel room, and that the set be rebuilt at a lower altitude so his lungs would be less taxed.

After only four days of filming, Wise demanded Strickling and MGM remove Tracy from the film. Strickling flew to Colorado to try to mediate the dispute, but after a day of meetings it was decided to fire Tracy. On June 25, 1955, Strickling fired Spencer Tracy in a Colorado hotel room. James Cagney took over Tracy's role.[25] Tracy retreated to the cottage on Cukor's estate, where he would die with Hepburn at his side on June 10, 1967. Studio publicists told the press Tracy was alone or was with his wife

Louise. When Louise finally spoke to Hepburn she said, "I thought you were a rumor."[26] Tracy was incorrigible to the end. Just before his death, he was offered the role of The Penguin on the television series *Batman*. Tracy said he would take the role only if he could kill Batman. Burgess Meredith got the role.

In the mid-1950s the MGM power structure was altered yet again. Mannix was helping Schary run the day-to-day operations and Strickling's people were still grinding away on behalf of the films. Nick Schenck had held onto his power after World War II but stubbornly refused to accept the threat of television and was oblivious to the changes in the way studios were run. The studio system was crumbling around him, and he seemed not to notice. Studios had already begun making cheaper package deals, purchasing a title that arrived with producer, director, and perhaps one or two stars. Schenck held on to the old way, but had to be moved aside as he had moved Mayer aside earlier. On December 14, 1955, he was unceremoniously removed and replaced by Arthur Loew. Things had come full circle; 30 years earlier Schenck took control after the death of Loew's father.

Spencer Tracy and Jean Harlow during the 1936 filming of *Riffraff*. He had not yet met Katharine Hepburn but his drinking and womanizing were already a major studio problem. By the 1950s Strickling could no longer afford to cover for Tracy, and he was fired.

The 1956 film *Diane* was Lana Turner's last under MGM contract. When it was done she left MGM to freelance. Her men — she would marry eight times— were still a problem in 1957. She had already been married once to Artie Shaw, twice to Steve Crane, and once to Bob Topping. On July 22, 1957, she divorced for the fifth time, jettisoning former *Tarzan* star Lex Barker after she discovered he had been molesting her teenaged daughter Cheryl Crane for years. During the divorce she met "John Steele," a charming man who owned a small gift shop in Westwood and bombarded Turner with flowers and gifts until she agreed to go out with him.

It was several months before Turner's friends told her that "John Steele" was Johnny Stompanato. The daily floral arrangements from him had come from mobster Mickey Cohen's flower shop. Cohen was Stompanato's boss. Stompanato grew up in Woodstock, Illinois, and was in the Marines during World War II. He converted to Islam to marry a Turkish woman before ending up in L.A. as a bouncer at one of Cohen's nightclubs. Cohen made him his personal bodyguard and his primary "bag man" (money carrier).

There was an immediate attraction between Turner and Stompanato. He was attractive and muscular, and given her amorality it didn't take long for the two to become intimate. Turner said the relationship took time to develop; Stompanato said they had sex the night they met. It was a mercurial relationship from the start and driven by sex. It was also violent, starting during the London filming of *Another Time, Another Place* (1958). During an argument Stompanato choked Turner. She told Scotland Yard he entered England using the false name John Steele, so he was deported for visa violations.

She knew he would be waiting for her — and angry — when she returned, so she arranged a secret trip to Mexico, telling only her MGM publicist, Betty Asher. But somehow when she got off the plane, Stompanato was waiting. At her Acapulco hotel he held a gun to her head and threatened to kill her. During the visit she learned that she had been nominated for an Academy Award for her role in *Peyton Place* (1957). The headlines in the *Examiner* when she returned from Mexico read "TURNER RETURNS FROM VACATION WITH MOB FIGURE." She knew that he could not accompany her to the awards, and a huge argument erupted when she told him so. It would end in death. Turner was not MGM property, but Mannix was still concerned about his old friend and she could still sell the MGM movies she did. Mannix reportedly approached Cohen through mutual "friends" to see if Cohen would stop the relationship. Mannix didn't know that Cohen was planning to blackmail the young actress. He planned to set her up in a compromising position to extort money from her.

Turner went with her daughter Cheryl to the March 26, 1958, Academy Awards, but when they returned home Stompanato was raging. He brutally beat her and yelled, "You'll never leave me home again! That's the last time." He left her black and blue and threatened to kill her daughter and mother. On Good Friday evening, April 5, the volatile relationship reached a deadly climax in the 730 Bedford Drive mansion Turner had moved into just four days earlier. The events of the night are still in doubt, but according to daughter Cheryl, when Turner tried to end the relationship, she listened outside the bedroom as he threatened to kill Turner,

Cheryl and her grandmother. Cheryl went downstairs and returned with a carving knife. In one swift motion she pushed past her mother and into the room and plunged the knife into Stompanato's chest. He muttered, "Oh my God Cheryl, what have you done,"[27] and collapsed dead on the floor.

When detectives arrived at the house they were greeted by Jerry Giesler. Turner's first call was reportedly to Giesler, but it's more likely she called Strickling, whom she had called in emergencies dozens of times. He would then have called Giesler. Turner would not have known how to reach Giesler, and it is not likely that Giesler would have taken her as a client given his relationship to the murder victim (he represented Mickey Cohen) unless someone like Strickling intervened. It is unclear how involved Mannix and Strickling were, apart from arranging for Giesler. Strickling arranged a steady stream of sympathetic articles and numerous tearful interviews that showed Turner as the abuse victim that she was.

There were rumors that Stompanato was actually killed by Turner and that Mannix arranged for Crane to take the fall, knowing that her age and their friends in the courts would make sure that she received the lightest punishment possible. As it was, an investigation by a coroner's jury resulted in a verdict of "justifiable homicide,"[28] and Cheryl Crane was released without charges or a trial. It is hard to believe Mannix would go to those troubles at a time when Turner didn't work for MGM. Also, it is doubtful Turner would allow her own daughter to go to jail for her. The result probably would have been the same whether Mannix and Strickling were involved or not, and Mannix was for all intents and purposes already retired.

By the time the dust had settled from the Turner-Stompanato fiasco, there had been so many changes at MGM since the glory days of the 1930s that it was barely recognizable as the mighty force it had once been. There were still stars but not enough to fill the heavens. Gone was much of the glamour, gone was the need for protection of their stars, and gone was the power once held by many of the studio executives. By 1959 Mannix and Strickling were all but retired from the studio they had quietly controlled for so long. Eddie's health kept him away except for a very few days a month. What was left for Strickling was mundane publicity work. There were no "fixes" needed with the disintegration of the studio system — except for maybe one more.

Strickling was then white-haired and 63 years old, and he and Gail were living on a secluded ranch at 5230 Louise Street in Encino. It was a quiet place, although just a half a mile north of bustling Ventura Boulevard. The sprawling ranch house with its big front porch sat well back from the street, surrounded by groves of fruit trees. Every weekend they entertained old friends like Clark Gable at their quiet retreat. The valley was home to dozens of stars. The Strickling's ranch had belonged to Paul Muni. Don Ameche lived nearby in a home once owned by Al Jolson and Ruby Keeler, and further up the street John Wayne owned a hilltop colonial mansion. Barbara Stanwyck, Chico Marx and writer Edgar Rice Burroughs had ranches close by.

Mannix was by then 68 and living quietly in the El Retiro Way mansion with Toni. He had emphysema and his heart was growing ever weaker; he spent his free time visiting and playing cards with his old Hollywood friends. He ventured outside infrequently. He only occasionally visited MGM, so weak was his heart that even mild exertion would bring on painful angina attacks. But he could still be a powerful force in Hollywood, and still retained the same connections on both sides of the law that had made him someone to fear for almost 40 years. And he was still tough. Even into his late 60s, if Schary's new MGM needed to fire someone, Eddie was called in to handle the unpleasantries.[29]

Toni was as much a caretaker as a wife, and the two had long since abandoned any sexual relationship. They loved each other very much, according to Jack Larson, but she also loved George Reeves. The Mannixes and Reeves still socialized as an odd threesome, and Reeves was a regular visitor to the El Retiro mansion that Toni assumed they would someday share. By 1959 Reeves and Toni had been together for over seven years. According to the wife of one of Reeves' *Superman* costars, Reeves and Toni were "very much comfortably married." In the years between 1951 and 1959 he had also become an internationally recognized star. But he was recognized for one role, and was not happy about that. He drank even more than he always had. Reeves had always been able to drink prodigious amounts of alcohol without visible impairment. Aside from getting a little grumpy, it was hard to tell whether George had had two drinks or ten.

By 1959, *The Adventures of Superman* was a sensation. The first year's 26 episodes were filmed between July and October of 1951. When filming ended, everyone went on to other things, assuming not much would be heard from the show. Reeves and Toni Mannix continued their relationship, doing everything together. If Eddie was feeling all right, he often came along. Toni did everything she could to become "George's girl." Mickey Cohen said she was "the only woman in Hollywood with any balls,"[30] but she offered a refined veneer for Reeves. She became involved in his pet charities like his favorite City of Hope research hospital. She read books he suggested she read. She spent hours at the Benedict Canyon house she had bought him, planting flowers and tending to the garden. They entertained friends there as if they were a married couple. The Benedict Canyon house was "theirs," but Toni paid the bills.

Barely a month after filming ended for the initial series episodes, the movie *Superman and the Mole-Men* made its L.A. premiere. Viewers loved it, so the television premiere was moved up six months, debuting in different cities between late 1952 and early 1953. The actual premiere was on September 19, 1952, on WENR-TV in Chicago. It made its West Coast debut on February 9, 1953, on KECA-TV in Los Angeles. By the time it reached New York on April 1, 1953, on WABC-TV, it was a huge success. Overnight, a half dozen unknown actors were celebrities.

Larson had returned to New York to concentrate on stage work. Unaware of the success of the show, he was in a small diner when he noticed over his shoulder a large crowd of people outside, pointing inside, at him. He was recognized everywhere as Jimmy Olsen. People shouted at him from every street corner.[31] He was so afraid the role would typecast him that even in the very beginning he refused to do interviews about the show. All of the major cast members were enveloped by their roles. In May 1953, the *Newark Star-Ledger* published a front-page article titled "SUPERMAN'S GIRL FRIEND TO DYE HAIR TO AVOID CROWDS." Underneath was a photograph of Phyllis Coates and her two year-old daughter.[32] Within a few weeks she was replaced by Noel Neill though.

Everyone benefited financially. On April 13, less than two weeks after the show went national, Kellogg's paid the unheard-of sum of $1,350,000 to sponsor 100 additional episodes. That meant that the show would run for at least another four years, and meant the stars would earn more. Larson's salary increased from $250 to $350 an episode, and Reeves got a raise to over $55,000 a year plus royalties from the sales of thousands of Superman-related items. It was good money, but he was far from the wealthy movie star his fans thought him to be. Also, Reeves spent money, according to friend, stuntman and special effects master Thol Simonson, "like Gene Autry."

It had been almost two years since the crew had even seen each other, but after the Fourth of July, 1953, everyone was back in Culver City filming another year's episodes. All of the episodes for the 1953 season, the show's second, were filmed between July and September 24, 1953. They began airing on September 14, 1953, with "Five Minutes to Doom." The demanding shooting schedule would be repeated every year for the next four years. The crew would gather and film all 26 episodes during two months. Five episodes were completed in a week or so, followed by four or five days off. Then back for another five, a break, and five more, and so on., until a season's 26 episodes were completed. The third season was filmed during the fall of 1954 and aired beginning in April 1955. The fourth season was filmed in the fall of 1955 and premiered in February 1956. Likewise, the fifth season was filmed between September and November of 1956 and began airing in March of 1957.

It was physically most grueling for Reeves. Superman's "muscles" were in fact weights sewn into a form that Reeves wore under the costume made by Thol Simonson, one of Hollywood's great prop men. His "muscles" weighed almost 15 pounds, so by the end of the day his arms were exhausted. To film Superman "taking off," a camera was set up beneath a diving board. Reeves, in costume and including the extra weight of his costume muscles, ran off the board, jumping over the camera and landing with a drop and roll on several mattresses laid on the floor. Landings were faked by swinging himself from a bar and dismounting like a gymnast. But Simonson remembered that Reeves never complained. During the episode "Man in the Mask," he had to wear a 200-pound suit of real armor. When Reeves was unable to remove the heavy leaden mask, he panicked and literally ripped it off of his head. In the process, he also tore off a dime-sized piece of his nose!

If Superman had to fly during the first season, Reeves was hoisted up by a wire harness and filmed in the air. During filming of "Ghost Wolf" (near the end of the original episodes) Reeves was filmed flying over some trees on the Forty Acre lot. He was suspended 15 feet above the ground when the wire snapped, hurtling him to the ground. He landed flat on his stomach, the wind knocked out of him. Had he not been in such good physical shape he would have been seriously hurt by the fall. Hal Humphrey's popular movie column in next day's *L.A. Mirror News* reported that Reeves had been injured in an on-set accident. Thereafter, Reeves refused to fly via wire harnesses. Scenes were filmed in front of a filmed backdrop, with Reeves lying outstretched on a fiberglass body pan.

Between 1951 and 1957 Reeves tried to maintain a movie career. His television celebrity got him movie roles but most have been forgotten, such as *Bugles in the Afternoon* (1952), *The Blue Gardenia*, *Forever Female* and *From Here to Eternity* (all 1953). The *Eternity* premiere offered a glimpse of his future. Whenever he appeared on screen, shouts of "Superman!" filled the theater. What had originally been a substantial role was edited down to a walk-on by the final release.[33] Reeves surrendered to the obvious and during 1954 starred in five different *Superman* films, including *Superman Flies Again*, *Superman and the Jungle Devil*, and *Stamp Day for Superman*. He did one final non–Superman role, in a Disney movie *Westward Ho, the Wagons* (1956), with six Disney Mouseketeers.

During *Superman* production Toni was still a daily presence on the set. Everyone knew that Toni was George's girl but nobody knew about the arrangement between Toni, George, and Eddie. Toni was a fun and feisty visitor to the set, and the ritual of Toni bringing George's brown-bag lunch to the set continued without fail. Toni had a well-known raunchy side. During lunch in George's dressing room with Neill and Larson the conversation turned to aging. Toni told Larson she was in such good condition that she did not have to wear a bra. With Reeves looking on bemusedly she took Larson's hand and put it inside her blouse on her breast so he could tell "firsthand."[34] According to a mutual friend "that was Toni. She was obsessed with physical features, and with herself." She also enjoyed teasing Reeves about their lovemaking, wanting everyone to know their sex was to be envied. To 18-year-old Larson, her stories were out of place.

People liked George Reeves. Those who knew or worked with him remember him as genuinely nice, likeable, and funny, a practical joker but a total professional. According to Reeves biographer James Beaver, he was "the salt of the earth." Reeves tried to keep everyone in a good mood during the often-difficult shooting. Simonson recalled Reeves made it fun for the entire crew and everyone looked to him to pull them through the usually long days.

Jack Larson told me that Reeves was a "sucker for a hard-luck story. He was always loaning money to almost anyone who asked. He rarely got his money back." He seldom complained and didn't seem to care. Reeves' closest friend, Natividad "Nati" Vacio, told writers Sam Kashner and Nancy Schoenberger that "George was an easy touch for a hundred, any time, day or night." He could afford to be generous; bills for his house, food, liquor, everything, were paid by Toni.

When Reeves was not busy with *Superman* duties he was a tireless fundraiser for a variety of charities and made dozens of publicity appearances. His schedule during the summer of 1955 was typical. On May 31, he appeared as Clark Kent in Tulsa, Oklahoma. On June 1, he appeared in Memphis, Tennessee, for a City of Hope Hospital benefit and made three television appearances. On June 6, he was in St. Louis, on June 7 in Battle Creek and Lakeview, Michigan, and on June 30 and July 1 visited a hospital back in Tulsa. On July 15 he appeared at Disneyland, and there were a number of other personal appearances between August 1 and September 6, when filming for the fourth season began. On November 4, 1955, he made one of his rare appearances in character, at the Arizona State Fair. He didn't like to appear in costume, not because he disliked the character, but because he worried how children would react. According to Larson, at one of the first appearances in costume a young boy stood in line with his father's pistol in his pocket! He wanted to see the bullet bounce off Superman's chest just like on television. A terrified Reeves himself talked the boy into giving up his pistol by telling him that one of the other kids might get hurt when the bullet bounced off. Reeves almost never appeared in costume after that episode. However, he didn't mind showing off his "super powers." According to Simonson, he created hundreds of replica metal bars and fake baseball bats made out of balsa wood for Reeves to bring to publicity stops. Reeves delighted in the children's reaction to people breaking bats over his head and his bending of "iron" bars.

His relationship with Toni offered George the needed escape from life as Superman. Their relationship was initially forged of sex and escape, but love developed and they were close friends. It reached a peak during late 1955 when they (as usual with Toni's money) bought a large piece of land at the top of Laurel Canyon near Mulholland. Toni had decided against living in the El Retiro Way house after Eddie died. She never really liked it, with its two bedrooms separated by a long red-carpeted hall she called the Red Sea. She decided she and George would build their own house.

In 1956 it seemed that the blissful love affair would last forever, but by the next year the first cracks began to mar the facade. The first occurred during the 1956 Christmas holidays when George's mother came for a visit from Illinois. She dangled a recently inherited million dollars over his head, and George always needed money even though Toni paid the bills and he lived in a house she paid for. He had never introduced his mother to Toni, knowing they would hate each other. As expected, Helen's visit was a catastrophe. Reeves arranged a cruise to Catalina Island, but between her skin-tight Capri pants, climbing all over Reeves in front of his mother, and getting drunk, Toni made the worst possible impression. Not that she cared; she told a friend that she got a glass of water for a seasick Helen from the ship's toilet.

Shortly after Helen returned home, on March 7, 1957, the first episode of the fifth season aired. Six months later on September 23, the crew gathered to film the episodes for the sixth season. The first episode filmed was "The Last Knight," and after completing episodes like "The Mysterious Cube," "The Gentle Monster," and "The Brainy Burro," filming was completed on November 9, 1957. The final episode filmed was "All That Glitters." The last two lines of dialogue, between Larson as Jimmy Olsen and Reeves as Superman, were prophetic. Olsen said to Superman, "Golly, Mr. Kent, you'll never know how wonderful it is to be like Superman." Reeves replied, "No Jimmy, I guess I never will."

Reeves was clearly tired of his character, like all of the actors who knew by then that they were typecast. Each had made his individual deal with his own individual devil, trading the money and fame for other roles.

Reeves was bored, telling a friend he was "wasting his life." But during the 1957 filming he found a new calling, directing three of the episodes himself, and interestingly, the three — "The Brainy Burro," "The Perils of Superman," and "All That Glitters" — were the best of the 1957 episodes. He was thrilled about his prospects as a director, and according to Larson, "Reeves had a big future in directing."[35] He had other reasons to go to the other side of the cameras. By 1957 he could no longer get in costume by himself. The excesses of life with Toni and his worsening drinking had combined to add considerably to his waistline. By 1957 Reeves had to wear an uncomfortable corset and needed help getting it on.

Toni was changing physically as well. Now into her 50s she was positively "matronly" according to Phyllis Coates.[36] When Toni and Reeves first met she was a young-looking 46-year-old with an insatiable appetite for sex and a bottomless pocketbook, all very appealing attributes to Reeves. At the end of 1957 she was still wealthy but not as much fun to look at, and sex was a chore for Reeves. The monthly visits to the Laurel Canyon site had all but ended. Between their aging, the cooling of the sex, affairs with other women, and Helen Bessolo's obvious displeasure, by late 1957 the relationship was ending. Toni still believed George would marry her when Eddie died, but after surviving a first heart attack in 1954 and several since, Eddie was showing no signs of dying anytime soon. It was then that Reeves met Leonore Lemmon.

The 1958 episodes filmed in 1957 began airing in February 1958. In October of 1958 Reeves went to New York for a publicity visit. By his October 15 return, he had fallen in love with someone else. Leonore Lemmon was born in 1919 and grew up a child of privilege, a Manhattan socialite who could charitably be described a party girl. She was beautiful; tall, raven-haired with deep dark eyes. But she had a loud personality and a foul temper. By the mid-1940s she was a tabloid favorite. At age 17 she was named a correspondent in a divorce filing. By age 20 she was barred from The Stork Club and El Morocco for punching other women. At age 21 she married a Vanderbilt but discovered her husband was broke when he was arrested for passing bad checks to pay for the honeymoon. Through the 1940s she traveled the globe, tried her hand at painting, acting, and nightclub singing, took golf lessons from Olympic champion Mildred Didrikson Zaharias, and married and divorced again in 1951. Lemmon was 38 when she met Reeves at Toots Shor's in early October 1958. Their affair started that night when Lemmon arrived unannounced at Reeves' hotel room with leftover chicken and champagne. They were inseparable during Reeves' two-week visit.

Reeves was taken by her wealth, wildness, disrespect for authority, and probably most by her nymphomania. Toni was in trouble; Leonore was a shapely 38 while she was a matronly 53. Somehow Reeves convinced himself Toni would understand his leaving her for Leonore. On October 15, just two days after his return, John Hamilton —*Daily Planet* editor Perry White — died of a heart attack in his Hollywood apartment. According to Larson, at Hamilton's funeral Reeves first went public about his new girlfriend, telling him at the gravesite that he was getting married. Larson, of Reeves' friends the closest to Toni and George, was stunned.[37] Reeves' friends did not know Lemmon had returned from New York with him. She had checked into a Hollywood hotel, waiting for the "all clear" from Benedict Canyon. Reeves sat down with Toni the day after his return. When she walked out an hour later, Reeves had less than eight months to live.

Toni took the news badly. At first stoic, then crestfallen, Toni became the model spurned women. She raged to her friends, threatening to tell the press Reeves was gay, and screaming about "that pig, that slut" that stole "her boy." She said she would cut his throat. She blamed the breakup on temporary insanity brought on by the pressures of being Superman.

She asked friends to help her get "the boy" back. She even turned to the retired Strickling, ordering him to orchestrate a media campaign to get Reeves back. When he told her he could do nothing she refused to speak to him again. Strickling told friends that Eddie was furious Reeves had broken it off with Toni. He must have felt badly for Toni, but Eddie was also upset that the delicate balance between George, Toni, and Eddie had been disrupted. How angry, we don't know.

Larson told me that Reeves said that Lemmon "made him feel young again." Toni asked him to "help me bring that boy to his senses," and Larson felt great sympathy. He obviously liked Eddie and Toni. When first approached for an interview he told me, "I want you to know that I loved Eddie Mannix."[38] Larson thought Toni's reaction a logical product of having a decade of dreams shattered. She lived for years confident she would marry Reeves one day, and a week after he met Lemmon that dream went away. It was understandable that she was angry, but was she angry enough to have him killed?

Lemmon moved into the Benedict Canyon house a few days after Reeves' break-up with Toni. There were no *Superman* duties in the spring of 1959, so they settled into a routine that revolved around drinking. His liquor bill was still being paid for by Toni, who still believed that her boy would return to her.

The house at 1579 was not the typical movie star mansion nor did its rustic design lend itself to use as a party house. It was modest, very small inside, and sat on a small lot just a few feet off of a busy street. The small backyard had a patio just large enough for a table and four chairs, and a small sauna unit Reeves installed. The back yard was only about 25 feet deep and backed up to a steep canyon wall rising several hundred feet above the house. The impassable hillside was completely covered with brambles and underbrush. Because of the location in the canyon it was only in sunlight for four months during the year. For entire seasons the house was out of direct sunlight for weeks at a time. The house was a split-level ranch with five rooms. The garage was at street level. The front door, five or six steps up from the driveway, opened into the living room, which took up most of the first floor. There was a small den to the right and a small kitchenette behind the garage to the left rear. The entire back side of the house was lined with windows looking into the back yard. There were three doors into the back yard, from the kitchen, living room, and den.

The second floor had just the master bedroom. The stairway from the garage side of the living room was split; halfway up it passed a small guest room above the garage before continuing in the opposite direction to a surprisingly small master bedroom. It was 13 feet square with a very low, beamed ceiling. Reeves could walk end to end in three steps. At the time, there were no windows on that floor other than a tiny one in the bathroom. The only way in or out of the master bedroom was down the stairs and through the middle of the living room.[39]

With Toni still paying the bills the house was the neighborhood party house, filled almost every night and known as "Grand Central Station of Hollywood." The noise and loud music led to frequent police visits to the quiet canyon. Reeves sent them along with autographed pictures of Superman. As the weeks went by, fewer of Reeves' friends attended the soirées. The house was usually filled with strangers and on most nights Reeves had no idea who they were. Partying was all Lemmon knew how to do, and though Reeves also enjoyed it, after seven months he was growing weary.

The stress was not helped by Toni. Her bizarre campaign to get "the boy" back had disintegrated into stalking. She called at all hours, 30 or 40 times a day, all hang-ups. Reeves changed his phone number but within a day the calls resumed. He finally asked his agent Art Weissman to hire an attorney to stop the harassment. The calls still came so Weissman asked city attorney Noel Slipsager to keep Toni away. Toni received a letter warning, "Mr. George Reeves ... has complained to this office about telephone calls by you to his place of residence." She acknowledged receiving the letter, but denied making the calls.[40] The phone calls continued. Toni was technically correct when she said she did not make the phone calls: according to Larson, she had her longtime groundskeeper Santiago make the calls for her. Lemmon began calling Toni at all hours and hanging up. The tension was unbearable.

In addition to his relationship issues with Toni and a growing disenchantment with Lemmon, a string of odd "accidents" began haunting Reeves. In late 1958 on the Hollywood Freeway, Reeves' Alvis— the long-ago gift from Toni—was sandwiched between two large trucks. Reeves slammed the brakes and slid to the side of the road as the trucks drove off into the night. Reeves brushed off the incident, but just a few weeks later, as he drove down the steep canyon road from Mulholland toward his house another large truck tried to run his car off the road. He was barely able to avoid hurtling off the street down into the deep ravine below. Again, the truck disappeared. Just before Christmas 1958, a black sedan appeared out of the shadows on Benedict Canyon and tried to hit Reeves as he stood in front of his house. The car careened down toward Beverly Hills after just missing the shaken Reeves, who had to dive onto his front lawn to escape it. The incidents were eerily similar to the "accident" that befell Bernice Mannix a decade earlier.

On January 22, 1959, the *Los Angeles Herald* reported that Sam, Reeves' beloved one-eyed schnauzer, had been stolen from the front seat of his new Jaguar X140 convertible, bought to replace Toni's Alvis, demolished in the earlier accident. Reeves never went anywhere without Sam, who was recovering from the loss of an eye in one of the earlier auto accidents, and Reeves left him in the car while he ran into a shop at 1627 Vine Street to pick up a razor.[41] Reeves was inconsolable and angry. He knew then that Toni was behind at least some of his recent misfortunes and assumed she had stolen Sam. The dog was fiercely loyal and would not have gone with anyone he did not know—like Toni. Friends of Toni and Eddie were aghast; they all believed she was behind Sam's dognapping. Nobody ever saw the dog at El Retiro but several friends were alarmed to hear a small dog barking as they spoke on the phone. Toni blamed neighbor's animals, but everyone knew it was poor Sam howling mournfully in the background. At some point, she apparently had him put to sleep.

Toni was also following Reeves. He saw her sitting in her car, parked across from his house, near friends' homes, or outside restaurants he was visiting. When he approached, she sped off. In April and May of 1959, Reeves filed formal complaints with police naming Toni Mannix. Police could do nothing, but Reeves' public accusations and the police involvement brought the Reeves-Toni affair into a public forum. Eddie was furious. It was bad enough that Reeves dissolved the "arrangement" but now Eddie had to watch Toni break down in public. At his age it was the last thing he needed. He was mad, but how mad?

If there was any doubt that *someone* wanted Reeves dead, it disappeared early in the morning of April 9, 1959, when Reeves' Jaguar piled into a cement light pole at Benedict Canyon and Easton Drive, a half mile north of his home. As he sped down Benedict Canyon — Reeves was notorious for driving too fast — he realized his brakes were not working. Trying vainly to slow the car down as he hurtled down the winding hill, he lost control and the car slammed into the pole. Reeves was thrown almost all the way through the windshield, suffering a severe concussion and a five-inch gash on his forehead that required almost 30 stitches. He could easily have died in the wreck. When a mechanic inspected the demolished Jaguar he found that all of its brake fluid had been drained. As an associate mentioned at the time, "It looked like someone wanted George dead."[42]

Lemmon's nonstop partying added to his tension. They began quarreling, often in front of the friends or the strangers filling their house. Reeves became more and more surly. According to Larson, by early June 1959 the "bloom was definitely off the rose" between Reeves and Lemmon.[43] His opinion is supported by the press. In early 1959 a UPI story headlined "SUPERMAN TAKES A BRIDE" indicated Reeves would marry Lemmon in Tijuana, Mexico. But as early as April 28, the *Los Angeles Examiner* reported that the wedding "between George Reeves and Lenore [sic] Lemmon was called off."[44] Reeves never confirmed any wedding. He said, "You didn't hear it from me," when asked. His close friends, Weissman, Vacio, and trainer Gene La Belle were unanimous in saying that he had no intention of marrying her. June 19, 1959, has been mentioned repeatedly as the date of the marriage but it has never been confirmed. Lemmon herself only first mentioned the date during a telephone interview with columnist Earl Wilson the day *after* Reeves died.[45] There were no concrete plans for Reeves to marry.

In the two months after the Easton accident Reeves was tormented by severe, blinding headaches. He escaped by lying on the cool tile floor of his bathroom, his head wrapped in a wet towel. He also took powerful painkillers and since he still drank heavily, the combination left him surly and unable to sleep. It was a very difficult time for him, as his life hurtled out of control: the accidents, Toni's stalking, Sam's kidnapping, Leonore, a wedding he didn't want, the stream of strangers partying in his house — everything came to a head at 1:30 in the morning on June 16, 1959, when one — or perhaps two or three — gunshots echoed through Benedict Canyon. Superman was dead. How and why has been a mystery for almost 50 years.

What really happened in the house that night will probably never be known. All we really know is George Reeves was dead with a bullet hole in his skull, and there were five drunk people there; Leonore Lemmon, Carol Von Ronkle, William "Bill" Bliss, Robert "Bobby" Condon, and Reeves. There may or may not have been someone else there.

Carol Von Ronkle was a casual friend of Lemmon's. She and her husband Albert ("Rip") lived a mile and a half further up Benedict Canyon. He was a writer 35 years older than his 25-year-old wife. Rip did not know Carol was having affairs. Bobby Condon was a writer from New York working on a book about boxer Archie Moore. Reeves was scheduled to participate in several exhibition matches against Moore and allowed Condon to stay in his guest room. Writers have described Condon as "Reeves' best friend" or "Reeves' expected best man," but they are incorrect; the two barely knew each other. Carol Von Ronkle also met Condon the week before, but the two were already having sex. Police never learned of the affair. Little is known about Bill Bliss. He lived up on Easton Drive and showed up that night. He was an electrical equipment manufacturer and Lemmon herself said she had absolutely no idea who he was when she opened the door to find him there.

Police were called at about 1:30 on the morning of June 16. The caller was identified as Mr. Bliss, who described himself as a houseguest and said the owner committed suicide by shooting himself in the head. Police arrived at the house at 1:59 A.M. and were let in by Bliss. They found a nude body on the bed in the bedroom. Stepping gingerly into the tiny room — they had to step over the edges of the bed and slide by furniture — all they saw at first was the blood. It was splattered everywhere. There was a huge pool on the sheets mixed with brain matter. Blood was splashed over the wall and the ceiling, and had drenched the carpet at the dead man's feet. There was a bullet hole on the right side of the head and an exit wound on the left. One of Reeves' eyes was open, staring into space. The other was empty. The left eyeball was stuck to the wall above and behind the body.

The fatal bullet had passed through the dead man's head and lodged in the ceiling above. The detectives mentioned that it was "certainly an odd upward trajectory for a bullet to take ... if this is a suicide." Lifting the body, they found the bullet's shell casing — ejected from the chamber when the fatal shot was fired — lying underneath. They also thought that strange; when a pistol ejects a casing it is projected out to the side and up. It would be extremely unlikely (but not impossible) for an ejected casing to travel in an arc that ended up *beneath* the seated body of the person firing the pistol. A cursory look at the gun showed it so well-oiled that there were none of the visible smudges or prints one would expect to find. It was oddly clean.

Police realized that all of the people were drunk, but they each told the same story. From the smallest detail to the motive, the three drunken witnesses gave the same account. Lemmon said she couldn't round up enough people for a official party so she and Reeves went to the Scandia Restaurant for dinner. They returned just before midnight and went to bed, but she went back downstairs to fix herself a drink, unable to sleep. She was careful not to wake Condon as she walked down the stairs past his room. She turned the front porch lights on and made herself a drink. It was just the first Lemmon comment that didn't make sense. The front porch lights were the unofficial welcome sign at 1579; if the lights were on, the party was on. Why would she turn the lights on if she was only down-stairs because she couldn't sleep? Unless she was expecting company, she would not have crossed the room away from the bar to turn them on. Could the light have been a signal? Something other than "welcome"?

She said that less than five minutes later the doorbell rang and she found Carol Von Ronkle and Bill Bliss there. She was surprised to find anyone there, and said she had no idea who the man was. How Carol met up with Bliss has never been explained. Lemmon said the three sat down for drinks and were soon joined by Condon. Soon after, an angry Reeves came down in his bathrobe and loudly objected to the party, snapping, "Get out. It's too late for this nonsense." The guests apologized, but Lemmon said she gave Reeves a "tongue-lashing" and ordered *him* to apologize. The guests said he meekly complied, saying he had a headache and retreating back upstairs.[46]

According to everyone there, as soon as Reeves left the room, Lem-mon said, "He's going to shoot himself." One told L.A. Police Detective Johnson that they heard a rustling—the sound of a bureau drawer being opened—and Lemmon said, "He's getting the gun now and he's going to shoot himself." Seconds passed, and a resounding explosion echoed from the upstairs. Lemmon ordered Bliss to go upstairs and he later told police he went upstairs alone. None of the other guests—all knew Reeves better than Bliss—went upstairs. Bliss found the actor lying on the bed drenched in blood. On the floor some distance away was a .30-caliber handgun. Bliss allegedly ran back downstairs and screamed to the others, "My friend is dead! My friend is dead!"

Each guest told Johnson the same story. They also told him, without being asked, that Reeves killed himself because he was despondent about being typecast as Superman. Police did not know that two of the guests barely knew him and the third was just a casual friend. So the comments were taken at face value. After the interviews the death was classified as an "indicated suicide" though no note was found.

The police work at the house was at best incompetent. The witnesses were all drunk, their stories rehearsed, and the scene a little too staged, but only a cursory look was taken. One of the most famous actors in the world lay dead, but the police did not request that investigators check for fingerprints. No photographs were taken of the body. The guests were not separated and interviewed alone. A Gates, Kingsley and Gates mortuary driver came and took body away. Notes given to him indicated a "non-suspicious death" and a "poss. suicide."[47]

The morning headlines screamed "SUPERMAN KILLS SELF!!!" The *Los Angeles Times* thundered "REEVES, SUPERMAN OF TV, KILLS SELF AT HOME!!!" Another noted "TV SUPERMAN ENDS LIFE AFTER PARTY!!!" Still another mentioned "'SUPERMAN' KILLED BY BROKEN HEART" and "SUPERMAN'S FIANCEE HAS PREMONITION—HE KILLS SELF!" The *Mirror News* offered up "TV'S SUPERMAN, OUT OF WORK, KILLS SELF!!!"

The official version of Reeves' death had a familiar ring. As a suicide that ultimately protected a woman allied with MGM, it was reminiscent of Paul Bern's death 25 years before. Coincidentally, Reeves' near-fatal car accident occurred at the bottom of Easton Drive, the same street where Bern was murdered and where houseguest Bill Bliss lived. Also like Bern, Reeves took the blame for his own murder. Mannix and Strickling both knew the Reeves story was untrue — just like they knew the Bern story was untrue when they orchestrated it.

Friends and coworkers who knew Reeves questioned Lemmon's story from the start. The controversy spread so rapidly that the L.A. tabloids printed extra editions just to address rumors. Rory Calhoun said that "No one in Hollywood believed the suicide theory." Agent Art Weissman never believed the suicide story and put the blame on Toni. Gig Young emphatically told reporters Reeves was incapable of killing himself. Alan Ladd called the suicide theory "bullshit," saying, "I talked with him just a few days ago, and he'd bought $4,000 worth of traveler's checks for an upcoming trip. He was never happier." Superman director Whit Elsworth said that it was impossible that Reeves had killed himself. Actor Robert Shayne — Superman's Inspector Henderson — and his wife Betty were Reeves' and Toni's closest friends. The foursome spent every Sunday afternoon together, and Shayne was adamant Reeves would not kill himself. He said, "George wasn't the suicide type. Nothing bothered him that much." It was whispered Reeves was killed by a "jealous woman." But who was this mystery woman?

Leaving Illinois for Beverly Hills, Helen Bessolo told a reporter her son did not kill himself. The next day she hired Jerry Giesler, who told the *Beverly Hills Citizen News* that the Reeves case had too many "phony angles."[48] Bessolo also hired the Nick Harris Detective Agency, telling them "I don't care what it costs. Find my son's killer." Harris eventually billed Bessolo $49,000, and though he didn't find much, what he did was a bombshell. Harris uncovered that the police had found *three bullet holes* in Reeves' bedroom, not just the one.

According to Jack Larson, Toni's reaction was "total devastation."[49] But there is a question as to when and how she learned about Reeves' death. Police were called to the house at 1:30 in the morning and arrived just before 2:00. The body was released to the funeral home at 3:30, just as the guests were allowed to leave the house. At 4:30 Toni called Phyllis Coates, hysterical. Coates was surprised to hear Toni wailing that "George is dead. The boy's dead. He's been murdered."[50] Toni wanted Coates to drive to the house with her but Coates declined. How did Toni know about the death so quickly and that he was "murdered"?

The coroner's processing of Reeves' body was as peculiar as the police work. It was not brought to the county morgue but taken to Gates, Kingsley and Gates Funeral Home, where a junior medical examiner went to examine the body. Only a cursory physical examination was done and two photographs—one each of the entrance and exit wounds—were taken. The wounds were sewn shut with twine and the body washed. No test for gunpowder residue was done on the hands (once the body was washed, the test would have been useless anyway). Finally, the mortician embalmed the body. A full set of photographs should have been taken. A total examination of the body should have been done. The wound should not have been tampered with at all, and the body should not have been washed. Embalming was against California law without family permission. All physical evidence was lost forever. The examiner stated that death was from a single gunshot wound entering above the right ear and exiting above the left ear and that the death was a suicide.

Lemmon would be on a train for New York within 48 hours, but before leaving she went back to the house in the dead of night. Lemmon cut through the police evidence tape and broke in. She found—and stole—$4,000 in traveler's checks that Reeves had purchased the day before. She also removed the bloody sheets from the bed and put them in the bathtub for reasons unknown. Her illegal visit was interrupted when she found Weissman sitting in the den. Weissman, the executor of Reeves' estate, threw the "vulture" out of the house.[51] She assumed Weissman would go to the police, since it was obvious he thought she had something to do with the death. Realizing she could easily be implicated in the death, she went to the press. She left Weissman and drove to the Von Ronkle's nearby house. She called an old friend, *New York Post* writer Earl Wilson, and between hysterical crying jags denied the comments about Reeves going upstairs "to kill himself." She told Wilson the "wife of a studio executive" had been harassing them and called his death "a tragedy." She believed that he died of "a broken heart. Hollywood cuts them down. The system killed him."

Wilson's "It Happened Last Night" column that week mentioned that Lemmon "bitterly denied ... forecasting that he was going to kill himself ... and ... was to have married the handsome but unemployed actor on Friday." Wilson added that "Leonore Lemmon has all the tough breaks. Back home in New York mourning the suicide of 'Superman' George Reeves, her apartment was flooded when a water main burst and most of her clothes were ruined."[52] Lemmon's bizarre interview raised more questions than it answered. The press wondered about the murder. Why was she at the house? What was she looking for? Why did she strip the bed of the bloody sheets? Did she forecast Reeves' suicide? Was it really a suicide? By the time Helen Bessolo arrived on June 25 the death had become a "mystery" and was front page news everywhere.

Lemmon was shocked to learn that Reeves left everything to Toni. His estate was small, consisting of the house, an Oldsmobile convertible, and $25,000. Bessolo and Lemmon were left nothing. Helen had her millions but Lemmon was crushed; she thought she would receive some money. She told Wilson, "Toni got a house for charity. She got the car and the bank account, and I got a broken heart." At first, she argued that another will existed, saying "Something's fishy here. George told people he made out a new will leaving everything to me."[53] The day after the will was read she left L.A. She had the stolen $4,000 in traveler's checks. She never returned.

Now people wanted to know why Reeves left everything to someone else's wife. Eddie called on Strickling, who stepped in to provide a statement for the *Los Angeles Times.* It noted that "Mr. Mannix and I have been friends of George Reeves for a number of years. I was particularly interested in and supported the work he was doing for children through the Myasthenia Gravis Foundation and the leukemia research work of The City of Hope, as well as the many appearances he made on behalf of charities and aid to stricken children. I intend to continue his work."[54] Strickling then ordered Toni to lie low; she was under heavy sedation anyway. He did not want it to look like Toni was hiding, but when she made her infrequent public appearances she was forced to wear a wedding ring. Also, she had to wear a large crucifix pin.[55] She appeared for all intents and purposes a grieving widow.

Toni was able to see the house a week later; she owned it anyway and asked Larson to take her there. The door was still wrapped in crime scene tape. When Larson had heard the news he was in Rome after doing a play in London and filming a movie at Bavariafilmwurk in Munich.[56] He returned to find Toni "absolutely and totally devastated and sedated for quite some time after the death." Toni asked Larson to take her to the house. Larson said the police had not cleaned anything. He said, "the bloodstains on the floor made me sick, and when I went to the bathroom, the bathtub was full of bloody sheets. It made me even sicker so we had to leave."[57] His story confirms Weissman's accusation that Lemmon put the bloody bed sheets into the tub. Larson said Toni was "totally ruined" by the visit.

The death became a prominent public mystery. Police Chief Parker — a close friend of both Mannix and Strickling — blocked further inquiry though his own police were expressing doubts, but growing public furor forced him to order Coroner Thomas Curphey perform a second autopsy. It occurred on June 24 and dutifully described the injuries: "perforating wounds ... multiple skull fractures ... extensive laceration of brain." But he did note something interesting. He noted "focal ecchymoses and abrasions of head, trunk and extremities." Reeves had bruises covering his right shoulder, his forehead, and the left temple.[58]

To a nonprofessional Curphey's autopsy appeared thorough, but to a trained pathologist what *wasn't* done stood out. He never examined the head wound; never checked for the stippling present in a close-contact head wound; never looked for gunpowder residue inside the wound, which one would expect to find; never even checked the wound track, the route the bullet took through Reeves' brain. He never checked Reeves' hand for gunpowder residue, and he never even addressed whether Reeves was killed by a shot from six inches, six feet, or six yards. Afterwards Curphey avoided the 50 reporters and wouldn't comment. A brief press release from his office indicated his opinion that "the wound was self-inflicted."

Parker miscalculated if he thought Curphey's autopsy would stop the controversy. It raised even more questions. Sgt. Victor Peterson went to the house and on a whim rolled up the rug in Reeves' bedroom. He was shocked to find two more bullet holes (the holes publicized by the Harris Agency). Both shots pierced the floor boards; one went into the wall above the fireplace in the living room and the other entered a beam across the ceiling there. Even with this remarkable new evidence, Parker refused to investigate. When Lemmon was asked about the holes (interestingly, by Parker himself), she suddenly remembered accidentally firing a shot "fooling around" with the gun. "I wanted to see what the Lugar sounded like," she said, but she couldn't remember where she was standing or where her shot went. And she said she only fired once, which left one bullet hole still unaccounted for.[59]

Lemmon also mentioned that Reeves often sat on the bed pretending to shoot himself in the head with the gun loaded with blanks. She offered, "Maybe someone slipped into his bedroom and replaced the blank with a real bullet." Nobody took the ridiculous idea seriously. Even so, blanks (wadding and gunpowder) can be lethal. Actors Jon-Eric Hexum and Brandon Lee were both killed after being shot with "blank" wadding. When Parker still refused to investigate, Det. Peterson asked him personally for an inquest and was thrown out of his office. What Parker was covering up and at the request of whom is unknown. The more questions, the more Parker retreated, finally saying defensively, "This is not a conspiracy!"[60]

Several days after the second autopsy a funeral service was held at the Gates, Kingsley and Gates Funeral Home. Helen had an open casket service even though Reeves had been dead for two weeks. The only way he could be presented was by covering his face with a wax mask. Only 20 or so of Reeves' closest friends attended the service. Lemmon and Toni were absent. After the funeral Helen refused to have the body interred. It was sent to a storage mausoleum at Westwood Memorial. She would not bury her son until she knew who killed him.

But who did kill George Reeves? Where to begin? Three things have to be addressed: physical evidence, eye-witness testimony, and Reeves' mental state, in the context of a question: Does the evidence fit a suicide in this case, as described in the autopsy report?

Reeves' body raises several questions. First, he was nude. It is rare for a suicide to be found nude. A veteran Chicago policeman told me that in over 300 suicides he had never found a nude victim. It didn't fit Reeves' personality and vanity, according to friends. Second, the position of the body is suspect. Reeves evidently pitched backwards after being shot; he was found on his back with his legs over the edge of the bed as if he was seated when shot. Given the route of the bullet, one would expect him to have fallen forward given where the bullet ended up. It's not impossible that he pitched backwards, it's just not normal.

The ballistics evidence is troubling. First, it was never confirmed that Reeves fired *any* gun that weekend. Second, the bullet track makes no sense. The wound was through-and-through, entering just above the right ear and exiting above the left. Lining up the entrance and exit wounds with the point where the bullet ends up indicates trajectory. Extending the line indicates Reeves' head had to be almost sideways on the bed with the gun below. If he had been sitting upright, the bullet would be in the wall to the side of the head, not near the ceiling above it. A much more likely scenario matching Reeves' wound pattern and the bullet near the ceiling would be a fatal shot during some sort of struggle in which Reeves dropped his head. The fresh bruises on Reeves' body indicated a recent struggle. Reeves' personal trainer indicated that he had no bruises anywhere on his body earlier that day.

No powder burns or gunshot residue were found on Reeves' head. This indicates that the fatal shot was fired at some distance. According to the Harris Detective report, that distance was at least 16 inches and probably several feet. The autopsy report noted "no evidence of stippling (tiny burns from heated gunpowder) on the wound of entrance." Since the only photographs—the entrance and exit wounds in his head—disappeared shortly after the second autopsy, these questions can't be fully answered. When a reporter inquired about the photos from a friend in the department he was told the studios ordered them destroyed. Giesler noted, "To not leave powder burns, the gun has to be held at least three feet from his head, at arm's length." Wound evidence indicates Reeves could not have fired the shot. Even at the minimum distance—18 inches—he didn't have enough room beneath him to fire into the side of his head, given the head position confirmed by the bullet track.

The gun is also a problem. Strangely, it was allegedly registered to Eddie Mannix according to police Sgt. Peterson, but Toni could have brought it into the house. There were no prints of any sort anywhere on the gun. It's impossible not to leave *something* without intentionally cleaning a gun. A partial. A smudged remnant. *Something.* The gun was cleaned. Giesler wondered in the press how many suicides clean their guns. It was found beneath and slightly beyond Reeves' feet on the floor at the bottom of the bed. If Reeves did shoot himself, given the position of the body after the fatal shot and the track of the bullet, the gun should have landed on the *side* of the bed, about 5 feet away. Also, almost all handgun suicides result in the weapon dropping near or on the body, and most remain in the hand. And the Lugar had a very low recoil. It should have been on the bed, or in his hand, or to the side. Not to the front.

The position of the spent shell adds to the ballistics dilemma. The Lugar ejects a shell each time a round is fired. Police found an ejected shell beneath the body. Remembering the bullet path leading up to the ceiling, an ejected shell under the body is unlikely. The Lugar ejects shells *upwards and to the side.* If Reeves held the gun a foot and a half from his head and fired, the shell would have been ejected away from the bed and some distance onto the floor. For the shell to wind up below Reeves' body with Reeves firing the shot, the gun would have to have been held backwards and upside down. Police never test-fired to gun to check ejection trajectory either.

Ballistics and physical evidence points away from suicide. It indicates another shooter. Circumstantially, it appears the shooting took place during a struggle of some sort. Three shots may have been fired. The crime scene was then arranged and the gun cleaned of prints.

On January 23, 1960, the *Los Angeles Herald* reported that Helen Bessolo was taking the body to Cincinnati but would first have an independent autopsy done. By then the body had begun decomposing and Helen's doctors could make no conclusions. Interestingly, just before this final autopsy began, an L.A. policeman gave one of the doctors a note with a phone number on it and asked the doctor to call the number if he found anything to contradict the earlier determination. When he dutifully called and reported that the condition of the body prevented any meaningful analysis, the voice on the other end of the line said, "That's good news." The phone number was the private number for Police Chief Parker.

The eye-witness testimony is very troubling. Lemmon stated Reeves came downstairs at about 12:30 A.M., had a quick drink and returned upstairs. The shot was heard seconds later, at approximately 12:45. Police were called at 1:30. Why did it take so long to call police? That question was never asked. Police noted everyone was "very drunk" and given that they waited an hour to call police they must have been extremely drunk when the gun was fired if they were only *very drunk* an hour later. Reeves' blood alcohol level was .27. He was legally drunk, but not drunk enough to kill himself in an alcohol-addled stupor. His ability to imbibe massive amounts without effect was legendary. He had been drinking a lot for years, and his friends all knew about his "wooden leg." He was a .27 most nights.

The questions that arise from contradictions in the guest statements are mind-boggling. How did Carol Von Ronkle and Bill Bliss arrive at 12:00, minutes after Lemmon turned on the lights? Maybe they were already there — or at least she was. Von Ronkle was having sex with Condon that week. Had she arrived early and spent the evening with Condon while Reeves and Lemmon had dinner at Scandia? I think Lemmon accidentally answered that question when she told police and reporters later, "I had no idea what Bill Bliss was doing on my doorstep." She didn't say, "with Carol"; just "Bill Bliss." Carol was already there.

Of all of the people available to send upstairs, Lemmon said she chose Bliss. He was the only one in the house who did not know Reeves. Lemmon said she had never met him until she opened the door to find him there. But an hour later she chose Bliss to check on Reeves. How did he even know where to go? He ran up the stairs and when he returned cried out, "My friend is dead. My friend is dead!" He had never met his "friend." Bliss did not go upstairs and find the body.

Each of the party guests told police that Reeves was despondent over his failing career and typecasting. How could Bliss have any opinion on this subject? He had never met Reeves. It is equally unlikely the others knew him well enough to have an opinion. But let's look at his mental state on the night he died anyway, to dispel that notion once and for all.

Dozens of friends who had seen him in the weeks before said Reeves was in unusually *good* spirits. He was upset about Toni, but more annoyed than depressed. None of his friends thought he was depressed: not his oldest friend Natividad Vacio, not the trainer he had been with every day, not his agent Art Weissman, not the doctor who treated him for the injuries from his car accident — nobody. In fact, just the day before he died, Reeves had promised Nati Vacio's son Alejandro he would attend his high school graduation on June 17. Reeves would never have missed Alejandro's graduation; he was a second father to the boy.[61]

There are other similarly ridiculous motives offered for Reeves' suicide. He was said to be upset that children had killed themselves by jumping out of windows wearing Superman costumes. Since nothing like that ever happened — though there were reports of children jumping off roofs, none died — this is not a reasonable motive. People still believe the series had been canceled and he was broke. Neither could be further from the truth. There is absolutely no doubt the show had been contracted for another season. There were to be at least 26 new episodes filmed, to air in 1960. The month before, Reeves knew that scripts were being prepared; he told UPI reporter Henry Gris in May that they had been approached to do another season. Weissman confirmed the same. Noel Neill (Lois Lane) and Bob Shayne (Inspector Henderson) both reported another season was confirmed. John (Perry White) Hamilton had died earlier; Neill even knew a character actor was hired to play White's brother while Perry was written out on a vacation. The week before his death Reeves bumped into Fred Crane, an old friend who had starred as his twin Tarleton brother in *Gone with the Wind*. Reeves told Crane about the new season and that he was excited about going back to work.

The people closest to *Superman* all said the same thing. Notes dated May 29 from the production company indicated scripts for a fall season were being prepared. Neill said she saw Reeves there in the weeks before he died, preparing for the season. Phyllis Coates also spoke to him during the same time and was aware he was going back to work. Jack Larson confirmed that another season was in the works, and also noted that

Reeves would not only star but direct. Reeves was excited about directing, the excitement Crane noticed. About a month after the death, Larson was approached to star in *Superman's Pal, Jimmy Olsen*. According to Larson, *Superman's* original sponsor, Kellogg's, was using money already put up for *Superman*.[62] There is no doubt that *Superman* had not been cancelled.

It was also rumored that Reeves was broke. While he was not wealthy, he had plenty of money. Toni was still paying most of his monthly bills and his mother sent him money as well. Weissman said that Reeves had "socked away his money and was well-fixed." He had recently begun receiving residuals from the earlier shows, the only cast member who had demanded payments (Audrey Meadows was be the only *Honeymooners* regular to demand residuals and when she died in 2002 was a multimillionaire). In addition, *Superman* had been sold to an Australian network just the month before, from which Reeves was to receive in excess of $20,000 (perhaps $200,000 today). In early 1959 Reeves signed to do a movie in Spain, for which he was to be paid $75,000. That trip was planned for the week after his death. Lemmon told people her honeymoon was a film shoot. The day before he died he bought $4,000 ($30,000 today) in traveler's checks for the trip to Spain. Part of that was for Lemmon's best friend Gwen Dailey, who had asked him to pick some up for her, since she was coming along. The trip to Spain was not a honeymoon.

He was also being paid $25,000 for the exhibition boxing matches with Archie Moore (Condon was in L.A. writing about Moore). Reeves was a former champion boxer and anxious to get into the ring with one of his heroes. Speaking like the fan that he was, he said, "The Archie Moore fight will be the highlight of my life." Over the years this rumor has been falsely updated to describe his depression that he had to box Moore in his Superman costume.

The most prevalent rumor is that Reeves was suicidal because he was typecast. Reeves probably was disappointed; Larson and others in the same position have confirmed as much and it is not hard to envision. But I don't think Reeves was depressed enough to kill himself. Condon told police he was admiring the large painting of Reeves in costume that dominated the living room wall. It is hard to believe that Reeves would hang a life-size image if he hated the role. Also, Reeves routinely posed happily in costume for charity functions. In March 1959, he appeared in the Beverly Hills Easter Parade. He was not the least bit upset and seemed to bask in the children's adulation. Just three days before he died Reeves was at a dinner party at the home of a friend. At the request of the children there he agreed to "wrestle" with one another guest so the children could see "how strong

Superman was." He even allowed his opponent to throw him around for the squealing kids.

The show was not going to be canceled, Reeves had plenty of money, and his overall prospects were bright. He had no motive to kill himself. Among his friends only Larson today thinks that he *may* have killed himself. Not that he did, but that he could have. Larson echoed Reeves' problem finding other work when he said, "I knew that I would always be Jimmy Olsen. I went through a terrible depression, and maybe George did too."[63] But in the months and years after Reeves' death, Larson was one of the most vocal opponents of the suicide theory. His change of heart may have had more to do with his lifelong friendship with Eddie and Toni. During my first interview with Larson he prefaced his comments by saying, "I want you to know that I loved Eddie Mannix."[64] Larson, treated like a son by Eddie and Toni, has remained loyal to them for 50 years.

At the time of the death, arguing against suicide didn't mean involving the Mannixes. Other than Toni being "handled" by Strickling, the Mannix name was infrequently mentioned. It was not until the 1980s that Larson changed his mind and agreed with suicide. In the intervening years Toni's relationship with Reeves has become much better detailed. Rarely is the death mentioned without a reference to his longtime affair with the Eddie Mannix's wife. Even today people do not know of the arrangement between Reeves, Toni, and Eddie. As the affair became more visible, Toni became the target of contempt, Eddie's real role as an MGM "fixer" became better documented, and a tawdry air arose. The natural question came up: "Did Toni ask Eddie to kill George?" The only way for Larson to defend his old friends was to support suicide; if Reeves killed himself, neither Mannix was involved. It must have been difficult for Larson to weigh his friendship with Reeves against the loyalty he still feels for Eddie and Toni.

There is always the possibility, however unlikely, that Reeves did kill himself. Reeves researcher Jim Nolt summed up this possibility when he told me, "Friends say that he was not the kind to commit suicide ... but what do friends really know? How does anyone know what's going on inside someone's head. How often do we hear reports of people doing horrible things, followed by remarks from friends indicating they never thought he/she was capable of something like that?"[65] Even so, Nolt does not believe Reeves killed himself, nor do I. Based solely on the physical evidence, it is unlikely that George Reeves *could have* killed himself. The circumstantial evidence supports something else also. If George Reeves didn't kill himself, who did? Like policemen, let's look at motive, opportunity, and ability to kill.

First, could Reeves have been killed by someone other than the people in the house that evening? An outside shooter could not have gotten into the house without someone knowing. Even if a killer could negotiate the new locks installed just the day before, he would have passed a living room full of people. The house was never empty that night, not for a moment. Condon remained there while Reeves and Lemmon went to Scandia for dinner. He may have been with Carol Von Ronkle. Bliss arrived shortly after Reeves and Lemmon returned.

Even assuming the unlikely scenario that the killer snuck in without being noticed to lie in wait, there was no place to hide in the bedroom; and Lemmon said she was in the bedroom with Reeves. An intruder would face the same problems exiting the house as entering. The only way out was down the stairs and through the living room full of people.

Could it have been an accident? Reeves was not a gun expert but knew enough, so he didn't kill himself accidentally while he cleaned the gun. His prints were not on the gun, and he was nude. People rarely clean their guns in the nude. Lemmon mentioned he might have died playing Russian roulette, and Toni would later accept this conclusion. But you wouldn't play Russian roulette with a Lugar. Unlike a cylinder pistol, the Lugar forces bullets into the chamber by pressure, one at a time. If the gun is loaded a bullet is always in the chamber.

If not suicide or accident, then who killed Reeves? Whoever it was had the power to convince Jerry Giesler to back off. The same Giesler that represented Bugsy Siegel and Mickey Cohen, who handled the biggest scandals for the biggest stars from Charlie Chaplin to Errol Flynn, was scared off of the Reeves death. Less than a month after the murder Giesler quit, even though Helen Bessolo paid him $50,000. But Giesler walked away, telling Bessolo, "There are some dangerous people involved ... drop the case ... you don't want to know."[66] Giesler was a shameless self-promoter but completely ignored the high-profile death in *The Jerry Giesler Story*, even though the book was published only eight months later. Every single famous case was discussed except Reeves'. Who convinced Giesler to back off? Probably the same person that convinced Police Chief Parker to back off: Eddie.

Only two possible solutions remain: someone in the house killed Reeves or he was killed at the behest of the Mannixes after breaking off with Toni. I believe that all of the evidence, physical and circumstantial, points to Leonore Lemmon killing George Reeves during a fight that began at the Scandia Restaurant and ended in their bedroom. Lemmon had a terrible temper, and liked guns and knew how to use them.

Eddie didn't have Reeves killed, nor do I think that Toni would have asked him to do so. He could have; one of his closest friends in L.A. was

Cohen, a friend from his New Jersey youth. Eddie frequented Cohen's Carousel Ice Cream Parlor, a small "front" where the West Coast mob hung out. I do think that Eddie engineered a cover-up, but not to cover his own tracks or involvement by Toni. Eddie protected the Mannix name from investigations that would unearth her real relationship with Reeves— the "arrangement." If Lemmon was known to be the killer, everyone would learn about the Reeves-Mannix relationship. Eddie could not allow that to happen. He worked with the same police, coroners, attorneys, and press he had worked with for 40 years. I'm sure a story was "suggested" to the people in the house that night to ensure that the death would remain a suicide and keep Reeves' private life a secret.

Unfortunately, when Eddie orchestrated a suicide verdict, Lemmon was taken off the hook by accident, and worse, it appeared that Mannix was hiding something else he had done. The result has been 40 years of baseless "Mannix had him killed" theories. Without question, Eddie could have had Reeves killed if he had wanted to. There is circumstantial evidence to suggest that *something* was going on in the six months between the time that Reeves returned from New York with Lemmon and his death. The strange car accidents made it look like someone was trying to harm Reeves, and Eddie may have been involved. He certainly had the wherewithal, and the reason, to be angry with Reeves. But, simply put, if Eddie wanted Reeves dead, Reeves would have been dead.

Writers Kashner and Schoenberger made the case that Toni Mannix planned Reeves' death in *Hollywood Kryptonite: The Bulldog, the Lady, and the Death of Superman,* theorizing that she hired one of Eddie's mob friends to kill Reeves. The killer got into the house through one of the back doors, killed Reeves and escaped without being seen. Neighbors told police they had heard the sound of someone driving away. Ignoring the fact that it is unlikely Toni could have hired one of Eddie's minions to kill *anyone*, there are logistical problems with this theory. It is conceivable that a killer could have gotten into the house through the back doors, which were routinely unlocked; in fact, they were the only locks that *hadn't* been changed the day before. The killer could have gotten upstairs and waited for Reeves, but what about Condon? He was in the guestroom just steps away, perhaps with Carol Von Ronkle. What about Lemmon, who was in the bedroom? Where did the killer hide? The closet was too small, and Reeves was in the closet changing out of his dinner clothes. There was no room in the bathroom either. And why didn't he shoot Reeves right away?

An outside killer couldn't have done it. He went unseen by Condon and maybe Von Ronkle. He hid where there was no place to hide. He waited for Lemmon to leave the bedroom, for Reeves to change into his bathrobe, and for Reeves to try to sleep for 30 minutes before getting up, all the while hearing the sounds of a growing party downstairs. Only then did he shoot Reeves. He shot him in the head while Reeves sat on the bed, with no struggle. He left a gun registered to Eddie even though Eddie's wife hired him. Lastly, he escaped out a tiny bathroom window in less than the 30 seconds it took Bliss to get upstairs. Neighbors that heard a car heard no gunshots. It's all impossible.

Toni's actions were over the top. Agent Weissman blamed the death on a thinly-veiled real-life "fatal attraction." There were hundreds of harassing phone calls. She was following him and having him followed. She stole his dog. All of these were obsessive actions but none involved violence except for the poor dog. Her closest friends believe it "inconceivable" that she would arrange for Reeves' death. According to Larson, Toni loved him too much to kill him. He told me, "She admittedly didn't take the breakup very well, and was kind of a diva, but she could never have killed George. She didn't do it. It never happened."[67] She was devastated by his death. And she would not have asked Eddie to have him killed. Some believe Eddie arranged the murder without involving Toni, but that makes no sense. He must have known that Toni's bizarre behavior would only have gotten worse (which it did) with Reeves dead.

Like Larson, I've come to believe that the Mannixes did not kill George Reeves. But unlike Larson I don't believe Reeves killed himself. I think Leonore Lemmon killed George Reeves. The two had been arguing earlier in the evening during dinner at Scandia Restaurant, probably about the upcoming wedding that I do not believe was going to take place. That's why Lemmon was angry. She had a history of asking boyfriends to marry her right after meeting, and took a non-response to mean yes. She always referred to her boyfriends as fiancés. But Reeves was not marrying Lemmon. The trip to Spain the next week wasn't a honeymoon. He was shooting a movie, and Lemmon's best friend was coming.

Had he simply grown tired of her? According to Larson it was no secret that "the bloom was off the rose."[68] That opinion was echoed by other friends, and supports Toni's defense. If she knew there were problems between Reeves and Lemmon, there was a shred of hope that her "boy" would return. The initial heat of the relationship was cooling and Reeves saw Lemmon for what she was: a manipulative, insecure, jealous and spoiled 38-year-old party girl with a terrible temper. I think he was trying to end the affair. Whatever started the argument at dinner, it continued when the couple got home, and at some point Lemmon shot Reeves. Who was in the house at the time isn't known. Bobby Condon was there. Carol Von Ronkle was there. Bill Bliss arrived either as a remarkable coincidence or was used by Carol as her excuse to get out of her house to see Condon.

I believe part of Lemmon's story is true. I think that after arguing at the restaurant throughout dinner, they returned home and he went to bed. She stayed up drinking with Condon, Von Ronkle, and Bliss. Reeves did indeed come downstairs, still angry after his fight with Lemmon, to voice displeasure about the party. Lemmon followed him back to the room, a scuffle followed, and she shot him in the head. One, and possibly two, other shots were fired through the floor during the scuffle. The party guests raced upstairs after hearing the roar of gunfire and found Reeves in a pool of blood and Lemmon holding a gun. They retreated downstairs to figure something out before calling the police. They may have framed their suicide theory during those first few minutes, or they may have had help.

Some murder cases are clear-cut. There is a motive specific to one person and that person kills. But when there is more than one person with reason to kill, the truth becomes murkier. Various possible motives are not necessarily mutually exclusive. The reason the Reeves case has lingered for so many years is that the assumption has always been that only one of the two theories could be true. Either Toni and Eddie Mannix were involved, or Leonore Lemmon killed him in anger. But what if there was truth to both, and the events took place together? That is what I think occurred.

Leonore Lemmon killed George Reeves after an argument. The police knew about the relationship between Toni and George for years before he approached them about her harassment. If a call came in that George Reeves was dead, it is inconceivable that Eddie Mannix would *not* be called. He and Strickling would have known within minutes, as they did 25 years earlier in the case of Paul Bern. They did the same thing to protect Toni they did to protect Jean Harlow. Police were directed to announce a suicide and the press was manipulated to say that Reeves killed himself because he was typecast.

Critics of the Lemmon theory claim that there was no reason for the people in the house to lie. That is part of the hidden fallacy. They were *given* a reason to lie for Lemmon. They lied because they were told to lie. It's possible that the people in the house called police and admitted that Reeves had been killed by Lemmon, although I don't think that's likely. I think that, after the group gathered again downstairs, they agreed upon a suicide story and called the police. But police would have immediately noted the inconsistencies—normally. But this was not a normal killing. Eddie knew that if police *really* investigated and learned that Lemmon was the killer, Toni's involvement with Reeves would be front page news. He offered police a clean suicide, and Strickling's press supported that version. Eddie probably didn't go to the house. Police cars in the cramped neighborhood woke everyone and alerted the press, so it's likely he engineered it from afar.

This scenario is not the most intriguing of explanations. It would have been a better story for Toni Mannix, jilted lover, to have her mob-connected studio boss husband hire a hit man to kill Reeves. But the truth is not always sexy, and my scenario is the only one that leaves no open questions, nor requires a leap of faith. It explains the slipshod investigation, police accepting stories that were clearly lies, unprofessional autopsies, why the D.A.'s office was never involved, and perhaps why Jerry Giesler removed himself from the case.

And it is the only solution that explains why Toni knew what she knew when she knew it. According to Phyllis Coates, at 4:30 that morning Toni "woke me up ... hysterical ... [she said] 'the boy is dead ... George was murdered.'"[69] And Larson told me that during a visit to the house a week later she told him where two almost invisible bullet holes in the floor were — bullet holes underneath a rug.[70] Toni couldn't know any of it unless Eddie already told her. Eddie knew because the police had called him. Eddie knew because he made sure Toni's name was kept out of the press. Twenty years later Strickling told his pal Sam Marx, "Of course, Eddie did it." But he didn't mean that Eddie killed Reeves, just Reeves' reputation.

It was only the Mannixes personal relationship with Reeves that led to Eddie and Howard's involvement in the murder. It would be the last time that either man would involve themselves in such a predicament. Even before Reeves' death, Eddie had suffered several heart attacks. His friends had lost count, between hundreds of bouts of serious angina and at least a half dozen actual attacks. Within a year Eddie was virtually housebound, stuck in a wheelchair inside the El Retiro mansion. On his one or two good days a month he joined his old friends at the racetrack or at Chasen's for lunch. But for the most part, he sat in his bedroom, watching television and yelling across the "Red Sea" for Toni or the servants.

At the same time, Howard's domain at MGM had become a pale version of the once colorful operation he lorded over for 35 years. The publicity department actually did just that; it publicized movies. No more cover-ups. No more payoffs. No more problems. Just publicity. By the mid-1950s, all MGM did was make movies. By the late 1950s Howard had almost nothing to do but go to the office and hang around. He retired to a ranch even farther away than the valley in 1963.

By the end of the 1950s, Eddie, Howard, and their ilk had become dinosaurs. By that time it was a rare MGM employee who even knew what they had done in the decades previous. The studios made movies, that's all. The actors' agents and publicists had to clean up after them. The studios didn't even *own* them anymore, since the studio system had been dismantled by the courts and by demanding actors and actresses. The once-grand MGM name meant little to moviegoers. None of the studios meant anything to the viewers. Who made a movie was not important anymore. The stars were. The movies themselves were. That's the one thing that hadn't changed in the 40 years since Eddie and Howard got into the business. It used to be about "all the stars in heaven." By 1960 it was just about "the stars."

Postscript

Fade Out

Few people with firsthand knowledge of the work that Eddie and Howard did during their decades at MGM are still alive. In fact, most of the people involved in their final project, the cover-up of the George Reeves murder, are gone. Leonore Lemmon left L.A. within days of the murder and returned to New York. She never again set foot in L.A. Unsuccessful in her attempts to change Reeves' will, she took up with married theatrical agent Jack Whittemore. She lived in his apartment at Thirty-Ninth Street and Park Avenue, where she stayed for the rest of her life. After his death, she reportedly resorted to prostitution, becoming a fixture in the nearby hotel bars. She died on January 1, 1990, alone in her cluttered apartment.

Helen Bessolo carted George's body back to Cincinnati for burial in a family cemetery. She first paid for a third — private — autopsy, but the results were inconclusive. It was rumored that she kept George on ice for five years searching for the truth, but in reality after the inconclusive Ohio autopsy he was cremated. She carried him back to L.A. on her lap in a brightly polished brass urn. It stayed on the mantelpiece of the Pasadena house they had shared when he was a boy, and where she died on June 19, 1964. She and her son now rest together at the Mountain View Cemetery in Altadena. Reeves' urn reads simply, "My Beloved Son, Superman, George Bessolo Reeves, January 6, 1914 — June 16, 1959."

Police Chief Parker's stranglehold on the L.A. police gradually weakened during the early 1960s, and he was caught in the swirl of controversy when Marilyn Monroe was found dead in her Brentwood hacienda in 1962. As in the Reeves case, he and Coroner Curphey directed the investigation away from the truth and tried to convince a disbelieving public of a questionable suicide verdict. Again like Reeves, the real truth of Monroe's tragic death was lost in a maze of lies, half truths, and an attempt to protect someone only marginally involved. Like Reeves, trying to keep names *out* guaranteed that they remained solidly *in*.

Monroe's death was probably the result of an accidental drug over-dose administered by her housekeeper Eunice Murray. Murray was planted in Monroe's house and life by Monroe's psychiatrist Ralph Greenson, who directed his former secretary to (illegally) administer Monroe's prescription drugs. Monroe preferred taking her drugs by enema and when Murray accidentally overdosed Marilyn and she died, Parker directed a cover-up to protect Jack and Robert Kennedy, both of whom had had affairs with the unstable actress, against even the perception that they had been involved. But the more Parker tried to hide the Kennedy involvement, the more they became suspected, and the more the real truth faded. To this day, people believe that the Kennedys had Monroe killed.

Parker spent his remaining years defending himself and the police department against a growing chorus of complaints of LAPD misconduct. During a particularly impassioned speech at the Statler Hilton on July 16, 1966, he keeled over dead at the podium in mid-sentence. He died before he hit the floor.

For Eddie Mannix, the 1960s were a haze of drug-addled days sitting in his wheelchair in his stifling El Retiro mansion. On August 30, 1963, he suffered a final massive heart attack at the house. He had had two strokes in the previous week. Eddie's funeral was held on July 3 at the Church of the Good Shepherd in Beverly Hills. His pallbearers were actors James Stewart and Robert Taylor, MGM sound director Douglas Shearer (brother of Norma), William Morris Agency owner Abe Lastfogel, and producers Maurice Benjamin and Charles Boren. He was interred in the mausoleum at Holy Cross Cemetery in Culver City.

The conspiracy mill was at full throttle in the months after Eddie's death with stories that Toni had killed him, too. Unsubstantiated and pointedly silly stories suggested Eddie was poisoned by Toni. Toni inherited the entire estate, and remained in the El Retiro house for another 20 years.

Howard and Gail Strickling sold their Encino ranch in the early 1970s. The San Fernando Valley suburban sprawl had gradually encircled their once-secluded ranch with tract homes over the 20 years that they lived there. Nearby Ventura Boulevard had been transformed from a two-lane valley thoroughfare into a four-lane blacktop packed with traffic. Gail could barely get to the grocery store by the time they moved. In 1971, 50 years after Howard arrived to work in "the movies," he and Gail left L.A.

The rest of Howard's family had remained in the far reaches of San Bernardino County, living in and around Ontario, where his parents had first settled before 1920. Both of his parents had died in the late 1950s, but three brothers and a sister were still living within a few miles of the 1919 family home. In fact, Howard had returned from his mother's 1959 funeral just a day before he received the telephone call about George Reeves.

His brothers lived on ranches in San Joaquin, San Bernardino and Gardena. Howard and Gail moved onto a 120-acre farm property south of Chino in the hills of Los Serranos, not too far from the brothers.[1] The ranch was located at 3660 Valle Vista Avenue, a winding hilltop road that meandered along the crest of the Los Serranos hills. Spread out beneath the property to the south is the vast Chino Hills State Park. To the north are the majestic San Bernardino Mountains. The area has become heavily populated since the 1970s, but at the time the Strickling property was secluded and quiet.

Howard spent his days tending to his ranch and visiting with family and old studio friends who made the two-hour jaunt out to the Chino Hills. For the rest of his life his memoirs were the target of dozens of serious offers from publishers. He often spoke of putting his stories on paper but never did. Strickling rarely spoke about the things he saw and did during his years at MGM, even to his closest friends. He told friends, "My fifty years in the entertainment business were wonderful, but as Irving Berlin said, 'You can't live there.'"[2] By the 1980s the visits from the studio friends had largely ended, and Howard Strickling was largely forgotten by Hollywood.

Gail had a heart attack at the ranch and died on April 15, 1980, at age 71. Howard lived another few years, visited daily by his two nieces. On July 15, 1982, Strickling died of congestive heart failure at a nearby hospital. He was 84. He is buried next to his beloved Gail at the Bellevue Cemetery in Ontario.

When Howard died, Toni Mannix was still living in the El Retiro house. After Eddie died what was left of Toni's social life all but ended and she retreated behind the always-closed curtains. Like Norma Desmond in *Sunset Boulevard*, the once powerful tiger-lady of MGM spent her nights watching reruns of *Superman* on tape machines from the studio. She kept all of Reeves' clothes in Eddie's old closets. She kept his books. And she had the gun. She quietly watched the same flickering episodes over and over. Art Weissman, Reeves' former manager and one of Toni's few friends, shared several of those evenings and remarked that "she watched Reeves transfixed, as if he were still alive."[3]

Toward the end of her life Toni deeded her entire estate over to St. John's Hospital in Santa Monica. In 1981 she moved into one of the special suites the hospital kept for celebrity patients. There she lived out the last few years of her life, still watching old *Superman* episodes and reminiscing about George with whomever would listen. She repeated to all of her visitors that George "was one hell of a good-looking guy."

On December 27, 1983, Toni Mannix died in her bed inside her private suite at St. John's. She was 75 but appeared much older. After a small funeral — less than a dozen people showed up — she was buried next to Eddie at Holy Cross. Her crypt says simply, "CAMILLE TONI MANNIX 1906–1983 God Bless."

By then the original MGM was itself a relic, bearing no resemblance to the MGM of old. When millionaire Kirk Kerkorian — who had worked as a handyman at MGM as a youth — purchased the studio in 1969 he didn't even want it; he needed MGM's resources to build a $125 million MGM-themed Grand Hotel in Las Vegas. At the first stockholder's meeting in January 1970, Kerkorian's hand-picked president announced that half of the remaining MGM staff would be fired, most of the larger films in production canceled, and the foreign and music divisions sold off.

Then he began selling everything in Culver City. Back lots were sold to real estate developers. Condominiums and houses were built on top of old MGM sets. What used to be Lot 2 would become a two-mile-long row of car dealerships. But Kerkorian didn't stop by selling the land.

Auctioneer David Weisz paid Kerkorian $1.5 million for 12,000 props and 120,000 costumes, most of which had been sitting in huge warehouses for decades. Beginning in May 1970, Weisz began selling off his collection of over 30,000 items that he could authenticate as having been in a particular movie or belonging to a specific star. Everything was sold.

Some stars scrambled to buy relics of their films. Debbie Reynolds borrowed $100,000 against her house to buy as much as she could for a long-dreamed-about Hollywood museum.

A chariot from *Ben Hur* sold for $4,000. A clock from Garbo's *Ninotchka* earned $3,750. A dress worn by Lana Turner in *The Bad and the Beautiful* sold for $225. Fred Astaire's hat from *Easter Parade* garnered $250. The blue-and-white-checked gingham dress Garland wore as Dorothy in *The Wizard of Oz* went for $1,000, the wizard's suit for $650, and the Cowardly Lion's costume $2,400.

Garland's ruby slippers had been discovered wrapped in a Turkish towel in a bin in the basement of the wardrobe department. When they were dug out in the spring of 1970 they didn't even have a label attached. During the week-long auction held at one of the massive sound stages, the slippers lay in a glass case with a spotlight shining on them. Weisz's son-in-law Dick Carroll said, "Hundreds of people crowded around the case; some stayed fifteen minutes,"[4] just staring at the famous shoes. They were one of the last items sold. Almost 3,000 people crowded the floor on Sunday night, May 17, 1970, as the bidding reached $15,000. It took 46 seconds.

For the year 1970, MGM lost $8,228,000 on its films. It made $9,801,000 selling its assets, and some said its soul.

By the time Toni died in 1983, Howard and Eddie were long forgotten by almost all of Hollywood. The new stars barely knew the names. An old woman dies in a hospital room in Santa Monica. An old man dies out in San Bernardino. Two anonymous deaths, mostly ignored. But the most celebrated secrets in Hollywood and movie history died with them.

Howard once described his job metaphorically, saying, "Talent is like a precious stone, like a diamond or a ruby. You take care of it. You put it in a safe, you clean it, polish it, look after it. Who knows the value of a star?"[5] According to him, since "there only one of each" Garbo or Gable, they had to be protected. That's just what he and Eddie did.

Notes

Chapter One

1. Sam Kashner, *Hollywood Kryptonite: The Bulldog, the Lady, and the Death of Superman*, p. 5.
2. A. Scott Berg, *Goldwyn*, p. 29.
3. Paul Zollo, *Hollywood Remembered: An Oral History of Its Golden Age*, p. 13.
4. Bob Thomas, *King Cohn*, p. 3.
5. A. Scott Berg, *Goldwyn*, p. 29.
6. Paul Zollo, *Hollywood Remembered: An Oral History of its Golden Age*, p. 12.
7. Robert Henderson, *D.W. Griffith: The Years at Biograph*, p. 103.
8. Ibid., p. 22.
9. Gavin Lambert, *Norma Shearer*, p. 102.
10. Coy Watson, *The Keystone Kid*, p. 13.
11. Robert Henderson, *D.W. Griffith: The Years at Biograph*, p. 97.
12. Gabe Essoe, *DeMille*, p. 22.
13. A. Scott Berg, *Goldwyn*, p. 36.
14. Paul Zollo, *Hollywood Remembered: An Oral History of Its Golden Age*, p. 19.
15. A. Scott Berg, *Goldwyn*, p. 40.
16. Gabe Essoe, *DeMille*, p. 24.
17. A. Scott Berg, *Goldwyn*, p. 41.
18. Miriam Cooper, *Dark Lady of the Silents*, p. 44.
19. Cari Beauchamp, *Without Lying Down: Francis Marion and the Powerful Women of Early Hollywood*, p. 161.
20. Neal Gabler, *An Empire of Their Own: How the Jews Invented Hollywood*, p. 47.
21. Michael Blake, *Lon Chaney; The Man Behind the Thousand Faces*, p. 53.
22. Gavin Lambert, *Norma Shearer*, p. 69.
23. Neal Gabler, *An Empire of Their Own: How the Jews Invented Hollywood*, p. 156.
24. Roland Flamini, *Thalberg: The Last Tycoon and the World of M-G-M*, p. 24.
25. A. Scott Berg, *Goldwyn*, p. 33.
26. Ibid., p. 28.
27. John Eames, *The MGM Story*, p. 7.
28. Diana Altman, *Hollywood East: Louis B. Mayer and the Origins of the Studio System*, p. 55.
29. Ibid., p. 67.
30. Neal Gabler, *An Empire of Their Own: How the Jews Invented Hollywood*, p. 113.
31. Gary Carey, *All the Stars in Heaven*, p. 123.
32. Marion Meade, *Buster Keaton: Cut to the Chase*, p. 67.
33. Gary Carey, *All the Stars in Heaven*, p. 121.
34. Peter Hay, *MGM*, p. 14.
35. Neal Gabler, *An Empire of Their Own: How the Jews Invented Hollywood*, p. 89.
36. Samuel Marx, *Mayer and Thalberg: The Make-Believe Saints*, p. 6.
37. Gary Carey, *All the Stars in Heaven*, p. 13.
38. Charles Higham, *Merchant of Dreams: Louis B. Mayer, M.G.M. and the Secret Hollywood*, p. 17.
39. Samuel Marx, *Mayer and Thalberg: The Make-Believe Saints*, p.12.
40. Charles Higham, *Merchant of Dreams: Louis B. Mayer, M.G.M. and the Secret Hollywood*, p. 26.
41. A. Scott Berg, *Goldwyn*, p. 43.
42. Diana Altman, *Hollywood East: Louis B. Mayer and the Origins of the Studio System*, p. 48.

Chapter Two

1. Gary Carey, *All the Stars in Heaven*, p. 54.
2. Roland Flamini, *Thalberg: The Last Tycoon and the World of M-G-M*, p. 10.
3. Gavin Lambert, *Norma Shearer*, p. 127.
4. Samuel Marx, *Mayer and Thalberg: The Make-Believe Saints*, p. 40.
5. Neal Gabler, *An Empire of Their Own: How the Jews Invented Hollywood*, p. 222.

6. Charles Higham, *Merchant of Dreams: Louis B. Mayer, M.G.M. and the Secret Hollywood*, p. 59.
7. Samuel Marx, *Mayer and Thalberg: The Make-Believe Saints*, p. 45.
8. Diana Altman, *Hollywood East: Louis B. Mayer and the Origins of the Studio System*, p. 95.
9. Roland Flamini, *Thalberg: The Last Tycoon and the World of M-G-M*, p. 51.
10. Diana Altman, *Hollywood East: Louis B. Mayer and the Origins of the Studio System*, p. 52.
11. Peter Hay, *MGM*, p. 15.
12. Michael J. Mann, *Wisecracker: The Life and Times of William Haines, Hollywood's First Openly Gay Star*, p. 73.
13. Charles Higham, *Merchant of Dreams: Louis B. Mayer, M.G.M. and the Secret Hollywood*, p. 105.
14. Gary Carey, *All the Stars in Heaven*, p. 124.
15. Maurice Rapf, interview with author.
16. Sam Kashner, *Hollywood Kryptonite: The Bulldog, the Lady, and the Death of Superman*, p. 5.
17. Charles Higham, *Merchant of Dreams: Louis B. Mayer, M.G.M. and the Secret Hollywood*, p. 86.
18. U.S. Census, New Jersey, Bergen County, 1920.
19. Maurice Rapf, interview with author.
20. Samuel Marx, *Mayer and Thalberg: The Make-Believe Saints*, p. 72.
21. Terry Ramsaye, ed., *1936–37 Motion Picture Almanac*, p. 579.
22. Roland Flamini, *Thalberg: The Last Tycoon and the World of M-G-M*, p. 73.
23. Samuel Marx, *Mayer and Thalberg: The Make-Believe Saints*, p. 72.
24. Maurice Rapf, interview with author.
25. Samuel Marx, *Mayer and Thalberg: The Make-Believe Saints*, p. 22.
26. Ibid., p. 67.
27. A. Scott Berg, *Goldwyn*, p. 76.
28. Samuel Marx, *Mayer and Thalberg: The Make-Believe Saints*, p. 109.
29. Cari Beauchamp, *Without Lying Down: Francis Marion and the Powerful Women of Early Hollywood*, p. 101.
30. Samuel Marx, *Mayer and Thalberg: The Make-Believe Saints*, p. 51.
31. Robert Barnes, *Maryland Marriages 1778–1800*, p. 220.
32. John Vogt, *Frederick County, Maryland Marriages 1738–1850*, p. 247.
33. Wes Cochran, *Washington County, Ohio Marriages, 1789–1918*, p. 245.
34. Wes Cochran, *Pleasants County, WV: Marriages 1863–1899*, p. 43.
35. U.S. Census, California, Los Angeles County, 1910.
36. Samuel Marx, *Deadly Illusions: Jean Harlow and the Murder of Paul Bern*, p. 150.
37. U.S. Census, California, San Bernardino County, 1920.
38. Maurice Rapf, interview with author.
39. U.S. Census, California, Los Angeles County, 1920.
40. Ibid., p. 108.
41. Frank Capra, *The Name Above the Title*, p. 118.
42. Samuel Marx, *Mayer and Thalberg: The Make-Believe Saints*, p. 42.
43. Neal Gabler, *An Empire of Their Own: How the Jews Invented Hollywood*, p. 81.
44. Samuel Marx, *Mayer and Thalberg: The Make-Believe Saints*, p. 32.
45. Neil Gabler, *An Empire of Their Own: How the Jews Invented Hollywood*, p. 209.
46. Jane Ellen Wayne, *Ava's Men: The Private Life of Ava Gardner*, p. 21.
47. Samuel Marx, *Mayer and Thalberg: The Make-Believe Saints*, p. 22.
48. Gavin Lambert, *Norma Shearer*, p. 184.
49. Charles Higham, *Merchant of Dreams: Louis B. Mayer, M.G.M. and the Secret Hollywood*, p. 207.
50. Ibid., p. 167.
51. Charles Higham, *Merchant of Dreams: Louis B. Mayer, M.G.M. and the Secret Hollywood*, p. 98.
52. Barney Oldfield, interview with author.
53. James Spada, *Peter Lawford: The Man Who Kept the Secrets*, p. 78.
54. Samuel Marx, *Mayer and Thalberg: The Make-Believe Saints*, p. 59.
55. James Spada, *Peter Lawford: The Man Who Kept the Secrets*, p. 59.
56. Bob Thomas, *King Cohn*, p. 165.
57. James Spada, *Peter Lawford: The Man Who Kept the Secrets*, p. 79.
58. Bob Thomas, *King Cohn*, p. 115.
59. Charles Higham, *Merchant of Dreams: Louis B. Mayer, M.G.M. and the Secret Hollywood*, p. 371.
60. Sharon Rich, *Sweethearts: The Timeless Love Affair— On Screen and Off— Between Jeanette MacDonald and Nelson Eddy*, p. 12.
61. Samuel Marx, *Mayer and Thalberg: The Make-Believe Saints*, p. 52.
62. Samuel Marx, *Mayer and Thalberg: The Make-Believe Saints*, p. 59.
63. Ibid., p. 77.
64. Neal Gabler, *An Empire of Their Own: How the Jews Invented Hollywood*, p. 223.
65. Samuel Marx, *Mayer and Thalberg: The Make-Believe Saints*, p. 49.
66. Neal Gabler, *An Empire of Their Own: How the Jews Invented Hollywood*, p. 225.

67. Barney Oldfield, interview with author.

68. Neal Gabler, An Empire of Their Own: How the Jews Invented Hollywood, p. 227.

69. Gavin Lambert, *Norma Shearer*, p. 78.

70. Roland Flamini, *Thalberg: The Last Tycoon and the World of M-G-M*, p. 75.

71. Frank Capra, *The Name Above the Title*, p. 117.

72. Gary Carey, *All the Stars in Heaven*, p. 77.

73. Samuel Marx, *Mayer and Thalberg: The Make-Believe Saints*, p. 134.

74. Gary Carey, *All the Stars in Heaven*, p. 77.

75. Gavin Lambert, *Norma Shearer*, p. 37.

76. David Stenn, *Bombshell: The Life and Death of Jean Harlow*, p. 100.

77. Charles Higham, *Merchant of Dreams: Louis B. Mayer, M.G.M. and the Secret Hollywood*, p. 67.

78. Frank Capra, *The Name Above the Title*, p. 118.

79. Samuel Marx, *Mayer and Thalberg: The Make-Believe Saints*, p. 133.

80. Ibid., p. 134.

81. Bill Davidson, *Spencer Tracy: Tragic Idol*, p. 103.

82. Busby Berkeley archives, author's collection.

83. Samuel Marx, *Mayer and Thalberg: The Make-Believe Saints*, p. 79.

84. Marion Meade, *Buster Keaton: Cut to the Chase*, p. 110.

85. Barry Paris, *Louise Brooks*, p. 228.

86. Marion Meade, *Buster Keaton Cut to the Chase*, p. 75.

87. U.S. Census, California, Los Angeles County, 1930.

88. Marion Meade, *Buster Keaton: Cut to the Chase*, p. 153.

89. Gary Carey, *All the Stars in Heaven*, p. 135.

90. U.S. Census, California, Los Angeles County, 1930.

91. Neal Gabler, *An Empire of Their Own: How the Jews Invented Hollywood*, p. 62.

92. A. Scott Berg, *Goldwyn*, p. 31.

93. *Photoplayers Weekly*, June 24, 1915.

94. Cari Beauchamp, *Without Lying Down: Francis Marion and the Powerful Women of Early Hollywood*, p. 46.

95. James Robert Parish, *The Fox Girls*, p. 23.

96. Anita Loos, *Cast of Thousands*, p. 32.

97. Gary Carey, *All the Stars in Heaven*, p. 107.

98. Ibid., p. 107.

99. Fred Guiles, *Joan Crawford: The Last Word*, p. 55

100. James Spada, *Peter Lawford: The Man Who Kept the Secrets*, p. 79.

101. Maurice Rapf, interview with author.

102. Barney Oldfield, interview with author.

103. Ibid.

104. Charles Higham, *Merchant of Dreams: Louis B. Mayer, M.G.M. and the Secret Hollywood*, p. 433.

105. Ibid., p. 108.

106. Gavin Lambert, *Norma Shearer*, p. 112.

107. Gavin Lambert, *Norma Shearer*, p. 228.

108. A. Scott Berg, *Goldwyn*, p. 80.

109. Michael Munn, *The Hollywood Murder Casebook*, p. 43

110. W.A. Swanberg, *Citizen Hearst*, p. 445.

111. Michael Munn, *The Hollywood Murder Casebook*, p. 50.

112. W.A. Swanberg, *Citizen Hearst*, p. 57.

113. Michael Munn, *The Hollywood Murder Casebook*, p. 57.

114. Roland Flamini, *Thalberg: The Last Tycoon and the World of M-G-M*, p. 37.

115. Sam Kashner, *Hollywood Kriptonite: The Bulldog, the Lady and the Death of Superman*, p. 6.

116. Sam Kashner, *Hollywood Kryptonite: The Bulldog, The Lady, and the Death of Superman*, p. 6.

117. Alex Madsen, *The Sewing Circle: Hollywood's Greatest Secret, Female Stars Who Loved Other Women*, p. 18.

118. Maurice Rapf, interview with author.

119. Bob Thomas, *King Cohn*, p. 61.

120. Diane McLellan, *Hollywood East: Louis B. Mayer and the Origins of the Studio System*, p. 122.

121. Ibid., p. xvii.

122. Maurice Rapf, interview with author.

Chapter Three

1. Miriam Cooper, *Dark Lady of the Silents*, p. 48.

2. David Stenn, *Clara Bow: Runnin' Wild*, p. 11.

3. Scott Eyman, *Mary Pickford: America's Sweetheart*, p. 126.

4. Cari Beauchamp, *Without Lying Down: Francis Marion and the Powerful Women of Early Hollywood*, p. 124.

5. Charles Higham, *Merchant of Dreams: Louis B. Mayer, M.G.M. and the Secret Hollywood*, p. 45.

6. Andre Soares, *Beyond Paradise: The Life of Ramon Novarro*, p. 19.

7. William Mann, *Wisecracker: The Life and Times of William Haines, Hollywood's First Openly Gay Star*, p. 114.

8. Irving Shulman, *Valentino*, p. 136.
9. Diana McLellan, *The Girls: Sappho Goes to Hollywood*, p. 39.
10. Maurice Rapf, interview with author.
11. U.S. Census, State of California, L.A. County, 1920.
12. Betty Harper Fussell, *Mabel: Hollywood's First I-Don't-Care Girl*, p. 126.
13. Andy Edmonds, *Frame-Up! The Untold Story of Roscoe "Fatty" Arbuckle*, p. 143.
14. Scott Eyman, *Mary Pickford: America's Sweetheart*, p. 98.
15. Cari Beauchamp, *Without Lying Down: Francis Marion and the Powerful Women of Early Hollywood*, p. 102.
16. Betty Harper Fussell, *Mabel: Hollywood's First I-Don't-Care Girl*, p. 139.
17. Robert Giroux, *A Deed of Death: The Story Behind the Unsolved Murder of Hollywood Director William Desmond Taylor*, p. 37.
18. Betty Harper Fussell, *Mabel: Hollywood's First I-Don't-Care-Girl*, p. 138.
19. Robert Giroux, *A Deed of Death: The Story Behind the Unsolved Murder of Hollywood Director William Desmond Taylor*, p. 39.
20. Andy Edmonds, *Frame-Up! The Untold Story of Roscoe "Fatty" Arbuckle*, p. 157.
21. Ibid., p. 247.
22. Letter from Minta Durfee Arbuckle, author's collection.
23. Betty Harper Fussell, *Mabel: Hollywood's First I-Don't-Care Girl*, p. 145.
24. Robert Giroux, *A Deed of Death: The Story Behind the Unsolved Murder of Hollywood Director William Desmond Taylor*, p. 13.
25. Robert Giroux, *A Deed of Death: The Story Behind the Unsolved Murder of Hollywood Director William Desmond Taylor*, p. 47.
26. Sidney Kirkpatrick, *A Cast of Killers*, p. 170.
27. *L.A. Examiner*, March 27, 1926.
28. Robert Giroux, *A Deed of Death: The Story Behind the Unsolved Murder of Hollywood Director William Desmond Taylor*, p. 128.
29. *Chicago News*, March 24, 1926, and *Chicago Herald Examiner*, March 25, 1926.
30. Ibid., p. 254.
31. Andy Edmonds, *Frame-Up! The Untold Story of Roscoe "Fatty" Arbuckle*, p. 145.
32. Gavin Lambert, *Norma Shearer*, p. 48.
33. Roland Flamini, *Thalberg: The Last Tycoon and the World of M-G-M*, p. 85.
34. Richard J. Maturi and Mary Buckingham, *Francis X. Bushman*, p. 15.
35. Samuel Marx, *Mayer and Thalberg: The Make-Believe Saints*, p. 63.
36. Bob Thomas, *Joan Crawford*, p. 48.
37. William Mann, *Wisecracker: The Life and Times of William Haines, Hollywood's First Openly Gay Star*, p. 86.
38. Diana McLellan, *The Girls: Sappho Goes to Hollywood*, p. 152.
39. William Mann, *Wisecracker: The Life and Times of William Haines, Hollywood's First Openly Gay Star*, p. 40.
40. Diana McLellan, *The Girls: Sappho Goes to Hollywood*, p. 36.
41. Maurice Rapf, interview with author.
42. Fred Lawrence Guiles, *Joan Crawford: The Last Word*, p. 56.
43. William Mann, *Wisecracker: The Life and Times of William Haines, Hollywood's First Openly Gay Star*, p. 61.
44. Andre Soares, *Beyond Paradise: The Life of Ramon Novarro*, p. 56.
45. William Mann, *Wisecracker: The Life and Times of William Haines, Hollywood's First Openly Gay Star*, p. 62.
46. Maurice Rapf, interview with author.
47. William Mann, *Wisecracker: The Life and Times of William Haines, Hollywood's First Openly Gay Star*, p. 78.
48. Miriam Cooper, *Dark Lady of the Silents*, p. 173.
49. Barney Oldfield, interview with author.
50. John Gilbert in Flamini, *Thalberg*, p. 76.
51. Michael Mann, *Wisecracker: The Life and Times of William Haines, Hollywood's First Openly Gay Star*, p. 133
52. Andre Soares, *Beyond Paradise: The Life of Ramon Novarro*, p. 140
53. Michael Mann, *Wisecracker: The Life and Times of William Haines, Hollywood's First Openly Gay Star*, p. 117.
54. Ibid., p. 64.
55. Ibid., p. 143
56. Barry Paris, *Garbo*, p. 114–16.
57. Leatrice Gilbert Fountain, *Dark Star: The Untold Story of the Meteoric Rise and Fall of the Legendary John Gilbert*, p. 102.
58. Ibid., p. 114.
59. Ibid., p. 125.
60. Fred Lawrence Guiles, *Marion Davies*, p. 170.
61. Leatrice Gilbert Fountain, *Dark Star: The Untold Story of the Meteoric Rise and Fall of the Legendary John Gilbert*, p. 102.
62. Charles Higham, *Merchant of Dreams: Louis B. Mayer, M.G.M. and the Secret Hollywood*, p. 112.
63. Leatrice Gilbert Fountain, *Dark Star: The Untold Story of the Meteoric Rise and Fall of the Legendary John Gilbert*, p. 132.
64. Barry Paris, *Garbo*, p. 138.
65. Ibid., p. 139.
66. Eve Golden, *Mary Nolan, Tragic Star*.
67. Neal Gabler, *An Empire of Their Own: How the Jews Invented Hollywood*, p. 147.
68. U.S. Census, California, L.A. County, 1930.

69. Gavin Lambert, *Norma Shearer*, p. 80.
70. Samuel Marx, *Mayer and Thalberg: The Make-Believe Saints*, p. 98.
71. Roland Flamini, *Thalberg: The Last Tycoon and the World of M-G-M*, p. 105.
72. Samuel Marx, *Mayer and Thalberg: The Make-Believe Saints*, p. 121.
73. Charles Higham, *Merchant of Dreams: Louis B. Mayer, M.G.M. and the Secret Hollywood*, p. 74.
74. Bob Thomas, *The Clown Prince of Hollywood*, p. 61.
75. Roland Flamini, *Thalberg: The Last Tycoon and the World of M-G-M*, p. 110.
76. Diana McLellan, *The Girls: Sappho Goes to Hollywood*, p. 94.
77. Roland Flamini, *Thalberg: The Last Tycoon and the World of M-G-M*, p. 112.
78. Ibid., p. 111.
79. David Stenn, *Clara Bow: Runnin' Wild*, p. 151.
80. Diana McLellan, *The Girls: Sappho Goes to Hollywood*, p. 95.
81. Leatrice Gilbert Fountain, *Dark Star: The Untold Story of the Meteoric Rise and Fall of the Legendary John Gilbert*, p. 132.
82. Roland Flamini, *Thalberg: The Last Tycoon and the World of M-G-M*, p. 117.
83. Barney Oldfield, interview with author.
84. Samuel Marx, *Mayer and Thalberg: The Make-Believe Saints*, p. 117.
85. Maurice Rapf, interview with author.
86. Fred Lawrence Guiles, *Joan Crawford: The Last Word*, p. 40.
87. Lawrence J. Quirk, *Joan Crawford: The Essential Biography*, p. 46.
88. Axel Madsen, *The Sewing Circle: Hollywood's Greatest Secret, Female Stars Who Loved Other Women*, p. 116.
89. Diana McLellan, *The Girls: Sappho Goes to Hollywood*, p. 173.
90. U.S. Census, California, L.A. County, 1930.
91. Charles Higham, *Merchant of Dreams: Louis B. Mayer, M.G.M. and the Secret Hollywood*, p. 135.
92. David Stenn, "It Happened One Night—at MGM," *Vanity Fair*, November, 2002.
93. Sam Kashner, *Hollywood Kryptonite: The Bulldog, The Lady, and the Death of Superman*, p. 28.
94. Ibid., p. 29.
95. Jack Larson interview with author.
96. Sam Kashner, *Hollywood Kriptonite: The Bulldog, The Lady and the Death of Superman*, p. 153.

Chapter Four

1. Diana McLellan, *The Girls: Sappho Goes to Hollywood*, p. 117.
2. Cari Beauchamp, *Without Lying Down: Francis Marion and the Powerful Women of Early Hollywood*, p. 104.
3. Samuel Marx, *Mayer and Thalberg: The Make-Believe Saints*, p. 165.
4. Maurice Rapf, interview with author.
5. Budd Shullberg
6. Tichi Wilkerson, *The Hollywood Reporter*, p. 4.
7. William Mann, *Wisecracker: The Life and Times of William Haines, Hollywood's First Openly Gay Star*, p. 101.
8. Ibid., p. 187.
9. Barry Paris, *Garbo*, p. 247
10. Floyd Conner, *Lupe Velez and Her Lovers*, p. 50.
11. Ibid., p. 138.
12. Jane Ellen Wayne, *Cooper's Women*, p. 34.
13. Floyd Conner, *Lupe Velez and Her Lovers*, p. 86.
14. David Stenn, *Clara Bow: Runnin' Wild*, p. 94.
15. Floyd Conner, *Lupe Velez and Her Lovers*, p. 124.
16. Ibid., p. 130.
17. Ibid., p. 138.
18. Bob Thomas, *Joan Crawford*, p. 95.
19. Garson Kanin, *Hollywood*, from *The Grove Book of Hollywood*, Christopher Silvester, ed.
20. Warren G. Harris, *Clark Gable: A Biography*, p. 21.
21. Lyn Tornabene, *Long Live the King*, p. 108.
22. Warren G. Harris, *Clark Gable: A Biography*, p. 37.
23. Roland Flamini, *Thalberg: The Last Tycoon and the World of M-G-M*, p. 132.
24. Ibid., p. 136.
25. Jane Ellen Wayne, *Cooper's Women*, p. 37.
26. Michael Mann, *Wisecracker: The Life and Times of William Haines, Hollywood's First Openly Gay Star*, pp. 217–218.
27. Fred Lawrence Guiles, *Joan Crawford: The Last Word*, p. 75.
28. Warren G. Harris, *Clark Gable: A Biography*, p. 72.
29. Ibid., p. 105
30. Bob Thomas, *Joan Crawford*, p. 93.
31. Warren G. Harris, *Gable and Lombard*, p. 34.
32. Lyn Tornabene, *Long Live the King*, p. 34.
33. Lawrence Quirk, *Joan Crawford: The Essential Biography*, p. 68.

34. Warren G. Harris, *Clark Gable: A Biography*, p. 83.

35. Ibid., p. 88.

36. Fred Lawrence Guiles, *Joan Crawford: The Last Word*, p. 78.

37. Charles Higham, *Merchant of Dreams: Louis B. Mayer, M.G.M. and the Secret Hollywood*, p. 174.

38. Gloria Swanson, *Swanson on Swanson*, p. 61.

39. Cornelius Schnauber, *Hollywood Haven*, p. 6.

40. Barry Paris, *Garbo*, p. 184.

41. Diana McLellan, *The Girls: Sappho Goes to Hollywood*, p. 61.

42. Ibid., p. 74

43. Ibid., p. 62.

44. Ibid., p. 68.

45. Barry Paris, *Garbo*, p. 255

46. Maurice Rapf, interview with author.

47. Barry Paris, *Garbo*, p. 257.

48. Diana McLellan, *The Girls: Sappho Goes to Hollywood*, p. 20.

49. Alex Madsen, *The Sewing Circle: Hollywood's Greatest Secret, Female Stars Who Loved Other Women*, p. 10.

50. Michael Mann, *Wisecracker: The Life and Times of William Haines, Hollywood's First Openly Gay Star*, p. 185.

51. Ibid., p. 175.

52. Barry Paris, *Garbo*, p. 264.

53. Maria Riva, *Marlene Dietrich*, p. 38.

54. Barry Paris, *Garbo*, p. 101.

55. Steven Bach, *Marlene Dietrich: Life and Legend*, p. 62.

56. Donald Spoto, *The Life of Marlene Dietrich*, p. 86.

57. Diana McLellan, *The Girls: Sappho Goes to Hollywood*, p. 113.

58. Maria Riva, *Marlene Dietrich*, p. 77.

59. Diana McLellan, *The Girls: Sappho Goes to Hollywood*, p. 331.

60. Barry Paris, *Garbo*, p. 285.

61. Maria Riva, *Marlene Dietrich*, p. 154.

62. Barry Paris, *Garbo*, p. 135.

63. Les Israel, *Miss Tallulah Bankhead*, p. 95.

64. Barry Paris, *Garbo*, p. 145.

65. Axel Madsen, *The Sewing Circle: Hollywood's Greatest Secret, Female Stars Who Loved Other Women*, p. 112.

66. Diana McLellan, *The Girls: Sappho Goes to Hollywood*, p. 158

67. Samuel Marx, *Mayer and Thalberg: The Make-Believe Saints*, p. 119.

68. David Stenn, *Bombshell: The Life and Death of Jean Harlow*, p. 10.

69. Jane Ellen Wayne, *Gable's Women*, p. 90.

70. Samuel Marx, *Deadly Illusions: Jean Harlow and the Murder of Paul Bern*, p. 99.

71. Jane Ellen Wayne, *Gable's Women*, p. 20.

72. David Stenn, *Clara Bow: Runnin' Wild*, p. 179.

73. Richard Hack, *Hughes: The Private Diaries*, p. 75.

74. Roland Flamini, *Thalberg: The Last Tycoon and the World of M-G-M*, p. 144.

75. Samuel Marx, *Deadly Illusions: Jean Harlow and the Murder of Paul Bern*, p. 18.

76. Roland Flamini, *Thalberg: The Last Tycoon and the World of M-G-M*, p. 158.

77. David Stenn, *Bombshell: The Life and Death of Jean Harlow*, p. 118.

78. Cari Beauchamp, *Without Lying Down: Francis Marion and the Powerful Women of Early Hollywood*, p. 297.

79. Samuel Marx, *Mayer and Thalberg: The Make-Believe Saints*, p. 47.

80. Cari Beauchamp, *Without Lying Down: Frances Marion and the Powerful Women of Early Hollywood*, p. 121.

81. Frank Capra, *The Name above the Title*, p. 134.

82. Jane Ellen Wayne, *Gable's Women*, p. 89.

83. Roland Flamini, *Thalberg: The Last Tycoon and the World of M-G-M*, p. 145.

84. David Stenn, *Bombshell: The Life and Death of Jean Harlow*, p. 55.

85. Ibid., p. 86.

86. Cari Beauchamp, *Without Lying Down: Francis Marion and the Powerful Women of Early Hollywood*, p. 297.

87. Jane Ellen Wayne, *Gable's Women*, p. 89.

88. David Stenn, *Bombshell: The Life and Death of Jean Harlow*, p. 106.

89. Samuel Marx, *Deadly Illusions: Jean Harlow and the Murder of Paul Bern*, p. 4.

90. David Stenn, *Bombshell: The Life and Death of Jean Harlow*, p. 107.

91. Ibid., p. 119.

92. Ibid., p. 154.

93. Charles Higham, *Merchant of Dreams: Louis B. Mayer, M.G.M. and the Secret Hollywood*, p. 184.

94. Samuel Marx, *Mayer and Thalberg: The Make-Believe Saints*, p. 191.

95. Charles Higham, *Merchant of Dreams: Louis B. Mayer, M.G.M. and the Secret Hollywood*, p. 183.

96. David Stenn, *Bombshell: The Life and Death of Jean Harlow*, p. 108.

97. Testimony of Irving Thalberg, Coroner's Inquest, September 8, 1932.

98. Gavin Lambert, *Norma Shearer*, p. 179.

99. Charles Higham, *Merchant of Dreams: Louis B. Mayer, M.G.M. and the Secret Hollywood*, p. 185.

100. Ibid., p. 186.
101. Roland Flamini, *Thalberg: The Last Tycoon and the World of M-G-M*, p. 161.
102. Samuel Marx, *Deadly Illusions: Jean Harlow and the Murder of Paul Bern*, p. 93.
103. Charles Higham, *Merchant of Dreams: Louis B. Mayer, M.G.M. and the Secret Hollywood*, p. 186.
104. Ibid., p. 187.
105. Samuel Marx, *Mayer and Thalberg: The Make-Believe Saints*, p. 192.
106. David Stenn, *Bombshell: The Life and Death of Jean Harlow*, p. 111.
107. *Los Angeles Record*, September 8, 1932.
108. Charles Higham, *Merchant of Dreams: Louis B. Mayer, M.G.M. and the Secret Hollywood*, p. 188.
109. Jane Ellen Wayne, *Gable's Women*, p. 91.
110. Samuel Marx, *Mayer and Thalberg: The Make-Believe Saints*, p. 194.
111. David Stenn, *Bombshell: The Life and Death of Jean Harlow*, p. 100.
112. *Los Angeles Record*, Sept. 6, 1932.
113. Charles Higham, *Merchant of Dreams: Louis B. Mayer, M.G.M. and the Secret Hollywood*, p. 184.
114. *Los Angeles Evening Herald*, May 9, 1931.
115. Maurice Rapf, interview with author.
116. Roland Flamini, *Thalberg: The Last Tycoon and the World of M-G-M*, p. 143.
117. Michael Mann, *Wisecracker: The Life and Times of William Haines, Hollywood's First Openly Gay Star*, p. 210.
118. Michael Mann, *Wisecracker*, p. 210 and Charles Higham, *Merchant of Dreams: Louis B. Mayer*, MGM and the Secret Hollywood, p. XX.
119. Charles Higham, *Merchant of Dreams: Louis B. Mayer, M.G.M. and the Secret Hollywood*, p. 174.
120. Gavin Lambert, *Norma Shearer*, p. 190.
121. Roland Flamini, *Thalberg: The Lost Tycoon and the World of MGM*, p. 184.
122. Charles Higham, *Charles Laughton*, p. 25.
123. Diana McLellan, *The Girls: Sappho Goes to Hollywood*, p. 36.
124. Lyn Tornabese. *Long Live the King*, p. 51.
125. Charles Higham, *Merchant of Dreams: Louis B. Mayer, M.G.M. and the Secret Hollywood*, p. 201.
126. Lyn Tornabene, *Long Live the King*, p. 237.
127. Warren G. Harris, *Clark Gable: A Biography*, p. 109.
128. Shaun Considine, *Bette & Joan: The Divine Feud*, p. 47.
129. *Los Angeles Post-Record,* December 1, 1933.
130. Floyd Conner, *Lupe Velez and Her Lovers*, p. 139.
131. Sharon Rich, *Sweethearts: The Timeless Love Affair— On Screen and Off— Between Jeanette MacDonald and Nelson Eddy*, p. 20.
132. Ibid., p. 73.
133. Ibid., p. 130.
134. Sharon Rich, *Sweethearts: The Timeless Love Affair-on screen and off-between Jeanette MacDonald and Nelson Eddy*, p. 128.
135. Charles Higham, *Merchant of Dreams: Louis B. Mayer, M.G.M. and the Secret Hollywood*, p. 212.
136. Barney Oldfield, interview with author.
137. *Los Angeles Evening Herald Express,* September 22, 1933.
138. *Los Angeles Evening Herald Express,* September 29, 1933.
139. Lawrence Grobel, *The Hustons*, p. 159.
140. Ibid., p. 160; also, Barney Oldfield, interview with author.
141. Michael Mann, *Wisecracker: The Life and Times of William Haines, Hollywood's First Openly Gay Star*, p. 212.
142. Ibid., p. 243.
143. Ibid., p. 187.
144. *Los Angeles Evening Herald Express,* December 4, 1933.
145. Sam Kashner, *Hollywood Kryptonite: The Bulldog, The Lady, and the Death of Superman*, p. 7.
146. Jack Larsen, interview with author.
147. Gary Carey, *All the Stars in Heaven*, p. 124.
148. Jack Larsen, interview with author.
149. Roy Drachman, *Just Memories: Hollywood Memories*, part 3, unpublished memoirs.
150. Barney Oldfield, interview with author.
151. Ibid.
152. *Los Angeles Evening Herald Examiner,* May 1, 1934.
153. *Los Angeles Examiner,* May 10, 1934.
154. Barry Paris, *Garbo*, p. 310.
155. Hedda Hopper, *From under My Hat*, p. 190.
156. Charles Higham, *Marlene: The Life of Marlene Dietrick*, p. XX.
157. Joe Morella and Edward Epstein, *Loretta Young*, p. 209.
158. Warren G. Harris, *Clark Gable: A Biography*, p. 126.
159. *Los Angeles Evening Herald Express,* March 26, 1935.
160. Ibid., October 5, 1934.
161. Floyd Conner, *Lupe Velez and Her Lovers*, p. 115.
162. Davidson, Bill, *Spencer Tracy: Tragic Idol* ,p. 64.

163. Warren G. Harris, *Clark Gable: A Biography*, p. 162.
164. Sharon Rich, *Sweethearts: The Timeless Love Affair — On Screen and Off — Between Jeanette MacDonald and Nelson Eddy*, p. 152.
165. Cari Beauchamp, *Without Lying Down: Francis Marion and the Powerful Women of Early Hollywood*, p. 221.
166. Judy Lewis, *Uncommon Knowledge*, p. 57.
167. Joe Morella & Edward Epstein, *Loretta Young*, p. 92.
168. Warren G. Harris, *Clark Gable: A Biography*, p. 138.
169. Judy Lewis, *Uncommon Knowledge*, p. 60.
170. Andy Edmonds, *Hot Toddy*, p. 21.
171. Ibid., p. 24.
172. Correspondence, R. Schafer to B. Drinnon.
173. Barney Oldfield, interview with author.
174. Maurice Rapf, interview with author.
175. *Los Angeles Evening Herald Express*, December 16, 1935.
176. Leatrice Gilbert Fountain, *Dark Star: The Untold Story of the Meteoric Rise and Fall of the Legendary John Gilbert*, p. 229
177. Barry Paris, *Garbo*, p. 296.
178. Maria Riva, *Marlene Dietrich*, p. 373.
179. Leatrice Gilbert Fountain, *Dark Star: The Untold Story of the Meteoric Rise and Fall of the Legendary John Gilbert*, p. 255.
180. David Stenn, *Bombshell: The Life and Death of Jean Harlow*, p. 203.
181. *Los Angeles Evening Herald*, July 13, 1936.
182. Richard Hack, *Hughes*, p. 102.
183. Cari Beauchamp. *Without Dying Down: Francis Marion and the Powerful Women of Early Hollywood*, p. 221.
184. Roland Flamini, *Thalberg: The Last Tycoon and the World of M-G-M*, p. 270.
185. Ibid., p. 273.
186. Gavin Lambert, *Norma Shearer*, p. 274.
187. David Stenn, *Bombshell: The Life and Death of Jean Harlow*, p. 220.
188. Ibid., p. 235.
189. Ibid., p. 237.
190. Bill Davidson, *Spencer Tracy: Tragic Idol*, p. 2.
191. Sharon Rich, *Sweethearts: The Timeless Love Affair — On Screen and Off — Between Jeanette MacDonald and Nelson Eddy*, p. 142.
192. Patricia Douglas story from *Vanity Fair*, November, 2002, It Happened One Night At MGM, David Stenn.
193. Judy Lewis, *Uncommon Knowledge*, p. 71.
194. Warren G. Harris, *Clark Gable: A Biography*, p. 304.

195. Barney Oldfield, interview with author.
196. Jeff Forrester, and Tom Forrester, *The Three Stooges*, p. 28.
197. *Los Angeles Daily News*, December 23, 1937.
198. County of Los Angeles, Registrar-Recorder, death certificate, Ernest Lee Nash, December 23, 1937.
199. Jeff Forrester, and Tom Forrester, *The Three Stooges*, p. 69.
200. Jane Ellen Wayne, *Gable's Women*, p. 172.
201. Sharon Rich, *Sweethearts: The Timeless Love Affair — On Screen and Off — Between Jeanette MacDonald and Nelson Eddy*, p. 225.
202. Ibid., p. 208.
203. Edward Baron Turk, *Hollywood Diva: A Biography of Jeanette MacDonald*, p. 231.
204. Coward quoted in Axel Madsen, *The Sewing Circle: Hollywood's Greatest Secret, Female Stars Who Loved Other Women*, p. 18.
205. Gary Carey, *All the Stars in Heaven*, p. 245.
206. Emanuel Levy, *George Cukor: Master of Elegance*, p. 117.
207. Charles Higham, *Merchant of Dreams: Louis B. Mayer, M.G.M. and the Secret Hollywood*, p. 294.
208. Lyn Tornabene, *Long Live the King*, p. 252.
209. Axel Madsen, *Stanwyck*, p. 115.
210. Gary Carey, *All the Stars in Heaven*, p. 118.
211. Ibid., p. 181.
212. Warren G. Harris, *Gable and Lombard*, p. 97.
213. Lyn Tornabene, *Long Live the King*, p. 257.
214. *Fort Wayne News Sentinel*, March 30, 1939.
215. Warren G. Harris, *Clark Gable: A Biography*, p. 238.
216. Axel Madsen, *Stanwyck*, p. 169.
217. Donald Spoto, *Laurence Olivier: A Biography*, p. 95.
218. Charles Higham, *Howard Hughes: The Secret Life*, p. 47.
219. Richard Hack, *Hughes: The Private Diaries*, p. 121.

Chapter Five

1. *Los Angeles Daily News*, January 23, 1940.
2. Charles Higham, *Merchant of Dreams: Louis B. Mayer, M.G.M. and the Secret Hollywood*, p. 248.
3. David Shipman, *Judy Garland: The Secret Life of an American Legend*, p 46.

4. Charles Higham, *Merchant of Dreams: Louis B. Mayer, M.G.M. and the Secret Hollywood*, p. 279.

5. Gerald Clark, *Get Happy: The Life of Judy Garland*, p. 168.

6. Axel Madsen, *The Sewing Circle: Hollywood's Greatest Secret, Female Stars Who Loved Other Women* p. 171.

7. Gerald Clark, *Get Happy: The Life of Judy Garland*, p. 164.

8. David Shipman, *Judy Garland: The Secret Life of an American Legend*, p. 105.

9. Gerald Clark, *Get Happy: The Life of Judy Garland*, p. 165.

10. Jane Ellen Wayne, *Gable's Women*, p. 174.

11. Lana Turner, *Lana Turner: The Lady, the Legend, the Truth*, p. 63.

12. David Shipman, *Judy Garland: The Secret Life of an American Legend*, p. 109.

13. Michael Munn, *Hollywood Rogues*, p. 36.

14. Barbara Leaming, *Katharine Hepburn*, p. 273.

15. Ibid., p. 270.

16. Axel Madsen, *Stanwyck*, p. 236.

17. David Shipman, *Judy Garland: The Secret Life of an American Legend*, p. 128.

18. Roland Flamini, *Ava: A Biography*, p. 49.

19. Jane Ellen Wayne, *Ava's Men: The Private Life of Ava Gardner*, p. 36.

20. Ibid., p. 41.

21. Lyn Tornabene, *Long Live the King*, p. 275.

22. Jane Ellen Wayne, *Gable's Women*, p. 173.

23. Warren G. Harris, *Clark Gable: A Biography*, p. 245.

24. Wes D. Gehring, *Carole Lombard: The Hoosier Tornado*, p. 12.

25. Warren G. Harris, *Gable and Lombard*, p. 12.

26. Lyn Tornabene, *Long Live the King*, p. 286.

27. Warren G. Harris, *Clark Gable: A Biography*, p. 250.

28. Warren G. Harris, *Gable and Lombard*, p. 150.

29. Jeffrey Meyers, *Bogart: A Life in Hollywood*, p. 79.

30. Stephen Humphrey Bogart, *Bogart: In Search of My Father*, p. 221.

31. Michael Munn, *Hollywood Rogues*, p. 115.

32. Stephen Humphrey Bogart, *Bogart: In Search of My Father*, p. 92.

33. *Los Angeles Daily News*, January 8, 1943.

34. Hedda Hopper, *The Whole Truth and Nothing But*, p. 86.

35. John Kobler, *Damned in Paradise: The Life of John Barrymore*, p. 364.

36. Axel Madsen, *Stanwyck*, p. 117.

37. Axel Madsen, *The Sewing Circle: Hollywood's Greatest Secret, Female Stars Who Loved Other Women* p. 171.

38. Diana McLellan, *The Girls: Sappho Goes to Hollywood*, p. 280.

39. David Shipman, *Judy Garland: The Secret Life of an American Legend*, p. 139.

40. Warren G. Harris, *Clark Gable: A Biography*, p. 257.

41. Ibid., p. 261.

42. Warren G. Harris, *Gable and Lombard*, p. 161.

43. Warren G. Harris, *Clark Gable: A Biography*, p. 271.

44. Gavin Lambert, *Norma Shearer*, p. 255.

45. County of Los Angeles, Registrar-Recorder, Woodbridge Strong Van Dyke death certificate, February 5, 1943.

46. *Los Angeles Daily News*, February 3, 1943.

47. *Los Angeles Evening Herald Express*, February 3, 1943.

48. *Los Angeles Evening Herald Express*, February 6, 1943.

49. Michael Munn, *Hollywood Rogues*, p. 21.

50. James Spada, *Peter Lawford: The Man Who Kept the Secrets*, p. 93.

51. Floyd Conner, *Lupe Velez and Her Lovers*, p. 229.

52. Charles Bickford, *Bulls, Balls, Bicycles and Actors*, quoted in *The Grove Book of Hollywood*, Sylvester, Christopher, ed., p. 114.

53. Charles Higham, *Merchant of Dreams: Louis B. Mayer, M.G.M. and the Secret Hollywood*, p. 346.

54. David Shipman, *Judy Garland: The Secret Life of an American Legend*, p. 137.

55. Ibid., p. 173.

56. Warren G. Harris, *Clark Gable: A Biography*, p. 275.

57. Lyn Tornabene, *Long Live the King*, p. 321.

58. *Hollywood Citizen News*, March 26, 1945.

59. Lyn Tornabene, *Long Live the King*, p. 318.

60. *Los Angeles Evening Herald Express*, July 17, 1946.

61. Barney Oldfield, interview with author.

62. James Spada, *Peter Lawford: The Man Who Kept the Secrets*, p. 88.

63. Ronald L. Davis, *Van Johnson: MGM's Golden Boy*, p. 151.

64. James Spada, *Peter Lawford: The Man Who Kept the Secrets*, p. 88.

65. Ibid., p. 116.

66. Charles Higham, *Howard Hughes: The Secret Life*, p. 94.
67. Warren G. Harris, *Clark Gable: A Biography*, p. 292.
68. Lee Server, *Robert Mitchum: Baby, I Don't Care*, p. 158.
69. Ibid., p. 168.
70. Kirk Crivello, *Fallen Angels*, p. 90.
71. Alexander Walker, *Fatal Charm*, p. 134.
72. *Hollywood Citizen News*, June 30, 1941.
73. Alexander Walker, *Fatal Charm*, p. 101.
74. Bill Davidson, *Spencer Tracy: Tragic Idol*, p. 105.
75. Ibid., p. 101.
76. Hedda Hopper, *The Truth and Nothing But*, p. 126.
77. David Shipman, *Judy Garland: The Secret Life of an American Legend*, p. 207.
78. Ibid., p. 225.
79. Hedda Hopper, *The Whole Truth and Nothing But*, p. 122.

Chapter Six

1. Jane Ellen Wayne, *Grace Kelly's Men*, p. 109.
2. James Spada, *Grace: The Secret Lives of a Princess*, p. 100.
3. David Shipman, *Judy Garland: The Secret Life of an American Legend*, p. 256.
4. *Los Angeles Mirror*, June 20, 1950.
5. Hedda Hopper, *The Truth and Nothing But*, p. 127.
6. Ibid., p. 128.
7. Jack Larson, interview with author.
8. Sam Kashner, and Nancy Schoenberger, *Hollywood Kryptonite: The Bulldog, the Lady, and the Death of Superman*, p. 19.
9. Jack Larson, interview with author.
10. Ibid.
11. Sam Kashner, and Nancy Schoenberger, *Hollywood Kryptonite: The Bulldog, the Lady, and the Death of Superman*, p. 20.
12. Jack Larson, interview with author.
13. Jim Nolt, letter to author.
14. Jack Larson, interview with author.
15. Elsa Maxwell, *R.S.V.P.*, p. 129.
16. W.A. Swanberg, *Citizen Hearst*, p. 617.
17. *Life* magazine, August 15, 1951.
18. Lana Turner, *Lana Turner: the Lady, the Legend, the Truth*, p. 160.
19. James Spada, *Grace: The Secret Lives of a Princess*, p. 95.
20. Warren G. Harris, *Clark Gable: A Biography*, p. 331.
21. Ibid., p. 335.
22. Barbara Leaming, *Katharine Hepburn*, p. 452.
23. Jane Ellen Wayne, *Grace Kelly's Men*, p. 210.
24. Ibid., p. 213.
25. Bill Davidson, *Spencer Tracy: Tragic Idol*, p. 134.
26. Ibid., p. 497.
27. Ibid., p. 240.
28. Michael Munn, *The Hollywood Murder Casebook*, p. 98.
29. Sam Kashner, and Nancy Schoenberger, *Hollywood Kryptonite: The Bulldog, the Lady, and the Death of Superman*, p. 31.
30. Ibid., p. 29.
31. Jack Larson, interview with author.
32. *Newark Star Ledger*, May 14, 1953.
33. Sam Kashner, and Nancy Schoenberger, *Hollywood Kryptonite: The Bulldog, the Lady, and the Death of Superman*, p. 22.
34. Jack Larson, interview with author.
35. Ibid.
36. Sam Kashner, and Nancy Schoenberger, *Hollywood Kryptonite: The Bulldog, the Lady, and the Death of Superman*, p. 47.
37. Jack Larson, interview with author.
38. Ibid.
39. Jim Nolt, *The Adventure Continues Newsletter*, house description text and graphic by Koza, Lou.
40. Sam Kashner, and Nancy Schoenberger, *Hollywood Kryptonite: The Bulldog, the Lady, and the Death of Superman*, p. 97.
41. Ibid., p. 85.
42. Sam Kashner, and Nancy Schoenberger, *Hollywood Kryptonite: The Bulldog, the Lady, and the Death of Superman*, p. 97.
43. Jack Larson, interview with author.
44. *Los Angeles Examiner*, April 29, 1959.
45. Sam Kashner, and Nancy Schoenberger, *Hollywood Kryptonite: The Bulldog, the Lady, and the Death of Superman*, p. 107.
46. Ibid., p. 111.
47. Ibid., p. 113.
48. *Beverly Hills Citizen News*, June 20, 1959.
49. Jack Larson, interview with author.
50. Sam Kashner, and Nancy Schoenberger, *Hollywood Kryptonite: The Bulldog, the Lady, and the Death of Superman*, p. 111.
51. Ibid., p. 118.
52. *New York Post*, June 23, 1959.
53. Ibid.
54. Sam Kashner, and Nancy Schoenberger, *Hollywood Kryptonite: The Bulldog, the Lady, and the Death of Superman*, p. 154.
55. *New York Post*, June 23, 1959, photos, 114(iii).
56. Jack Larson, interview with author.
57. Ibid.
58. Sam Kashner, and Nancy Schoenberger, *Hollywood Kryptonite: The Bulldog, the Lady, and the Death of Superman*, p. 134.

59. Ibid., p. 137.

60. Ibid., p. 140.

61. Jim Nolt, *The Adventures Continue Newsletter.*

62. Jack Larson, interview with author.

63. Ibid.

64. Ibid.

65. Jim Nolt, letter to author.

66. Sam Kashner, and Nancy Schoenberger, *Hollywood Kryptonite: The Bulldog, the Lady, and the Death of Superman*, p. 181.

67. Jack Larson, interview with author.

68. Ibid.

69. Sam Kashner, and Nancy Schoenberger, *Hollywood Kryptonite: The Bulldog, the Lady, and the Death of Superman*, p. 115.

70. Jack Larson, interview with author.

Postscript

1. Lyn Tornabene, *Long Live the King*, p. 136.

2. Ibid., p. 34.

3. Sam Kashner, *Hollywood Kryptonite: The Bulldog, the Lady, and the Death of Superman*, p. 197.

4. Aljean Harmetz, *The Making of* The Wizard of Oz, p. 304.

5. Axel Madsen, *Stanwyck*, p. 117.

Selected Bibliography

Abrams, Harry N. *Front Page: 100 Years of the Los Angeles Times, 1881–1981*. New York: Abrams, 1991.

Adams, Alex. *Madam 90210*. New York: Villard Books, 1993.

Alpert, Hollis. *The Barrymores*. New York: Dial Press, 1964.

Altmann, Diana. *Hollywood East: Louis B. Mayer and the Origins of the Studio System*. New York: Birch Lane Press, 1992.

Anger, Kenneth. *Hollywood Babylon*. New York: Dell, 1981.

_____. *Hollywood Babylon II*. New York: Dutton, 1984.

Arce, Hector. *Gary Cooper: An Intimate Biography*. New York: William Morrow, 1979.

_____. *The Secret Life of Tyrone Power*. New York: Morrow, 1979.

Austin, John. *Hollywood's Greatest Mysteries*. New York: Shapolsky Publishers, 1993.

_____. *Hollywood's Unsolved Mysteries*. New York: Shapolsky Publishers, 1990.

_____. *More of Hollywood's Unsolved Mysteries*. New York: Shapolsky Publishers, 1991.

Bach, Steven. *Marlene Dietrich — Life and Legend*. New York: William Morrow, 1992.

Balshofer, Fred, and Arthur Miller. *One Reel a Week*. Berkeley: University of California Press, 1967.

Baxter, John. *Hollywood in the 30's*. New York: A.S. Barnes, 1968.

Beaton, Cecil. *Memoirs of the '40s*. New York, 1972.

Beauchamp, Cari. *Without Lying Down: Francis Marion and the Powerful Women of Early Hollywood*. New York: Scribner, 1997.

Behlmer, Rudy, ed. *Memo from David O. Selznick*. New York: Viking Press, 1972.

Bret, David. *Tallulah Bankhead: A Scandalous Life*. London: Robson Books, 1996.

Brooks, Louise. *Lulu in Hollywood*. New York: Alfred A. Knopf, 1982.

Brown, Pamela Ann, and Peter Brown. *The MGM Girls: Behind the Velvet Curtain*. New York: St. Martin's, 1983.

Brownlow, Kevin. *Hollywood: The Pioneers*. New York: Knopf, 1980.

_____. *The Parade's Gone By*. New York: Knopf, 1968.

Capra, Frank. *The Name above the Title: An Autobiography*. New York: Macmillan, 1971.

Chaplin, Lita Grey. *My Life with Chaplin*. New York: Bernard Geis Associates, 1966.

Cini, Zelda, and Bob Crane, with Peter H. Brown. *Hollywood: Land and Legend*. Westport, Conn.: Arlington House, 1980.

Clark, Gerald. *Get Happy: The Life of Judy Garland*. New York: Random House, 2000.

Cochran, Wes. *Pleasants County, WV: Marriages: 1863–1899*. Parkersburg, W.V., self-published.

_____. *Washington County, OH: Marriages: 1789–1918*. Parkersburg, W.V., self-published.

Cooper, Miriam and Bonnie Herndon. *Dark Lady of the Silents: My Life in Early Hollywood*. New York: Bobbs-Merrill, 1973.

Crivello, Kirk. *Fallen Angels: The Lives and Untimely Deaths of 14 Hollywood Beauties*. Secaucus, N.J.: Citadel Press, 1988.

Crane, Cheryl. *Detour: A Hollywood Story*. New York: Arbor House, 1988.

Crowther, Bosley. *The Lion's Share: The Story of an Entertainment Empire*. New York: Dutton, 1957.

D'Agostino, Annette M. comp., *An Index to the Short and Feature Film Reviews in the Moving Picture World: The Early Years, 1907–1915*. Westport, Conn.: Greenwood, 1995.

Davidson, Bill. *Spencer Tracy: Tragic Idol*. New York: E.P. Dutton, 1987.

Davies, Marion. *The Times We Had: Life with William Randolph Hearst*. New York: Bobbs-Merrill, 1975.

De Acosta, Mercedes. *Here Lies the Heart*. New York: Reynal and Company, 1960 .

DiOrio, Al. *Barbara Stanwyck: A Biography*. New York: Coward-McCann, 1983.

Drachman, Roy. *Just Memories: Hollywood Folks,* Part 3. unpublished memoirs.

Eames, John Douglas. *The M-G-M Story*. New York: Crown, 1971.

Edmonds, Andy. *Frame-Up! The Untold Story of Roscoe "Fatty" Arbuckle*. New York: William Morrow, 1991.

Edwards, Anne. *The DeMilles: An American Family*. New York: Harry N. Abrams, Inc., 1988.

Eyman, Scott. *Ernst Lubitsch: Laughter in Paradise*. New York: Simon and Shuster, 1993.

_____. *Mary Pickford: America's Sweetheart*. New York: Donald I. Fine, 1988.

Faderman, Lillian. *Odd Girls and Twilight Lovers*. New York: Columbia University Press, 1991.

Fairbanks, Douglas Jr. *The Salad Days*. New York: Doubleday, 1988.

Farber, Stephen and Marc Green. *Hollywood Dynasties*. New York: Delilah Communications, Inc., 1984.

Feinman, Jeffrey. *Hollywood Confidential*. New York: Playboy Books, 1976.

Finch, Christopher and Linda Rozencrantz. *Gone Hollywood: The Movie Colony in the Golden Age*. New York: Doubleday, 1979 .

Flamini, Roland. *Scarlett, Rhett and a Cast of Thousands*. New York: Crown, 1990.

_____. *Thalberg: The Last Tycoon and the World of MGM*. New York: Crown, 1994.

Fountain, Leatrice Joy Gilbert. *Dark Star: The Untold Story of the Meteoric Rise and Fall of the Legendary John Gilbert*. New York: St. Martin's Press, 1985.

Fowler, Gene. *Father Goose: The Biography of Mack Sennett*. New York: Crown, 1934.

Fowler, Will. *Reporters: Memoirs of a Young Newspaperman*. Malibu: Roundtable Publishing, 1991.

Frank, Gerold. *Judy*. New York: Harper & Row, 1975.

Freedland, Michael. *The Warner Brothers*. New York: St. Martin's Press, 1983.

Friedrichs, Otto. *City of Nets: A Portrait of Hollywood in the 1940's*. Harper & Row, 1980.

Fussell, Betty. *Mabel: Hollywood's First I-Don't-Care Girl*. New Haven: Ticknor & Fields, 1982.

Gabler, Neal. *An Empire of Their Own: How the Jews Invented Hollywood*. New York: Crown Publishers, 1988 .

Garceau, Jean. *The Biography of Clark Gable*. New York: Little, Brown, 1961.

Gehring, Wes D. *Carole Lombard: The Hoosier Tornado*. Indianapolis: Indiana Historical Society Press, 2002 .

Geist, Kenneth L. *Pictures Will Talk: The Life and Films of Joseph Mankiewicz*. New York: Charles Scribner's Sons, 1978.

Giesler, Jerry. *The Jerry Giesler Story*. New York: Simon and Schuster, 1960.

Giroux, Robert. *A Deed of Death: The Story of the Unsolved Murder of Hollywood Director William Desmond Taylor*. New York: Alfred A. Knopf, 1990.

Golden, Eve. *Mary Nolan: Tragic Star*. Films of the Golden Age available at http://www.filmsofthegoldenage.com/foga/1999/winter99/marynolan.shtml.

_____. *Platinum Girl: The Life and Legend of Jean Harlow*. New York: Abbeville Press, 1991.

Goodman, Ezra. *The Fifty Year Decline and Fall of Hollywood*. New York: Simon and Schuster, 1961.

Graham, Shiela. *Confessions of a Hollywood Columnist*. New York: Bantam Books, 1970.

_____. *Hollywood Revisited*. New York: St. Martin's Press, 1984.

Grobel, Lawrence. *The Hustons*. New York: Avon Books, 1989.

Griffith, Richard, and Arthur Mayer. *Movies: The Sixty-Year History of the World of Hollywood*. New York: Bonanza Books, 1957.

Guiles, Fred Lawrence. *Jeanette MacDonald*. New York: McGraw-Hill, 1975.

_____. *Joan Crawford: The Last Word*. New York: Birch Lane Press/Carol Publishing Group, 1995.

_____. *Marion Davies*. New York: McGraw-Hill, 1972.

_____. *Stan: The Life of Stan Laurel*. Briarcliff Manor, N.Y.: Stein and Day, 1980.

_____. *Tyrone Power: The Last Idol*. New York: Berkeley, 1979.

Hack, Richard. *Hughes: The Private Diaries, Memos and Letters: The Definitive Biography of the First American Billionaire*. Beverly Hills: New Millenium Press, 2001.

Hadliegh, Boze. *Hollywood Babble-On: Stars Gossip about Other Stars*. Secaucus, N.J.: Carol, 1994.

_____. *Hollywood Lesbians*. New York: Barricade Books, 1994.

Harmetz, Aljean. *The Making of The Wizard of Oz*. New York: Alfred A. Knopf, 1977.

Harris, Warren G. *Clark Gable: A Biography*. New York: Harmony Books, 2002.

_____. *Gable and Lombard*. New York: Simon and Schuster, 1974.

Haver, Ronald. *David O. Selznick's Hollywood*. New York: Knopf, 1980.

Heimann, Jim. *Out with the Stars: Hollywood Nightlife in the Golden Era*. New York: Abbeville Press, 1985.

Henderson, Robert M. *D.W. Griffith: The Years at Biograph*. New York: Farrar, Straus and Giroux, 1970 .

Higham, Charles. *Bette*. New York: Macmillan, 1981.

_____. *Cary Grant: The Lonely Heart*. New York: Harcourt Brace, 1989.

_____. *Charles Laughton: An Intimate Biography*. Garden City, N.Y.: Doubleday, 1976.

_____. *Errol Flynn: The Untold Story*. New York: Macmillan, 1980.

_____. *Marlene: The Life of Marlene Dietrich*. New York: W.W. Norton, 1977.

_____. *Merchant of Dreams: Louis B. Mayer and the Secret Hollywood*. New York: Donald I. Fine, 1993.

Hoffman, Carol Stein. *The Barrymores*. Louisville: University of Kentucky Press, 2001.

Hopper, Hedda. *From Under the Hat*. Garden City, N.Y.: Doubleday, 1952.

_____, and James Brough. *The Whole Truth and Nothing But*. Garden City, N.Y.: Doubleday, 1962.

Israel, Les. *Miss Tallulah Bankhead*. New York: G.P. Putnam's Sons, 1972.

Kanin, Garson. *Hollywood*. New York: Viking Press, 1967.

Kashner, Sam and Nancy Schoenberger. *Hollywood Kryptonite: The Bulldog, the Lady and the Death of Superman*. New York: St. Martin's, 1996.

Kirkpatrick, Sydney D. *A Cast of Killers*. New York: Dutton, 1986.

Keats, John. *Howard Hughes*. New York: Random House, 1966.

Keylin, Arlene and Suri Fleischer, eds. *Hollywood Album: Lives and Deaths of Holly-wood Stars from the Pages of the* New York Times. New York: Arno Press, 1979.
_____, eds. *Hollywood Album 2: Lives and Deaths of Hollywood Stars from the Pages of the* New York Times. New York: Arno Press, 1979.
Koblar, John. *Damned in Paradise: The Life of John Barrymore.* New York: Atheneum, 1977.
Lambert, Gavin. *Nazimova.* New York: Knopf, 1997.
_____. *Norma Shearer.* New York: Alfred A. Knopf, 1990.
Lamparski, Richard. *Lamparski's Hidden Hollywood: Where the Stars Lived, Loved and Died.* New York: Fireside Books, 1981.
_____. *Whatever Happened To …,* various volumes. New York: Crown, various dates.
Lasky, Jesse L. *I Blow my Own Horn.* Garden City, N.Y.: Doubleday, 1957.
_____. *Whatever Happened to Hollywood?* New York: Funk & Wagnall, 1975.
Leaming, Barbara. *Katharine Hepburn.* New York: Crown Publishers, 1995.
Levin, Martin. *Hollywood and the Great Fan Magazines.* New York: Harrison House, 1970.
Levy, Emanuel. *George Cukor: Master of Elegance, Hollywood's Legendary Director and His Stars.* New York: William Morrow, 1994 .
Lewis, Judy. *Uncommon Knowledge.* New York: Pocket Books, 1994.
Lockwood, Charles. *Dream Palaces: Hollywood at Home.* New York: Viking Press, 1981.
Loos, Anita. *Cast of Thousands.* New York: Viking, 1977.
_____. *Kiss Hollywood Good-bye.* New York: Grosset and Dunlap, 1975.
Louvish, Simon. *Stan & Ollie: The Roots of Comedy; The Double Life of Laurel & Hardy.* New York: Thomas Dunne Books, 1991.
Madsen, Alex. *The Sewing Circle: Hollywood's Greatest Secret, Female Stars Who Loved Other Women.* New York: Birch Lane Press/Carol Publishing Group, 1995.
_____. *Stanwyck.* New York: Harper Collins, 1994.
Mann, William J. *Wisecracker: The Life and Times of William Haines, Hollywood's First Openly Gay Star.* New York: Viking, 1998.
Marx, Arthur. *The Nine Lives of Mickey Rooney.* New York: Stein and Day, 1986.
Marx, Samuel. *Mayer and Thalberg, The Make-Believe Saints.* New York: Random House, 1975.
_____, and Joyce Venderveen. *Deadly Illusions: Jean Harlow and the Murder of Paul Bern.* New York: Random House, 1990.
Morella, Joe. *The "IT" Girl: The Incredible Story of Clara Bow.* New York: Delacorte Press, 1976.
_____ and Edward Z. Epstein. *Gable and Lombard and Powell and Harlow.* New York: Dell, 1975.
_____ and _____. *Loretta Young: An Extraordinary Life.* New York: Delacorte Press, 1986.
Morris, Michael. *Madam Valentino: The Many Lives of Natacha Rambova.* New York: Abbeville Press, 1991.
Munn, Michael. *The Hollywood Murder Casebook.* New York: St. Martin's Press, 1988.
_____. *Hollywood Rogues.* New York: St. Martin's Press, 1991.
Navasky, Victor S. *Naming Names.* Penguin Press, 1991.
Noguchi, Thomas. *Coroner.* New York: Pocket, 1983.
Paris, Barry. *Garbo.* New York: Alfred A. Knopf, 1995.
_____. *Louis Brooks.* New York: Alfred A. Knopf, 1989.
Parish, James Robert, with Ronald L. Bowers. *The MGM Stock Company: The Golden Era.* New Rochelle, N.Y.: Arlington House, 1973.

Parish, James Robert, with Stephen Whitney. *The George Raft File.* New York: Drake Publishers, 1973.
Parrish, Michael. *For the People: Inside the Los Angeles Country District Attorney's Office 1850–2000.* Angel City Press, 2001.
Parrish, Robert. *Growing Up in Hollywood.* New York: Harcourt Brace Jovanovich, 1976.
Parsons, Louella. *The Gay Illiterate.* New York: Doubleday, 1944.
_____. *Tell It to Louella.* New York: Putnam, 1961.
Photoplay Magazine. Stars of the Photoplay. Chicago, 1924.
Quirk, Lawrence J., and William Schoell. *Joan Crawford: The Essential Biography.* Louisville: University Press of Kentucky, 2002.
Ramsaye, Terry, ed. *1936–37 International Motion Picture Almanac.* New York: Quigley, 1936.
_____, ed. *1942–43 International Motion Picture Almanac.* New York: Quigley, 1942.
_____, ed. *1944–45 International Motion Picture Almanac.* New York: Quigley, 1945.
_____, ed. *1947–48 International Motion Picture Almanac.* New York: Quigley, 1947.
_____, ed. *1948–49 International Motion Picture Almanac.* New York: Quigley, 1948.
Ragan, David. *Who's Who in Hollywood: 1900–1976.* New Rochelle, N.Y.: Arlington House Publishers, 1977.
Rapf, Maurice. *Back Lot: Growing Up with the Movies.* Lanham, Md.: Scarecrow Press, 1999.
Riva, Maria. *Marlene Dietrich.* New York: Alfred A. Knopf, 1993.
Robinson, David. *Chaplin: His Life and Art.* New York: McGraw-Hill, 1985.
_____. *Hollywood in the Twenties.* London and New York: Zwemmer and Barnes, 1968.
Ruuth, Marianne. *Cruel City: The Dark Side of Hollywood's Rich and Famous.* Malibu: Roundtable Publishing, 1984.
Schnauber, Cornelius. *Hollywood Haven: Homes and Haunts of the European Emigres and Exiles in Los Angeles.* Ariadne Press, 1997.
Sennett, Robert, S. *Hollywood Hoopla: Creating Stars and Selling Movies in the Golden Age of Hollywood.* New York: Billboard Books, 1988.
Server, Lee. *Robert Mitchum: "Baby, I Don't Care."* New York: St. Martin's Press, 2001.
Shipman, David. *The Great Movie Stars.* New York: Da Capo Books, 1982.
_____. *Judy Garland: The Secret Life of an American Legend.* New York: Hyperion Books, 1992.
Silvester, Christopher, ed. *The Grove Book of Hollywood.* New York: Grove Press, 1998.
Soares, Andres. *Beyond Paradise: The Life of Ramon Novarro.* New York: St. Martin's Press, 2002.
Spada, James. *Grace: The Secret Lives of a Princess.* Garden City, N.Y.: Doubleday, 1987.
Spoto, Donald. *Laurence Olivier: A Biography.* New York: Harper Collins, 1992.
_____. *Notorious: The Life of Ingrid Bergman.* New York: Harper Collins, 1997.
Springer, John, and Jack Hamilton. *They Had Faces Then: Super Stars, Stars, and Starlets of the 1930's.* Secaucus, N.J.: Citadel Press, 1974.
Stenn, David. *Bombshell: The Life and Death of Jean Harlow.* New York: Doubleday, 1993.
_____. *Clara Bow: Runnin' Wild.* New York: Doubleday, 1989.
Swindell, Larry. *Screwball: The Life of Carole Lombard.* New York: William Morrow, 1975.
Talmadge, Margaret. *The Talmadge Sisters: Norma, Constance, Natalie.* Philadelphia: Lippincott, 1924.
Thomas, Bob. *King Cohn: The Life and Times of Harry Cohn.* New York: G.P. Putnam, 1967.

_____. *Selznick*. Garden City, N.Y.: Doubleday, 1970.

_____. *Thalberg: Life and Legend*. New York: Bantam, 1970.

Thomas, Tony. *Errol Flynn: The Spy Who Never Was*. New York: Citadel, 1990.

Thomson, David. *Showman: The Life of David O. Selznick*. New York: Knopf, 1992.

Tornabene, Lyn. *Long Live the King: A Biography of Clark Gable*. New York: G.P. Putnam's Sons, 1976.

Torrence, Bruce T. *Hollywood: The First 100 Years*. New York: Zoetrope, 1982.

Turner, Lana. *Lana Turner: The Lady, the Legend, the Truth*. New York: E.P. Dutton, 1982.

Turk, Edward Baron. *Hollywood Diva: A Biography of Jeanette MacDonald*. Berkeley: University of California Press, 1998.

Tygiel, Jules. *The Great Los Angeles Swindle*. New York: Oxford University Press, 1994.

Walker, Alexander. *Shattered Silents: How the Talkies Came to Stay*. New York: Morrow, 1979.

Warner, Jack. *My First Hundred Years in Hollywood*. New York: Random House, 1965.

Wayne, Jane Ellen. *Ava's Men: The Private Life of Ava Gardner*. New York: St. Martin's, 1990 .

_____. *Clark Gable: Portrait of a Misfit*. New York: St. Martin's Press, 1993.

_____. *Crawford's Men*. New York: Prentice-Hall, 1988.

_____. *Gable's Women*. New York: Prentice-Hall, 1987.

_____. *Grace Kelly's Men*. New York: St. Martin's Press, 1991.

_____. *Robert Taylor: The Man with the Perfect Face*. New York: St. Martin's Press, 1989.

Webb, Michael, ed. *Hollywood: Legend and Reality*. Boston: Little, Brown, 1986.

Zierold, Norman. *The Moguls*. New York: Coward-McCann, 1969.

Zollo, Paul. *Hollywood Remembered: An Oral History of Its Golden Age*. New York: Cooper Square Press, 2002.

Reference Materials

Chicago Herald-American, archival records.

Chicago News, archival records.

City of Los Angeles, Directory, various years 1925–1940.

Los Angeles Times, archival records.

Los Angeles Evening Herald, archival records.

Los Angeles Evening Herald Express, archival records.

Los Angeles Herald, archival records.

Los Angeles Record, archival records.

Movieland Magazine, archival records.

Photoplay Magazine, archival records.

United States Federal Census, Los Angeles County, 1910.

United States Federal Census, Los Angeles County, 1920.

United States Federal Census, Los Angeles County, 1930.

Other Materials

Meyers, Laura. "Holey Matrimony." *Los Angeles Magazine*, February, 2000.

Stenn, David. "It Happened One Night ... at MGM." *Vanity Fair*, April, 2003.

Index

Abbott, Eve 216
Acker, Jean 56
Adair, Ada 30
Adair, Ida 70, 71
The Addams Family (television series) 135
Adoree, Renee 22
Adrian, Gilbert 22, 206
The African Queen (1951) 242
Ainsworth, Phillip 67
Albert, Kathleen 130
Alexandria Hotel 11, 55
Algonquin Hotel 113, 122
Alias Jimmy Valentine (1928) 80, 90
All Quiet on the Western Front (1930) 207
Allen, Elizabeth 147, 150, 209
Allen, Kirk 235
Alsop, Carelton 233
Ameche, Don 247
American Feature Film Corporation 17
American Mutoscope and Vitascope Company 7
Anderson, Bob 159
Anderson, G.M. 8
Andy Hardy (1940) 29
Anna Christie (1930) 108
Annabella 205; sexuality of 206
Annie Get Your Gun (1949) 227
Another Time, Another Place (1958) 245
Anthony and Cleopatra (1908) 41
Apfel, Oscar 11, 12
Apger, Virgil 116, 118
Arbuckle, Roscoe 46, 54, 58, 62, 63, 64; and Rappe scandal 58, 59, 60
Armstrong, Robert Z. 22
Arnaz, Desi 234
Arnst, Bobbe 93
Arzner, Dorothy 108
As You Desire Me (1932) 109
Asher, Betty 50, 193, 194, 198, 206, 207, 214, 245; affairs of 194, 195; as informant for Edgar J. Mannix 207; lesbian

affairs of 205; sexuality of 213; spies on clients for studio 193, 213; suicide of 207
Asher, Ephraim "E.M." 193
Astaire, Fred 233, 278
Asther, Niles 141; child of 142; divorce from Vivian Duncan 142; homosexuality of 41; released by MGM 142; studio-arranged marriage of 141
Astor, Mary 68, 195
Atwill, Lionel, sex parties of 195
Ayres, Lew: biography of 207; World War II service of 207

Babes in Arms (1939) 188
Bacall, Lauren 204
Bacon, James 219
The Bad and the Beautiful (1952) 278
Bad Day at Black Rock (1955) 242, 243
Baer, Max 142
Bakewell, William 114
Ball, Lucille 234
Bankhead, Tallulah 65, 83, 93, 108, 110; lesbian affairs of 109; sexuality of 106, 130
Banksia Place Sanitarium 63, 67
Banky, Vilma 79
Bara, Theda 42
Barbier, Larry 65
Barker, Lex 244
Barondess, Barbara 123, 125
The Barretts of Wimpole Street (1933) 129
Barrymore, Ethel 17
Barrymore, John 105; death of 204, 205
Barrymore, Lionel 17, 28, 37, 80, 97, 189, 195
Barthelmess, Richard 47, 58, 67, 68
Batman (television series) 244
Baum, Vicki 37, 102
Bautzer, Gregson 194; affairs of 222
Baxter, Ann 222
Bayne, Beverly 64, 65, 74

BBB's Cellar 108, 187
Beaton, Cecil 109, 127
Beery, Wallace 1, 101, 141, 160, 161, 170, 171, 172, 189; alcoholism of 101, 175; involvement in murder of Ted Healy 175; marriage to Gloria Swanson 174; personality of 174; rapes wife Gloria Swanson on wedding night 101; sent out of country after Healy murder 177
Bel Air Hotel 242
Belasco, David 14
Bell, Alphonso 13
Bello, Marino 111, 115, 121, 126
Ben-Hur (1926) 56, 66
Ben-Hur (1959) 278
Benchley, Robert 37
Bendix, William 234
Benjamin, Maurice 276
Bennett, Billie 95
Bennett, Constance 184; fight with Lilyan Tashman 126
Bergman, Ingrid 196; affairs of 196, 204
Berkeley, Busby 39, 206, 227; affairs of 220; alcoholism of 161; automobile accident of 161; suicide attempt of 216
Berlin, Irving 277
Bern, Henry 121, 122
Bern, Paul 3, 33, 35, 67, 68, 111, 112, 114, 125, 142, 166, 259; alleged sadomasochism of 120; allegedly beats Jean Harlow 119; biography 112; common-law marriage to Dorothy Millette 117; death of 4, 116; death of mother 113; friendship with Irving Thalberg 111; funeral of 122; marriage to Jean Harlow 115; murder cover-up 117; note written by 118; problems with women 113; relationship with Dorothy Millette 113; reported suicide attempts 114; rumors of impotency 120, 121; suggested homosexuality of 120; works for Irving Thalberg 113
Bessolo, Helen 251, 252, 259, 260, 261, 263, 269, 275
Beverly Hills Hotel 91, 238; construction of 10; early development of 9; growth of 10
Beverly Wilshire Hotel 98, 167
Bey, Turhan 218
Bickford, Charles 213
The Big House (1930) 175
The Big Parade (1925) 66, 71, 79
A Bill of Divorcement (1932) 196
Bioff, Willie 158
Biograph Studio 10, 41
Birdwell, Russell 182

The Birth of a Nation (1915) 17, 18, 28, 55, 58
Bison Studios 10
The Blackbird (1925) 66
Blane, Sally 152, 173
Blattner, Oscar 40
Blind Husbands (1919) 19
Bliss, William "Bill" 257, 258, 259, 265, 266, 271, 272
block booking 229
Blondeau Tavern 11
Blondell, Gloria 177
The Blue Gardenia (1953) 249
Boardman, Eleanor 22, 68, 73
Bogart, Humphrey 149, 203; accused of being Communist 189; affairs of 204
The Bohemian Girl (1935) 160
Boren, Charles 276
Borgnine, Ernest 243
Bosworth, Hobart 25
Bow, Clara 54, 56, 79, 92, 96, 169
Box Office Attractions Studio 42
Boy Meets Girl (1938) 221
Boyer, Charles, affairs of 196
Boys Town (1938) 242
Brabin, Charles 209
Brand, Harry 218
Brecht, Berthold 102
Brice, Fanny 143
Bringing Up Baby (1938) 149, 196
Broadway Melody (1928) 80
Broadway Melody of 1938 (1938) 221
Broccoli, Albert 175, 177
Brooks, Louise 127
Brown, Betty 177
Brown, Chamberlain 97
Brown, Clarence 22, 72, 165
Brown, Gilmore 183
Brown Derby 182
Brown of Harvard (1926) 69, 90
Browne, George 158
Browning, Tod 37
Bruce, Nigel 103
Bruce, Virginia 183
Bugles in the Afternoon (1952) 249
Bull, Clarence 38, 203
Burke, Marcella 125
Burkhardt, Hans 102
Burns, L.L. 11
Burroughs, Edgar Rice 91, 247
Busch, Mae 22
Bushman, Francis X. 17, 41, 64, 65, 74, 111
Butler, Betty 217

C.C. Julian Petroleum scandal 75, 84
Cabot, Bruce 210

Cagney, James 115, 234; accused of being Communist 189
Calhoun, Rory 259
The Call of the Wild (1935) 146, 147, 151
Calling All Husbands (1940) 234
Camille (1937) 183
Cantor, Eddie 88
Capone, Alphonse 158
Capra, Frank 31, 114, 127
Captain from Castile (1947) 218
The Captain Hates the Sea (1934) 162
Captains Courageous (1937) 167, 179
Carmen, Jewel 154, 157, 159
Carmichael, John 3, 116, 118, 121, 122
Carmichael, Winifred 3, 116, 118, 121, 122
Cass Timberline (1946) 226
Cassini, Oleg, affairs of 243
Centaur Film Company 11
The Champ (1931) 101, 175
Chandlee, Esme 225
Chandler, Raymond 160
Chaney, Lon 22, 66, 80, 84, 87, 147
Chaplin, Charlie 3, 9, 46, 47, 48, 54, 55, 60, 64, 108, 149, 184, 229, 269
Chateau Elysee Hotel 48
Cherrill, Virginia 149; divorce from Cary Grant 149; marriage to Cary Grant 149
Chester, George Randolph 20
Chickens Come Home (1930) 154
China Seas (1933) 125, 150, 151, 169
Christian, Linda 218
Ciro's Restaurant 173
Citizen Kane (1941) 178
City Lights (1931) 149
Clark, Dave 89
The Clock (1944) 214
Coates, Phyllis 235, 248, 252, 260, 273
Cochran, Margaret 26
Cody, Lou 69
Cohen, Mickey 88, 143, 245, 246, 247, 269, 270
Cohn, Harry 5, 6, 28, 31, 114, 176; and "casting couch" 51; funeral of 51
Cohn, J.J. 115
Cohn, Joseph 39, 40
Colbert, Claudette 95
Colby, Anita 216
Cole, Ben 240
Cole, Jack 194
Collier, Constance 243
Collins, Victor 172
Colman, Ronald 103
Colonial Theater 17
Colton, Jack 95, 106
Columbia Pictures Corporation 17, 23, 28, 114, 162, 176

Condon, Robert "Bobby" 257, 258, 267, 270, 271, 272
Connelly, Walter 162
Converse, Lawrence 67
Conway, Jack 76, 95, 165
Conway, Virginia 165
Coogan, Jackie 22
Cooper, Gary 92, 93, 95, 117, 125, 133, 168; bisexuality of 92
Cooper, Jackie 31, 101, 194
Corbaloy, Kate 33
Cortez, Ricardo 66
Cosmopolitan Pictures 22, 36, 46
Coward, Noel 181
Cowl, Jane 97
Crandall, Sophia 26
Crane, Cheryl 204, 245; molestation by Lex Barker 244
Crane, Fred 266
Crane, John 204
Crane, Steve 244
Crawford, Charles, murder of 89
Crawford, Joan 29, 65, 68, 70, 79, 80, 90, 95, 98, 109, 119, 130, 132, 141, 169, 182, 189, 195, 207; abortions of 133; affairs of 96, 99, 130, 133, 222; drunken driving accident of 83; feud with Clark Gable 133; leaves MGM 83; lesbian affairs of 66, 131; marriage to Douglas Fairbanks, Jr. 82; marriage to Franchot Tone 133; porn film of 82, 83; pregnancy of 100; sexual appetite of 65; sexual reputation 82, 83, 190; sexuality of 99, 104, 106, 131
Crews, Laura Hope 79
Crocker, Harry 108, 109
Crosby, Bing 218, 234; affairs of 241, 242
The Crusades (1935) 148, 151
Cukor, George 110, 129, 181, 242; fired from *Gone with the Wind* by MGM 182
Culver, Harry M. 34
Culver, Roland 223
Culver City, history of 34
Curley, Mary 146
Curley, William 146
Curphey, Thomas 262, 275

Daly, Blythe: lesbian affairs of 109; sexuality of 130
Dana, Viola 22
Dance, Fools, Dance (1930) 98, 99
Dancing Lady (1933) 132
Dandridge, Dorothy 170
Dane, Karl 79; death of 80, 145
The Dangerous Little Demon (1920) 33
Daniels, Bill 37
Dante's Inferno (1935) 150

Danziger, Daisy 56; mysterious death of 56
Darnell, Linda 51
Daugherty, Jack 67
Davenport, Dorothy 63
David Copperfield (1933) 129
Davies, Marion 22, 36, 46, 47, 48, 73, 79, 85, 101, 127, 145, 148, 168, 239; affairs of 101; alleged children of 146; death of 240; pregnancy of 145
Davis, Betty 187
Davis, Clifton 3, 116, 118, 119, 121, 122, 124
Davis, Roger 90
de Acosta, Mercedes 106, 109, 110; lesbian affairs of 105, 106, 107, 109; sexuality of 104
Deeley, Ben 67
DeHavilland, Olivia 182, 190
Delmont, Bambina Maude 59
Del Rio, Dolores 139
DeMille, Cecil B. 1, 5, 11, 12, 13, 14, 39, 63, 111, 151, 160
Desert Nights (1928) 84
Desire Me (1946) 219
Devil in the Deep (1933) 93
The Devil's Pass Key (1920) 19
de Vorak, Geraldine 145
Diane (1956) 244
DiCicco, Pasquale 154, 156, 158, 164, 175, 177, 178
Dickson, William K.L. 6, 7
Dies, Martin 189
Dietrich, Marlene 57, 89, 95, 110, 163, 164, 195; appears in lesbian reviews in Europe 108; early childhood of 107; and John Gilbert's death 162; lesbian affairs of 104, 107, 108, 109; relationship with John Gilbert 163; sexuality of 104
Dietz, Howard 25, 32, 43, 49, 69, 72, 110
Dillon, Josephine 96, 97, 99, 100
Dinner at Eight (1933) 142, 175
Dockweiler, John 190
Dr. Jeckyl and Mr. Hyde (1941) 195, 196, 242
Dr. X (1932) 195
Don Juan (1927) 77, 78
Dorfler, Franz 96
D'Orsay, Fifi 105
Double Whoopee (1929) 112
Douglas, Kirk 99
Douglas, Melvyn 189; accused of being Communist 189
Douglas, Patricia 170, 171
Dove, Billie 187
Drachman, Roy 144

Dragna, Jack 88
Dressler, Marie 108, 141; relationship with Greta Garbo 108; sexuality of 108
Duke, Doris 146
Duncan, Isadora 106; lesbian affairs of 106
Duncan, Vivian 141, 142; divorce from Niles Asther 142
Durbin, Deanna 191
Durfee, Minta 59
Dwan, Allen 24
Dyreda Art Film Company 17

Easter Parade (1948) 227, 278
Eddington, Nora 210; relationship with Errol Flynn 211
Eddy, Nelson 31, 134, 197, 209; beats Gene Raymond 180; marriage to Ann Franklin 181; personality of 135; relationship with Jeanette MacDonald 136; sexuality of 134, 167, 168; strange relationship with his mother 134, 135
Edison, Thomas Alva 6, 7, 8, 41, 77
Edmunds, Larry, death of 195
Edwards, Frances 38
Elam, Jack 219
Elsworth, Whit 259
Engstead, John 187
Esmond, Jill 186
Essanay Studio 8, 41, 46, 64
European salon crowd in Los Angeles 57, 102, 103, 104
Excellent Pictures 138
Excess Baggage (1928) 80
Exeter Theater, Boston 13
Eyton, Charles 60, 62

Fairbanks, Douglas 3, 30, 54, 55, 58
Fairbanks, Douglas, Jr. 83, 99, 100, 109, 130, 132
Famous Players Company 15
Famous Players–Lasky Studios 20, 41, 60; drug dealers serving 57
Famous Players Studio 15
Farnham, Joseph 38
Farnum, Dustin 11, 12
Farnum, William 41
Fast Workers (1933) 82, 162
Father of the Bride (1950) 242
Fay, Frank: divorce from Barbara Stanwyck 183; marriage to Barbara Stanwyck 130, 131
Faye, Alice 95
Faye, Hughie 57
Ferguson, Bill 130
Feuchtwanger, Lion 103
Fields, W.C. 129, 160, 195

The Fighting 69th (1940) 234
Film industry, influence of Communist scare on 189
Fine, Larry 175
Fire Over England (1936) 186
First National Pictures 19
Fischer, Robert E. 159
Fitts, Buron 83, 84, 89, 121, 122, 123, 137, 156, 158, 160, 161, 171, 172, 189, 190; suicide of 190
Fitzgerald, F. Scott 37, 76, 102
Fitzgerald, Zelda 203
The Flame Within (1935) 129
Flamini, Roland 21
Fleishman, Harry 208
Fleming, Victor 22, 76, 182, 196
Flesh (1932) 129
Flesh and the Devil (1926) 72
Flint, Motley 75
Flying Down to Rio (1934) 139
Flynn, Errol 48, 95, 103, 204, 269; death of 211; fondness for teenaged girls 210, 211; rapes Nora Eddington 211; residence of 205; statutory rape trials of 210; voyeurism of 205
Fontaine, Joan 225
A Fool There Was (1915) 42
Foolish Wives (1922) 19
Ford, John, military service of 209
Ford, Martha 159
Ford, Wallace 159
Forest Lawn Cemetery 167
Forever Female (1953) 249
Fort George Amusement Park 16
Foster, Norman 152
Fountain, Leatrice 70
The Four Horsemen of the Apocalypse (1920) 43, 56, 65
Four Jills in a Jeep (1944) 222
Fowler, Gene 205
Fowler, William 40
Fox, William 6, 18, 42, 78, 81, 82
Fox Studios 81, 95, 103, 112; drug dealers serving 57
Francis, Kay 108
Francis, Lee 94, 127; arrest of 96
Franklin, Ann Denmitz, marriage to Nelson Eddy 181
Franklin, Sydney 22
Frederick, Pauline 97
Freed, Arthur 214
Friedman, Harry 214, 215
From Here to Eternity (1953) 249
Frost, David 99

Gable, Clark 1, 4, 48, 52, 91, 95, 96, 101, 114, 119, 122, 126, 130, 131, 141, 146, 147, 151, 166, 168, 169, 180, 184, 189, 191, 195, 199, 200, 202, 208, 214, 232, 247, 279; affairs of 98, 99, 100, 101, 115, 130, 133, 147, 148, 153, 166, 209, 215, 241, 242; alleged automobile accident 136; almost dies from mouth infection 132; asks MGM to fire George Cukor 182; automobile accidents of 137, 214, 215; child of 150, 151; daughter of 172, 173; death of 216; and death of Carole Lombard 203; divorce from Ria Langham 153; exiled to Columbia as punishment for something 140; feud with George Cukor 182; feud with Joan Crawford 133; hatred of homosexuals 151; homosexual affairs of 110; hypochondria of 132; informed of birth of his child 153; leaves MGM 242; liaison with William Haines 141, 182; loaned out to Columbia Pictures Corporation 136; marriage to Carole Lombard 133, 185; marriage to Ria Langham 100; meets child with Loretta Young 164; military service of 207, 208; obsessive behavior of 132; payoff to Josephine Dillon 100; removal of teeth of 132; reported sexual liaison with William Haines 98; as Rhett Butler 181; rumored love child with Adela Rogers St. Johns 98; signs with MGM 98; uses women to advance career 96, 97; as womanizer 96
Gable, Will 131, 132
Gandolfi, Alfred 11
Garbo, Greta 1, 37, 56, 57, 66, 73, 74, 80, 85, 89, 91, 95, 98, 106, 108, 110, 126, 141, 145, 162, 167, 188, 189, 207, 278, 279; discovery by Louis B. Mayer and arrives in America 72; on European sexuality 103; first speaking role of 108; hides in Harry Crocker's mansion 109; lesbian affairs of 104; moves into John Gilbert's mansion 73; relationship with John Gilbert 72, 73, 81, 104; relationship with Lilyan Tashman 105; relationship with Marie Dressler 108; sexuality of 104
Garden of Allah Hotel and Apartments 79
Gardner, Ava 187, 198, 241; abortions of 241; divorce from Mickey Rooney 199
Gardner, Reginald 189
Garland, Judy 1, 31, 45, 50, 180, 189, 194, 197, 207, 217, 278; abortions of 198, 207, 212, 218; affairs of 190, 206, 213, 214; biography of 191; death of 234; divorce from David Rose 205, 212; drug addictions of 192, 213, 216, 226, 227, 228, 233; emotional problems of 192, 206,

212, 227, 233; family of 191; fired by
MGM 233; lesbian affairs of 205; mar-
riage to David Rose 198; marriage to
Vincent Minnelli 214; medical problems
of 228; pregnancy of 216; relationship
with Artie Shaw 193; sexuality of 213;
suicide attempts of 227, 233, 240
Garrison, Harold "Slickem" 35, 36, 116,
121, 122, 123, 125
Garson, Greer 211; relationship with
Louis B. Mayer 135
Gaynor, Janet 91; arranged marriage to
Gilbert Adrian 206; sexuality of 206
Gem Theater 17
Genthe, Arnold 72
Gibbons, Cedric 22, 39, 163
Gibran, Kahlil 105
Giesler, Jerry 84, 161, 216, 219, 220, 246,
259, 264, 269, 273
Gilbert, John 1, 22, 30, 66, 68, 70, 71, 75,
76, 80, 81, 82, 84, 92, 95, 113, 115, 119,
122, 167, 225; death of 82, 162, 163;
emotional problems of 74; funeral of
163, 164
Gilbert, Walter 71
Girl Crazy (1943) 206, 213
Gish, Dorothy 41
Gish, Lillian 41, 54
Gleason, Jackie 234
Glorifying the American Girl (1929) 91
Glyn, Eleanor 47, 56, 70
Goddard, Paulette 184, 195, 214, 222
Godsol, F.J. 21
Goetz, William 160
Golden Boy (1939) 184
Goldwyn, Samuel 5, 6, 11, 14, 15, 31, 34,
35, 79, 88
Goldwyn Studios 15, 21, 43, 161
Gone with the Wind (1939) 39, 180, 181,
186, 188, 201, 234, 266
A Good Catch (1912) 64
Goulding, Edmund 127, 161; fired by
Louis B. Mayer 165; return to U.S.
arranged by studio 128, 129; sent to En-
gland 126, 128; sex addiction of 127; sex
parties of 127; women injured at his
S&M party 127
Grable, Betty 51
Grand Hotel (1932) 127, 175
Granger, Stewart 238
Grant, Cary 93, 103; homosexual affairs
of 108, 163; homosexuality of 89; mar-
riage to Virginia Cherrill 149; sexuality
of 110, 149; suicide attempt 149
Grauman, Sid 88
Grauman's Chinese Theater 112, 209
Gray, Hubert 183

The Great Dictator (1940) 229
The Great Secret movie (serial) 64
The Great Train Robbery (1903) 7, 8
The Great Ziegfeld (1936) 143, 169
Green, Burton 9, 10
Greenburg, Ralph, murder of 190
Greenson, Ralph 276
Greenstreet, Gail 144; marriage to
Howard Strickling 144
Greenwood, Martin 121
Grey, Virginia 215
Grieve, Harold 73
Griffith, D.W. 5, 6, 10, 17, 28, 34, 41, 54,
56, 58, 68, 209
Gris, Henry 266
Gwenn, Edmund 22
Gwinn, Edith 89, 223, 224

Haines, William 22, 68, 69, 70, 76, 80, 85,
86, 90, 98, 101, 108, 110, 132; arrests of
90, 91, 216; death of 141; dropped by
MGM 140; homosexual affairs of 110;
homosexuality of 90, 140
Hall, James 112
Hamilton, John 236, 266; death of 253
Hanley, James 40
Hanson, Betty 210
Harding, Laura 196
Hardy, Oliver 49, 112, 154, 170
Harlow, Jean 4, 29, 37, 47, 52, 110, 111, 116,
117, 120, 121, 122, 123, 142, 147, 150, 166,
169, 187, 209, 244; abortions of 112, 120,
163; affairs of 112, 115, 120, 142; alleged
beatings by Paul Bern 119; alleged fight
with Paul Bern 124; death of 167, 172;
discovered by studio 112; final illness
and death of 166; given nickname "Platinum Blonde" 114; hires prostitutes
from the House of Francis 94, 95; ices
nipples 115; learns of Paul Bern's murder 119; marriage to Charles McGrew
111; marriage to Paul Bern 115; refusal
to assist conspiracy against Paul Bern
120; relationship with co-workers 115;
returns to work after Paul Bern's murder 126; signs with MGM 114; studio-
directed marriage to Harold Rosson
142; youth 111
Harlow, Mama Jean 111, 112, 115, 116, 121,
166, 167
Harris, Mildred 55
Harris, Nick 260
Harrison, Ethel 60
Harrison, Irene 117, 122
Harrison, Rex, affairs of 223
Harron, Charles 58
Harron, Robert 58

Hart, Moss 37
Hart, William S. 71
Having Wonderful Crime (1944) 221
Hawks, Howard 76, 203
Hay, Mary 68
Hays, William H. 63, 110
Hays Office 63, 228
Hayward, Leland, affairs of 196
Hayworth, Rita 213
He Who Gets Slapped (1924) 65, 71
Healy, Ted: alcoholism of 175; death of
    176; fight and death of 175; fight with
    DiCicco, Broccoli, and Beery 176; fu-
    neral of 177
Hearst, Bill 240
Hearst, David 240
Hearst, Millicent 146, 240
Hearst, Richard 240
Hearst, William Randolph 22, 36, 46, 47,
    48, 73, 88, 108, 109, 123, 127, 139, 140,
    145, 148, 168, 178; death of 239, 240;
    moves Marion Davies' dressing
    room–house 36, 148; rumored children
    of 146
Hell's Angels (1930) 112, 163
Hemingway, Ernest 183
Hendry, Whitey 38, 39, 88, 89, 116, 150,
    161, 165, 167, 215, 226
Henley, Hobart 22
Hepburn, Katharine 95, 187, 219, 241,
    242, 244; affairs of 196, 197, 224; cares
    for Spencer Tracy 225; family of 196;
    first marriage of 196; lesbian relation-
    ships of 196
Her Rise and Fall (1930) 98
Herald Square Theater 14
Hermann, Eva, sexual relationship with
    Aldous and Maria Huxley 103
Hesse, Paul S. 187
Hexum, Jon-Eric 263
Hickman, Betty 176
High Sierra (1941) 140
Higham, Charles 125
Hill, George 22
His Brother's Wife (1935) 183
His Glorious Night (1929) 80, 81
Hitchcock, Alfred 184; affairs of 241
Hoffman, H.W. 176
Hohmann, Arthur 190
Hold Your Man (1932) 142
Holden, William 234; affairs of 241, 242
Holleran, Walter 153
Hollywood: early attitude toward movie
    people 12, 13; growth of 8, 18
Hollywood Forever Cemetery 146
Hollywood Party (1930) 129, 176
The Hollywood Reporter 46

The Hollywood Review of 1929 (1929) 80
Hollywood Victory Committee 200
Holman, Libby: lesbian affairs of 109;
    sexuality of 106
Honky Tonk (1941) 200
Hoover, Herbert 31, 32, 81, 82
Hoover, J. Edgar 83
Hope, Bob 218
Hopper, Hedda 22, 31, 49, 92, 146, 178,
    198, 199, 226, 243
Hopper, William DeWolfe 178
Hoppy Serves a Writ (1942) 219
Horse Feathers (1932) 154, 155
House of Francis brothel 50, 94
*How the Porto Rico Girls Entertain Uncle
    Sam's Soldiers* (1894) 7
Howard, Jerome (real name Horwitz,
    Jerome) 175, 176, 178
Howard, Leslie 186
Howard, Moe (real name Horwitz,
    Moses) 175
Howard, Shemp (real name Horwitz,
    Samuel) 175, 176
Howell, Dorothy 34
Howland, Jobyna, sexuality of 110
Hudson, Sharlay 217
Hughes, Howard 32, 112, 114, 163; affairs
    of 196, 218, 241; automobile accidents of
    164; hires private detectives to follow
    his girlfriends 187; homosexual affairs
    of 108, 187, 218; sexuality of 164, 186
Humphrey, Hal 249
The Hunchback of Notre Dame (1939) 130,
    188
Hurrell, George 38
Huston, John 138, 140; possible involve-
    ment in Clark Gable automobile accident
    138, 139
Huston, Walter 139
Huxley, Aldous 37, 102, 103
Huxley, Maria 103
Hyde, Johnny 194
Hyman, Bernie 33, 40, 123, 125, 165

I Love Lucy (television series) 234
In the Good Old Summertime (1949) 227
Ince, Thomas 5, 34, 35, 71; mysterious
    death of 46, 47, 48
Independent Moving Picture Company
    (IMP) 14, 41
Ingersoll, Rick 183
Ingram, Rex 22, 43
Intolerance (1915) 35, 58, 209
The Island of Lost Souls (1932) 130
It Happened One Night (1933) 140, 150
It's a Wonderful Life (1939) 28
Ivano, Paul 56

Jannings, Emil 91
The Jazz Singer (1927) 77, 78, 79
Jesse L. Lasky Feature Play Company 14, 15
Jezebel (1938) 140
Jimmy's Backyard 86
Johnny Belinda (1948) 207
Johnny Eager (1942) 197
Johnson, Van: homosexual relationships of 216; sexuality of 211, 217
Jolson, Al 78, 247
Jones, Edward B. 120, 132, 166, 192
Jones, Jennifer 214
Joy, Leatrice 120
Joyce, Peggy Hopkins 76
The Joyless Street (1925) 104, 108
Judith of Bethulia (1914) 56

Kahn, Gus 78
Kalem Productions 8
Karloff, Boris 103, 196
Katz, Otto 107
Kaufman, George S. 37
Kaye, Danny, relationship with Laurence Olivier 186
Keaton, Buster 22, 30, 40, 65, 76, 79, 80, 239
Keaton, Frank 75
Keeler, Ruby 247
Keenan, Frank 216
Kelly, Gene 226, 227, 228
Kelly, Grace 232; affairs of 241, 242, 243; amorality of 241
Kelly, Patsy 160
Kennedy, John F. 276
Kennedy, Madge 55
Kennedy, Robert 276
Kennedy, Willard "Bill" 236
Kenyatta, Jomo 241
Kerkorian, Kirk 278
Keyes, Asa 62, 64, 75, 83, 84
Keystone Studio 10
Khan, Aly, affairs of 241
kinetascope 6
King Kong (1933) 39
King of Kings (1925) 39
The Kiss (1930) 207
Klemperer, Otto 102
Kley, Fred 11
Knudsen, Vern 80
Knute Rockne All-American (1940) 234
Kono, Toriachi 47
Kosloff, Theodore 47
Koster & Bial's Music Parlor 7
Koverman, Ida 31, 32, 37, 45, 81, 97, 99, 183, 185, 227, 232; discovers Judy Garland 191; discovers Nelson Eddy 135

La Belle, Gene 256
La Boheme (1925) 66, 71, 79
Lachmann, Harry 150
Lackey, Ken 175
Ladd, Alan 241, 259
Laemmle, Carl 6, 8, 13, 14, 19, 20, 41, 87
Laemmle, Rosabelle 20
Lake, Arthur 146
Lake, Patricia 146
Lake, Veronica 234
LaMarr, Barbara 66, 67, 68, 69, 90, 113, 119, 120, 151; death of 67
Lamarr, Hedy 67, 135, 183, 189
Lamour, Dorothy 222
Lanchester, Elsa: discovers Charles Laughton's homosexuality 130; marriage to Charles Laughton 129, 130
Landau, Arthur 115
Landis, Carole: affairs of 221, 222; biography of 220, 221; marriages of 222; and Rex Harrison 223; suicide of 223; World War II, volunteering in 221, 222
Lang, Fritz 102
Langham, Ria 97, 98, 99, 101, 132, 136, 148, 150, 152, 153, 184; divorce from Clark Gable 153
Lanier, Toni 127, 143, 236, 237, 249, 254, 255, 259, 260, 261, 262, 263, 264, 268, 269, 270, 271, 272, 273, 279; affairs of 238, 238; burial site of 278; death of 278; last years of 277; moves in with Eddie Mannix 145
Lanza, Mario 31
La Roque, Rod 79
Larson, Jack 85, 143, 234, 236, 237, 239, 247, 248, 250, 251, 253, 260, 262, 266, 267, 268, 271, 273; biography of 235
Lasky, Jesse 5, 11, 12, 14, 58, 59, 179
The Last Laugh (1924) 91
Lastfogel, Abe 276
Laugh, Clown, Laugh (1926) 141, 147
Laughton, Charles 93, 129, 151; homosexuality of 129; marriage to Elsa Lanchester 129, 130
Laurel, Stan 49, 112, 154, 170
Laurents, Arthur 217
Lawford, Peter 44; sexuality of 211, 216, 217
Lawler, Anderson 92
Lawler, Andy 182
Lawrence, Eddie 107
Lawrence, Florence 41
Lee, Brandon 263
Leeds, Lila, drug arrest of 219
Le Gallienne, Eva 105, 109

Leigh, Vivien 182, 186; mental problems
of 186; as Scarlett O'Hara 181
Lemmon, Leonore 252, 253, 255, 256,
257, 258, 260, 261, 262, 263, 265, 269,
270, 271, 272, 275; as prostitute 275
Leo the Lion 25
Leonard, Robert 22
LeRoy, Mervyn 97, 162, 179
Letty Lynton (1932) 100
Levee, Art 132
Lewin, Al 33, 113
Lewis, Tom 173
Life with Riley (television series) 234
Lillie, Bea 65
Lindbergh, Charles 78, 85
Lindquist, Edward 171
Little Caeser (1930) 179
Loeb, Edwin 20
Loew, Arthur 244
Loew, Marcus 5, 15, 16, 19, 20, 21, 24, 32,
77, 81; death of 76
Loews, Inc. 16
Lombard, Carole 1, 48, 52, 95, 141, 184,
199, 200, 214, 216; death of 201, 202,
208; funeral of 203; jeolousy of 200,
201; marriage to Clark Gable 133, 185;
miscarriages of 200
London After Midnight (1928) 80
Loos, Anita 37, 43, 54, 127
Louis B. Mayer Pictures 18, 19, 20, 21
Love (1927) 73
Love, Bessie 76
Love Finds Andy Hardy (1938) 191
Love Me Tonight (1932) 135
Love on the Run (1936) 209
The Love Parade (1930) 135
Lowe, Edmund 86, 193; studio-arranged
marriage to Lilyan Tashman 104
Loy, Myrna 98, 142, 143
Lubitsch, Ernst 102
Luciano, Charles "Lucky" 114, 154, 156,
157, 158, 159, 160, 213
Lupino, Ida 153, 156
Lyon, Gene, affairs of 241

Maazal, M. 138, 139
MacDonald, Anna 135
MacDonald, Blossom 135
MacDonald, Jeanette 29, 134, 197, 209;
abortions of 168, 180; alleged frigidity
of 135; beaten by Gene Raymond 180;
call-girl rumor of 134; marriage to
Gene Raymond 168; pregnancies of 180;
promiscuity of 167; relationship with
Nelson Eddy 136; sleeps with Louis B.
Mayer 134, 135; suicide attempt of 181;
uses sex to advance her career 135

MacLean, Douglas 60
The Madness of Youth (1922) 71
Mae's Brothel 95, 96, 170
Magnificent Obsession (1935) 183
Main, Marjorie 65; sexuality of 106, 130
Malloy, Dick 204
Malloy Brothers Mortuary 204
The Maltese Falcon (1941) 140
Maltin, Leonard 190
Manhattan Melodrama (1935) 209
Mankiewicz, Herman 30
Mankiewicz, Joseph 190, 213
Mann, Thomas 102
Manners, Dorothy 152
Mannix, Bernice 24, 40, 41, 88, 126, 144,
255; death of 178; files for divorce from
Edgar J. Mannix 173; leaves Eddie Man-
nix 145; mysterious death of 174
Mannix, Edgar J. 31, 34, 40, 43, 49, 67,
73, 75, 79, 80, 82, 85, 86, 88, 89, 90, 95,
97, 98, 101, 105, 106, 110, 112, 116, 117,
121, 122, 136, 143, 148, 154, 165, 167, 170,
193, 194, 195, 196, 198, 202, 206, 208,
209, 210, 212, 217, 226, 228, 232, 233;
affairs of 23, 25, 50, 75, 84, 88, 126, 127,
144, 173, 207; alleged marriage to Toni
Lanier 237; arranges for other studio to
fire Mary Nolan 84; and "casting couch"
51 consolidates power after removal of
Irving Thalberg 129; covers up Ted
Healy murder 176; death of 276; early
jobs of 16; feud with Mary Nolan 84,
85; fight with Frank Fay 182; fires William Haines 141; first marriage of 24;
friendship with Charles "Lucky" Luciano 160; friendship with Johnny
Roselli 160; friendship with Pasquale
DiCicco 160; friendship with Thelma
Todd 154; funeral of 276; has employees
followed 175; health problems of 246,
247, 273, 276; hides rape at studio gathering 169; hides Van Dyke suicide from
press 210; hires Victor Fleming for *Gone
with the Wind* 182; included in rape
lawsuit against MGM 172; meets Toni
Lanier 127; office of 35; opinion of Irving Thalberg 19; organized crime
friendships of 88, 160, 270; pallbearer
for Ted Healy 177; personality of 27, 85;
promoted to General Manager 128; protects Lana Turner 245; purchases Joan
Crawford porn film 161; reports to Irving Thalberg 24; residences of 24, 40,
239, 247, 276; rumored involvement in
death of young actress 89; search for
Joan Crawford porn film 82, 83; servants of 40, 41; spies for Schenck 24;

temper of 144; treks to Carole Lombard
death site 202; works with Schenck in
New Jersey 23
Mannix, Elizabeth, death of 178
Mannix, John, death of 178
Mannix, Ruth 40, 210
March, Fredric, accused of being Com-
munist 189
Marie Antionette (1938) 166
Marion, Francis 13, 22
Marlowe, Alona 126
Marsh, Mae 54
Marsh, Oliver 37
Marston, Maybelle 168
Martin, Mary, lesbian affairs of 206
Marty (1955) 243
Marx, Chico 165, 247
Marx, Groucho 96, 154
Marx, Harpo 155
Marx, Sam 28, 29, 32, 98, 119, 273
Marx, Zeppo 155, 179
Marx Brothers 88
The Marx Brothers at the Circus (1939) 188
Masden, Leo 163
Mathis, June 56
Maxwell, Marilyn 215
Mayer, Irene 104
Mayer, Louis B. 1, 2, 5, 6, 12, 16, 17, 18, 19,
20, 21, 22, 23, 24, 28, 30, 32, 33, 36, 39,
43, 44, 46, 49, 55, 63, 64, 66, 68, 72, 76,
78, 79, 82, 84, 86, 87, 88, 95, 100, 104,
105, 110, 111, 114, 116, 117, 118, 119, 121,
122, 125, 135, 137, 148; affairs of 29, 77,
114, 134, 135, 168; arranges marriage of
Nelson Eddy 134; and "casting couch"
51; chicken soup promise 38; contract
battle with Clark Gable 136; contract
battle with Joan Crawford 136; crying
for sympathy 30; daily schedule of 40;
demands Nelson Eddy marry 181; dislike of Charles Laughton 129; dislike of
other's weaknesses 29; effectively de-
motes Irving Thalberg 129; feelings
about homosexuality 69, 70; feelings
toward homosexuals 142; feud with
Buster Keaton 40; feud with Edmund
Goulding 127, 129; feud with Francis X.
Bushman 74; feud with Irving Thalberg
128, 165; feud with John Gilbert 30, 70,
72, 73, 74, 80, 81, 82, 162, 163; feud with
Lon Chaney 87, 88; feud with Niles Asther 141; feud with Tallulah Bankhead
83, 110; feud with William Haines 68,
70, 86, 90, 141; gets into fights 55; hires
Mervyn LeRoy 179; intervenes in Jeanette MacDonald–Gene Raymond marriage 168; involvement in Clark Gable

accident 139; leaves MGM 240; loses
power at MGM 230; management style
of 25, 28, 32, 230; maternal feelings of
30; office of 31, 32; orders Barbara Stanwyck and Robert Taylor to wed 185; orders Clark Gable to divorce Ria Langham
and wed Carole Lombard 184; orders
Eve Wynn to divorce Keenan Wynn and
marry Van Johnson 217; orders Jeanette
MacDonald abortion 168; orders Joan
Crawford and Douglas Fairbanks, Jr. on
honeymoon 100; prevents John Gilbert
from getting other work 162; prohibits
Lew Ayres from working at MGM 207;
reduces Irving Thalberg's power 128; re-
lationship with Greer Garson 135; rela-
tionship with Jeanette MacDonald 135;
simplistic views on film-making of 29;
talks Douglas Fairbanks, Jr. out of ex-
posing Joan Crawford affair with Clark
Gable 132; uses own attorney to quash
rape case against MGM 172
Mayer, Margaret 17
McArthur, Charles 129
McAvoy, Freddie 210
McGrew, Charles 111
McHugh, Frank 162
McIntyre, Andrew 208
Me and My Gal (1942) 205
Meadows, Audrey 267
Meet Me in St. Louis (1944) 213
Meredith, Burgess 244
Merry-Go-Round (1923) 20
The Merry Widow (1925) 71, 98
The Merry Widow (1952) 241
Methot, Mayo: assaults Humphrey Bog-
art 203, 204; death of 204
Metro Company 19
Metro Pictures Corporation 17
Metro Studios 16, 20, 21, 27
Mexican Spitfire Sees a Ghost (1942) 211
Mexican Spitfire's Blessed Event (1943) 211
Mexican Spitfire's Elephant (1942) 211
Meyer, Gabe 164
MGM Annual Sales Convention, 1937 169
MGM Studio 1; birth of 20; casting office
of 35; daily production schedules 51, 52;
doctors hide rape at studio gathering
171; early production 65; feud between
New York and Los Angeles offices 24;
founding of 21; growth of studio 88;
hiring voice coaches for actors 79; move
to sound movies 78, 80; opening of 22;
physical plant 35, 36, 37, 38, 39; police
department of 38, 88; sale of 278, 279;
studio commissary of 38
Milland, Ray, affairs of 241

Miller, William 138
Millette, Dorothy 113, 117, 118, 121, 122, 123, 124, 125; murders Paul Bern 125; suicide of 122
Min and Bill (1930) 175
Mineo, Sal 217
Minnelli, Liza 216, 227
Minnelli, Vincent 207, 226, 227, 233; biography of 213; marriage to Judy Garland 214; sexuality of 214, 216
Minter, Mary Miles 17, 60, 61, 62, 63
Mr. Smith Goes to Washington (1939) 188
Mitchell, Margaret 181
Mitchell, William 82
Mitchum, Robert 234; biography of 219; drug arrest of 219
Mogambo (1952) 241
Monesco, Al 208
Monkee Business (1931) 154
Monohan, Henry 240
Monroe, Marilyn 131, 218, 232, 235, 275; affairs of 276; death of 276
Monte Carlo (1930) 135
Monte Cristo (1922) 71
Montemarte Café 94
Montgomery, Robert 100; military service of 200
Moore, Archie 257, 267
Moore, Colleen 112, 119, 120, 147
Moore, Grace 29
Moore, Owen 58
Moorehead, Agnes, sexuality of 104
Moran, Polly 69
Moreno, Antonio 55, 56, 62
Morgan, Frank 166
Morgan, Ira 85
Morocco (1930) 108
Movie industry, mob infiltration of 158; payments to District Attorney's offices 160
Mrs. Miniver (1942) 211
Muir, Florabelle 190
Muni, Paul 247
Murder in the Big House (1942) 216
Murnau, F.W. 91; death of 91
Murphy, George 189
Murray, Eunice 276
Murray, Mae 22
Mussolini, Benito 31
Mutiny on the Bounty (1935) 130, 151, 153, 169
Mystery of the Wax Museum (1933) 195

Nagel, Conrad 22, 32
Naldi, Nita 63
Nance, Frank 139, 164, 177
Naughty but Nice (1927) 147

Naughty Marietta (1934) 136, 167
The Navigator (1924) 65
Nazimova, Alla 56, 57, 79, 105
Negri, Pola 56
Neilan, Marshall 22, 28, 29
Neill, Noel 236, 250, 266
Never Let Me Go (1953) 242
The New Adventures of Superman (television series) 234, 235, 236, 247
New York Moving Pictures Company 10
Newcomb, Vivian 34
Niblo, Fred 22
nickelodeon theaters 8, 16
Ninotchka (1939) 188, 278
Nissen, Greta 138
Nitti, Frank 158
Niven, David 103; affairs of 166
Nolan, Mary (real name Mary Imogene Robertson) 75; death of 226; lawsuit versus Eddie Mannix 84
Nolt, Jim 237, 268
Norberg Pictures 10
Normand, Mabel 41, 42, 57, 60, 69
Nosferatu (1922) 91
Novarro, Ramon 22, 55, 56, 69; death of 142; homosexuality of 90, 142; released by MGM 142

Oakie, Jack 148, 160
O'Brien, Dolly 216
O'Brien, Pat 149, 162, 221
Oldfield, Barney 44, 68, 137, 182
Olivier, Laurence: relationship with Danny Kaye 186; sexuality of 186
One the Night Stage (1915) 71
O'Neill, Eugene 234
Oppenheimer, George 34
Orpheum Theater 17
Orry-Kelly, Jack 149
Orsatti, Ernie 30
Orsatti, Frank 88, 160
Orsatti, Victor 160
O'Sullivan, Maureen 92
Ott, Fred 7
Our Dancing Daughters (1928) 80
Owen, Seena 47

Palace Theater, Los Angeles 13
Palisades Park 5, 24
Palmer, Lilli 223
Pankey, Fred 190
Paradise Park 16, 23
Paramount Pictures Company 15
Paramount Studios 62, 81, 87, 108, 137, 140, 145, 167, 229, 230; drug dealers serving 57
Parker, Dorothy 37, 196

Parsons, Louella 46, 48, 49, 86, 148, 153, 168, 172, 178, 212
Pasadena Playhouse 234
Pat and Mike (1952) 242
Pathé Studios 8, 41
The Perils of Pauline serial 41
Persson, W.F. 159
Peters, Bessie 200, 201
Peterson, Les 193, 198, 199
Peterson, Victor 262, 264
Peyton Place (1957) 245
The Philadelphia Story (1940) 196
Pickfair 100
Pickford, Jack 57, 58
Pickford, Mary 3, 10, 28, 30, 41, 46, 54, 55, 57, 58, 61
Pidgeon, Walter 166, 189
Pierce Brothers Mortuary 204
The Pirate (1947) 226
Pitts, ZaSu 151
The Plastic Age (1925) 96
Platinum Blonde (1931) 114, 147
Polly of the Circus (1932) 101
Popular Plays and Players Company 17
Porter, Edwin S. 7, 8
The Postman Always Rings Twice (1946) 218
Powell, Dick 168
Powell, Eleanor 29
Powell, Frank 42
Powell, William 22, 79, 143, 163, 167, 209
Power, Tyrone 103, 166, 205, 207, 212; affairs of 206, 218; military service of 206; sexuality of 183, 206
Power, Tyrone, Sr. 205
Preminger, Otto 102
Prevost, Marie 33
Price, Kate 69
Pringle, Aileen 22, 47
The Prisoner of Zenda (1922) 56, 66
Pruig, Joseph 40
The Public Enemy (1931) 97
Publicity stunts, first 41, 42
Purviance, Edna 60

Quality Pictures Company 17
Quarberg, Lincoln 114
Queen Christina (1933) 145, 162

Rachel and the Stranger (1948) 219
Rachmaninoff, Sergey 102
Raft, George, affairs of 166
Rain (1931) 100
Rainer, Luise 135, 143
Rambova, Natacha 56
Ramond, Harold 212

Rapf, Harry 19, 21, 25, 32, 33, 34, 35, 40, 44, 65, 82, 85, 88, 177
Rapf, Maurice 34, 44, 50, 51, 82, 126
Raphael, Stephen 210
Rappe, Virginia 58, 59, 60
Rathbone, Basil 103, 195
Ray, Man 102
Raye, Martha 194
Raymond, Gene: marriage to Jeanette MacDonald 168; sexuality of 167, 168, 180
Reagan, Ronald 234
Red Dust (1932) 119, 126, 142
Redemption (1913) 23
Red-Headed Woman (1932) 114
Reed, Donna 31
Reeves, George 235, 263; and affair with Leonore Lemmon 252, 253, 271; and affair with Toni Mannix 236, 237, 238, 239, 247, 250, 251, 268, 269, 270; affairs of 234; automobile accidents of 255, 256; autopsies of 260, 262, 264, 265, 275; Benedict Canyon residence of 238, 239, 247, 248, 254, 269; biography of 234; death of 257, 258, 260, 271, 272, 275; finances of 267, 268; funeral of 263, 275; health issues of 256; last will of 261, 275; personality of 250; type-casting of 251, 252, 266, 267; volun-teerism of 250, 261, 267
Reid, Wallace 41, 57, 63; death of 63
Reinhardt, Gottfried 29
Reiver, Harry 11
The Revenge of Tarzan (1920) 91
Reynolds, Debbie 235, 278
Rice, Florence 22
Riffraff (1936) 244
Rinaldi, Mary 63
Ripon College 149
Riptide (1934) 129
Ritchie, Bob 135
RKO Studios 32, 87, 106, 167, 183, 219, 230
Roach, Hal 12
Roach, Harold 157, 160, 169, 170, 171, 222
Roberti, Lyda, death of 160
Robinson, Edward G. 19, 97, 179
Rogers, Charles "Buddy" 160
Rogers, Earl 88
Rogers, Ginger 95, 187
Rogers, Will 22, 35
Roland, Gilbert 67, 184
Rolfe's Picture Company 17
Romance (1930) 105
Romeo and Juliet (1906) 41
Romeo and Juliet (1937) 169
Romero, Cesar, homosexual affairs of 218

Rooney, Mickey 31, 96, 189, 190, 193, 194, 206; affairs of 166, 198; divorce from Ava Gardner 199
Roosevelt, Eleanor 107
Roosevelt, Franklin D. 203
Rose, David 194, 197; divorce from Judy Garland 205, 212; marriage to Judy Garland 198
Rose Marie (1936) 167
Roselli, Johnny 158
Ross, David 170, 172; accused of rape 171
Rosson, Hal 37, 142
Roulien, Raul 138
Roulien, Tosca 138, 139
The Round-Up (1919) 56
Rowland, Richard 17, 20
Royal Wedding (1952) 233
Rubens, Alma 47
Rubin, J. Robert 21, 22
Ruskin, Harry 166
Russell, Rosalind 189
Rutherford, Ann 28, 194

The Saga of Gosta Berling (1923) 72
St. Johns, Adela Rogers 59, 66, 88, 92, 95, 98, 99, 120, 212, 213
St. Johns, Ivan 88
Sally, Irene and Mary (1925) 68
Sanborn, Pansy 175
Saratoga (1937) 133, 166, 209
Satterly, Peggy Lee 210
The Saturday Night Kid (1929) 112
Schafer, Rudy 157
Schary, Dore 230, 232, 240, 242, 243, 244
Schenck, Joseph 15, 16, 21, 39, 40, 67, 68, 76, 79, 82, 86, 88, 160; tries to buy MGM 81
Schenck, Nicholas 15, 16, 21, 22, 23, 24, 46, 49, 76, 81, 114, 127, 128, 129, 207, 230, 240, 244
Schindler, Rudolph 102
Schoenberg, Arnold 102
Schumm, Gloria 177
Schuster, Joe 235
Schwab's Drug Store 179
Scott, Randolph 186; relationship with Cary Grant 89, 149; sexuality of 149
Seastrom, Victor 22, 34
The Secret Six (1931) 114
Sedgewick, Edward 85
Seiter, William 112
Selig, William 10, 18
Selig Film Company 8, 10
Selwyn, Edgar 15
Selznick, Danny 28
Selznick, David O. 1, 39, 115, 116, 119, 128, 181, 196, 214

Selznick, Irene Mayer 112, 115, 214
Sennett, Mack 5, 6, 10, 29, 34, 59
Sergeant York (1941) 140
Shaw, Artie 193, 244; divorce from Lana Turner 194
Shayne, Betty 259
Shayne, Robert 236, 259, 266
Shearer, Douglas 78, 92, 101, 276
Shearer, Marion, suicide of 101
Shearer, Norma 22, 29, 37, 65, 69, 71, 76, 77, 98, 119, 129, 148, 165, 189, 276; affairs of 165, 166
Sheehan, Winfield 150
Shelby, Charlotte 60; as suspect in William Desmond Taylor murder 61, 62
Shepard, Christy 187
Sherlock, Jr. (1924) 65
Sherman, Lowell 86
Shields, Jimmy 70, 90, 141
Shubert, Lee 21
Shulberg, B.P. 62, 137, 140
Shulberg, Budd 62, 83, 89
Shuler, Deborah 26
Shulman, Irving 119
Sieber, Maria 107, 108
Sieber, Rudolph 107
Siegel, Benjamin 190, 269
Siegel, Jerry 235
Silberberg, Mendel 172
Simms, Ginny 29
Simonson, Thol 248, 249
The Single Standard (1928) 141
Skelton, Red 51
Skolsky, Sydney 123
A Slave of Fashion (1925) 69
Slide, Kelly, Slide (1927) 69
Slipsager, Nip 254
Smashing the Money Ring (1939) 234
Smith, C. Aubrey 102
Smith, Charles 157, 159
Smith, Jim 62, 65
Smith, Pete 25, 27, 31, 32, 43, 88, 130
Solvason, Sigrid 145
Somewhere I'll Find You (1942) 200, 216, 218
Son of Frankenstein (1939) 195
The Son of the Sheik (1926) 79
The Song of Bernadette (1943) 214
sound pictures, development of 77, 78
Soup to Nuts (1930) 175
Spencer, Herbert, murder of 89
Spreckels, Kay 216
Spring Fever (1927) 69
The Squaw Man (1914) 11, 12, 18
Stamp Day for Superman (1956) 249
Stand Up and Fight (1938) 184
Stanwyck, Barbara 65, 83, 95, 195, 241,

247; arranged marriage of 197; beaten by Frank Fay 131; divorce from Frank Fay 183; lesbian affairs of 131, 182; marriage to Frank Fay 130, 131, 182; marriage to Robert Taylor 185; relationship with Robert Taylor 184; sexuality of 104, 106, 110, 130, 182, 186; suicide attempts of 197

A Star Is Born (1937) 131, 221

A Star Is Born (1954) 234

State of the Union (1948) 242

Stein, Gertrude 107

Stella Dallas (1937) 184

Stenn, David 169

Sternberg, Josef von 108

Stevenson, Garcia 91

Stewart, James 276; affairs of 166; military service of 200

Stiller, Mauritz 72, 74

Stock Market Crash of 1929 82, 87

Stompanato, Johnny 245; death of 246

Stone, Lewis 29, 174

Strand Theater, New York City 13

Strange Interlude (1930) 98

Stravinsky, Igor 102

Strickling, Gail 246, 276; death of 277

Strickling, Howard 25, 31, 38, 65, 67, 69, 75, 81, 82, 83, 86, 88, 89, 93, 101, 105, 106, 108, 110, 112, 116, 118, 119, 120, 121, 122, 123, 148, 149, 161, 167, 172, 192, 195, 200, 204, 208, 209, 218, 232, 233, 234, 244, 246, 253, 259, 261, 268; ancestry 26; arranges abortion for Jeanette MacDonald 168; arranges abortion for Joan Crawford 100, 133; arranges abortion for Judy Garland 198, 207; arranges abortions 163, 194; arranges annulment and re-marriage for Lana Turner 204; arranges dates for Robert Taylor 183; arranges divorce for Keenan Wynn and re-marriage of Eve Wynn to Van Johnson 217; arranges final Loretta Young adoption 171; arranges for Loretta Young to adopt own child 151, 164; arranges funeral for Karl Dane 145; arranges marriage for Barbara Stanwyck and Robert Taylor 185; arranges marriage for Judy Garland and Mickey Rooney 198, 199; arranges marriage for Nelson Eddy 181; assists William Randolph Hearst 145, 146; burial site of 277; and "casting couch" 51; changes Clark Gable's image 98; covers up automobile accident 136; covers up Clark Gable automobile accident 215; covers up Marlene Dietrich's involvement in John Gilbert's death 162; covers up

murder of Ted Healy 176, 177; covers up stormy relationship between Johnny Weissmuller and Lupe Velez 133, 134, 136; dealing with actors 52; dealing with William Haines 90; death of 277; and death of Carole Lombard 202; designs cover-up of Paul Bern murder 117, 125; designs massive *Gone with the Wind* publicity campaign 181, 182; designs publicity campaigns for Lana Turner 179; develops final version of Paul Bern's death offered to press 121; early jobs of 27; early responsibilities of 43; early schooling of 26; fictional account of Irving Thalberg's death 165; fires Spencer Tracy 243; forces Clark Gable to marry Ria Langham 99, 100; and Gail Greenstreet 144; gathers information from subordinates 50; has Clark Gable removed from company of Marino Bello 126; hides birth records 153; hides Charles Laughton's private life 130; hides details of Lupe Velez suicide from the press 212; hides Greta Garbo's lesbian affairs 107; hides Judy Garland suicide attempts 227; hides rape at studio gathering 169; hides Woodridge Strong Van Dyke suicide from press 210; makes Loretta Young adoption arrangements 173; marriage to Gail Greenstreet 144, 179; meets new MGM hires 44; negotiates divorce for Clark Gable from Ria Langham 184; personality of 27, 44; plans Niles Asther studio-arranged marriage and honeymoon 141; protects Barbara Stanwyck 197; protects Jeanette MacDonald 167; protects Joan Crawford 130; protects Judy Garland 191; protects Lana Turner 241; protects Loretta Young 152; protects Marlene Dietrich 163; protects Mickey Rooney's step-father 190; protects Nelson Eddy 167; protects Niles Asther 141; protects Ramon Novarro 142; protects Spencer Tracy 150, 225, 226, 243; as publicist 45; recovers nude photos of Lupe Velez 94; relationship with Eddie Mannix 45; relationship with Louis B. Mayer 43, 44, 45; residences of 26, 27, 76, 88, 246, 276, 277; suggests marriage to Nelson Eddy 168; suggests that Judy Garland have a child 214; tries to change image of Robert Taylor 183; uses gossip writers 49; uses Louella Parsons and Hedda Hopper 178; uses movie magazines 46; uses payoffs 83, 94, 123, 127, 137, 151; Strickling, John 26

Strickling, John B. 26
Strickling, John Howard (Howard) 26
Strickling, John Wesley 26
Strickling, Joseph 26
Strickling, Joseph Wesley 26
Strickling, Margaret Edythe 26
Strickling, Roy Eugene 26
Stromberg, Hunt 33, 160
studio tours, birth of 13
Summer Stock (1950) 228, 233
Sunrise (1927) 91
Superman (television series) 39
Superman and the Jungle Devil (1956) 249
Superman and the Mole Men (1951) 235, 236, 248
Superman Flies Again (1956) 249
Susan Lenox (1930) 98
Sutherland, Eddie 57
Swanson, Gloria 10, 56, 63, 79; marriage to Wallace Beery 101, 174; raped by Beery on honeymoon 174
Sweedie Goes to College (1915) 174
Sweet, Blanche 22, 54, 65
Sweethearts (1939) 180

T&M Studio 96
Tabu (1931) 91
Talmadge, Constance 40, 76, 77, 79, 86
Talmadge, Natalie 40, 76, 79
Talmadge, Norma 15, 40, 54, 67, 68, 76, 79
Talmadge, Peg 40, 79
Tarzan of the Apes (1917) 91
Tarzan the Ape Man (1932) 91, 92, 209
Tarzan the Mighty (1928) 91
Tashman, Lilyan 86, 94, 193; death of 126; fight with Alona Marlowe 126; fight with Constance Bennett 126; lesbian affairs of 109; sex parties hosted with Edmund Lowe 105; sexuality of 104; studio-arranged marriage to Edmund Lowe 104
Taylor, Denis 60
Taylor, Don 226
Taylor, Elizabeth 31
Taylor, Robert 31, 189, 197, 276; affairs of 197; marriage to Barbara Stanwyck 185; personality of 183; relationship with Barbara Stanwyck 184; sexuality of 183, 186, 197
Taylor, William Desmond 60, 61, 62, 63, 64; family of 60; murder of 60
Ted Healy's Stooges 175
television, impact on movie studios 229, 230, 234
Tell It to the Marines (1926) 69

The Temptress (1926) 56, 72
Terry, Alice 22
Tess of the d'Urbervilles (1924) 65
Thalberg, Henrietta 20, 77; protective of Irving Thalberg 20
Thalberg, Irving 13, 14, 19, 20, 21, 22, 24, 32, 34, 35, 36, 38, 39, 46, 49, 52, 69, 70, 72, 75, 78, 79, 80, 87, 88, 90, 91, 95, 96, 97, 98, 100, 103, 106, 108, 109, 110, 111, 112, 113, 114, 115, 116, 117, 118, 119, 120, 122, 123; battles with von Stroheim 19, 20; convinces Louis B. Mayer to pass on *Gone with the Wind* 181; feud with Louis B. Mayer 128; final illness and death of 165; first heart attack of 66; hires Spencer Tracy 150; inner circle of 33; makes people wait for appointments 34; management style of 25, 28, 32; marriage to Norma Shearer 76, 77; meets Louella Parsons 48; and Norma Shearer 29; office of 34, 35; opinion of writers 37; personal bungalow of 36; removed from power by Louis B. Mayer 129; second heart attack of 128; self-promotion of 20; working anonymously 33; writes with psuedonym 33
Thau, Benjamin 35, 128
Thaw, Evelyn Nesbitt 23
They Won't Forget (1937) 179
The Thin Man (1934) 22, 209
Thirty Seconds Over Tokyo (1944) 216
Thomas, Olive 57, 58, 63
Thomson, Fred 13
Three Musketeers (1921) 66
Thy Name Is Woman (1923) 66
Tierney, Gene 222
To Catch a Thief (1954) 243
Toch, Ernst 102
Todd, Thelma 154, 161, 164, 176; affairs of 154; beatings by Pasquale DiCicco 154; divorce from Pasquale DiCicco 154, 158; marriage to Pasquale DiCicco 154; murder of 153, 156, 159; police handling of murder of 155
Toklas, Alice B. 107
Tone, Franchot 83, 133, 136; accused of being Communist 189
Top Hat Café 179
Topping, Bob 240, 244
The Torrent (1925) 66, 72
Tracy, Carroll 167
Tracy, John 226
Tracy, Louise 179, 190, 224, 241, 244; charitable work of 197
Tracy, Spencer 95, 99, 147, 179, 191, 192, 196, 232; affairs of 190, 196, 197, 224, 241, 243; alcoholism of 95, 149, 167, 197,

225, 242, 243; arrest at House of Francis brothel 149; death of 243, 244; destroys hotel room 150; destroys studio set 150; fired by Fox 149; fired from MGM 243; first arrest of 95; hidden in sanitarium 167; illnesses of 149; marriage to Louise 190; medical problems of 242; signs with MGM 149, 150; and the "Tracy Squad" 150; tries to kill his brother 167
Trader Horn (1928) 75, 91
Trader Vic's 163
Treasure Island (1934) 175
Triangle Studios 34
Tribute to a Bad Man (1955) 243
Trocadero Restaurant 150, 154, 175, 176
Turner, Lana 22, 48, 50, 193, 196, 278; abortions of 194, 204, 218; affairs of 193, 197, 200, 204, 211, 218; beaten by Johnny Stompanato 245; divorce from Artie Shaw 194; I.R.S. problems of 240; image as "Sweater Girl" 179; infected with syphilis 218; joins MGM 179; leaves MGM 244; marriage to Artie Shaw 194; marriage to Bob Topping 240; marriage to John Crane 204; marriages of 244; sexuality of 194; suicide attempt of 240
Twentieth Century Fox Studios 51, 87, 146, 149, 218, 220, 222, 230, 234, 235

Unaccustomed as We Are (1929) 154
Undercurrent (1946) 219, 225
The Unholy Three (1925) 66
United Artists Studio 87, 131
Universal City, development of 13
Universal Picture Company 14
Universal Studios 13, 20, 36, 87

Vacio, Alejandro 266
Vacio, Natividad ("Nati") 250, 256, 266
Valentino, Rudolph 43, 47, 55, 63, 65, 71; death of 56; homosexual relationships of 56; homosexuality of 55; marries lesbians 56
Valley of the Giants (1920) 63
Vanderbilt, Gloria 187
Van Dyke, Woodridge Strong ("Woody") 22, 91, 180, 211; suicide of 210; biography of 209
Vargas, Alberto 57
Velez, Lupe 92, 117, 125, 133, 134, 211, 213; affairs of 212; divorce from Johnny Weissmuller 173; feud with Lilyan Tashman 94; fights with Johnny Weissmuller 133; marriage to Johnny Weissmuller 133, 173; pregnancy of 212; relationship with Gary Cooper 92; relationship with John Gilbert 92; rela-

tionship with Johnny Weissmuller 92, 93, 94; suicide of 212
Victorine Studios 43
Vidor, King 22, 37, 66, 73
Viertel, Peter 103
Viertel, Salka 57, 85, 103, 106, 107, 109
Vignola, Robert 47
Vincent Benet, Stephen 37
Virtuous Wives (1927) 178
Vitagraph Studios 13, 41, 60
vitascope 7
Voice of the Millions (1912) 56
Voight, Hubert 72
Von Ronkle, Carol 257, 258, 260, 265, 270, 271, 272
von Stroheim, Erich 19, 20, 22, 24, 102
Vorkapich, Slapko 117, 122, 124

Wagner, A.F. 155
Waldof, Claire 107
Walker, Robert, emotional problems of 211, 214
Wallis, Bert 155
Walsh, Raoul 185, 204, 205
Walter, Bruno 102
Walters, Charles 227
Warner, Al 6
Warner, Harry 6, 77
Warner, Jack 6, 77, 131, 160, 199, 234
Warner, Sam 6, 77, 78
Warner Brothers Studios 36, 77, 131, 148, 161, 179, 199, 203, 221, 230, 234
Way Down East (1920) 58
Wayne, John 197, 247
We Who Are Young (1940) 194
Webb, Clifton 186
Webb, Watson 205
Weekend at the Waldorf (1945) 216
Weissman, Art 254, 256, 259, 260, 262, 266, 267, 271
Weissmuller, Johnny 91, 93, 133, 134, 153, 209, 211, 213; divorce from Lupe Velez 173; fights with Lupe Velez 133; marriage to Lupe Velez 133, 173
Welles, Orson 178; affairs of 213
Wellman, William 147, 148, 150
Wertheimer, Al 174
West, Mae 95, 97
West, Roland 154, 155, 157, 159
West of Zanzibar (1928) 84
West Point (1928) 69, 85
Westward Ho, the Wagons (1956) 249
Wheeler, Arthur 222
Wheelright, Ralph 215
Whitbeck, Frank 43
White, Pearl 41
White, Stanford 23

White Shadows of the South Seas (1928)
  80
Whittemore, Jack 275
Why Be Good (1929) 112
A Wicked Woman (1934) 183
Wilcox, Daeida 9
Wilcox, Horace 9, 12
Wilder, Billy 102
Wiles, Buster 210
Wilkerson, William 46, 89, 90, 179
Willat, Irving 187
Willebrandt, Mabel 82, 128, 229
Williams, Blanche 120
Williams, Hope 105
Williams, Kay 215, 216
Wilson, Carey 22, 70, 113
Wilson, Earl 256, 261
Wilson, Tweed 202
Winchell, Walter 223
Wings (1927) 178
Winkler, Jill 208
Winkler, Otto 185, 199, 201, 202, 208
Winwood, Estelle 65, 109
Wise, Robert 243
Withers, Grant, marriage to Loretta
  Young 147
Without Love (1945) 216
The Wizard of Oz (1939) 180, 188, 191,
  192, 278
A Woman of Affairs (1928) 73, 80
Woman of the Year (1941) 196, 199
The Women (1939) 188
Wood, Sam 22, 165
Woolwine, Thomas Lee 61, 62, 64
World War II, impact on movie industry
  199, 200, 207
Wray, Fay 68

Wright, Frank Lloyd 102
Wuthering Heights (1939) 186, 188
Wyatt, Ginger 170, 172
Wyler, William 102
Wynn, Ed 216
Wynn, Eve: as manager for Keenan 217;
  sexual relationships of 217
Wynn, Keenan: homosexual relations of
  216; sexuality of 211, 217

Young, Clara Kimball 41
Young, Gig 259
Young, Judy 164
Young, Loretta 164; adoption of two children to hide adoption of her own child
  171, 172; affairs of 147, 148, 150; biography of 147; gives birth 153; hides in
  Venice Beach awaiting birth of child
  152; image of 146, 147; marriage to
  Grant Withers 147; pregnancy of 150,
  151; returns one adopted child to birth
  mother 173; secreted back to Los Angeles for birth of child 151; sent to Europe
  to hide pregnancy 151
Young, Polly Ann 147
Young, Robert 189

Zaharias, Mildred Didrickson 252
Zanuck, Darryl 51, 97, 131, 160, 222, 223
Ziegfeld Follies 57
Zeigfeld Follies (1946) 213, 216
Ziegfeld Girl (1941) 194
Zinnemann, Fred 102; affairs of 241
Zukor, Adolph 6, 12, 15, 20, 41, 53, 58,
  59, 229
Zweig, Stefan 103
Zwillman, Abner 114, 120